DEAD MEN
HIKE NO TRAILS

2006 Jigglebox Press
jigglebox.com
P. O. Box 4101
Bisbee AZ 85603

DEAD MEN
HIKE NO TRAILS

RICK McKINNEY

In the United States a person somebody loved dies by their own hand every 17 minutes.

***

It is said that one who hikes the entire length of the Appalachian Trail from Georgia to Maine ascends 89 vertical miles or the equivalent elevation of Mount Everest 17 times.

AUTHOR'S NOTE

They'll tell you this book is a work of non-fiction, but take it from me, the author: It isn't. I mean, how could it be? A ghost talks my ear off in the fourth chapter, and another ghost drives me to the airport in Chapter 13. In another instance, I claim to have played 18 holes of golf with Adam Sandler then gone pole-vaulting over livestock with my cousin, all in the same day. Unlikely! Speaking of faerie tales, this book is full of them. There's a faerie in one chapter, a gnome in another, angels everywhere, and if you're paying attention you'll note that I'm walking and talking with dead people throughout.

Librarians and bookstore employees will either shelve this book under Depression Self Help, or they'll stick it with Appalachian Trail guidebooks. There are problems with both placements, the main problem being the NF word: non-fiction. If this were a work of fiction, it could simply be shelved by my family name and you, The Reader, could discern for yourself just what it is. But here's the bugger: it isn't fiction either. It is the true yet subjective story of one man's journey through the tangible forests of Appalachia and the intangible deep woods of a tormented and beautiful mind.

"This is NOT" he stated emphatically, "an Appalachian Trail guidebook!" Use this book to guide you on the trail, and you will grow horns and a tail and become limited sexually to arousal by only the most odiferous hikers. Bears and all other order of animal life will run from you, and you'll get lost. Often. Also, you'll no doubt be lured in by the author's subliminal call to his secret cult of Heaven Junkies. You'll find yourself buying the book by the dozen and depositing one at every shelter like zealots distributing The Holy Bible. Result: I'll be branded a pariah for accessory to pollution, and Julia Butterfly will get word of my eco-transgression and hate me without ever even having gotten to know me, and I'll cry.

As for the Depression Self Help categorization, I don't know. Time and my readers will have to tell, because I can't.

Claiming my book will help other depressed people makes me feel like Ferris in the film *Ferris Bueller's Day Off*. While all the doctors and shrinks and pharmacists and my parents and Principal Rooney and all but a few close friends thought I was sick in 2004, I was out having the time of my life and loving life and getting healthy and singing *Danke Schoen* into the Universe with all my might and meaning it. It was the best six-month-long day of my life.

Truth is, however, when I hit that trail at Springer Mountain, Georgia on March 20, I was suicidal. I was no Ferris Bueller. I was Susanna Kaysen, Sylvia Plath, Anne Sexton, Kurt Cobain and the 30,000 uncelebrated Americans who annually take their own lives, most due to mental illness. Could this book be helpful to the suicidally depressed reader when its author drank beer prodigiously at every supply town and self-medicated aplenty when physical pain proved intolerable? Yes, I believe it could. For though neither practice is productive to any path to improved mental health, they are a reality. Lump together the statistic that one in four Americans suffer from some form of mental illness with the fact that 90 percent of the population self-medicates in some form (How's that chardonnay taste?), and you can bet that 90 percent of depressed people self-medicate and/or supplement their meds with something Dr. Prozacflinger didn't prescribe.

Whatever this book is, it is honest. Despite flights of fancy, fireflies, faeries, poetry and a little wishful thinking, it is my truth, and it is told as much to entertain as to elevate, to lift You, The Reader, up out of yourself, and carry you aloft to a quite lofty finish. "Know this," he again stated emphatically, "There's not a finger prick blood-droplet of insincerity in anything written herein on the subject of suicide, depression, anxiety, the will to live or die, love of life and friends, the healing power of movement and nature, and my own love and empathy for all who suffer as I have."

In these pages, may you find an epic adventure outside the office cubicle; an honest letter of confession to lend perspective to your own personal Hell (should you be in one); a fun and sometimes downright silly campfire story (should you be unacquainted with Hell); a novice's introduction to long distance gear and hiking life; all the steamy hot makings of a romance novel minus the bad writing; an almost certainly criminal amount of inspiration to get you to chuck it all and hit the trail for yourself; and finally the coordinates to navigate the parallel universe of the Realm of the Appalachian Thruhiker. Alas, the latter are encoded in poetry and entirely lacking in longitude and latitude.

Just walk north following the white markings on the trees for 2, 174 miles, make your first right at the ranger station beneath Mount Katahdin, and climb on.

Vaya con Dios.
Rick "Peregrine" McKinney

For Luciano

ZERO

Zero is when a 150-foot-tall cannon shaped liked a clenched fist blasts the ashes of your mentor into the Colorado night sky with you one of the lucky few there and close enough to feel the fallout.

Ground Zero. This is where it ends, a man's life, his legacy, and all the fear and the loathing that made of him an icon. With the cannon smoke still wafting, I grab Stevie's cell phone and dial my cousin in New Hampshire as promised. The signal is poor, but just enough. The small crowd gathered at the entrance to Owl Farm is singing now. "Justin? Justin can you hear me? This is it!" I hold the phone high above my head and join in as Bob Dylan's *Mr. Tambourine Man* is broadcast through the canyon, a weird funeral dirge for a man whose journalistic legacy will always carry with it visions of violence, drugs, insanity. But hey, it was his favorite song.

I came a long way to be here, some 500 miles over the Continental Divide. As my mentor had in his youth traveled to Hemingway's home in Idaho to pay his respects in the wake of the man's suicide, so, too, did I come to bid Hunter Thompson farewell. But I came not by car, but on foot. And I did it for more than just an eyewitness account of the cannon blast. I attached meaning to my journey, garnering media attention with a hike sometimes reaching heights of 14,000 feet to raise public awareness of the stigma of depression as one of the chief triggers of suicide. Though I believe that Thompson's suicide was more of what Karl Menninger called an organic suicide, one in response to a physical illness or infirmity, I seized upon the occasion of his memorial to call attention to all suicide, a cause of death statistically epidemic in America.

"Justin! You still there?"

"Yeah, I'm still here. That was great, cuz. You made it! You really DID IT! I'm proud of you, man."

I thanked Stevie as I handed her back her phone. The buzz in the air was intoxicating. Earlier, before sunset when several of my fellow non-VIPs had begun chanting, "Hunter this sucks!" I'd been quick to remind them in an authoritative voice that surprised even me that outside the gate was the right place to be; that we had the best seats in the house. "Hunter isn't in *there!*" I shouted. "He's out here with us, with his kind of people." It felt right. Besides, as per the view, the cannon was 150-feet tall, and we couldn't have been more than a football field away. Now as we walk down the hill back toward the Woody Creek Tavern with the shadow of the Gonzo fist projected by giant spotlights against the low-lying clouds above us, I've no doubt in my mind. Hunter was with us. It felt so good to be with him, on his turf, in his town on that night. To try and describe it better would be moot. Hunter himself said it best:

> *...no explanation, no mix of words or music or memories can touch that sense of knowing that you were there and alive in that corner of time and the world. Whatever it meant...*

It was only much later as I bade my fellow Gonzo Junkies farewell that I began to ponder just what *had* it meant. I took Justin's words and, as a chronic depressive will do, turned them against myself. What had I accomplished, really? Thanks primarily to Denver's Westword, The Aspen Times and the Steamboat Chronicle, I'd gotten my 15 minutes out of this one. With help from the Internet, my name would be forever folded into the footnotes of Thompson's farewell. But what had I accomplished for the 30,000 annual suicides? Had I done anything to help them? How many had I saved?

Walking away from the Woody Creek Tavern and down the dark road, my brain answered, "Zero." I began going into a tailspin when somehow I stopped the spiraling sinkhole of my mind and shouted, "No! You're not going there! You've helped somebody, somewhere. You may never know their names or how many or how much, but you did something GOOD!"

I had tried. After nearly a decade of oft-crippling depression, I had reached inside myself and pulled out not the usual woes but a strength I hardly thought possible. And with it I had come along way. A long, long way. Further than just the 500 miles to Aspen from the north.

In fact, I had walked a lot further in the past year and a half than most people will walk in their lifetime. And I had written a book, this book.

Zero is how many miles of long-distance hiking I had ever done before this story began. Zero then, is not only the end but also the beginning.

It was to be a struggle, a battle of wits between my full-of-life self and that part of me that would just as soon have been dead. For death, it could be said, is what started it all. As with many a battle, it all began with one gunshot.

Zero is the beginning of this story, the story of the greatest journey of my life.

***

ONE

Driving Myself Crazy and Sleeping Around...The Four Billion Pound RV Mistake...A Hole in the Water and No Woman...Seven States in One Year? Let's Make it 14! Liberals, Jesus and Lovers Who Go Home to Other Men...A Crash Course in Long-Distance Hike Preparation...A Blood-Soaked Sponge for the Sadness of the World.

Having thoroughly exhausted myself with consumer culture and driving back and forth from the Palm Springs area 500 miles each way to the San Francisco Bay 10 times in the past four months (that's 10,000 miles since Thanksgiving), I have decided to sell the $1000 barely-habitable sailboat, park the old BMW, hop the train to Georgia, and hike the Appalachian Trail to northernmost Maine this spring and summer. With a self-inflicted shotgun wound to the head, my sweet songster friend Luciano has, like the parrot in the Monty Python sketch, gone and joined "the choir invisible." Feeling strongly that I may join him any day, I have nothing to lose.

I bought a sailboat to get out of my head and onto the water, but more immediately to live cheaply in the prohibitively expensive San Francisco Bay Area. I'd also bought a used Winnebago in January for similar reasons: to live cheaply and see the West in comfort and style. It was an endeavor that lost its charm immediately with the dawning realities of six miles to the gallon, parking hassles, and consequent cop harassment on the streets of Berkeley. I sold it a month later and, thanks to my mechanical prowess, sold it at a profit.

The boat, like the RV, is undoubtedly a very worthy and inexpensive urban living solution for many. There are many shadowy figures skulking around on my dock pretending not to live aboard their boats. And why not? At $5/foot/month for a 25-foot boat, it is a rent that Zilchville, Nebraska, would have a hard time undercutting. But I have learned in my recent acquisitions that no amount of dressing or chic naming (sailboat! Winnebago!) can hide the fact that the indweller is essentially homeless. It is neither legal to live aboard my boat nor to live on the streets in a Winnebago. While this must work for many, I learned that for me it just plain sucked. While I hardly claim to be a strictly law-abiding citizen, I cannot daily go to sleep beneath the radar and rise the same. I need a place to call home, one that doesn't require skulking in and out of or moving every three days to avoid a parking ticket.

So why the Appalachian Trail?

Because, believe it or not, thruhiking, the term given to walking a long trail end-to-end in one season, either the Pacific Crest Trail from Mexico to Canada or the Appalachian Trail from Georgia to Maine, has long been a secret dream of mine. Ever since hiking chunks of the Sierra Nevada with a field botany class in 1987 and later hikes of northern California's Trinity Alps, Marble Mountains, and Lost Coast, I have secretly longed for the epic, mind-blowing gigantor hike. Yet somehow, thanks to art, cars, beer, women, and gonzo journalism, a decade has passed since my last big hike.

But I haven't answered the question of why a vagabond hiker's trek when what I seem to need most now is a cozy cabin to myself somewhere. The answer, I suppose, is that when you're really good at one thing, and the other thing you desire is as yet unattainable, you may as well keep up what you're good at, especially if next year or the year after you might not have the physical or mental stamina to do it. This thing for me, of course, is motion. The journey. The road.

Where the road is concerned, I am an undisputed duke, a lord of the court, a king. Though my relationship with this kind of motion is certainly of the love-hate variety, I'm a traveler. The ability to travel as I have been doing for years is a gift of freedom.

Freedom, free travel especially, is a grace afforded us by a combination of external tranquility (national peace, as it were) and inner courage. Obviously, we don't have world peace. Sadly, we are at war. But that's for later in the story.

Proficiency at the art of travel is a badge of immense freedom, of freedom exercised. When a public official recently expressed disbelief that one so dollar poor as I could travel to and live in (albeit briefly) seven states in one year's time, I replied, "You would be amazed how little money a resourceful person can live on." Likewise, it takes little money to traverse the entire country if one has friends and/or is patient. Kerouac's gypsy lifestyle of the 1950s is easily replicated today.

As the seed of interest in thruhiking has grown in me in recent months, accelerated by the looming early-spring departure dates of March or April, I have been reading up. The list of would-be sacrifices to comfortable suburban life intrigues me:

- Sleeping in a sleeping bag in a different place every night (Ha! Between the boat, the RV, friends' houses, the ground, the car, and a few motels, I've been doing this for months.)
- Eating like a squirrel with a cook stove, often without even that (With no kitchen of my own and too poor to eat in restaurants, this would be me.)
- This ain't no Winnebago camping! (Owning an RV briefly was a great lesson. I learned that I felt absurd carrying around such a huge shell, and the gas mileage cinched the deal.)
- The beverage choices on the trail: water, coffee, and tea (I already drink water like a fish, never drink soda pop, love tea, prefer instant coffee or "mud" to a latte any day, and lately my beer consumption has declined dramatically due to my ongoing battles with chemical depression.)
- No flush toilets on the trail (There are scant more satisfying and simple acts of freedom than peeing in the woods.)
- No TV, no radio, no movies on the trail (I've sat down in more movie theaters in recent months than ever before. Why? To escape the dismal realities of a muddy spectrum of world problems and the reality of my own lonely, disjointed, and insecure existence. I love movies, but I know myself enough to know that in the natural world, I won't need movies to escape. Anyone who knows me knows I haven't watched 20 hours of TV in 20 years. I am blessed with a passion for writing, both blessed and cursed. As Hunter S. Thompson told George Plimpton, "Wanting to write and having to are two different things." I most certainly crash-landed out of the womb and into the latter category. Writing not only has kept me from jumping off many a bridge, but it long ago eliminated the need of television to entertain.) I haven't watched television in 20 years.

Doing without music will be difficult at first, I am sure. One could wear a Walkman on the trail, but this brings three problems to mind immediately. Plugged in, you are not in touch with your surroundings, a weakness that rattlesnakes and bears won't respect. Aside from the obvious weight issue of player, CDs, and batteries, how many conversations have you ever had or entered into wearing a Walkman? I want to meet people on the trail. I want to dialogue with like-minded wanderers.

Which begs the question, "Why a nature hike when you're lonely?" and why have I chosen the Appalachian Trail over the Pacific Crest. Answers: because a nature hike can be more social than you'd think, and because the AT is hands down the more social of the two.

As much as I crave a "place" to call home right now, I know my heart enough to know that the right people can be just as much "home" to me as any place on Earth. I have traveled extensively in this country, yet when it comes time to decide where to live, I have no answer. Not now, anyway. Why not now? Because I have friends EVERYWHERE. Wherever friends are feels like home. Ipso facto, my problem is not homelessness but that I have too many homes!

In the past year, I have lived in a small town in the mountains where locals know of me as "the guy with the weird car," yet nobody really knows me at all. I've lived in Berkeley, California, where a handful of very busy friends I rarely see know me, and the only strangers who approach me are panhandlers and crazy people. I have never been lonelier in my life.

Both Berkeley and the small mountain town of Idyllwild are places I love as well as the people therein, and I have thus tried to make a go in them both. Yet both have left me feeling hollow. Thus, for the time being, I have given up on the idea of finding a place to call home. Back to nature then. Back to people.

It is a weird irony of life that you can be lonelier in a crowd than when alone. City life for the no-small-talk and rarely chatty me has proved excruciating. I walk through oceans of people in a horrific bubble of solitude every day here. The current political polarization of those for and against war only makes it worse. Even in my mother's house, I feel obliged to stuff my feelings, my angst, my ire, as my stepfather, bless his otherwise kind soul, eviscerates left-wingers and daily sings a kind of Hail to the Chief in his own, non-lyrical way. Thanks to his influence, Rush Limbaugh is now a favorite of my mother, who in turn dismisses my extreme discomfort with the man's hate-engendering language, saying, "Well, of course, you're a liberal."

Sadly for me, the very things that seem to have strengthened Hunter Thompson, or at least kept his motor of righteous mayhem and libel running, have caused me to wither and damn near die. I chose a hero I couldn't possibly keep up with, not, anyway, in his tolerance for fear and loathing, doom, failure and drug abuse. I just wanted to watch people, write about them, and whenever possible, lose myself in torrid, stormy sex in an Amtrak bathroom with a Joffrey Ballet contender in her late teens with flower-patterned skirt and no panties.

But, lately, the bubble of solitude has crept into my love life as well.

I don't date. I don't pick women up in bars, or anywhere. I've met what women I've been with over the years largely through friends or small social gatherings. We meet, and if the chemistry is right, we crash into one another like plutonium atoms, lighting up the night sky with terrifying joy and splendor. If we're lucky, the sex and mutual respect turns to love and carries us through for a few months or a year. But I digress.

From the material I've been reading, the Appalachian, for its proximity to cities and population centers all up the East Coast is anything but empty of people. Thousands of people hike the trail every year, all around the same time. Unlike the sad mass of humanity around me, their war-waging guilt soothed by shopping and reality TV in this so-called "culture" of ours, the handful of people who nightly come to rest at shelters all along the AT route appear cemented together by the common bond of their very uncommon pursuit. I have read as much, and I know it is so, based on a lifetime of swimming from one funky freak community to another, finding them with ease as a dowser finds water with a stick.

Another social horror I've been living with lately is boredom. Boredom has never had a place in my life, and before it takes root and drives me to the nuthatch, I'm going to kill it like the scurvy dumb drooling dog it is. As monotonous as a 2,000-plus mile walk might sound, it will probably be anything but. I don't like repeating my steps. When driving a distance, I will do almost anything to avoid turning back even one freeway exit. Thus, the thruhike, 2,000 miles north, every step and every day different from the next. I don't know this by experience. But all evidence points to its truth.

If all of this sounds as if I am rationalizing aloud to myself, I am.

The first day of spring and the trailhead of the Appalachians is but a short 18 daze away. Suddenly, I have a schedule. I've got a lot of work to do and fast. But today I have accomplished the first, or perhaps the first, second, and third steps toward this new mad vision of mine, The Appalachian Trail. I have made the commitment in my mind, begun to verbalize it, sold my boat, and come south to Idyllwild where I will leave my car and set out via train to Georgia. Here at Bruce's house, I have a room to myself, floor space on which to spread out, inventory my gear, and pack. I am very excited about this next step.

Getting down here wasn't easy. After a panic attack night in the ER at Berkeley's Alta Bates Hospital, I awoke to transact the sale of the boat in the downtown Berkeley rain, the BMW overheating from a blown hose, then sickness, a short-lived stomach flu of sorts and last-minute dental work, and then the road, all of it too much. I caved in on the southbound I-5 near Bakersfield, opting out of the remainder of the drive to Idyllwild (another four hours) to take my nodding head and ill guts to bed at Buttonwillow's $25/night trucker motel. Twelve hours I slept, then caught *The Man Who Knew Too Little* on cable, a helluva deal at roughly $2/hour for divine sleep and a movie. Finished the drive today, the day's end wrapped in irony, back in Weirdsville again. But this time I have a six-month-long goal ahead, half a year away from here. I can't wait.

> *Morning. Dreams of her last night. I was in a theater, darkened, after a show, the last one in there when a woman entered to inquire why I was still there. Then my wife (as yet a vision, a dream) entered and gestured for the woman to relax, saying, "He is still here." Curly dark shoulder-length hair, eyes soft and dreamy, a warm smile, all I can recall.*

Now morning and I feel as though I am already on the mountain, the 2,000-mile trail ahead truly overwhelming. But it is a definite goal and, as such, attainable. It is infinity that most frightens the task-oriented mind. Give us a goal, a job to do. Even we free-spirited greyhounds need a bunny to chase. So, now to the bunny, several baby steps at a time. Today then, reading, acquisition of a sewing machine, perhaps a supply run, though more likely a day of list-making.

> *anotheer day has passd. Last night islept in the mtns. night before that i slept ina moetl bed on a lonesome stretch of interstate 5. night before that i slept ona boat, my friend's boat, having just sold mine that morning. night before that i was on my boat, as i was for the week predceding. before tath it was the mtns of socal again. and before that in my tent in the desert of joshua tree. before taht in suburbia at my sister's house. and before thtat it was the boat again. i am a nomad, always on the*

road.. this trail will be the same, but new, trading the car for a pair of boots and a pack. better.

The above material was written last night in a new form I am experimenting with, in which I place the keyboard and gingerly cradled Palm Pilot on my chest whilst lying on my back in bed. The challenges to such a technique are many. For one, it's dark. Also, the keyboard is out of my line of sight even in light, so finger placement on the keys is crucial. Then there's still the question of hitting the right keys given the alien positioning of the hands, alien to the brain's normal grasp of touch typing. I am blessed to know how to touch type. No hunter-pecker would stand a chance of typing like this.

This new technique is one I would like to master soon for its usefulness on The Trail. There's not likely to be a lot of desks and chairs in the wilderness, and typing like this on my chest should beat hunching over in my tent. We'll see.

It's so hard to see progress in this vague procession of days and in the casual and unclocked, unrecorded manner in which I go about doing things each day. I work, but, without pay or boss, it's hard to see that I'm getting anywhere. With a half-dozen unpublished manuscripts in my bone closet, even very real tangible accomplishments don't feel like success. On The Trail each day, at day's end, I hope to feel that sense of having done something, gotten somewhere, and been bedazzled in the doing.

Two weeks until spring. Just got into a Jesus discussion with my only sister. Since my last visit here, there appeared a poster on the boys' door featuring a race car with Jesus Christ slapped all over it where Pennzoil and Taco Bell logos might normally be. Sis has been slipping the Jesus into everything these days, and I asked her about it. "It's not about religion or people at church," she said. "It's about my personal connection with God through Jesus Christ." I said that's wonderful, that I was glad for her. We talked at length about it, about our religious upbringing and the teachings of our parents, and all went relatively well. I had meant to more or less wrap up the discussion when I said, "I just hope your faith in Christianity doesn't reach a point where you shun people with other belief systems, non-Christians as it were."

For starters, I was referring to our late grandmother Selena, a Jehovah's Witness. But this only lit the fuse, and she responded, "But it's biblical, says right there in the Word of God that the only path to salvation is through Jesus Christ." I realized then that my little sister was already gone, already swaddled in Christian conviction, protected and assured by its iron clad exclusivity clause. "Don't you believe that Jesus is the Son of God?" After an admittedly long pause, I said that I did. How could I not? Years and years of Christian summer camp and youth group, the blissful memories of my nightmare adolescence. I added, "I also believe that a million-score dead who never knew Jesus have found their way to God just fine, my beloved Selena not the least of them." Then we were interrupted in our discussion.

It's been nearly an hour since, and my sister has not reappeared. But when she does, and even if she doesn't, I would like to say this: I believe in God and Jesus. I also believe in a Universal Good, a force working toward the divine in all of us.

Furthermore (and here I would have lost her altogether, but what the hell, she's absent), I believe in faeries and angels and lovers pining from the grave. I believe in ghosts. I believe that Heaven will be there for those who seek it, just as life here on Earth is either Heaven or Hell depending upon how we perceive it, and to some extent the plate we're dealt. I believe in Cause and Effect and in Chaos and The Gonzo Embrace of the Epic Adventure of Man. I believe we are all lost and hungry but that faith in something drives us on, and that is both amazing and beautiful. I believe that Jesus meant what he said when he said that the Kingdom of Heaven exists inside every one of us. I believe that everyone who believes in something has as much a chance at redemption as any zealot touting his or her exclusive truth of the path to salvation.

Nearly a week later, and The Machine rolls forward with fantastic ease and great result. I now have tickets in hand for a four-night rail journey to Atlanta by way of Chicago, and the trail is so close I can smell the moose scat. In the past week I have accomplished a number and variety of preparatory tasks unimaginable in sum over the past year or so of crippling fear and loathing. I have smogged the BMW, had a bad wisdom tooth pulled, had a full medical exam and been given a clean bill of health by local Dr. Joe, rounded up and purchased almost a thousand dollars in supplies for the trek (including $160 in granola), packaged said supplies in seven parcels ready to mail to myself at points along the trail, and rescued Duke the Art Car from his cage of trees by the restaurant, towing him here to Bruce's where he'll be quite safe and happy in my absence. Let's not forget the hours and hours spent preparing *Jigglebox.com* for "live from the trail" postings, many of said hours spent creating a way for my editor, attorney, and gonzo cousin Justin to easily post the words I'll be e-mailing him from the trail.

I am Bill Murray as phobia-addled Bob. Baby steps toward the trail. Anything is possible, even in this kind of crash course pace I've set for myself. Dream big, act fast, search for what you want and need; and if it doesn't feel right, move on to the next thing. Waste not, want not of time. Preliminary pack weight estimate based on full gear load plus food but without water: 22 pounds. Twenty-two pounds!! This I owe to reading Ray Jardine's book and taking his "go-lite" philosophy seriously (and spending the extra bucks on the ultralight gear). My favorite item? The Pocket Rocket butane-fueled stove, weighing just three ounces and fitting in the palm of my hand like a badminton shuttlecock, its extending wings retractable until the tiny stove resembles little more than a handful of metal darts. Bitchin'!

Friday the 12th THE JACKET arrives. I do mean THE JACKET! Easily worth twice what I won it for on auction at eBay, my new-to-me North Face 700-fill down warmed its former owner on his trek of the Himalayas and will now warm me in the Blue Ridge Mountains and points north! I'm so excited I could wet my pants. To meet me now, tonight, you'd never know I just got out of oral surgery and have been spitting blood for two hours. I'm pumped!

In little over a week, I've divested, plotted, planned, invested, packed, listed, shopped, arranged, run ten dozen errands, and even managed to see a doctor, three dentists, my nephews, and my mother in preparation for a departure date now just four days hence. I even devoured two fat books on the subject of the AT, and a third arrived today. Blessed with a fair budget from a hard-won NEA grant, and nothing but free time, I have accomplished in the short term what should take months to plan. Now we'll just see if it works. I could very well be completely delusional, and there's no way in hell one can succeed at such a major endeavor as this in such short order. But screw that! I've never been one to color inside the lines, so why start now? I'm only concerned that of all the advice imparted (and followed by me) by author and thruhiker Ray Jardine, his conviction that hiking without months of prior training is a sure recipe for disaster. Unfortunately, this is one piece of advice I cannot follow. It's not possible. Not this year, anyway. THIS YEAR is the year Rick McKinney walks from Georgia to Maine and tells the tale on *Jigglebox.com.* This is the year. This is the time. The first day of spring is the day.

The main focus of Ray's philosophy is pack light! Pack light and travel far faster, better. This I have done. Where the author of *On the Beaten Path* set out carrying a 60-pound load (not to mention his own 275 pounds of body weight), I have achieved a base pack weight of 15 pounds, an amount which the addition of food and water will no more than double, leaving me to carry 30 pounds tops after each resupply. As I move a-hiking and consume supplies, my pack will lose up to 10 pounds. What about my lack of training? Well, at a relaxed pace, the AT takes six months to hike. That means departing from the Georgia trailhead no later than early April. When I learned that the first day of spring was March 20, the die was cast. I have to go. No time to train. Jardine reasons that the untrained muscles require a day of rest between each day of hiking. While I respect his authority and agree with him on every other count, my imminent departure leaves me no choice but to defend my position as a "cold starter." So here's my rebuttal: Who says the body counts in 24-hour days? Why isn't it enough to give the muscles eight to ten hours of horizontal rest in the form of exhausted slumber? I say it is. I've learned this truth about my body: It pretty much does whatever my mind tells it to do. So I say I'm going to be just fine starting cold. I'm going to rise each morning early, hike until midday with a dozen or so two-minute breathers, rest an hour or more midday with my feet elevated and my keyboard on my chest and type away, then resume a moderate pace until sundown. My days of rest will be my nights, just so.

Just so. Just.... I hope so. Now to go divide up two pounds of Hadley dates into seven Ziploc baggies, one for each of seven 10-pound resupply boxes I've been packing this week. If 70 pounds of food doesn't seem enough for six months out, you're correct. Being closely woven into the populated fabric of the American East Coast, the AT provides thruhikers with many opportunities for resupply along the trail. So I have packed mostly specialty items, things I can't be sure I'll find at Jethro's Corner Store in Deep Woods, Tennessee. Additionally, my resupply plan extends only to the halfway point on the trail. If I make it that far, I will break for Independence Day and spend a week packing a second round of self-made care packages. To the packing!

> *I. No, not I. She. She has me in her grip. She has enslaved me. She the dream, and she doesn't even know who I am. I am. I am a little man. I am a man perched on the edge of an abyss, and I am going to jump. It is my nature. I am a jumper. I am a gambler who never touches money. I am the gamble. I gamble on me. I am Evel Knievel. I am the space monkey ready to be shot into orbit. I am game.*

I packed my bags tonight, pre-flight. I unloaded a chock-fulla-crap BMW into a chock-fullera-crap seventies model Ford Granada specially equipped with a 120-cubic-foot "camper shell" made of antique luggage. This is Duke, my art car. (Duke is a whole other book unto himself, but you may learn all about him and other art cars at *Jigglebox.com* or *Artcars.com*.) I broke down everything I own and everything I've recently acquired into the aforementioned seven separate baggies, all to be packed into two-week parcels and shipped to me en route. I don't what the hell I'm doing.

Bruce assures me that I DO know what I am doing. He is a dynamite cheerleader. Tonight at the restaurant I fell for a bus girl with Cleopatra eyes and a long angular face, thinking, "I want HER as my cheerleader." I was devastated to learn she was only 14. No Bruce, I don't know what I am doing. Obviously.

I pack and I pack. I plan and I plan and I pop another Klonipin. I drink an IPA and mash together hamburger and raisins and crushed up pretzels and garlic and onions and form them into patties for our dinner. The sun sinks below the mountains to the west and its setting makes me sad.

Oh, did I mention that there are about a billion things that make me sad, at least a million that make me cry? Yeah. Cry just about every day. I wish I could say it was just mood swings, but no. The shrinks refer to it as "severe chronic depression aggravated by acute anxiety disorder and periodic suicidal ideation." Something like that. That public official I mentioned earlier? That was a federal judge. According to her ruling based on my lengthy psychiatric history, mine is "a condition presumed to result in death." I love that last bit. So dramatic! As though we all aren't dying a little bit every day.

But not to mock myself, or my condition. It is indeed likely that I will die before you. I'm comfortable with that. Inasmuch as I have suffered from an imbalance of neurotransmitters in my brain, inasmuch as I've been on my knees in mental anguish, death no longer frightens me. Life does though, much of it.

Anyway, I sold my boat in Berkeley because I felt, in the words of Bay Area local Tom Waits, "lonelier than a parking lot when the last car pulls away." I had a boat! Women love a man with a boat, right? That's what I had heard. I didn't meet any women. I didn't meet anyone at the marina. Everyone who "appeared" to live there (albeit illegally like me) skulked around the place never returning my sheepish hellos, never making eye contact. I felt like an asshole. I felt like a trespasser. I felt lonelier than a, you know. It didn't help my mental health.

At my age it doesn't make you feel very good when you fall for a 14-year-old. I mean, you knew she was young. But, man o man, I had no idea she could have been that young. They build them seriously and prematurely equipped these days.

I think about Bronwyn Lea, my girlfriend in the early 90s and the love of my life. Had she and I conceived a child, it would now be nearly a teenager. Scary.

But mostly scary that it DIDN'T happen. Scary it is that I am now more than a decade older and not a whit wiser it would seem, falling bleary-eyed for a girl not much older than my would-be child. That's grounds for some serious loneliness.

Don't get me wrong. I fall in love easily and often. I fell in love with a woman my mother's age just a few weeks ago. I am hungry. I have never felt loneliness like this. It's terrible. I wouldn't recommend it to anyone. Depression is bad enough with a supportive partner.

I saw Mike at the restaurant tonight. Mike is a very successful something-or-another. Mike, without meaning to I'm sure, makes me feel very unsuccessful. He thinks highly of me as a writer. Over the summer, he made several references about wanting me to write something for him so that he could make a short film. I finally had to confront him with the reality that I was living on about $20 a week scrounged out of Duke's donation can, and that at that income level I could scarcely write for myself. I told him that if he wanted me to write him a short script he would have to "make my life a little easier" in the form of a couple of C-notes. It took this kind of bluntness to get him to understand the vast discrepancy in our financial situations. But it worked, and I almost fell out of my chair when one night he slapped down three bills for a short script. Flattered, honored, and just plain pleased as punch at the respect that $300 showed me, I pumped out a seven-minute script for him in one day.

It has been like summer here in the mountains of southern California this past week. I imagine Pacific Crest Trail thruhikers trickling down from the peaks above town to get their mail and supplies and try to imagine what my life will be like when, one week from tonight, I am the thruhiker, spending my first of some 170 nights in a tent. Will there be snow in Georgia? Likely. Will I make it through the first week even? Will I be lonesome?

I'm entering new territory now. Efficiency has guided me this far these past weeks until the pieces are almost all in place. But what of me? What of the reality of this hike? What and why am I doing this? I'm not scared.

I'm terrified. Terrified of my own conviction, of the apparent self-confidence with which I dive into the unknown again and again. Jesus. God help me.

I just happened upon the following, written on the back of a happy hour menu from a historic fish restaurant in Berkeley. This gist of it reminds me of

WHY I am venturing east for a long, long hike in nature, away from cities dense with crazy people who seem to seek me out, as though they can read my medical chart in my blue eyes of pain.

January 28, 04
Guy my age approaches me at corner of Shattuck and Kittredge looking troubled. He places a box cutter razor knife to his neck and says he's gonna commit suicide right then and there because he hasn't eaten in a week. Myself, just fresh from the lobby of Berkeley Mental Health, I tell him to go there and get help. "Too late for that" he says, then adds, "but if you got 50 cents...." I give him the 50 cents and he departs. I am badly shaken by the incident. Horror is everywhere. I walk to the cinema and pay $10 to escape this horror, to escape into the fiction of film. I choose badly, picking the latest film by Clint, Mystic River. *Damn depressing. Back at the marina on the payphone, Rock tells me that a mutual friend of ours is trying to psychically steal his kidneys. I can't take much more of this.*

Chest Test. One week now and I'll be on the trail. So I figured out a way to improve on this typing on my chest idea. In order to keep the Palm Pilot from dislodging from its precariously perched position on the keyboard, I rigged it with two stays, one pulling in each direction to keep the unit from slipping off its perch either to the left or the right. I cut the snaps out of a couple of little plastic thrift store purses, superglued them to the top face of the Palm, and to each a line extending down to the keyboard and glued in place there. Improvisation. MacGyver would have survived just fine in the wilderness with only his paper clip and shoestrings. So will I. My chest typing method works. Now it's as though I am typing blind, and, in fact, I am. Blind and reclined. This will likely be the only way I'll want to type when on the trail after a hard day of peak bagging. Hallelujah for technology. Kudos for improv.

Too damn early the next morning. Bruce is off to work at some ungodly predawn hour. Ever the light sleeper, I lie awake with codeine constipation. The rotten wisdom tooth is out though, so no complaints. Rotten wisdom. Now there's an irony. Bossa Tres jazz mnemonic in my dawn-addled ears. Just 36 hours now til I board the train that'll deliver me into the unknown. Georgia. Jesus. Who woulda thought it. The train, the walk. The Auschwitz transport train to the Bataan Death March. Okay. I'm getting a little dramatic, even for me. Apologies to those living and dead who suffered those real horrors. This, however, will end up being a central theme of this book: the incredible freedom we Americans enjoy and how, at the time of this writing anyway, we are all still free to hike the Appalachian, Pacific Crest, or Continental Divide trails.

This is BIG. The commitment: six months, more than two thousand miles. The pack: even at only 30 pounds, it's going to be a bad-back nightmare for the first month. We built an anti-mice food container, Swami and I. I call it the Howitzer. I had called it the Bomb initially, but with today's search engine hyper climate of fear and Patriot Act McCarthyism, probably best not to call it that. No, instead let's name it after some military gun freak's crowning achievement. Yeah.

Anyway, it's fairly low-tech and no doubt the least expensive and most durable piece of equipment in my pack: two big-ass coffee cans that come together to form one long can. To ensure they stay together, to further guard against them crafty mousers, a tiara-sized hose clamp cinches up the middle and we're ready to rock and roll. Okay, so much for the go-lite philosophy on that one. But hey, there are remnant cabins and shelters all along the trail, and, by golly, I'm going to use them. After all, I'm not going to meet the Granola Girl of My Dreams stealth camping way off away from the gang, am I? The shelters are where the mice live, where they live and have developed paramilitary-like food infiltration tactics, or so I've read.

My last night in a bed for the foreseeable future. Not a good time to pop a codeine and watch *Requiem for a Dream*. Ugly flick. Brilliant but disturbing. Morning now. March 16. Crunch Time. Battle fatigue, the kind of battle where the enemy is YOU, is fear. Too many questions without answers, that dead zone before or between, rather, the guidebooks and the real jungle...

I wish my mother had come up to see me off this weekend. Methinks she doth protest too much when unavailable I am. For when available for her to see me, she will not make the trip, the 90-minute trip from Fallbrook along lovely country roads up into the forested town of "Idleweird." I miss my mother and my father, the parents I had before they dwindled on shortened leashes, leashes of love and codependence to their Nuevo Spouses.

But mostly on this journey I will miss Jacob and Matthew, my nephews, two shiny, bright-eyed, fresh-brewed souls in rapidly expanding Earth suits, growing, growing up and swathed in parental love and the innocence of pre-school days. In six months they will have grown a foot. Jim Morrison called it the "wooly cotton arms of infancy" and Myk Loutzenhiser, friend and poet wrote, "Children skip rope and grow scales for the future." Wow.

Today I meet with O for coffee and a strange farewell of sorts. Despite all the love I mustered for this woman over the past six months and in the virtual reality of my imagined dream of us, I kinda dread this meeting. I feel as though I fell in love with a pinup girl, a celebrity musician, a New York powerbroker and a supermom all tied into one. A big city powerbroker she is not, but her constant reminders to me of her tight, tight schedule hearken back to the day I left Susan Jenks, my old summer camp love, on a commuter train in Boston, she transformed that morning from weekend jeans and flannels and falling curly black hair to power suit, corseted curls, businesslike manners, and a coolness that shocked me, a personality switch so common to the business world, yet something I will never understand. O is nothing like that. Pardon the tangent.

O is a musician, a poet and a sculptor of lovely found-object art. O is a good mother to her wise and handsome 8-year old son. O loves me back, loved me forward I should say, before I even realized I was there with her in that blind and blissful place. In a singularly unique moment in my life, O asked me to marry her. I wanted so badly to say yes. But O is unavailable and thus a Siren on the rocky shore calling to me, her straight-jacketed muse, unwittingly of course, never understanding that with her lovely song she will smash my tiny boat in shallow water and I, without arms, will drown in her. Word to the wise, a word, a phrase no doubt spoken in warning many times throughout history: Don't fall in love with unattainables, unavailables, married and/or mostly married people, male or female. The side-dish lover loses every time.

So, in the words of Chris McCandless, who walked north through California and Oregon, Washington and Canada to his destination, Alaska, back in 1991 while I was in college, and who kept walking deep into the deepest shit that Mother Nature has to offer: "Now I walk into the wilderness." The *New Yorker* article about his illogical but forthright and convictional quest toward some cold but perhaps blissful death in the "wooly cotton arms" of snowy nature, away from all this consumer-driven shit down here in the Lower 48, struck me deeply, still does.

Now I walk into a tamer, more populated wilderness "not to die but to be reborn, away from the world so tattered and torn." (Jimi Hendrix) I walk for another brilliant guitarist and songwriter, 27-year-young Luciano Lenchantin, brother of Paz, who died for lack of a hardened shell round that swollen heart of his, so full of love, compassion, and pain. I walk away from unattainables and a patterned and deeply grooved past of my own pain. I walk into the future, into the unknown future, and though I take ME with me, I fully plan to slough off a few layers of dead skin and demons along the way.

To be sure, I walk for sad people everywhere, for sufferers of the disease of depression, be it ever so unrecognized despite epidemic suicide rates. I walk to bring you hope, a virtual forest, new friends, a few laughs, and perhaps even by my example, the courage to walk a long trail yourself.

I walk also for all of you who need such a journey but cannot make the time or find the freedom. On my Web site, *Jigglebox.com*, I have been accused of self-righteously lording over the consumer-trapped masses locked in cubicles and kitchens and factories and mortgages. If you have had this impression of me from my crying out against things incomprehensible to me, then I am truly sorry. I never meant to come off "holier than thou." Rather, I unwillingly capture as does a giant satellite dish all the pain and unhappiness in our culture. It enters me like blasts of dental office radiation penetrating the skull in search of cavities. It finds them. Forgive my presumption, but there has GOTTA be a whole lot of dissatisfied people in this country, people with big dreams now dwindled by the crushing reality of an uncaring money-driven world. There has to be a lot of this, because this overwhelming and collective sadness fills me like a blood-soaked sponge. It hurts me. It has nearly killed me on more than one occasion, unwitting receptor that I am. Too sensitive as a child, twice as bad as an adult, I am helpless to suffer the ills of the world. So I write. Starting in three days, I walk and write.

I write out this pain, bang it out onto plastic keys in some hope that in the doing some of it will leave me. I write it out so that it will not kill me. I try to phrase things in a way that sheds light or sounds familiar and perhaps strikes a poignant chord in readers who may be host to that sorrow themselves. I don't try to change anyone. I sure as shit don't try to say that I am right, that my wholly unstable and broken life is any better than one lived in a cubicle or a stucco suburban cookie cutter home. My life is a nightmare, but it is also an ever-changing and fluxing adventure, and it is mine and mine alone. If I could shut off the stream of ugly images and pain and sorrow that flood my heart and head like so many radio waves and x-rays and cell phone wireless words and thoughts flying through the air, if I could tell all that to go away and leave me in peace, I would. But for me there is no peace, there is only hope that I can keep a few steps ahead of the sorrow, far enough ahead to smile and see the beauty that's out there beyond the cloud of human suffering.

Now let's go climb a mountain or two. Or a bazillion! Georgia, here I come!!!!

TWO

Amtrak Incongruities: Let the Smokers Drink, You Geeks!
Albuquerque: Heartache Ground Zero...Who Would Have
Thought It Would End on the Set of *Red Dawn*? Heavily
Medicate Me, Please! Weird Memories in Chicago's Union
Station and the Affection of a Dying Girl...A Monster Diesel
Millipede Sucking Poison From a Bad Brain...Jamaica Lust and
Grandma Irena...First Contact.

Amcrack Arizona-New Mexico border. Little hexagonal reservation homes
sit queerly on the Old West train set landscape just beyond the I-10 canyon
intersection of these two dry and stunning open states. Once again aboard the
Jigglebox (my pet name for Amtrak). Passed out hard atop my six-month pack
not long after boarding last night in San Bernardino. A largely empty train
means two seats to myself. Not counting on it lasting, but hallelujah for now.
Rose with the sun at Flagstaff, kind of bleary, kind of freaked. Then rolling
into view from the northern window there appears that magical motel from
my youth. Now a Travelodge (and perhaps always that, I don't recall), the
horseshoe- shaped inn once had swings in the wide grassy courtyard where a
young man, a boy of 13, sat swinging and watching, counting the cars as
endless processions of boxcars and locomotives rolled east and west. The boy
was bound for California and a new life, a transition time, the end of one life,
the beginning of a new. I remember it with the fondness of a sweet dream of
Heaven.

Next we ride out a few not-so-sweet recent memories of Flagstaff, like the
arduous and angst-ridden hump across New Mexico and Arizona in a dying
art car. Poor Duke. Poor me riding the train through here nearly a year ago on
that ugly mission of mental health, that cruel test, that sadistic audition for the
lead role in a nightmare I'd been fighting alone for years.

But aaauurrgh! The hell with all that! To better days. Beside me sits a
backpack loaded with all the love and logistical genius necessary to sustain
one on a six-month trek. In my lap a yard of fleece, a needle, and thread with

which I stumble untrained through the creation of a camping pillow soft and small. Gallup now, TG&Y Hardware, Busy Bee Laundromat, The Road Runner Motel, and tough love over the Amtrak public address system (this stuff always makes me laugh):

"This is the conductor speaking. There is no drinking of any beverages or eating food in the smoking car. The smoking car is for smoking cigarettes only. No cigars, no pipes, no children. If we find remnants of food items or drinks in the smoking car, we'll shut down the smoking."

Aside from smoking the children, this strikes me as the most absurd rule on Amtrak. I don't smoke, yet even I can plainly see that smoking and drinking go hand in hand. Yet the drinkers can't smoke in the cocktail lounge, and the smokers can't drink in the austere iron lung prison cell of a room downstairs they call the Smoking Room. Whatever.

Paula is a painter who paints in oils and rarely shows, the disappointment of years creating for little or no audience or praise shows in her soft eyes, her gently resigned face. I know this look well. It is the face I see in the mirror these days. She asks about my writing and have I been published. I give her the Cliffs Notes version of the unsung and unrequited. We compare heartaches briefly, then sit bonding silently, our stillborn dreams conversing subliminally whilst her husband talks of wind sprints and pains more physical. All this over breakfast at one of those cramped little dining car tables where Frau Glotzenboza the Dining Car Steward seats you with the warning that she WILL be seating others with you.

The first to the table, I respond to her threat with "Lucky me!" She doesn't like this and is quick to penetrate my American-bred dining space privacy bubble. Paula and David turn out to be fine company, however, so all's well. When asked where I'm headed, I offhandedly relate the details of my mission as though it were a trifle. I'm kidding myself, of course. The journey ahead is mammoth, the biggest thing I've ever undertaken. As the red bluffs, tumbleweeds, and trailer homes of the West roll away, I feel very little, am almost numb.

Perhaps this numbness is the key. The numbness says: "It's time for a change of perspective." I numbly roll toward Albuquerque, my city of failure full of snapshots and people and stuff, memories just as well forgotten. Maybe this is the source of the numbness, a defense mechanism, a deadening of the heart set to last out the afternoon and into night until the train has carried me far away to the east and the blissfully unknown, unscarred, unscathed. My heart is black and blue and smiling still, hopeful, like a toddler badly beaten but beaming with love unconditional for its rotten, abusive parents. So near to where mankind detonated the first atom bomb, Albuquerque, New Mexico, is my own personal Ground Zero of Heartache in America. God grant me the serenity.

Dear Mr. McKinney,

It has come to our attention that you will shortly be embarking on a treacherous lengthy journey. Sheer cliffs, poisonous snakes, deer ticks, and siren-like women will abound on your journey. We at Mutual of Omaha would like you to keep a few things in mind and in your backpack before you set out:

- *Proper walking shoes. No stiletto heels as you are often inclined to pack.*
- *DDT. Or whatever the properly approved politically correct insect energy zapping spray may be today. Keep that Lyme disease away!*
- *Plastic wrap. Siren-like women trap men with their baby makers. You must protect yourself from your unborn children.*
- *Bribes/gifts for rations from the stills. It's not physically possible to carry enough beer to last this entire journey. Or, at least for me, to carry enough even for one day of this journey. Wine maybe. But I digress. Porno would likely be a good bribe for some swill. Carry 2 or 3 mags with you and a page per bribe/per drink and you're set for probably a week. Beware of the still owner's daughters, however. We have some statistics on that topic.*
- *In instances of extreme danger, pretend to be mentally challenged. Truly evil people with bad intentions have an absolute fear of these types of handicapped people.*
- *Write to everyone on the outside. They really wish they could go with you and will be living vicariously through your words.*
- *Write to your Mutual of Omaha agent more often than everyone else. We at Mutual of Omaha always have your*

best interests at heart and truly want you to enjoy your lengthy treacherous journey.

Sister Maria Margarita aka Agent Red (Texas Region)
Mutual of Omaha Life Insurance; Dept. of Salvation and Copulation

Las Vegas, New Mexico. One more stop on the trail of tears and weirdness. LVNM, home to the location shooting of the film *Red Dawn*, now a lesser known eighties ratpack flick but one with a strong impact on my teenage years. *Red Dawn*, the tale of the commie invasion of America, setting: a rural town in "Colorado." If you've seen the flick, you'd need only a short stroll through downtown to know that you were there, standing smack in the heart of that fiction's real-life location. A weird town, Las Vegas. One of those last-stop settlements for freak healers and outlaws, and supposedly home to Val Kilmer. I'd heard strange tales of the place before visiting there, and now I have my own.

For some synchronistic reason I may never know, I took my love, my girlfriend, my common-law wife, K, there for her birthday for the novelty of the three-hour train ride and an overnight in the old historic hotel downtown. For reasons a little less murky and a whole lot more painful, as I stare at the town from the window of a train 2.3 years later, Las Vegas, New Mexico, is where that love ended for me, where I waited anxious for the last time for her midnight-whiskey-crossover.

Sick from worry the next day, I tipped the domino that sent the whole kit and caboodle and commitment ala carte tanking hard and fast like a chopper outta fuel. Out the window I'm staring at the faded sign proclaiming the identity of the no-doubt once-famous Castaneda Hotel, now boarded up. Inside, deep in my buckshot heart, I know that here, right here whilst waiting for this very train, here is where it ended. I wanna buy the old hotel and burn it to the ground.

But hey, Las Vegas, New Mexico, ain't all bad. There's the semi-public hot springs, some great old crumbling architecture, and, of course, the remnant memories of *Red Dawn*, the best of which for me came years after the film while dating Martin Sheen's daughter, Renee. At a private Sheen family dinner, I recognized the red Wolverine letterman jacket on Charlie's then-girlfriend, Kelly Preston. Without hesitation, Charlie took it off Kelly and put it on me. In my coming-of-age in the eighties pop culture consciousness, wearing that jacket (even for a minute) held more significance for me than the treasures of Tutankhamen or the Holy Shroud of Turin. So Vegas NM is all right. Or maybe it's the Vegas of fiction that I really like; and in the act of going there, the thinly veiled fictions of my own life just couldn't hold up.

Farther on down the track, or north of Vegas that is, a black on white railroad sign announcing the town of "Waltrous" or some such weird name. I can't deny that the landscape here is fascinating to me. I'm stupid with its blond beauty, its cliffs and buttes and sculpted rock faces forever, its deciduous trees now winter-barren of leaves, now branched and budded golden, and all the golden rocks and the streams running though it and dry desert scrub trees also golden or ochre or a green that borders on black, and all that blue, blue, blue sky above. I cannot deny that I am in love with New Mexico, much as I'd like to think I'm not. Worming into AlbuQ from the west and the south, I felt my numbness turn to nausea, vertigo, a dizzying sadness for all I had tried to be here, for all I thought I had going, and for the finger-snap fast conclusion of it all not two months after my sojourn in Kaseman Psychiatric Hospital. I didn't try and kill myself because of her, no, far from it.

Perhaps it was the change of meds. Perhaps it was that balloon crew job during Albuquerque's famed balloon festival and my instant subservience to so many privileged people, reminding me of my protracted status as a service industry drone. By now, I should be among the privileged. I could have written *Prozac Nation* instead of the esoteric, failed first novel I did write. I could have married Renee! I could have done a lot of things differently. Most definitely it was K's alcoholism, a bad mix with my depression.

There with K on the grounds of the Castaneda awaiting our return train, it was a few well-phrased words by Hermann Hesse that triggered that "abandon ship" sensation in me. Abandon ship, in the wake of so many whiskey psycho drunk episodes of abuse. Abandon ship from all the hate-filled curses out of the mouth of babes, from the mouth of my lover, my friend, my abusive and amnesiac alcoholic mate, K.

To infuse the story with a little humor here, as Tom Waits said, "Ah, there's nothing wrong with her a hundred dollars won't fix." The train is well past Las Vegas now, and I wonder, "How much will it cost to fix me?" Anyway, I am glad. There are no more scary "scene(s) of the crime" for me now, not on this train route anyway. I am relieved.

Part of me hoped against some silly hope that Dave, who came late to visit me at the station in AlbQ and saw me thus for only a moment, would have roared north in his sleek black Volvo to intercept me there and ride with me a while. But this, like so much of my life, was just a fantasy, based on no amount of everyman's reality, and far too much of mine, of my imagined movie version of my life. K and our house and the bottle room I built, they're all gone now.

They're there, back there in that weird little city that to rock bands represents (I'm told) a necessary evil, a throwaway performance waypoint between bigger cities to the east and to the west. They're there indeed, not really gone but there.

Either way, Georgia awaits. With her a dream, like the tiny Tinkerbell in my pocket, purloined from my art car Duke to charm my voyage strange. Tinkerbell in her tiny lamp, a little piece of a far greater magic. I carry her with me, and faith will carry us both.

Farewell then, New Mexico. Farewell, Castaneda Hotel. Farewell, Hesse and sweet love's dying duress. Farewell, Mrs. Woulda-been McKinney. The horizon then is bright. It is blank as an empty page. I will write on it. Write on it I will.

I write-a too mucha today. I loosa my mind. the train jiggles to and fro and on the cafe car. I have always loved her with the love of a boy, the boy who watched her in *A Little Romance* with Olivier and fell hard at 13. "The train track through the Alps before there ever was a train." Turn me over, I'm done on this side. Boy, am I crocked. Scott Frank, famous writer and friend, greeted me on the platform in his straw hat and white beard, dark glasses, his blackjack winner getup, he calls it. So nice to see his face there in that queer and unsettling land where I've been through so much I would like to forget. Hopeful of Dave's arrival, but not confident of it, we ducked around the corner into some new Thai joint lorded over by two blatantly gay men who happily welcomed us in and poured me a sake and a Singha and Scott a sober iced tea. We drank and reveled in our relative wealth (he from gambling, me from government sponsored gonzo-ness). That sake and beer sure got me rolling at one o'clock in the afternoon.

Then it was time to chase the train, where of course we ran into Dave, late and waiting, but almost too late, as the train prepared to leave and did in fact pull out three minutes later. The boys in solidarity waited on the platform, and as we passed I threw open the downstairs window and howled a grateful "Hoorah!" It was a brief yet sweet moment, a snapshot of redemption to counter the numbness, the nausea, the rolling-into-AlbuQ blues. An hour later I awoke with a start from a drunken stupor by the too-loud and grammatically strained p.a. announcement about the night's dinner offerings. It was an auditory nightmare, especially fresh from a flash-fast gonzo noontime train drunk nap. Medication was definitely in order. Then music. Loud and of an infinite selection, the sort offered by my Archos, the 20-gig jukebox I swore I wouldn't carry on this long, long journey but which I realized in the last minute I just couldn't do without. Six months without music? No way! If some literature professor someday asks the question on an exam, "What were the principal influences of Rick McKinney's writing?" don't believe the bullshit about pain and depression. It was music that kept me writing. And beer. Hefe- Weizen, if possible. Naz Darovia. But definitely music, and all kinds. Rock, pop, punk, hardcore, swing, folk, jazz, classical. The cello, the sax, the fiddle, the bass, the banjo, the slide guitar!

I met an old cat named Bruce Lippincott, a jazz poet who recorded with Ferlinghetti and backed up Kerouac on sax. Bruce was older than gold and probably the closest I've ever come to meeting a real "Beat." After he'd read some of my work, he pronounced me a true jazz poet. Skeptic that I am, I later looked him up on the Web. He's for real. Bruce, whether or not you've joined your compadres up in Beat Heaven by now, I'll never forget you and will always be thankful that you heard music in my humble words.

This is what they do. They hurry you up, stick you in a gigantic concrete lung of a station that heaves and breathes, a million commuters its nervous blood pumping through, and they feed you booze, white beer at $2 a pint and serenade you with a cover band's renditions of "Hotel California" and "Comfortably Numb" and you get numb and loose and stupid, feeling all safe and happy. Then they make you wait. They delay your train and make you sit, you and two hundred others, all anxious, all waiting on line like eighties *Star Wars* ticket zealots camped on sidewalks for days. I've been "forced" by this situation to sit beside a sweet-smelling zit-faced beauty and her boyfriend, they from some foreign country for whose dialect there is no name, in the dimly lit dungeons of Amtrak, Chicago.

Day Two on the rails and I am falling asleep. No, really falling. After a handful of beers and songs and good fun with Alex and Rebecca at the upstairs bar, I am tanked and zonked and in real danger of losing consciousness if I don't get up now. Now! GET UP NOW!

Whew. That was a close one. Awake now and quite sure in recollection that I would have nose-dived the tile-on-concrete floor seconds later if the zit-faced Italian hottie hadn't reached over and twisted my left nipple. This, much to the abhorrence of her machismo boyfriend, but hey! The girl knew her

VEMT, man (that's short for Venetian Emergency Medical Training), and she acted quickly, purely duty-bound, of course. I say Venetian for I have by now discerned in their babbling something approaching Italian. Whatever. The nipple-twisty worked. Woke me right up. Good thing. My train was loading and the aggro-carnivorous sheep were clusterhumping through the gate like so much hamburger through a grinder. I just had to get in on that fun. But what happened next wasn't really fun.

You see, there was this little Asian girl, er, woman, I should say, name of Malu. Malu struggled with five suitcases and seven shopping bags such that she was blocking MY entry into MY train car. So, the gentleman that I am, I helped her transport her bags to her seat. However, idiot that I am, I didn't seize the Malu day. As crowded as the train quickly grew, it would have been a gimme to just sit down beside this Asian cutie and avoid the inevitable dead air loneliness that would (and did) ensue the moment I secured a two-seater all my own; and no one, I repeat, no one sat down beside me.

Backing up a bit, in the so-called 11th hour of my two-night train trek from soCal to Chi Town, I met Alex. Alex and Rebecca. These two friendly young ladies not only graced me with their company on and off the train but well into the beer-addled station layover hours that followed. They also kept me red in the face with compliments. Rebecca focused on my ass, whilst diminutive and well-proportioned Alex at 4-foot-11 seemed better stationed to see my heart, or its whereabouts. Alex went from catching my eye this afternoon to full out thrilling me tonight, all in a matter of just a few hours. As she herself noted, perhaps it was just the beer. But there was something there. It was GOOD. It was welcome, both her energy and Rebecca's. The farewell kiss I planted on Alex felt very like tonguing a ripe cloven mango. Why then am I alone again so soon? Welcome to the world of Amcrack, where in Chi Town everyone detrains and disappears, going their merry way without you.

A veritable tide of humanity, fast-footed commuters every one of them, trotted through that station in the two hours Alex and Rebecca and I sat there boozing and schmoozing. From 4:30 to 6:30 p.m, I toggled between guilt and giggling fits as we exercised criminal amounts of joy and freedom from The Big Business, Big Money, Big Debt Corporate Cubical World. When I'd cross that flow of Grand Central pedestrian traffic to relieve my bladder in the far-off men's room, I felt I was fording a dangerous river. Twas indeed a river of stress and haste and corporate gym muscle and sinew-filled suits that would stomp me like a rock concert neophyte if I didn't dodge and weave with the grace of a quarterback. It's weird how all the world is moving at such

27

a pace, going places, doing things, moving stuff around, making deals, and faking smiles, things I'll never understand. It's amazing and beautiful! I am glad they're out there, doing their thing. Someone has to run The Machine. I guess.

I am a thousand times gladder that I am not that person. I am Lost and Found Boy. I am Wal-Mart Boy abandoned in the store and roaming free, beneath the radar, confusing the calendar and dodging the clock. Thank you, Lord, that Thou hast given unto us the freedom of choice, the choice to be or not to be, to do or...not to give a shit. I choose the latter. Of course, I am lying through my teeth.

I care. I care like crazy. I care so much it hurts, that I double over in sobbing fits as waves of a sadness pandemic the Earth over find me wherever I am and howl through my hollow bones in yearning and grief.

When the professors entreat their English Lit grad students someday to dig through all this gibberish of mine and find meaning, they will find that I cared immensely, intensely, that I wrote and I loved and I lived. But mostly I cared. I wrote profusely to solve it all, and it killed me just the same.

Chicago's central station was a trip. I thought I'd left behind the weird heebie-jeebies of bungled ex-lives somewhere back near the northeastern edge of New Mexico. Not quite. A beer at the upstairs bar at Grand Central Station reduced my walk to a wobble, my stance to a hunch. For in a wave of uneasy nostalgia, I recalled the day in 1996 when there in that very train station bar I asked K to marry me. Poor as I was, I had naught to offer for a ring but a one-shot whiskey bottle screw-on cap, punched through and fashioned into a ring. I am sad just thinking about it. A woman as fine as K deserved so much more. A fine man, I should have had so much more to offer. But I was poor and struggling hard against a depressive mind, so hard that all I could do half the time was muster the will to breathe.

I remember that on that day in 1996 I had to go back to Arizona for some job, which meant regrettably leaving K in Chicago with her sister. So right there in the station with my train rumbling nearby, I asked the girl I loved to marry me, and she said yes. It was the first such request to cross my lips and may well be the last. As it happened, I got on my train and rode it as far as St. Louis before that same heart-wrenching love caused me to detrain and ride right back the way I came, back to K and a fair helping of the kind of awkwardness that comes with such rash romantic acts. Her family was stymied.

I never made good on my wish to turn that bottleneck ring into the real thing. Not a year later my mental battles were bad enough that I had to pull out of the engagement altogether.

Marriage is not the sort of decision one makes when half out of one's mind. Or it shouldn't be anyway. So that was I, in 1996 and there again today, sitting a few tables away and fully weirded out with disillusioning deja vu. Am I sorry for the pain? Yes and no. Every great moment in life simply IS and must be honored as it IS, not as it was later bungled, retracted or lost. That moment of pure love will always exist for me, and I am grateful for it. I must admit, however, that it was a little weird sitting there again, drinking beers and being flirty with Rebecca and Alex while out of the corner of my eye seeing very clearly the Rick and K of '96 going gaga and silly in love just a few tables away. I could see us clear as day.

Okay. That's enough of that. Let's have a laugh. Let's talk gear. Yes, of course, gear. I get the impression from my reading that the really well-hung thruhikers are super gearheads. They have to be. Just try throwing together a Coleman tent, $40 Wal-Mart sleeping bag, propane stove, army surplus mess kit, full-length foam mattress, fuel, canned tuna, canned chili, and a typical week's worth of your usual clothing: jeans, cotton shirts, cotton socks, lederhosen, jungle pith helmet, cast iron chastity belt, Kevlar vest, you know, the usual stuff, and just see how many megatons your pack weighs in at. Over 80 pounds I bet. More likely 100. So some smarty pants long distance trekkers started thinking light, figuring, I guess, that the lighter you packed the further you could go. These guys really got it down to a science, too. They started drilling holes in their watchbands, cutting the ends of their toothbrushes, severing superfluous limbs, a finger here, a little toe there, stuff like that. It got pretty out of hand.

Then I came along and revolutionized the whole thruhiker "thang." While everyone else was spending 10 times the money on ultralite gear like sleeping bags made out of origami paper, I invented "negative weight" gear, gear so light it actually subtracts pounds from heavy gear loads: a tent that weighs in at -5 kilos (that's measured in quantum Kelvin divided by the speed of light in the indeterminate atmosphere of a wormhole), a down bag made from the feathers of actual ghost geese (ectoplasm extracted, of course), and a cook stove so light it draws its fuel energy from the negative attraction of atoms in an inverse universe.

Anyway, every hydraulic system has its bleeder valve, and this train ride is mine. Four foul nights of scant sleep and insatiable questions across a country chock fulla dead dreams and broken love schemes. Yes, that's my kind of warm-up, my way of bleeding the brakes on this carbonate machine; bleed 'em now so we know they work, then never use them again, not once. Not for the entirety of the 2,200-mile walk. Just go go and go some more. Bad memories bled, masochistic impulses fed and then tucked away in a storage locker in Barstow, California. Got me my negative weight gear and eight six-packs of beer (for ballast of course, to keep me from floating away on a hot air balloon pack of negative weight). I'm gonna stomp on the terra!

Coursing along the Ohio River now, pea soup green and choked with skeleton trees beige and brown, gray skies, a bridge now and again, flood plains full of rocks and naked trees, moss and lichen and white caps over shallow spots. Aside from trash and the government-green and cement-gray dam ahead, there's no sign of man other than the tracks ahead. The tracks. The tracks on which this wiggly-jiggly train doth roll, this parade of water buffalo, this supersized cyborg witch on her crooked broom, a monster diesel millipede pulling an old silver toaster train of ten-score telltale hearts a-beating. Genius.

The forest is all around us now. Then we cross the river at last, slow as snails, the required speed for an ancient bridge no doubt. On the other side a sign: Hawk's Nest. Behind it in the woods a sign with a symbol...could it be? The symbol of the AT? I don't know. For all my planning and packing, I neglected to bring one map, not even just a xerox of the whole eastern seaboard. Nothing. So though I know this train will very soon pass right over the squiggly line of Earth that is my future home, I'm afraid I won't know it, not consciously anyway. Perhaps I will just feel it. Perhaps months from now while on foot near here, I will see the silver snake Am....trak its way right past me, and say, "Aha."

Well, please excuse my flight into fancy, but I needed that. The train crowded in thick in West Virginia, causing my space bubble to shrink by half, and, coincidentally and messily, a Budweiser burst in my bag. I shall return shortly with a full and serious list of my actual, real-life super-expensive high-tech ultralight gear. Over and Out.

First contact. Met Doug, don't yet know his trail name. He picked me out of a crowd boarding the train, this my last of three consecutive trains since leaving California Tuesday. Today is Friday. Yah. Do the math. Anyway, so Doug sights my pack and introduces himself. I'm awed and almost a little intimidated to find that not only is he an intended thruhiker like me, but this will be his second time! Holy moose doo-doo! Now that's gonzo dedication. Back in Charlottesville I dined out with Irena, a sweet grandmotherly woman from Canada who'd been across the aisle from me on the previous train. Both facing a four- or five-hour layover, we checked our bags at the station and set out together for a stroll down the town's restaurant row, as it were.

I let Grandma Irena pick the place, and well she did choose. Place turned out to be a brewery. Naturally I had to sample all their brews, each a six-ounce or so glass, but by the end of the taste test I was amply baked. Irena told me of her seven children, all well and alive, even her one "bugger of a son," as she called him, the 40-year-old, my age roughly, the bad seed. Observing Irena, I saw my idealized visions of both my grandmothers combined—sweet, happy-go-lucky, adventurous, and full of stories and enthusiasm for my stated journey. Ours was one of those fast friendships of convenience and trust that rarely occur in the real world. Such things happen only in movies, and I'm not talking about that stuff shot on film that you sit in the cinema and passively observe; I'm talking about "moving life" or life on the road, the rails, and likely, the Appalachian Trail.

Back on the train I offered to buddy up with her on a seat so she wouldn't have to be seated with a stranger. Having discovered once under way that other seats were free, I relinquished my seat to her that she may stretch out and get some rest. No doubt I should be doing the same. Myself now in a two-seater, I could lie down but my recent conversation with Doug has me all excited, thinking about the trail. Or maybe it was the two cups of coffee I sipped while slipping under the spell of Jamaica, the bartender at a cute little bistro across from the train station.

Jamaica. Gorgeous, sultry, wants to write freelance, be a photographer too. I should have been all over that, full of advice or at least inroads to conversation with this Virginia goddess; but, no, I was too busy stumbling, nay, stopping my sure-to-stumble tongue before it could say anything. She no doubt found me rather odd and boring. But maybe not. I just don't know anymore. It's been too long, and I haven't the faintest idea how women see me. Well, with the exception of Rebecca and Alex yesterday. But surely that was some freak anomaly! Surely those girls were drunk and their comments about my cute ass were said out of pity for my blatant humpback personality, all warped and freakish and sure to live out its life knocking around bell towers and laboratories of mad scientists!!

Okay. I'm getting weird. It's late and I've been on trains for TOO DAMN LONG. This rail gig is savage and unnatural, and I wouldn't recommend it to the Butcher of Lyon. Amtrak is degenerating. The curtness of its conductors is on par with every Schweinhund Greyhound bus driver I've ever met. Bitch, bitch, bitch. And control! Ah, there's nothing wrong with me a First Class upgrade wouldn't fix. Tomorrow morning, Springer Mountain. The beginning. And the end of trains, for a while. I hope.

So much for sleep. Four a.m. just south of Charlottesville, North Carolina, and I'm just about lobotomized with Amtrak hospitality. So, let's talk gear some more! You see, REI has this policy about ticking luggage, er, I mean about returning sleeping bags. Being one of those comfy owner-operated and year-end dividend-paying yuppie neato enterprises, REI promises a satisfaction guarantee on all merchandise. So it came to pass that back in January I splurged and bought myself a $240 down bag. It had some fancy name like the Ripcord or the Tiger's Ballsack or something and was all the rave with this year's mountaineers, or so I was told. I was thrilled. A damn-near lifelong dropout from The School of Consumerism, I'm so out of touch with shopping, I get very uneasy in stores that don't specialize in groceries and beer. But thanks to a recent influx of money and a couple of friends who guided me around department stores like steering an old-style robot that doesn't corner too well, I had been learning lately that buying stuff really can be cool! And, shallow as it sounds, buying new stuff really can make you feel better about yourself.

I slept in my new mummy bag for damn near a month on the boat, but I never felt quite at home in the thing. So, after I'd gotten it good and smelly from sleeping in it unshowered for weeks in the mildew-zealous environs of a sailboat berth in winter rains, I took it back. Oh, the girl at the REI counter loved me for that one. Actually, I think she really did. I think she was one of those kinky pheromone-junkies I've read so much about, you know, modern primitives who turn up their noses at perfumes and deodorants and prefer the good old-fashioned musky scents of the animals we really are (I would meet lots of these on the AT).

Okay, I confess. I'm really talking about ME. I mean, I think she and I were alike in this way. I've never gotten down and dirty with a woman cloaked in pseudo-smells, be it $1,000 an ounce perfume or teenage girl-tonic from Target. I hate the shit. A well-scrubbed woman to me is an invisible woman. Even if I can see the woman, I'd be hard-pressed to find her erogenous zones under perfumed-stinky sheets. Nope. Gimme a woman unshowered a day or two, and I'll show you a WOMAN! A smiling woman after I'm done sniffing her out.

Oops. Once again I seemed to have strayed far afield from my intended message tonight. Hmmm. Just what was I talking about? Oh, yes! Sleeping bags.

So REI takes back my Rick-ripened Ripcord (that's what it was called!), the blue and black straightjacket of a high-dollar bag, and just when I'm getting somewhere feeling out the selection for myself, this profoundly deaf sales clerk overcompensating for his handicap (barely improved by a set of honkin' hearing aids) touches the softie in me, and suddenly I'm following him around buying every vowel-heavy object he recommends. No matter that I can barely understand a word he's saying and that my deep-seated compassion for the disabled has completely blinded me to what I really came there to buy, buy I did.

It seems to make the kid really happy to be so adeptly helping me, so I don't fight it. I leave the store considerably lighter in pocket and with some weird synthetic-fill bag that's even more confining than its predecessor. The only thing the new bag has going for it is its name: The Nootsack. I dig the name. Something to do with my long-standing love of the film adaptation of Farley Mowat's Alaskan wolf study, *Never Cry Wolf*, in which the last civilized outpost before Mowat's character, Tyler, disappears above the Arctic Circle is a quirky "Northern Exposure-on-Acid" village called Nootsack.

Well, perhaps just to get back at REI for sicking that deaf kid on me, I keep the bag another couple of weeks and give it my own brand of moose-dander sweetness, then return it as well. At last alone with REI's fine selection of God's Gift to Outdoor Slumber, I happen upon the Big Cat, a pale olive green bag that's vastly wider in the shoulders than any other mummy they've got. This has been my problem with the other bags: waking up at night fully zipped in and experiencing about seven seconds of sheer hemmed-in horror as I struggle to get OUT of the damn thing, enough at least to free my arms. The Big Cat has an advertising ploy that penetrates even my titanium-tough anti-bullshit defenses: The Big Cat comes in two models, a left and right zipper option, so that when one big cat finds another big cat on the trail, you can zip your expensive-as-shit bags together and do the snuggle and the nasty right under Mother Nature's nocturnal nose. Cha-ching. Sold! To the biggest dreamer. You know what? I kept it and loved it the entire journey, and a year hence I sleep in it still.

THREE

The First of Five Million Steps to Maine...The Electric Monsoon Tent-Safe Test...Love at First Scent...Holy Jesus, I Have Knees! Fuman the Mad Sobo and the First of Many Trail Names...Hobbes on Catnip and Easter Eggs in Trees...And Yes My Son, the Pope Does Shit in the Woods.

I lie here in my new, untested tent deep in the mountains of Georgia. Energy in the air outside is both magnificent and threatening. Thunderheads prepare to christen our arrival here at Hawk Mountain Shelter. I made it, nine miles today, my first day on the trail and this after four days of scant sleep on Amtrak. I drift off to sleep now as I write. Shit. Thunderclaps growing closer. Lightning strobe-like. Lark is a young cutie who dropped out of Harvard to join us on the hike. Would already like to see more...(lapse of consciousness).

VWHHHAAAAAMMM! Down comes the jackboot stomp of Zeus. I'm wide awake now as the mother of all storms drops in with a bang! No warning. First lightning and thunder and now rain, trickling pitter pat, then wind torn out of some hole in the sky like a thousand screaming children released for summer break. Will my tent hold up? There's nothing to do now but pray. The roar of monsoon deluge has replaced the pitter pat, the roar and the crash as the storm moves directly overhead. Then POP! goes the sky, and the whole Hawk Mountain world explodes!! It suddenly occurs to me that I've left my little propane/butane stove outside the tent, not far from my head. If another lightning strike like that one hits any closer, it could hunt down that little bomb out there and boom! No more Rick. Probably blow my head off.

Wowwowowowow! Calming now, I give over to the forces of nature and choose not to worry but simply revel in the symphony of light and sound, one of the finest electrical storms I've experienced in years, not since that night in 1996 with Florence Drukas, we two huddled in a tent in the Shady Dell trailer park below Old Bisbee on my first night in a town that has long been a home to me.

Wow. Thank you, God. Thank you, LIFE, for guiding me here to this place, to this journey. I sit up and flick on my headlamp and take quick stock of the tent floor around the edges. Not a drop. Still down it comes in buckets and barrels, kegs and caboodles…remnants of creation, the Great Flood, and God made this…BOOM! God made that BOOM! God destroyed this and that and drowned damn near the sum of men, BOOM! And all the animals on the Arc went "Wheeee!" Wow.

I am screwed if this tent doesn't hold up against this onslaught. I have a down sleeping bag, useless when wet, a down Himalayan jacket, and a not-at-all-waterproof backpack.

I think of little Lark in her tent across the way. Little Lark bound for Harvard, ballsy enough to drop out when her heart wasn't in it, to drop out and head south to hike the AT, alone. My friends think *I'm* brave! I wonder how she's holding up in this onslaught? Hell, I've had to stop typing several times now, my heart in my throat as another bomb of electrical energy explodes overhead, seemingly right outside my tent. Today we, the dozen or so thruhikers camped here, all made the first big step on a daunting journey the likes of which few Earthlings will ever so much as consider. We are misfits most, as am I, like everyone I've met so far—Doug from the train last night who's doing the trek for the second time; Nathan, sweet as can be, out of shape like me and missing a few teeth, hiking to get over his lost love; John from Boston with his blinding white thighs, a narrow and angular guy, graduate of Tufts and transitioning, no doubt dissecting that special question that lives in all of us: "What next?" All told, there are perhaps two dozen camped here on this electric first night of spring, first night and first right!

The storm has largely passed now, and I give my tent an A plus plus. Worth every one of its $250 with its silicone-impregnated nylon and waterproof zippers and god knows what kind of super waterproof floor. I love it. God just dumped a Jacuzzi on me personally, and my down and I are bone dry. But we're tired too. Wiped out so bad from four daze on the train and so little sleep, we should have passed out an hour ago. But that was too good to miss. Ha! As if I could ever have slept through an event so alive as the cracking open of sky. Day One on the AT: finito et benne!

I needn't look at my new purchased-for-the-trail watch to know that it's apparently late in "AT Time." I am the absolute last man standing at Hawk Shelter here on the second morn of spring. Even Jackie is gone, she who confided to me, "It took me two hours to get ready this morning. I don't know what I'm doing." She hardly made a peep this morning while everyone packed around the table but then spoke briefly, almost soundlessly, to me when the others were gone. Last man standing. That's me. A merit badge for Day Two: Last Scout to Strike Tent. Thank you, Mr. Pederast Scoutmaster (mine was, apologies to those who aren't). I am proud to accept this honor on behalf of the me that doesn't give a rat's ass how fast he walks the trail, so long as he keeps moving and enjoys the journey the whole frikken way.

I hope last night's storm, a brilliant orgasm of light and crashing sound, sets the tone for my entire journey. "Concussion Bombs for Jesus!" Amen, and we thank thee, Oh Sacred and Indefatigable Tent, for keeping us snug and dry as a pit barbecue hog in the waterless Mojave.

I sense already a mentality, nay, an instinctual desire to keep up with the pack. This I imagine is going to be my daily sacrifice, both to taking it slow and safe and to keeping this story written down, every day. All right, so whilst we sit here and last night's gang gets ever farther on ahead, let's talk a bit more about gear.

For the sake of easing access to food during the day's hike, I spent $15 on a small fanny pack, just large enough to hold a day's worth of granola and dried fruit, including honey dates from Hadley's date palm farm in Coachella Valley, just down the hill from my home base, Idyllwild. Speaking of which, just as a matter of unique interest, I also carried here from California and am still sipping from two quarts of spring water pulled right out of a hole in the ground outside Idyllwild just a stone's throw from the Pacific Crest Trail, the AT's West Coast cousin. Thus, in me here today there exists a kind of a marriage of the two trails in water, as it were.

So there's the fanny pack round my waist full of snacks in easy reach as I hike. Another excellent item, one I can't imagine doing without is my Camelback, a two-liter water bladder with a line of blue transparent tubing running from the pack to the area of your mouth. You simply turn your head to the side, bite the nipple and you're drinking. I bought the thing years ago as a gift for K but kept it for myself when it turned out she wanted a bigger one. (Stop that! We'll have no penis jokes in this book.) Fanny pack of snacks plus water bladder equals hands-free hiking. This makes a big difference when you have a hefty load on your back and you don't want to offload and reload every time you want to nosh.

My pack is no mythical, high-tech thing. It's simply a pack, a black Jansport bag with no internal frame or space age accoutrements. It was a gift from friend Emelia years ago, I think from when we did some hiking together in northern Cal's Trinity Alps. I must have been pack-less and she had two. Emelia will no doubt pop to mind often on this journey. A dear friend, a beautiful lady with a spirit to match, she gave my latter college years depth, Zen wisdom, and the perspective of an older friend. Much or all of the simple yoga stretches I'll be doing often on this trip I learned from Emelia.

My "kitchenette" consists of one $40 MSR (Mountain Safety Research) "Pocket Rocket" stove, a tiny three-ounce miracle that screws onto a diminutive butane canister; one titanium cook pot, also feather light and also $40 (ouch); and one small stainless coffee mug, a splurge weight-wise but what the hell. For utensils I have one heavy-duty plastic spoon and my Swiss Army knife. That's it.

And that's it for this writing session. Close behind the storm last night was a cold front that currently has me sitting here freezing my ass off, even in the sun. Time to get hiking and warm up from within.

High atop some mountain in Georgia on Day Five, I contemplate the last four days of some kind of weird ecstatic granola-junkie dirty-sock boot camp. At Walasi-Yi hostel at Neel's Gap, we are all equal in stink. "What will you do with your shoes when you're done hiking," the Volcano Goddess asks. "I'll sell them on eBay," I say. "The shoes that made the whole trail from Georgia to Maine. Two thousand miler shoes." Casey, the border collie with the doggie food backpack, comes over and nuzzles my face, attempts to get the cashews from my closed hand. All around us, Goddess, Flowerpants, Underground Radio, and me, there spans out seemingly to forever the blue of the bluest sky, and below it layer after layer receding into the distance of blue-shaded mountains, mountains that to see them up close must be brown and gray like the forests we walk through, but in the distance and perhaps in the reflection of the sky, they roll on, blue, sleeping dreams of distant oceans.

I've been trying to find time to write for four days. But I've become a part of a tight little family of friends, all thruhikers, all traveling at roughly the same speed. They're pushing it, pushing me. Not in any zealous speed hiker sense, but enough, and more than what I would have done myself.

So much to tell after so few days. I'm seated now beneath this fantastic old oak tree, all gnarled and scraggly and full of personality. From my place here on the ground it climbs Beanstalk Jack-high and crazy like varicose veins on the blue skin of the sky. I type, finally using my laptop lying-down method after days of being so busy or tired I hadn't the strength.

I met Elly (my name for her, pseudo-named for her likeness to Jodie Foster and our mutual love of the film *Contact*) on my second day out. I wanted the Volcano Goddess the moment I spotted her. After spending an hour writing on Sunday morning, I'd made a shorter than expected day of seven miles to Gooch Gap Shelter. On Day One I'd done nine. On Day Two, seven. On Day Three, I did 12. Day Four was just four miles into Neel's Gap where we rested and "desupplied." John dubbed our new friend Nathan "Underground Radio" based on his claim to have buried his hefty radio the first day of the hike in an effort to reduce his pack weight. His comment about this odd but classic act: "The earth worms are groovin'!" Apparently he left the radio on. I'd like to think the hypocritical dope fiend Rush of Right Wing Radio was the last to go squawking into the dirt.

The shelter on Day Two at mile marker 14.6 was great, and I quickly claimed a spot in its loft. That night I sewed my loco fleece hat that has since become something of a trademark and is most certainly a colorful eye catcher. Hand-sewn with temperatures dropping rapidly at sunset, it was whipped together without regard for chic design.

When Elly arrived I was up in the shelter's loft, the shelter a kind of miniature barn with an open front and a picnic table beneath its overhanging roof. The first thing I noticed about Elly was her hair. A wild mane, very lion like, erotically reminiscent of my college girlfriend, Melissa Moore, from 1989, the only girl in a long history of lovers who truly broke my heart. Fifties librarian-style glasses, sexy, muscular, and slim, Elly hails from a commune in Virginia. At the right angle, she's a dead ringer for Jodie Foster but with a wild and uncombed mane.

Fate dropped this girl in my lap. Fate cleared the way and dropped Elly right beside me. She got to the shelter when there was but one space left for someone to throw down her bag, the space right beside me, and join the stinky-feet slumber party that was my second night on the AT. Late that night, the temperature dropped below 20 degrees F and had me snapping awake from dreams of sliding into this girl's bag for warmth. So real were those dreams, I woke embarrassed, damn nearly blurting out apologies for my forwardness.

Funny how fate works, for just one night later, after a brutal 12 miles and a cold and late arrival to the next shelter, I threw shyness to the wind and asked if she'd like to share a tent with me. She said yes. Now she nightly shares my tent. As a result I am not resting much. Perhaps those dreams were just premonition? Pity me my little sleep, I'm sure you will. Seriously though, it's been a lot more power-hiking than I had counted on, with days up to 12 miles so far. All this on knees not at all happy with me.

Last night's camp of some three-dozen tents has completely cleared out. Again, mine is the last tent standing. I feel bad, holding Elly back from her potentially much faster pace. But for now we tread some middle ground compromise. No, that's a load of crap. I'm slow as a slug and she, patient as rust. She must like me.

Underground and Flowerpants have gone, essentially busting up our little family of four for today anyway. There is a shelter much closer today, seven miles. Perhaps I will have time to write then tonight, given this more reasonable goal. Yesterday's 12 miles wiped me out, and then there was the tent to pitch, water to pump and treat, and so on. Elly made delicious black bean burritos for our supper, perhaps in trade for my pitching the tent. Overall I couldn't be happier, but I feel like a fat middle-aged man thrown into boot camp, and kept there, not by any mandate so much as a sweet cherry pie, steaming hot and waiting on the windowsill every night.

After repeatedly joking with south-facing hikers, none of whom were thruhikers, asking them, "So how was Maine?" today it really happened. There on the path appeared Fuman, who answered our query with "Great!" Yes, he had come from Kathadin. Wha-what? We couldn't believe it. Fuman of the blazing red hair and beard and snow-white legs hardly seemed to match the fiery spirit that must have driven this man to thruhike the AT not only in the opposite and thus less-social direction as us, but in the dead of winter, one of the harshest winters on the East Coast in years, says Elly. "What are your trail names?" he inquired. I said that we hadn't quite landed them yet. Fuman, without hesitation, looked at me and said, "Malcovich."

"Almost done," he said. "Just one more day." We all looked at one another in amazement. One day? It had taken us five. We shook his hand, congratulated him, and not long after parting ways, wished we'd taken a group photo with the one called Fuman, he who'd hacked through winter with an ice ax, lost his partner and his Chu.

Cheered from a grumpy slumber this morning by a vocal quintet, the sing-song joyous sounds of the Von Trapp Family, three children from ages 10 to14 (roughly) hiking with their parents. They sing a song about shaving cream, or at least one in which shaving cream is inserted every time the word should have been shit. Very funny stuff.

Thus far:
- Six days, no blisters.
- Temp in teens two mornings so far.
- Most every step of the way so far has felt like hiking a dead forest, all deciduous and bare in the dregs of winter.
- Cooking is hard when your hands are frozen and your brain is a meat Popsicle from hoofing it all day.
- I'm out of hot cocoa already on Day Five.
- Spent an additional $45 on stuff sacks at Neel's Gap – the magic result: everything once strapped to the outside of my pack now fits inside!
- One of the biggest subjects of conversation is pack weight. I am well ahead of the game with a pack fully loaded with food and water at 35 pounds. Many hikers, some of them women half my size, are still carrying 50 pounds.
- I took a self-portrait photo of my bare belly against the background of the AT route map from Georgia to Maine (my belly hung somewhere in Georgia). Why? Because when I reach the top of that map, I will have no belly and will have muscles in places I never thought possible.

Lark lay in her tent asleep. Its all-screen walls afford the passerby a full view of her reclining there angel-like on her back, closed lids skyward. I think to myself, "It's Sleeping Beauty on display here on the Nutball-Thruhiker-Terra-Stomping Appalachian Trail. Beauty's on 'medical leave' from Harvard, and doesn't she look peaceful, gentle and sweet?" (Don't believe it).

I met Lark on the evening of Day One as she fumbled with her gas stove before a macho and unhelpful audience of hiker men. The stove was a blazing mess, seemingly uncontrolled fire spilling out of it everywhere; and though everyone seemed to know how to work the thing, no one got down on hands and knees to help her. I didn't know the stove. Mine is of the propane canister variety. But I got down there with her anyway and did my best.

Later with the stove under control and her dinner cooking, I chatted her up a bit and learned that she had dropped out of Harvard to come and do the trail. Wow, I thought. What conviction, what courage. But when I showed her my little pocket stove (that looks so much like a little lunar lander) and said I like it because it's "sexy," she gave me such a dirty look (virgin) that I decided it best to leave her be. I mean, what was she, 18? Seventeen, maybe? I was 17 when I went off to Pepperdine U. and dropped out myself just one semester later. God bless Lark and her hike. If only I'd had such a lofty and cleansing goal at a young 18.

Today I sit atop a hill at some shelter whose name escapes me, napping and telling this tale in the sun and the relative warmth of March 25 at three thousand feet in the northern Georgia mountains. I hiked, driven on by Elly's unflagging pace, seven miles today, an easy day in the parlance of this rugged trail ripping crowd of Thoreaueans-on-crack. Some of these guys really move. Now on my sixth day, I've done 50 miles. I'm told the three young men who just arrived are on their third day. I don't have the stamina or the training to move that fast. My knees are a constant source of pain and psychological terror. If I continue to stop to rest them, I will lose Elly, the warm cherry pie at the end of a grueling day.

So, the Lekis. I have "crutched" my knees with a $129 pair of ski pole-like trekking poles that balance you and, in my case, bear a lot of the brunt of weight I place on my knees with every downhill step. In one day I have become quite proficient at this. I feel at times like Scrooge's Tiny Tim eagerly "four-stepping" (or did he only have one crutch?) toward Christmas turkey. More than once I've said to Elly, "Tiny Tim is ready for his morphine." The pain is that bad.

Somewhere down this hill the syncline of which is killing me, sending dagger-like stabs into my legs with every step, fresh, moist turkey awaits. Right? Or am I the turkey? Okay, McKinney. Be careful with your metaphors. Turkey hunting season just opened in these parts and continues for another couple of weeks.

It's strange that it has turned out to be knee problems. I've never had knee problems in my life! In the first two days, I went down twice on a turned left ankle. I've twisted ankles before and thought sure this would be the weak point. But aside from straight fatigue and major adjustments being made on the part of my lungs, I'm fine. Ankles now fine. Feet are fine, not one blister. But my knees! Mein Gott! It's like I never knew they existed, and suddenly, whammo! God says, "By the way, you have knees." In His typical omnipotent fashion, God don't serve up nothing new without a buttload of pain for a chaser.

On the evening of our resupply on Day Four in Neel's Gap, I actually had to excuse myself from my hostel company friends to go out back and bawl my eyes out. I cried for fear that this weird and sudden anomaly would stop me short, would rob me of this great journey I am on and the family of like-minded misfits from mainstream society that I have quickly come to love. The poles are helping. I leave the rest to God and hope He can take a joke.

I came to hike the AT knowing full well I would need a trail name, that everyone has one and so should I. It is a way of separating ourselves from the people we were in the outside world, in the crazed and sickly mainstream society that all of us have somehow, miraculously and through great effort, managed to escape for a time. But I didn't want to name myself.

Now nearly a week in, I am proud to have been "gifted" several names from which to choose. Thus far they include: Hammerhead (based on the hammerhead shark-shaped fleece hat I made myself); Tinkerbell (given me by the children of the Von Trapp family), based on the little Tinkerbell in a plastic lamp I have hanging round my neck, property of my art car Duke's dash but pilfered to bring me luck on my trip; Malcovich (explained yesterday); and Inspector Gadget, a name given me by Kristen due to the presence on my hip of this very device on which I now write. Before we got well ahead of them, Sam and Larrisa were calling me Jack, after Jack Sparrow, Johnny Depp's character in *Pirates*. I found that both ironic and flattering. I have temporarily dubbed Kristen "Flowerpants" by her flower-patterned shorts, though surely she is deserving of something better. I go undecided sensing more choices are coming.

An Appalachian Trail song, by me:
(to be sung to the tune of "Sunshine on My Shoulders Makes Me Happy")
Mouse turds in my coffee cup make me happy.
Mouse turds give you Hantavirus and make you die.
So throw some water in, boil 'em up good, ya-dee ya-dee.
Mouse turds in my coffee get me high. [repeat]

Morning and the coffee's on. Sleeping Beauty is now Dawn of the Dead, the fire 'round which we sat yakking is out, and last night's distant monkeys have been identified as turkeys (we think). I have manipulated carabineers to lower the cable lines which suspend our food high above nocturnal bear aspirations; and now, whilst others are chowing down carbos in preparation for "Big Miles," I am cooling my fingers on this keyboard to bring you, the reader, the latest from the Great Gonzo AT Romp. Elly, master of birdsong, gardener, and graduate of biochemistry, is a snuggler.

Elly laughs and smiles a lot in the tent at night, and thus far has stuck with me during the day, but I have no idea what she really thinks of me. I have asked much about her life and she offered still more, but not once that I can think of has she responded with a similar or related question about me. I find this odd and a little isolating, but have chalked it up to her somewhat reserved

Elly-ness, her quiet and angular beauty. I've even managed for the most part (so far) not to be hurt by her apparent total lack of interest in my stated goal of writing about this journey. It is no doubt odd having someone following your actions with pen and paper, but it IS what I DO, and I figure anyone sufficiently bothered by it will do well to just get the heck away from me.

This is my blessing. This is my curse. But to the obvious and rigid goal of everyone in these mountains—getting to Maine— I have the added goal of churning out a tome to match the trail in length and spirit. I may soon lose my thus far ad hoc hiking family because of this, because of the need to go a little slower, to smell the flowers, to stop and scribble. But I'll do whatever has to be done. Just as thruhiking the trail is really no more than a grand idea made real by daily walking, so is this idea. The practice of writing is no more than writing every day. Now for a handful of granola, striking the tent, and hitting the trail.

Walk and walk and walk some more, this seems to be the only real trick of the trail. For an entire business day we walk, and at day's end there's very little time before night. When the sun goes down in the forest, you go to bed. Just so. And awaken, as I have this morning, to the first rising of the sun, sometimes a little before. The woodpecker hammers: getup, getup, getup!

[The following incident calls to mind a Jim Morrison line about a "strange and overfriendly guest you brought to dinner." This really happened.]

A man sits trailside with a heavy pack and a four-pound Bible in his hands. "Lotta people on the trail this time of year," he says. "They're gonna hafta put in a superhighway here. The good news is there are about 150 ahead of you. The bad news is only about five of them are gonna make it. Jesus is the way and the truth, the only way. That's all that matters. Bible stands for Book of Instruction Before Leaving Earth."

Point: Typically garrulous and responsive, none of us have anything to say in response to this man. All I can think is: Leave it to a zealot to give us the grim news of how many of us will fail. Flowerpants says she had to resist telling the man that Jesus was too much pack weight. The man stays behind awaiting the next hiker. We walk on. As an afterthought up trail, I turn and shout aloud, "The Lord, Sir, lives in me every step of the way! I've got Jesus in my knees, Amen!"

Counterpoint: At the trailhead at Indian Grave Gap, we descend to a road and to the sight of Claire, "Hobbes on Catnip," and their dog, Matty, reclining roadside in matching blue lawn chairs. Hanging from a tree at the trailhead hangs an Easter basket full of colorful plastic eggs. In each egg, a handful of chocolates, Sweetarts, and other goodies. Claire and Hobbes hung their goodie basket the night before and have returned to fetch the leavings. Our arrivals have coincided. They pass out Frescas and we exchange laughs and, from us, gratuitous expressions of gratitude. Such a simple and selfless act is theirs. This is an incident of "Trail Magic," an apparently common phenomenon that strikes us as anything but common. Wonderful, rather.

Already today another man hiking a segment of the trail handed out "Cokes," the southern term for soda of any kind. He gave me a Pepsi. Hobbes hails from Clearwater, Florida, and will begin his thruhike in May, section hiking with his wife pacing him in an RV. "I'm lucky to be able to go at all. It's taken two years of planting seeds," he says, nodding over his shoulder at his wife and winking at us. We laugh and share a smile.

As we prepare to move on up the trail, another car pulls up and out steps "Queen Diva," a woman shuttling hikers around. She, too, offers us sodas and candy. We gratefully accept Oreos and Rice Krispie Treats and head on our way. An hour later up the trail, the sugar rush must still be on me. We've made today's goal, Tray Mountain Shelter, but it's early and I can't imagine stopping now. Elly is game to hike on. But Underground Radio is complaining of sore shoulders and wants to stay. The one I've been calling Flowerpants, Kristen, has her shoes off and is tendering a nasty ankle blister. She's having knee problems, too. Together, they stay. Together, Elly and I move on. Once again the family is broken, though almost certainly temporarily. I've suggested several trail names for Flowerpants, and she has found one to her liking: "Tumbling Tumbleweed." I don't think I've ever met a bigger female fan of the Cohen brothers' film *The Big Lebowski.*

Two hours later Elly and I stop with the setting sun at Addis Gap, 61.5 miles north along the AT. It was a 13-mile day, my longest yet. Seventy degrees in the shade at two o'clock this afternoon. That represents a 50-some degree temperature variance in just one week out here on the trail. I'm sweating like an Eskimo in New Orleans, and the flies are on me. It's March. I can't even begin to fathom what hiking will be like in the dead heat of summer: 100 degrees, insects in full force, the trail closer to cities and trash and tract homes. Dear God!

Okay, then. Tough as this early stretch of trail may seem to novice me, I must now vow to appreciate it every moderate step of the way. "Do you, Rick, promise to love and cherish this trail for as you long as you both don't hate one another?"

I do.

Ever hiked much? I thought I had, but most of it was short jumps and more than a decade ago. I ask because of a funny thing that I'd forgotten about hiking: You see a lot less of the forest than you'd imagine. What you do see is a lot of dirt. Earth, rocks, dead leaves, sticks. You come to know your shoes very well.

I have lagged behind the gang to rest a moment. A small black fly bites into my leg. The clink-clink of my trekking poles takes me in my mind to a ski slope of my youth, legs dangling from a chair lift, ski pole duels with the friend beside me. I imagine in this endless stepping rhythm and trance of the trail, I will travel to many places in my mind, see much that I haven't seen in years, all the while fully present in my slowly moving Appalachian world.

I stop on the crest of a hill and just breathe. Down by my sides extend arms misted in sweat connected to hands suddenly vigorous and vital in duty, gripping hard the cork grips of titanium trekking poles. Overnight the poles have become extensions of my arms, another pair of legs to support the week knees of the primary pair. Hot air heaves out of me in heavy gusts, and I am reminded that I have been breathing like this for days, for one full week now. I arise in the morning a muddle of mad exhaustion and even madder enthusiasm, and I do this every day, all day. I am becoming a machine. A hiking machine. Yet I haven't even been born into this yet. More than 2,100 miles to go, yet today my 70-mile feat feels a triumph unparalleled in my life.

A cooling breeze blows from the north and the west. My feet are throbbing, but this is okay, balanced by the fact that every muscle in my body is humming. At 37 I felt I was dying. Already I am no longer 37, no longer dying, no longer sick from the world. I forget to take the Prozac—I don't feel that I need it out here. I take them anyway. It's okay. No harsh changeovers necessary. Just walk. That's all I have to do each day: just walk.

Elly, all business one minute, now tender as can be, reminds me daily that I'll be just fine. When my knees felt ready to collapse descending Blood Mountain, she walked with me slowly and at the hostel assured me again that I would be just fine. Up here on this ridge just south of Plumorchard Gap Shelter, I feel like a man again, a man and a monster, a heaving, breathing, pulsating, well-oiled machine. Albeit a machine with very sore knees, but I think maybe I'll live.

Escaping 75-degree heat here on a late March day, I crawl inside a lush rhododendron grove, drop my pack on a flat spot in the leaves, and fall asleep. I have entered North Carolina today, having walked the full 80-some miles that the AT traverses northern Georgia. I am exhausted, sore all over, and thirsty for a beer (haven't had one in nearly two weeks). Gear, food, and knees are the principal topics of conversation among us thruhikers, a real switch from the usual outside world talk of sex, booze, and cop & lawyer TV shows (I generalize).

Elly and I switched places yesterday, no longer her leading at her Zen plodding pace and me in the rear. I took the lead and, much more true to character, began tackling the trail in leaps and bounds, interspersed of course by a zillion short stops for breath (at which point she'd catch up). Huffing and puffing is my daily due now; some eight hours a day I'm damn near hyperventilating. I know this will change with my metabolism. Pondering my trail name, the one I haven't quite settled on yet, I thought "Screaming Knees" would be good, if I were a Navajo or something. Met Squirrel Master going the other way yesterday (and hoofing it like all the obviously seasoned hikers do). Says he was finishing up his southbound thruhike, started in June of 2003. Wow! Said he was taking his time. I like that. He also said there was a "Gadget" last year, so I'm now somewhat disinclined to carry that name.

Met a guy named "Hard Tack Hank" from Buford, Georgia, yesterday, a congenial and funny guy who says he's a big fan of thruhikers and bade us please apologize to young Lark for him. Nineteen-year-old Lark is hiking alone, and apparently Hank figures he freaked her out when he said he'd be "stalking" her on the Internet all the way to Maine. I clued him in to *Jigglebox.com* so he could "stalk" my journey, too. What the hell. I knew what he meant. At least I thought I did. I later received an e-mail from Hank: "Have never read such egocentric drivel in my life but am sure to be drawn weekly if not daily to your rantings with, as Marlon Brando may have said in *Apocalypse Now* the horror of it all."

Dropping down into Dick's Gap, the hitchhike road-crossing into the nearest town of Haiwasee, I told John to have a hamburger and a beer for me. Elly said to please eat some sharp cheddar for her. We weren't going into town and he was. Not 20 minutes later when we dropped down to the highway crossing, we discovered more trail angels there to greet us with food and drink. "Tater from 2000," as he called himself (a former thruhiker of that year), was the first to chime in and offer me a hotdog and soda. I snapped up that dog so fast you would have thought I was a hummingbird. Then from a few picnic tables away came the voice of Queen Diva, offering the same. We all had a good laugh as I made a joke about our being fought over by competing angels, pulled from one to the other by free food. Over at her grill, I got my hamburger. Talk about rapid manifestation of desires. John appeared out of the forest having given up on the previous road. He did well, getting a burger and a ride into town with Tater.

Diva, it seems, is acting as a kind of roadrunner and trailside food supplier to a team of thruhikers she calls the "Fab Five." I am amazed to learn that she will be pacing these five hikers all the way to Maine at their set rate of 21 miles per day. Outstanding. Additionally baffling, because when I try and work out the mileage of this monumental undertaking and do the math with the days between now and October 15 when Mt. Katahdin, the northernmost point, closes for the winter, well…I just can't imagine how the hell I'm going to pull it off AND take my time and smell the flowers along the way.

I die each night with the setting sun. Down it goes, falling languidly toward my native California making me wonder, as I often do, what the hell I'm doing here. "Here" over the past many years has been many places, many places not California. I have roamed nomadic, at times ecstatic, others pathetic. Now at sunset on a Sunday in North Carolina on Standing Indian Mountain, I merely stare, stupefied, stoned by another eight-hour endorphin rush, the result better than codeine, Valium, any of that shit.

We clean our pots and hang our food against the bears, and I, somewhat against mountaineering protocol, leave out a pre-made cup of coffee for myself, sugared and creamed instant, cold but conveniently located for that early morning groggy grab out the tent, lighter in hand, pocket rocket propane stove on, coffee hot. If the bears come after that, well, let 'em have it. Then it's down like a fighter throwing the fight, into the tent, out like a light. At 7:30 p.m. Astonishing.

How does that song go? "New morning, new day, gonna do things my way…." Who's that? Foreigner? Yeah. Ok, I'm old. What am I talking about? The frikken Stones are STILL performing! Feeling better today, way better. Feeling like $37 instead of the $3 I felt like yesterday when I woke up. Although "woke up" isn't quite correct since I NEVER SLEPT! But that's another story, one I'll tell when I get over the shock of it.

On today's forecast, ladies and gentlemen of the Vicarious Trek, Elly and I and a handful of other insane misfits and Ameri-Cuban boat refugees from the Bush Disaster will be Romper Rooming it over not one, but two mile-high peaks in our overpriced sneaks. The AT, I have found, has a penchant for outrageous ups and downs. Its "authors" or trail volunteer engineers, as it were, seem to enjoy sending its adherents way up and then way down again in roller coaster fashion. When I heard someone speaking of "The Roller Coaster" the other day, I was sure they were speaking of a stretch over which I had already climbed. But nooo.

THE roller coaster yet awaits us, apparently an 18-mile stretch somewhere in the Smokies featuring no fewer than 18 mountains. Eighteen mountains, eighteen miles. How many psycho-fitness nuts did it take to screw in that topographic light bulb? I wonder.

Woke up last night to the sound of drops hitting the tent canopy. Just an occasional "pop" of a raindrop, but it was enough to jerk me straight out of bed, shoes on and out of the tent. I grabbed our packs and stowed them under this tiny vestibule of a canopy at the tent's feet end, grabbed Elly's shoes and tucked them in her side of the tent, and did the same with mine on my side. Then I peed. You pee a lot out here. Or maybe you notice it more. Because every movement of bladder or bowels out here is an undertaking, some more major than others.

Getting up in the middle of the night to tinkle is one thing. It's cold and, as in the case of last night, damp, and dark and spooky and all the rest, but once past the pain of wrenching oneself out of one's toasty mummy bag, it's bearable. But a midnight movement, that's a real pain in the ass and usually requires twice the "enthusiasm" to get out of the bag. After a largely sleepless night (night before last) I NEEDED sleep BAD. So last night, after lying there a while entertaining the various pains in feet and knees and so on, I said screw it, and popped a codeine (leftover from recent wisdom tooth pull). Aside from pain reduction, codeine, a vastly watered down cousin of morphine, is nonetheless an opiate derivative and thus has the added "benefit" (in this case) of stopping you up. Result: no nocturnal interruptions of my deep sleep campaign to answer any unwanted call from, you know…Nature.

So much for my highfalutin talk about endorphin highs at sunset. The high only lasts about half an hour. Beyond that, you're on your own. Like a good Boy Scout, I come prepared.

FOUR

Elly Flies Over the Cuckoo's Nest…The Irksome Nocturnal Visit of the Ghost of Boudreau…Lily-Me and the Barrymore Connection… The Sarge-Little Engine Love Conundrum…Nantahala, my Narnia! The Big Miles Obsession…Elly Outa Joint & the Delayed Explanation…

Then just like that, Elly is gone. The walk in the woods today was strange. No, she didn't go "off trail," the gentle vernacular for quitting. No, she didn't disappear. Like that old joke where a guy asks his buddy if he lost his job and he answers that no, he knows where his job is, there's just someone else doing it now, well, I have a pretty good idea where Elly is.

Do I miss her? Yes. I'm lying here in a shelter on some mountain at around mile 110. Beside me lies a man rumored to be a gargantuan snoring machine. Yikes. I could have set up my tent, but it rains now, and it could freeze tonight, bringing snow. In a way it is symbolic. I met Elly in a shelter and haven't slept in one since. I slept with Elly. We shared my groovy little two-person tent every night. Have I mentioned that I miss her?

The boys out around the fire are talking about Bill Bryson's book A *Walk in the Woods*. The review is largely critical. We are laid out here in the old wooden shelter like bagged corpses after a massacre. Our packs hang from large nails driven into the wall above us such that my pack is suspended right over my head. The wall is not much longer than my body and laid out lengthwise to my left, the back hanging wall at my head. A third wall is six sleeping-bag-widths away to my right. I am in the leftmost corner. Rain dances on the tin roof overhead. The roof extends farther than the walls, almost by double, creating a covered cooking area, what some call a pavilion.

Some guy from south Boston with the thickest "Mass-accent" I've ever heard and a thus far curt demeanor loiters at the butcher block-like table in the center of the open area. He eats and paces, his bright headlamp beam scanning the darkness. If I were a narcissistic severe depressive with acute anxiety and fits of paranoia, which modern medicine claims I am, I'd say he was doing it specifically to annoy me. Ha. Ha.

49

I don't know where to begin in telling you why Elly is gone. It was getting quiet between us toward the end. Now it's dead quiet without her.

I've heard chainsaws are verboten out here. Not even the trail volunteers who clear fallen trees from the trail are allowed to use them. There is only birdsong. Woodpeckers mostly. The clink-clink of my titanium poles on the trail. I look at myself and feel I must look like every kid I knew in school with arm-brace crutches, kids with CP, leukemia, what have you. But I am not disabled, not physically. So I walk on, steady and sturdy, determined to make a good go of this for the physically disabled everywhere, for every limping, crutch-addled person I've ever seen on the street whose infirmity has set me teary-eyed and smacked my blues across the face with the sting of shame. Incidentally, Duke, the tiny action figure from "Doonesbury" that I stole from my art car to carry on my pack, has lost both his arms. Poor Duke, modeled after writer Hunter Thompson, is now a paraplegic. He has stuck with me, however, riding proud. [Postscript: Little did I know at the time that in Colorado the real Duke, my mentor, was growing infirm, increasingly reliant on a wheelchair and not long for this world.]

"When you goad me I start farting," says Fast Eddy from Louisiana. Navigator is giving him shit about snoring, as he is rumored to do. Aha, so he's the gargantuan! There are two tiny dogs running around. They belong to Dirtnap, an alleged law student gone native now running around the Appalachians in shorts and Tevas and a mop of brown hair stoking a smoky fire to cook his food (he carries no stove). He has been hiking north since January, having begun in the Florida Keys. Says he walked some stretches in a foot or more of water for miles at a time through the swamps of that state, Jeb's wet Bush Empire.

Tinker is a very hungry 19-year-old with great enthusiasm for gear. He made his own alcohol stove based on recent popular soda can designs published in *Backpacker* magazine and on the Boy Scout Web site. When I arrived today he was surveying a massive sprawl of food before him. "This is four days' worth," he explained to me. "That's why my bag weighs 45 pounds." For my whole first hour here, he was eating, trying to force down as much as possible to reduce his pack weight. Tinker is in the National Guard and may get called off the trail at any moment to go serve his country in Iraq or elsewhere.

Sanguine is a schoolteacher from Providence, Rhode Island, taking a year off to go get dirty and cold and sore in the mountains. She has a big bright lime green pack cover that made me want to call her Miss Margarita coming down the trail today. Hiking with her is Navigator of Seattle. I'd like to call him Yodeler for his classic Swiss Alps hiker look.

I want to talk about Elly. But I can't. I miss her. But, then again, I don't. It's hard to mesh two people from totally different worlds together for 10 days, 24/7, as it were, especially in this pressure cooker first month wherein the attrition rate is 40 percent. We're all just too unique and too full of our own ghosts and quirks and demons and doubts. We tried.

The smoke from the wood fire outside drifts into the shelter in sufficient quantities that I feel ready to sneeze at any moment. The little dogs pace parabolas between our mummy bags looking for someone to snuggle up with. Campfires are a good thing to a point. They warm us and give us a little nightlife where normally there is none. But the eight o'clock zonk bell goes off in my now deep woods-conditioned head, and I want the fire to die out and the boys to go to bed. Their dialogue is far too clear and, like the wind, it howls Elly's absence. For the first night on the Appalachian Trail, I go to sleep truly sad.

I covered 18 miles on this, the last day of March, for a total thus far of 127 miles. Six of us cram into Wessar Mountain Shelter under frigid conditions. Sarge, Little Engine, Boudreau, Doug, Tinker, and me.

Boudreau the "Sobo" or southbounder is telling the story of the origin of his name, of one John Baptiste Boudreau, his apparent 5th generation great-grandfather. Somewhere in the story there's talk of Grandpa Boudreau selling in the slave trade. Cautious in the company of a black man, Boudreau the storyteller tries to explain. Sarge, big, black, 72 years old and once a Marine sergeant, don't sling bullshit: "Slaves are slaves, Boudreau, but let's just get on with this story."

Pardon me, Dear Reader, if this seems selfish, but I'd like to tell the story of my day. I walked in snow all day today. I walked in a blizzard. I walked in a period of sunshine when the sun melted the snow on the branches and snow avalanched down on the trail like a frozen waterfall. It was stunning, magical.

Boudreau's story, however, goes on and on. I am sure it is a good story. But I walked 18 miles today! I want to rest. I want to write and then rest. To varying degrees, the others are listening. Doug later tells that the story kept his mind off the bitter cold. Tinker must be listening because when, after an hour of exposition, Boudreau poses a question to his captive icicle audience: "And what do you think those secret orders said?" Tinker yells out, "Kill him!" So they did. Sarge later told me he had his earplugs in by then. Little

Engine keeps murmuring "uhum" from her facedown position in her mummy bag, either a good listener or one very polite girl.

My god. The story is finally over! But not before we got to hear three soldiers sawed in half and Boudreau's fifth generation great-grandfather bashed to bits "on the wheels," as it were. What a wretched gory nightmare! I can't even think of my day now. It's gone. I've lost it. Eighteen miles, my greatest achievement to date, bashed to bits by a long and passionate story about, well, about a guy who got bashed to bits! Oh, yah, and how that inspired his fifth generation grandson to take on his name for a trail name. I much preferred hearing Alice's story told me last summer about being the fifth generation grand-daughter of Lewis Carroll's Alice, told to me in sighs and moans as Mad Hatter-I thrust into her rabbit hole like it was the last tea party on Earth.

In the silence following the denouement of the seemingly endless tale of bashed-bones Boudreau, his odd descendent lets go a tremendous fart, long and loud. It is the perfect punctuation to his passionately told but too-long tale. Beside me to my left, Little Engine and Sarge. Sarge has hiked the trail from end to end before and now hikes a thousand or so miles of it every year since. He certainly seems to deserve his trail name. I got wet and cold as hell in today's snowstorm. Coming into the shelter, I had to undress quickly, shedding wet clothes and donning what little dry stuff I had, then dive straight into my bag before hypothermia set in.

Dinner was a mix of chicken noodle soup, dried potatoes, and dried refried beans. It was delicious and warmed me so inside. My shoes are soaked and I doubt they'll be any drier by morning. Of my three pair of socks, only one pair is mostly dry. I have them here in my bag with me to finish the job. The temp outside is likely in the teens. It was 28 degrees most of the day, through snow and snow and more snow. I hiked today without gloves, thanks to my one MasterCard, a Paypal card, being denied at the supply store back at Rainbow Springs. Today, more than ever, my trekking poles were essential, which meant going the storm with my hands exposed. I hiked 10 hours almost without stop. Today was the most foul-weathered, arduous day yet, but also one of the best.

April Fool's Day morning and oh! What do you know? Boudreau is gone. If I had to swear one way or another, I would say that Boudreau wasn't of this world. Boudreau was an X-file. There was just too much about Boudreau that didn't fit, or did fit, as it were, into some mystical scheme to make us all believe he was there in the flesh when in fact he wasn't. His skin for instance:

He was ghostly white. The whole southbound thing: What a perfect excuse for why we'd never see him again after that night. He arrived late, nearly dark, high atop a haunted mountain in a storm and greeted us all when our minds were too blown from battling the elements to be too discerning about who or what was yapping at us. I have heard it said of the dead that they cannot sleep head-to-head with the living. Boudreau, in a move I found quite odd, slept with his head at my feet. He was the only one so positioned.

You see, I believe in ghosts, and I believe that the alleged southbound hiker Boudreau is in fact the lingering spirit of the man he spoke of so passionately. I believe the spirit who visited Sarge, Little Engine, Doug, Tinker, and me that night was none other than John Baptiste Boudreau himself. For John Baptiste was a half-breed Indian at a time when the French still owned the Louisiana Purchase, and his work as peacekeeper between the French and the native tribes was of great importance. But the French killed him anyway. For days now we've been hiking over lands soaked in the blood of natives, French, English, and Civil War soldiers. Places with names like Indian Grave Gap and Blood Mountain. John Baptiste came out of his relatively warm earthen grave and into the cold night to tell us his tale, and I was too tired to listen.

My sleeping bag is a stinky sack of dirty clothes (now hopefully dry), my Palm Pilot, and me. I had to put my Palm Pilot between my thighs for five minutes to thaw it out. I suppose it works cold, but when it's cold, the LCD screen is ghostly faint. Which is fine, because I am now typing in the dark, this time inside the bag because the air temp outside is well below freezing.

Yesterday I walked through a brutal snowstorm. I became concerned because one inevitably gets wet from sweat in one's under layer, and I was soaked. Then my shoes got soaked. I just had to keep moving. Every now and then while I'd be worrying or wrestling in my mind about the possible mistake of letting Elly go, I'd remember Lionel Barrymore's character in that thirties film *You Can't Take It With You,* and I'd say to myself, "Just be like the lilies. Just be a lily and everything's going to be just fine,"

Ha. The gods just never quit with the irony. Be like a lily, Lionel said so long ago. Okay. I love Lionel. Fast-forward to the present and Lionel Barrymore's great-great-niece Drew goes to court and sues my best friend's dad for the rights to his 40-year-old documentary film company name and wins. The film company Les Blank forgot to copyright? Flower Films. Drew, thou art a lily, indeed.

Trekking poles, it turns out, make really good snow smacker-offers. Some parts of the trail are so dense they're like tunnels. Now add a layer of snow to the branches and you've got one narrow tunnel! I knock the snow off with my poles, and whoosh, up snaps the tree branch, up and out of my way!

Doug was amazed to find how many people had made their way through the storm and to the shelters, Cold Spring and Wesser Bald. "I was following two sets of prints in the snow, that's it," he says. "I figured it was just you and Tinker I was following," he told me. The snow was coming down that hard.

When the drinking tube from my Camelback water bladder froze (because it's so skinny it was the first thing to freeze), I took to lapping snow off rhododendron leaves for hydration. Underground Radio would have been fun to get through the snowstorm with. I miss him. I guess I never explained what happened to Tumbleweed and him. That day our foursome hit a shelter a little early in the day, and Tumbleweed and Radio wanted to stay. That was it for them. Elly and I went on. I haven't seen them since. Now I've lost Elly as well.

Everybody around me is talking about food. Desiring a vicarious feast, Tinker asks Sarge what he ate at Fat Willey's. Sarge says something, then Tinker says, No, I asked WHAT you ate. Little Engine, who appears to be Sarge's companion and young enough to be his granddaughter if not for their fairly obvious racial difference, goes into great detail about the exact food elements that comprised their dinner at Willey's, some restaurant in Franklin, North Carolina. It's brutally cold out and I have to go to the bathroom. Food is the last thing from my mind.

To sleep, I remove my Himalayan down jacket, zip it back up, and slip the foot of my bag into it, thus doubly warming my feet. I put on my "smart wool" long johns and dry socks if I have them. In the case of last night when I didn't have dry socks, I tucked my feet into the legs of my other long johns whose hip area needed drying anyway. I wear nylon spandex shirts because they dry so quickly and are warm. I have only two long-sleeved warm shirt items, a wool sweater and a thermal turtleneck. Both were rather damp after yesterday's hike, but I wore the sweater to bed and the turtleneck lay drying somewhere in my mummy bag.

My bag is of the mummy type and thus has a "hoodie" area intended to be lain under and zipped up around one's head and neck. I sleep with the bag upside down such that the hoodie lies like a flap over my head. In windy, witch-tit cold weather like this, I hide inside. I'm taking the time to tell you all this just to avoid joining the crowd in the inevitable ice-cold packup of gear. Did I mention that Elly is gone? Yes, I suppose I did. But hey, maybe there's potential with Little Engine? She can't be Sarge's lover, can she? Nah! Too young. I like what I've heard of her so far. Sweet, attentive as hell to the old dude. Maybe mid- to late-twenties. Ahh, hell. I don't know. But there's a woman for me out here somewhere. I just know it.

Stepping up a craggy cliffside out and away north from the Nantahala Outdoor Center, North Carolina Mile 134.6, I feel a mixture of irony, satisfaction, gratitude, and the will to move forward. Fading below me as I rise in elevation come the strains of "Whiter Shade of Pale," that melodic and nostalgic seventies dirge that trips the light fandango and all that. The music is piped high and loud up through the canyon to be heard over the roar of the Nantahala River. I have stayed two nights at the NOC, taking a Zero Day primarily for the purpose of rest and to catch up on what seems to me days and days of stories untold, but also in hopes that Underground and Tumbleweed might catch me up. They did not.

That's right, they're gone, too. In just a matter of a few days, our cool little family foursome went dry like a keg of Blue Ribbon in a Wisconsin bowling alley on the day before Lent. Now there's nothing left but me: the tap. Or am I the empty keg? All right, enough of that analogy. Two nights at the NOC and I couldn't write diddlysquat. Now I'm just half a mile up trail and the words begin to flood in. I sit down on a leafy soft spot and pull out my "works" and shoot up some words. Round the corner comes No Beard and his pretty fair-haired, fair-skinned, fair-everything'd girlfriend, No Dog. They're a cute couple. Seem solid as oak and granite and colorful as fruitcake. Jesus! What am I saying?

Okay, time to hike up a jillion switchbacks. Two days at 15 miles/day will put me at Fontana Dam and the gateway to the Great Smoky Mountains National Forest, 70 miles of bear-infested and allegedly rule-crazed ranger territory. The prize at the far end is Hot Springs, North Carolina, where the whole town comes out to celebrate thruhikers on April 17. Sounds like a blast to me. One day soon, I'll catch you up on questions like: What happened to Elly? Where am I? Who am I? More importantly, who are all these crazed mutants huffing and puffing alongside me bound for Maine with nutty names like Dirtnap and IceBox?

Later, I sit on some high rock looking at ridge upon ridge upon mountain upon mountain. Old far hikers Mule and the Professor point at the snowline atop the highest mountain as far as we can see and say, "See that snow? That's where we walked from the other day." Indeed. Was that a nightmare or a lovely crystal white fluffy winter dream for which I should feel grateful for having been present? Truth is, I froze my ass off up on that mountain. I had wet everything—shoes, socks, and upper body garments from the sweat beneath my raingear. But I hiked my longest day that day: 18 miles. Hoo-frikken-ray.

And they're off! Right out of the gate and over Grassy Top it's Harvard Lark apparently inexhaustible after her much-celebrated 22-mile day. Right behind Lark is Beer Thirty from Jersey, bent trekking pole and all, he's making tracks like a champ. Third out the gate this morning here at Appalachian Downs it's Big Horn Wanderer, big, wandering, and, well, horny, I guess. Sarge is out there, holding back from his usual pace, throwing the race for the sake of Little Engine, the judge's daughter from Pensacola preparing for the big flip-flop half-way to Maine. She's smoking, but not in the way to win the race, if you get my meaning. In our next heat we have No Dog and No Beard, colorfully adorned in red and yellow Gortex jackets, sure not to be shot by any near-sighted turkey hunters this season. Initially ahead of them but now dropping back we have the Professor and Mississippi Mule, two daunting sixty-something studs, sure, by dint of age and determination, to win the Gold no matter how they place in this one-of-a-kind, 2,000-mile race.

But of course it ISN'T a race at all, is it? I just toy with metaphor. Or is this allegory? Someone back at the beginning said, "First one to Katahdin loses." I think they're probably right. For to run that fast would be to take all the fun out of it, and would also likely mean you got some big ugly responsibility awaiting you at home that's pushing you to finish. I'd rather finish last.

Most with whom I have hiked so far, myself included, have no deadline. Many of us have no homes, no phones, no nothing. That's why we will be the ones to make it. I both admire and turn a curious eye, however, on those who have spouses or lovers at home. I wonder how they'll do it. I admire them for trying. God bless the Von Trapps, who I hear tell lost their home and job of many years when the conference center they managed gave them the boot. Even after losing it all, they chose, as a family, to hike the AT. Wow! What those kids will learn!

Me, I'm not wired right for long-distance relationships. I gave up great love once (maybe more than once?) when I knew that our paths were dividing, geographically speaking. It's too hard on the poet's heart, on any heart, I suspect. But I did get lucky when on Day Two of this endeavor. I met Elly, with whom I hiked and camped for some 10 days. Then it was time for that to end, too. Our paces, our patience, our reasons, our ways, and our means, none passed the test of that grueling first week.

So I go it alone, now last in that little mock race I was just describing. My pace has quickened though, enormously. Now and again I remember that my stride measures far wider than I usually ask of it. Then into that stride I step, braking my fall with poles as I descend, pulling with poles as I climb. In no time I will have thighs of iron and biceps to match. The sun is out today, 70 degrees, light breeze, and we're cooking along. What a vast and incomprehensible difference from just two days ago when I descended through snow with a pack full of frozen-stiff socks and frozen, undrinkable water. Onward.

Thank God for small favors and the freaks who "invent" time travel with this whole daylight savings time shit. Today they have done my fellow hikers and me a favor. Starting today, our days no longer end so damn early. Of course, we'll still rise and set with the sun, but the sun will be around longer, or later. Whatever. Speaking of time and the whole game of reckoning progress, I came out here to relax and enjoy nature, (exfoliated and kind of winter-dead as it is right now - but SO WHAT?). On the contrary, the "whole-food crack heads," as I've come to call them, are up, stuffing their bags and wolfing down Cliff bars at the crack-o-dawn no matter what the weather, and then BAMM! THEY'RE GONE! Off and running. "BIG MILES today!" they say. "Gotta do big miles!"

I say, piss on Big Miles. Sarge is from the Big Easy and I think he'd agree. The whole "big mile" mentality is just another manifestation of the shop-til-you-drop, go-go-go, work-long-hours-for-the-man bullshit that I THOUGHT we were out here to escape. Of course, I never see those big milers again. They're way out ahead now. But every morning there's a new crop of dirt track crack heads, bustin' ass to get to Maine quick as bunnies so they can race home and bust ass back into jobs and cubicles and clichés. It saddens me to see this mentality. But more so, I suppose, it chafes at me, like jock itch, because many of these guys I'd like to see again on down the trail. But I won't. No way. They're gone.

Speaking of gone, and sadly so, Fast Eddy passed me going southbound yesterday as I was heading out of Nantahala. I said, "Hey, Fast Eddy, where you going?" He said, "Hey buddy! I forgot something back at the NOC." Just like that, chipper as can be. Away he went. I remember thinking right away, "Hey, he called me buddy. That's cool." Fast Eddy was the quietest, most soft-spoken giant of a man I've yet met on the trail. I liked him a lot and looked forward to getting to know him better.

I heard last night at Sassafras Gap Shelter that Fast Eddy had "gone off trail," sold his gear piecemeal to any hiker on hand, and headed home to Galliano, Louisiana. He hadn't forgotten anything back at the NOC. Too shy perhaps to say goodbye, he'd at least called me his buddy. Vaya con Dios, Amigo Eddy. You will be missed.

Written during one of the endorphin highs I've been getting in late afternoon:

It's 7 o'clock and I really should be going. I still need to make camp somewhere before dark. I've hiked 15 miles or so today and I feel okay. I really should be going, but I just felt compelled to stop and, if not capture it in words, at least admire the beauty before me. It's a mix of manmade and Heaven, this dazzling late afternoon scene.

There is a breeze, cool but not uncomfortable whilst I am seated in the sun in windbreaker and fleece hat. I hear no birds just now, likely tucking in for the night. There is only the light dance of dry leaves and the whisper of wind in the trees. To my right and ahead slips the sun from the day's sky, framed by mountains, poised almost as though to drive down the aptly named Yellow Creek Mountain Road that stretches onward below it. The sunlight has painted it, lit up all its yellow lines and shiny spots like a river or a silver ribbon through the forest. It is lined with trees, yet so perfectly aligned with the sun's path this afternoon that the shadow of not one tree nor outstretched branch touches it. The sun sinks dead ahead in perfect sync with the vanishing road.

Closer to me, a tiny little alley of dirt and twigs and dry leaves tumbles upward toward me from that road. This little alley is but a few short paces of the Appalachian Trail. On a tree beside me there stands painted into the bark a tiny white blaze, not much bigger than two business cards end to end. It is the simple white paint sign to all who hike that yes, this is the trail, this is the way to Maine. A few thoughts at a crossroads in North Carolina.

I learned a lot from Elly, like the names of a few birds and trees. She taught me about the junco, a little bird that gets its dinner from junk lying around on the ground, and about the pileated woodpecker, a big and beautiful thing that would sing to us through the jungle-like rhododendron groves of Georgia. That was before the snows of course, back in those first days when one might believe that Georgia knew no real winter.

From Elly I learned more than I may ever need to know about life on a commune, on one of the few still existing and apparently successful communes in the country, her home. I learned all about the The Rainbow Gathering and heard for the first time the term "spange," a short form of spare changing, the mainstay of the modern young hobo. Those are among the good things I learned about Elly, and most of them because I asked questions about her life and probed further when probing felt welcomed.

I rather quickly developed a kind of lonesomeness around Elly, however, stemming from something I don't often encounter in people of mutual attraction trying to get to know one another: Elly never asked me anything about myself. I learned that Elly had been hurt somehow, somewhere, quite badly it seemed. I learned this through her anger, of which she had plenty. We all deal with depression in different ways. Elly's way is anger. I've been forestalling this, but here goes. The night when things really fell apart for us went something like this:

We made camp and went about the business of cooking our separate meals and washing in the creek almost entirely without dialogue. For my part, I didn't know what to say anymore. I felt I had run out of I "interest" in this woman thanks largely to her seeming total lack of interest in me. If she didn't want to know about me, then I didn't really care to know much more about her. It seems a terrible thing to admit, but there it is.

Elly was sweet as a peach when we lay down together nights. She laughed and smiled a lot and was a totally different person than her hard-hiking day self. So it was that night of our demise, duties done, the last thing I wanted to do was get heavy on her when we lay down to watch the sunset. But I had to get the question off my chest. "How come you never ask me anything about myself?" I inquired. She didn't want to be invasive, she said. Hmm. Okay. "But you've asked me NOTHING about myself, nothing at all."

Elly explained that she had learned much about me by the stories I told, and that she hadn't felt comfortable asking more. Basically, she went on to explain away something that had really only required an apology, or some small balm on my ego with the assurance that in the future she looked forward to learning lots more about me and would do her best to ask.

Yeah, right, McKinney. Dream on.

The whole thing stank for me, and the combination of this problem and a lot of things I HAD LEARNED about her through incessant query and just plain observation 24/7 since we'd met had already likely sealed our fate. I felt it was time to move on, to say thank you both to one another and to the Universe for the great gift of companionship in getting through this difficult first stretch of the trail together, and say adieu. Despite appearances to the contrary, I don't easily make such decisions. But then Elly went batty, and that sealed the deal.

It should have been a non-event, a no-biggie. But the way she reacted just freaked me out. She rolled a joint and then lost it in the leaves. Okay, okay, let's put on our headlamps and look for it. "LIGHT IS NOT WHAT I NEED!" she railed. Shall we perhaps roll another one? NO! So it went, for an hour at least, a stomping, cursing, obsessive, and repetitive search, back and forth over the same bit of ground. After an unwelcomed attempt to help, I kept my distance. Amazingly, Elly found the thing at last, in her sleeping bag of all places! She lit up, we lay down, and I put my foot in my mouth in the worst way, throwing the car in reverse at 60 mph and proving for all eternity that timing is EVERYTHING and that I have no frontal lobe. I said, "I think starting tomorrow you and I should hike our own hike."

Wrong thing to say.

One long, sleepless, tear-filled night and three days of tense relations later, she accepted my wish that this be so and raced on ahead to avoid the pain of seeing me. It was terrible. I felt awful. She'd even threatened to quit the trail over it.

Elly's Terminator-tough exterior turned out to be a total facade, and I was left to break the heart of a girl as broken inside as I am. But Elly is a girl whose brokenness has manifested in ways utterly alien and quite frightening to me. Actually, not totally alien. I understand it, but I cannot be around it. From her sadness has grown anger; from mine, a turning inward, a quiet resignation and retreat. The two don't mix well.

Elly is lovely when she smiles. At times, she was the spitting image of Jodie Foster. Gross as this will sound to those of you out there in the scrubbed-clean world, I loooooved her several-days-unshowered smell. After her first 15-mile day (the night we met) she was ripe as hell. I loved it. She lay down beside me up there in the loft at Gooch Mountain Shelter, and I was in Heaven. I'd barely gotten a look at her before darkness, but I lay there basking in her scent and her stories, a man in a dream. Dream I did that night. I woke twice in the early morning totally convinced that I had somehow mounted her through our sleeping bags. (And why not? It dropped into the teens that night and that sweaty body 15 inches away meant more than sex, it meant warmth!)

I see Elly, now freshly showered and smiling in the afternoon sun at Rainbow Springs Inn looking beautiful as ever. "There's a couple of Coronas in the fridge in the yurt," she tells me, knowing full well I'm dying for a beer and there's none to be purchased for miles around. This is her gift to me, her concession, her sweetness after another angry freakout earlier that day that left us both mute as trees. But, sadly, it's too little too late. By the time I get to it, there's one beer left in the fridge. I drink it and am grateful.

The sun is setting on the cabins and the grassy grounds beside the river. John from Saco, Maine, plays Frisbee with his dog, Casey. Elly goes to the phone to call her mom. But the phone is occupied, and she returns to my campsite to say that she'll race on ahead tomorrow if that's what I'd like. "Just say it," she says. "Just tell me you want me to go away." I can't do it. I won't do it. It's not fair and it's not what I feel. I just want her to acknowledge my request of three days ago——that we walk our own walks now.

I say again what I've been saying for days: Thank you. Thank you for the gift of one great week together. I repeat some of what I've been saying about compatibility, that it's a miracle and a gift we lasted a week. Elly smokes pot; I drink beer. Elly is a vegetarian; I eat anything and everything. Elly wants to help the Earth; I think the Earth's just fine and it's we humans who are doomed. Elly is a self-described Luddite, one who avoids machinery; I carry a virtual laptop and modem in my pocket. Then the final big one: Elly is an atheist; I believe in God, and DAMMIT, I'M GOING TO FIND ME A WOMAN IN THIS MESSED UP WORLD WHO WILL TELL ME, ON MY DEATHBED, THAT I'M GOING TO HEAVEN AND SHE'LL SEE ME THERE! Is that so much to ask?

That's the story of Elly and me. Until I meet her up the trail. Which I probably will. Whether she likes it or not. [Postscript: I never saw Elly again.]

From a mountaintop overlooking Fontana Dam, North Carolina, and the only spot I could transmit from for the past 40 miles or so, this is Lord Duke "Jester" Jack Gadget Malcovich Tinkerbell Hammerhead Peregrine saying farewell, and see you on the other side of the Smoky Mountains if I am not eaten by a bear.

FIVE

Remember: They Turned Away Baby Jesus, Too...A Sure Sense of Doom at the Dam...Mainsail, Mockingbird, and the Great Race Against the Storms of the Smokies...Up on Rocky Top They Get Their Corn from a Jar! Bambi, the Close Encounter...Like Hell the AT is EASY! The Starship Clingman...Fear and Loathing in Gatlinburg...My Soul for a Saxophone...

Dinner tonight here at Mile 167 consists of tree bark shavings, hapless hibernating cicada pupae (plus a good a bit of the dirt I dug them out of), eye of newt, hearts of pinecone, oh, and, of course, granola. Actually the real ingredients are not much better. I started, as I often do for dinner, with a scant two tablespoons of rice in a cup and a half of water. Chopped in one clove of garlic and diced up a handful of those baby carrots that keep so well in a non-refrigerated pack, then came curry spice, pepper, and a wink of salt. Surveying what I have to eat over the coming week (all of it fitting in a nylon sack no bigger than a woman's large-sized purse), I foraged in my supplies for some dried berries—cranberries, raisins, blueberries. I think one strawberry even got in there. Threw them in the pot.

Then there's the teeny dope-like half-baggie of smoked salmon jerky that I hoard like a squirrel on methamphetamine. Crumbled a bit of that in there. In went some soy nuts, some sunflower and pumpkin seeds, and a bit of kamut to thicken it up. More water to make it go a little further. That's it. That's dinner out here on the trail for your author and friend. Actually, today that's dinner at the so-called "Fontana Hilton," a kind of hopped-up big budget version of the usual rangy old shelters found along the trail. The "Hilton" overlooks Lake Whatever-you-call-it, probably Fontana, and is full of all the amenities and personality of an interstate rest stop, things like concrete picnic tables and trash bins and a water fountain, simple things the dam-visiting public come to expect but that we, the few, the proud, the AT thruhikers, find ever-increasingly odd and alien and, well...plush. I have to laugh at the sign at the top of the road leading down here from the dam: "Shelter 300 Yards: Hikers Only." I feel like royalty.

I say all this with surprising good spirits considering that my introduction to Fontana Damn, er, Dam, was hardly pleasant thanks to one more meal of humble pie, a brief fit of paranoia, and the expenditure of my very last dollar bill. The latter came first when I excitedly spent my last dollar on the $1 shuttle from the trailhead two or three miles into town for a motel room and an ATM. A pick-it-up-and-dial-zero airport-like convenience telephone at the trailhead made this wonderfully simple and seemed to bode well for the day ahead. But I've had trouble with my credit card already on this trip, and although I knew a few hundred bucks had been deposited into my account three or four days back, I still went forth with apprehension. Sure enough, I was turned away at the Fontana Inn for insufficient funds. Embarrassed and upset, I fumbled for small change in the various folds of my pack. Trouble is, constant weight checks on the pack had me fully aware of everything that was and wasn't in the pack, and thus I knew that very little change, if any, was. I managed to scrounge 75 cents and asked shuttle driver Laurie to take me back to the dam. She kindly did.

At the dam phone I used my calling card, only to learn that I had, perhaps two calls before it, also, ran out. I chose to call Rocky, my pillar of strength and optimism in the West, and keeper of a small stash of backup money for me in cases of emergency. Standing there alone on the dead-vacant Fontana Dam with not a thruhiker in sight and no one else to boot, penniless and quite suddenly aware of how very far from home I was, I pressed the emergency button. He wasn't home, but I left a message: Please send cash ASAP, 911, to me c/o General Delivery, Hot Springs, North Carolina, etc, etc. Then I called PayPal, keeper of my one sacred piece of plastic money. Turns out it was just a matter of checking account monies clearing in time, or not in time, as the case was. The money would clear on the 7th they told me. Okay. Today is the 5th. Tomorrow I walk into the Great Smoky Mountains Wilderness not to reappear for a week. Standing there penniless and 2000 miles from home with no hope of money for a week, I realized something important: It just didn't matter. I would simply walk into the woods, light my stove, roll out my bag, and be once more a king.

In my mummy bag this morning I am a skydiver, belly toward the Earth, legs raised at the knees, feet elevated (in this case to keep them above my heart until time to use them), my hands folded beneath me for warmth. Skydiver, base jumper, nothing between me and the Great Smoky Mountains

Bear Enclosure but a few more minutes of snores, sleep-mumbles, and moans, and maybe even some real moans coming from the couple across the way, hard to tell. There are some two dozen of us out here at the "Fontana Hilton" this morning, still snozzling, still squirming on Thinsulate pads and wooden floors and bunks against the predawn cold. When I came here yesterday, I didn't like it. The scene creeped me out, and I wanted to flee immediately across the dam and into the Smokies.

But the Smokies have strict regulations regarding the "kindness" they afford thruhikers. The one big rule: We may sleep ONLY in shelters. There is no stealth camping allowed in the Smokies. I pulled out my mileage book, consulted my watch, and did the math. Nope. No way I would make it to the first shelter by dark. So with great restraint, I gave in to the forces of the Great Magnet, as Thompson called it, sat and made dinner at four in the afternoon.

At that time, there were only two other thruhikers here, Doyle and Sunset. Nothing against them, but I don't know either of them, and my recent credit card rejection experience had me weirded out, and the whole post-apocalyptic environment of the dam, well, I just wanted out of there. But I calmly cooked instead, and as I cooked a parade of familiar thruhikers began to appear from the south. Mockingbird, now Nathan, now Shortcake, now Southie, now the Newlyweds, now Breathless and Speed. Now the place felt okay. I was with my tribe again, or they with me. The evening went nicely with the one not so nice aspect of Shortcake's resignation. The trail hadn't turned out to be as much fun as she'd hoped, and that was that. Sounded like as good a reason as any. It would definitely be one of mine, should it occur to be less fun.

This morning the birds begin to sing, and outside the mummy-wrapped womb of my bag I hear the troops beginning to move about. A peek out of my hoodie reveals a lot more light in the room than I wish to see. The sun is by no means UP yet, no way. But it's coming. Soon I will be diving, for real. Jumping off the dam as it were and into 70 miles of Smokies, the much-touted and rather haunted-sounding Smokies with all them bears and scary rangers and regulations and bears and, well, bears. Part of me envies little Shortcake. She gets to go home now, no harm, no foul, no shame; and from the sounds of it, she even has a home to go to. Most of these folks do. Most are much younger than I and thus still have the parental option. Most are in semi-daily contact with their parents to assure them that they are well and alive.

I e-mailed my mother a week ago and still haven't heard back from her. But this goes both ways. She hardly got more than a minute's notice from me that I was departing on this "little hike" and not much of a farewell visit at that.

But Mom's got her husband and her life, and Dad the same, and I'm too frikken old to be phoning the parents all the time. As safety nets go, they're not there for me anymore. So it's back to the freefall metaphor. Back to the skydiver's crouch, or whatever that would be called, legs up, arms out, eyes Earthward; look out, Appalachia, here I come.

Fontana Dam, North Carolina, is what Hoover Dam or any damn dam will look like if some hellish virus wipes out every living creature on Earth someday. It is a strange and eerie place. A giant concrete monument to...to what? Ugliness. The dam is ugly and the body of water it creates, by very nature of being manmade and awkwardly so with its telltale dirt skirt shoreline where the waters recede, is ugly. Shortcake says the whole dam complex reminds her of Stephen King's Langoliers. A place where nothing lives yet everything is still intact and all the machines still hum along, stupid, irreverent of our absence.

Okay, the shower there last night was heavenly and hot. But it was like showering in a mausoleum, all marble walls and steel doors and concrete structure. There wasn't a soul in sight last night when I walked the half-mile down from the shelter to the dam and the showers. I'm not complaining. It was peaceful in the way I imagine is death. I told the others it reminded me of Logan's Run, of the underbelly beneath the city full of weird, twenty-something people. But that reference was too distant perhaps for young Shortcake and Danny from Massachusetts, both nearly two decades my junior. Whatever. Someday somebody's going to walk across a dam like this and say the same thing about us, about me perhaps, about the free people who used to walk the now-gnarled and overgrown trail from Georgia to Maine.

In that future time, perhaps there will be no such freedom, or perhaps so few people that humankind once again will have clustered together in fear and be afraid of the woods. Or perhaps it will go the other way, the way of too many. In this latter scenario, I don't see the dam or the trail. I don't see anything. Anything but people. But that's not my hunch. My hunch is that this dam will always be a spooky, haunted place and that the trend toward gross overpopulation will continue into the coming decades and end, tragically probably, leaving the dams and other self-running machines to go on humming quietly in a silent world.

Afterthought:
There are thousands of people walking this trail, all of them having started around the same time as I did and headed in the same direction. I see a dozen or so every day. But on the trail, all I need do is stop a moment to write or

push on ahead a little, and suddenly I am the only man left in the world. It's baffling, really, how much space there is still left in the world, how much so-called emptiness that is alive and humming with living things with consciousness far beyond ours such that we call them vegetative or animal. While walking the Trail, I sometimes imagine that the trees are all actually moving very quickly, and that I am on such a different quantum time-space plane, that I cannot see their movement. I say all this both in support of my idea of the solitary nature of the dam, and in contrast to it. The dam therefore is a blight and a joke, a falsity and a lame attempt made by men who do not walk the woods, to conquer it, to stop Nature in her tracks. But Nature will never stop, of that I am sure. We are fooling ourselves with our dams. Nature has already destroyed them.

Time and again on the AT, I would be deep in some woods and come upon a sign informing me that I was standing in what was once vast, open farmland. Nature will never stop.

Heavy day. Spooked by that damn dam, I hoofed it hard up the first four miles, all ascent, straight up and into the Smokies. I passed the Honeymooners, Mainsail, Mockingbird, everybody it seemed. I was on a tear, ripping up the trail like the hare who got the slapdown from the savvy tortoise. Around mile seven I was feeling every bit tore up. I start slow mornings, typically feeling lousy for the first few miles. Today was no exception. But for some reason I was driven. All this jazz about being allowed to sleep only in shelters in the Smokies pushed me onward, knowing that I either had to make it 10 miles or 16 miles, and dreaming of achieving the latter. Mainsail is my new buddy. We gabbed all day about this and that, about women and beer and some of the places we'd both lived or visited, like Humboldt and Missoula. Mainsail's got a girl at home. He misses her, of course, but it sounds like they have a good chance of surviving this journey of his. Seems she's headed to Africa to do volunteer work for a few months. That ought to work. It's the hikers I meet that have a lonely spouse or mate at home that I worry about.

So today Mainsail reminded me of something I think I ought to explain to those of you who don't really know or understand what the AT is. Mainsail says even *Backpacker* magazine is sorely mistaken in their assessment of the AT's difficulty in reference to the Pacific Crest Trail or the Continental Divide. The AT is NOT the easiest of the three trails. Coming from the West Coast, I can attest that there are long stretches of flat or near-flat ground between mountain ranges, at least in California. While, out here, damn! I have done nothing but climb up one mountain and down another for nearly 200 miles, and there's no end of it in sight.

To look at a profile of the Appalachians is to see a never-ending roller coaster of "balds," or tops, and "gaps," or lower regions between mountains. It's frikken crazy! The AT of 60 years ago is apparently not the AT of today. Earl Schaeffer was first to hike the trail in the 1940s. Fifty years later he did it again to become not only the first hiker but also the eldest. His report upon hiking the lower regions especially, that is to say, the miles I've just completed, was not at all positive. He was downright pissed. According to Schaeffer, the trail engineers added all these unnecessary loops and trails straight up mountains, making every effort to complicate the trail that he had navigated easily in the 1940s.

Having looked at a few topo maps, I so far agree. There are some real bullshit east and west divergences. Allegedly these were added to discourage thruhikers right from the start, thereby minimizing impact later up the trail. I don't know. That sounds kind of hokey and conspiratorial, but I wouldn't put it past them. Them who, you ask? Men, most likely. Elitist trail engineers. Eco-Nazis. Health nuts more interested in the number of peaks bagged enroute than the immense and intense holistic triumph of simply walking nonstop from Georgia to Maine. If I am wrong in all of this, so be it. It is my opinion, and this is my book.

The AT is a monster, no shit. I'm doing it. It's all mountains, man. The trails go straight up, every one of them. So, just so you all know, this ain't no sidewalk I'm strolling down, or up, from Georgia to Maine. This is a beast, and today my feet felt every bit gnawed upon by that beast. I made my dinner lying down, just too wasted to stand or sit. Sixteen miles today. Probably 20 tomorrow. Must get out of the Smokies quick.

Aside from being home to apparently twice as many plant species as all of Europe, the Great Smoky Mountains National Park is also the most visited of all America's national parks, with around 20 million visitors per year. What this means for thruhikers is hike during the week and get out before the weekenders show up to stuff the shelters like sardines. Because, remember, you are allowed to camp only in shelters. Oh, and Big Horn just reminded me of the other thing pressing us to roar through here fast: the rainfall. The Smokies get more annual rainfall than almost anywhere else in the U.S. Thruhikers talk of it incessantly. Today it was sunny and clear. Tomorrow we might get lucky again. But then Thursday's another story. We still have 60 miles to go. This is Sir Hamburger Feet signing off from my bunk in an old stone shelter in the Smokies. G'night.

Having a hard time keeping my spirits up. Two guys from Gatlinburg, long like cigarettes and silent, sit chain smoking by the fire. They're cooking steak they hauled up from town. I'm eating granola. A short distance from the stone dungeon-like shelter at Mile 183, Circuit Rider reads aloud from the Bible to the boys of the so-called Fab Five. They need all the prayer they can get, I figure, staring at a 25-mile day tomorrow.

Already flies harass me. I can see insects bringing down my "big hike conviction" real easy some day when I am more tired and pained and feeling less purpose than today. Some day soon, perhaps. I sleep fitfully. In the night, one or both of the Gatlinburg boys is up for a smoke. I can smell it mingled with the stench of wood fire smoke. I rise to pee once in the night, go out through the chain link fence gate into the bear-infested night. The moon is nearly full. There are no bears. I begin to think the whole bear thing is a myth.

In the morning a doe trots into camp to say hello. "Bambi!" I call to her where she stands just a few feet away, and in an instant she bounds into the air, pirouettes, comes down, and does the wildest jig. All of us are stunned. A small group of other locals, probably two fathers and their boys, have been chuckling at my impressions of Gollum and Smoegel, and Bill Murray from *Caddyshack*. For a while over breakfast, I think I've lost my signature hat. Sewed myself and resembling that of a court jester, it has earned me the trail name Jester. Suddenly I remember that I've left it in the pocket of my rain jacket. I excitedly yank it out, place it on my head, and screech with Smoegel joy. After the Bambi incident the others look at me strangely, as though I really am crazy and have somehow spoken to this animal directly. It is just the sort of moment I enjoy.

On the trail again this morning I am a sloth. I simply cannot muster yesterday's power or enthusiasm. Mainsail and Mockingbird stay with me but are always just ahead and just out of audible range such that all I hear of their bubbling laugh-filled dialogue is unintelligible sounds. Their "sailing" pace "mocks" me.

When we are all together, we're always talking movies. At one point Maine Sail and I are discussing his recent trip to Disneyland with his girlfriend Krista. Maine Sail says a lot of the rides were closed when they went. I ask him if Pirates of the Caribbean was open. Nineteen-year-old Mockingbird chimes in, "They have a ride called Pirates of the Caribbean?"

Our finest moment together occurs atop Rocky Top Mountain in Tennessee as Mainsail sings an Appalachian song, and I laugh and try in vain to remember the lyrics as he repeats them. This much I get:

Corn don't grow at all on Rocky Top
Dirt's too rocky by far
That's why all folks out on Rocky Top
Get their corn from a jar

It goes on about moonshine makin' and sweet Appalachian girls and such. It makes the pain in my knees a little more bearable. But now I've lost the boys again, too far ahead in this hobbit-like ridgeline forest of strange grass hummocks and gnarled little trees like fruit trees bare in winter. The fields of blonde grass long and lopped over like seventies haircuts are not smooth but consistently bumpy, like a convention of 10,000 hedgehogs basking elbow to elbow in the mountaintop sun. There are patches of snow everywhere, and I eat from them; and when it's hot, I fill my hat with snow and let the icy coolness dribble down my neck.

I must retain my sense of purpose out here, or I am done for. It is hard, hard work and endless, and the candidates for Katahdin are dropping like flies. Yet just what is my purpose for doing this mad thing? Already I have forgotten. I have learned that Gatlinburg is not far off the trail and makes for a nice break in the Smokies with its Vegas-like atmosphere and Dollywood, the theme park homage to Dolly Parton. I resolve to stop there, rest, eat a burger, drink a beer.

Walking without a penny in one's pocket, even here in the free forest, is stressful. My experience of being denied a motel room in Fontana was degrading, however well I paved over the sting with words. To Gatlinburg then, to spend some money on myself (assuming the check has cleared) and give this aching body a night's coddling rest. Then it will be back into the Smokies for one more night straddling two 15-mile days. Just eight more miles today and 10 tomorrow, then I can rest my lonesome heart and dizzy head in Dolly Parton's ample...bed?

While sitting trailside writing earlier, a guy and girl with matching orange hats went zooming by me like they were just out for the weekend pulling a 30-mile day or so. I didn't think much of it. Then I met them both at Double Spring Shelter. We got chatting, and I learned that I was talking to Silver Girl and none other than Flyin' Brian, the legendary hiker who, in one 10-month stretch, hiked the Triple Crown: the AT, the PCT, and the Continental Divide. He is the only man to have ever done them all in one year, and with two months to spare at that! Needless to say, my morning musings of pain and sloth just went right out the window. Only recently introduced to this whole world of heavy-duty hiking, I admit I didn't know who Flyin' Brian was two months ago.

Bruce at Nomad Adventures in Idyllwild was the first to tell me of Brian's feat. Bruce knows a lot about his business and helped me get the right gear together. I think he would have liked to be a fly on my hat when Flyin' Brian blew by me and I didn't even know it. I won't soon forget Brian's look of consternation as he regarded the substance of my lunch: carrots, carob clusters, dates, Stilton cheese, and water crackers. The Triple Crown champion was impressed, stuck as he was with the Kraft cheese and chocolate-covered peanuts he'd acquired locally.

Funny day. And, of course, another super-painful day. For some reason, the miles went by a lot slower today and time went faster. I was humping it from eight in the morning until six at night, almost non-stop. I decided the word for the day was stamina, which fits into the sentence "I have no stamina." If I do succeed in hiking this whole trail, I have to do something fat to follow such an act, so to speak. Speaking more to Brian's achievement than talking about myself, I said to him, "Yeah, I was thinking if I successfully finished the AT this year, I would go run with the bulls in Pamplona."

I was baiting him. I mean, what do you do to top an act like the Triple Crown? Brian didn't bite. He just said I should go on and hike the PCT. Fuddy duddy.

Later when Mainsail asked him what he did with those two remaining months of the year he completed the Triple Crown, he replied that he went to Acadia National Park in Maine and did a buncha small day hikes while reacclimating to society. My uncle David drowned and was never found off the coast of Acadia in 1969. Small world. I bet Brian has seen the bronze plaque made for David situated on a cliff above where he drowned. Thought no doubt a needle in a haystack, it's apparently the only unnatural thing in the park.

The views here in the Smokies are incredible, just mountain after mountain after mountain. So of course my camera battery died. All I will have to remember the park by is some very, very sore feet. Maybe a postcard from Dollywood. Bunked up in another ancient stone shelter tonight, this one not so uglified by chain link fences. The privy, or shitter, is of the composting type, and sits up in the air. It's like an outhouse in a tree house. Which sure beats what I saw a few shelters back—a privy area minus the privy. The effect was a minefield of dangerous deposits only occasionally announced by tufts of TP. Very strange. I smell the mind of an eco-Nazi behind this field of feces. If there's no privy, why bother making an area? Why not just post a sign that says, "Please go shit far away from the shelter. Thank you." Whatever.

The boys are amazed at my fully reclined typing trick. It is pretty cool. But really it is the only way I can write. In as much pain as I am in daily, sitting up in bed is out of the question. When I am not lying down, I'm hiking. That's pretty much it. Huffing and puffing up one grade after another, or falling down to cook some gruel, brush my teeth, and collect water from the springs. That's all I do. That's all I can do after hiking all day. I guess Ray Jardine was right in his book. Hitting the trail like I did without any prior training makes for a hike that is nothing but survival. So I survive. But hey, I'm telling a story, too. So I guess I've got him beat on that.

It is April 8th when I clamber up Clingman's Dome, Mile 196.2, the highest elevation on the Appalachian Trail. A freaky spaceship-like tower rises from the top of the mountain like some replica of the *Enterprise* from *Star Trek*. The air up here on this cloudy day is, in the words of Tom Waits, "colder than a well-digger's ass." Three great old dudes named Badger, Papa Bear, and Spoon, all in their late sixties or early seventies, are up here with Maine Sail (as I now understand it is spelled), Mockingbird, and me. They're in this for the whole trip, too. Inspiring! I sang a bit on my way up here in Tom Waits's gravelly voice, something about "climbing through a dead forest on a snow-topped dome, a monk, two mutants, a jester, and a gnome." All right, enough silliness. Live from the top of the AT World, Frozen Fingers signing off.

Very strange rhythms here in Rocky Top, Tennessee. Gatlinburg, I mean. This is one very strange town. Extreme fear and loathing. Perhaps the pressure of this undertaking is getting to me. I mean, imagine the pressure: One toenail improperly clipped could take you off the trail. First you're in pain, then walking funny to compensate, then blistering, maybe losing the toenail. How is a brain to handle the kind of stress wherein every step along a hard and twisted, precipitous forest path could be the ONE, the one step that brings you down hard and spells the end. Every step. Every fast step, for they are nothing if not fast with 2,000 miles to go to Maine before autumn's end, could be the one that smashes a femur or wrenches a kneecap beyond use.

Perhaps this stress is what has me so nutty, so manic and insane today in this tiny tourist mecca of Tennessee. Perhaps this stress is what just made me insult, albeit unintentionally, two women hikers at the local brewery, telling their male companion that I'd meet him "later down the street at the titty bar to further celebrate (his) birthday." I.. just...don't...know. Such a statement isn't like me. I don't feel myself here at all in Gatlinburg. I feel like a speed freak, like a man torn from his natural habitat of tree and rock and thrust into THIS, this overblown pseudo-alpine tourist town, thrown here by sheer dying necessity to GET OUT of the woods for a day or two. But once out…I am out of control.

I order the sampler of the local brewery's offerings. I think I am so thirsty I could drink a keg. But when the beer comes I don't like any of them, not one of the eight. The waitress is kind and pretty and likes hikers. She is the one good thing I have felt since my arrival in Gatlinburg. She is tolerant of me when I ask, absurdly I guess, if the bar serves any other beer. No they do not. Okay. I order the beer I dislike the least. I devour a 12-ounce ribeye steak, potatoes, a salad, and some buffalo wings. I drink my one beer. I am suddenly overstuffed and mentally wrong. Am I drunk? No, not really. But while leaving I do manage that very-un-me comment about a titty bar. What then? What the hell is wrong with me? I come to "town" to feast after days of ramen noodles and packaged oatmeal. I dream…WE dream, Maine Sail, Mockingbird and I dream out loud as we hike of burgers and fries, steaks and beer. Now here I am! It's all too much.

A queer aerial tram drops out of the late afternoon sky from "Ober Gatlinburg" down here to Gatlinburg, Earth. Tourists, a preponderance of obese and obese-in-the-making, wander the sidewalks of this psycho-Disneyland, exhausted every one of them, towing kids, some carrying them in their bellies, shopping, dizzy, momentarily stunned by the sight of the weird and albeit dirty-looking REAL alpine hikers in their midst. Most don't even notice us. But I see them. They are tired, every one. I KNOW I am tired, and for good reason, physically exhausted from day after day of putting one foot in front of the other from sunup to sundown for nearly three weeks over mountain after mountain.

But why are they tired? Why do they look more tired than I? I'm just bloated from gorging on non-hiker food and, well, a little drunk, I guess, on two beers. But I look great! We three all look great. My face is bronzed from constant exposure to high- elevation ultraviolet light even though many a day is overcast. My beard is thickening. My muscles are changing overnight. My beer belly of three weeks ago, now nearly gone. These changes in my metabolism both frighten and thrill me. I rush back to the motel room and ferret out a Klonipin. Too much change, too soon, too much.

As I sprawl out on the motel bed and try to relax, my mind drifts to Benicio del Toro in *Fear and Loathing* as he admonishes Johnny Depp's Thompson.

You took too much, too much! If I put you in the pool now,
you'll sink like a stone.

In my case, I have to wonder, too much of what? Roaring down the trail at breakneck speed over tangled ankle-wrenching roots, down rockslides, over fallen trees, and through yesterday's foot of mud and melted snow for eight miles straight, the effect on the brain is like chewing, not on extract of some other poor bastard's pineal gland, as Thompson claims in *Fear and Loathing in Las Vegas,* but ON YOUR OWN pineal gland!

Flyin' Brian embodied this kind of wound-up teeth-grinding speed-talking, snap-synapse, pineal-chewing energy. The Champion truly is a machine. I imagine he suffers from a kind of impatience with the slowed-down world. His metabolism is jet fuel through a fire hose. I feel that I, too, am headed this way.

The boys return from their foray into downtown Gatlinburg. They report on the weirdness of it all. There is a wedding chapel downtown that offers weddings cheaper than the cost of a night's lodging, a mere $25. Two Baskin-Robbins in close proximity and dozens of fudge shops. Oh, and the Space Needle. Nineteen-year-old Mockingbird calls the needle "very seventies." We mustn't forget the chairlift that goes uphill to nowhere, appearing for a moment to indicate the presence of a ski resort, yet there is none. The list goes on. Not one, but half a dozen Ripley's museums and attractions of one sort or another. Everyone is consuming the pseudo-alpine product. We, the real thing, appear to be actors on a theme set, like dueling cowboys in full costume on the streets of Tombstone.

Yet we are freaked by it all. Or I am, anyway. Freaky Gatlinburg by 8 p.m. has provided a fantastic sort of counterpoint to the "point" of our trek of the Appalachian Trail. The metabolism of weirdness runs high. Just hours ago, wishing I could stay longer, I am already ready to be back on the trail tomorrow. "What do you think potatoes and tuna would taste like?" Maine Sail asks. The boys sort processed food items picked up at the same store in which, just an hour ago, fear-addled and freaked, I was barely able to fumble through the purchase of beer and half a dozen postcards I didn't want.

Calmed now by the beer and diazepam-related sedative, I see all these tired faces and I know exactly why they're so tired. They're dying. Death by shopping. Death by passive entertainment. Death by TV and total immersion in a culture that fosters and feeds on false experience, on vicarious living in the giant jungle, desert, alpine rainforest, Mediterranean "paradise" theme park that is America. They're tired because they are not engaged. Only their jobs, their 9-5 world, is tangible and real and irksome and perhaps even loathsome and painful, for it exists mostly to service the debt incurred to afford said passive entertainment. Their free time, their FREEDOM, has been prepackaged and planned and spoon-fed them until it is naught but FREE DUMB.

That's what Gatlinburg, Tennessee was: dumb. The freedom part is pure illusion anymore. How could some enterprising Mommy or Daddy motivate the "kinder" to go hike a mountain when TV tells the kids that Dollywood is the place to be? Good luck, Mom and Dad. Some snake is profiting in Gatlinburg, but it ain't the poor chubby tourist zombies shuffling its sidewalks in a commercial daze. In the words of Hunter S. Thompson, "The Circus-Circus [insert Gatlinburg] is what the whole hep world would be doing on a Saturday night if the Nazis had won the war."

It is a beautiful Good Friday here in the Smokies, April 9th, 2004. Stunning day. Warm sun. The slush of yesterday's trails largely melted. The scent of Christmas in the air with all the pine and fir trees responding to the warmth of the sun. The parking lot at Newfound Gap 12 miles above garish Gatlinburg looks like a day at the beach. It's like it's Family Day on the AT today. A short while back, a family stopped to ask where I was going. When they heard Maine, the little girl lit up with joy. "You see, honey, there you go. You wanted to see a thruhiker and now you've seen one!" Of course, I was pleased and played it up accordingly. "Well good," I think. "A couple of moms and dads did succeed in getting the kids out into the trees and away from all that consumer crap below."

The restroom at the Gap was like a reunion of many thruhiker friends, scattered over the past days here and there along the trail and trailside towns. Ry and Jackie, Rael, Sunset, Sanguine, Navigator, all were there. I always enjoy running into the young couple Ry and Jackie. Jackie bedazzles me. She is an astounding creature to behold, and I hope Ry will not hold me in ill regard for saying so. He should be flattered, that and proud to have her.

It is a day of ridge running, of skipping almost, the pain in my knees miraculously absent today, skipping along narrow ridges with giant, sweeping drops on both sides. The mountains, blue in this light, layer outward to forever. To the south, I look at them and say proudly, "I have walked them all." I reach a point on one ridge where the view is too incredible not to howl in triumphant gratitude to the Earth. Far ahead, thruhiker Sunset howls in response. We continue this for some time. Sunset hails from Mississippi and speaks an almost entirely unintelligible tongue. In the words of my language professor in Germany years ago, "Er spricht mit Kartofeln in Mund," he speaks with a potato in his mouth. My teacher was referring to all Americans and our poor enunciation. Sunset's potato is particularly large.

The day astounds me with its beauty and the varying environments I pass through. The first 40 miles or so of the Smokies kind of sucked. But this ridgeline dance in flawless weather, wow! I have in mind to make it 16 miles today, but I didn't get started until nearly one o'clock thanks to morning supply shopping in Gatlinburg and an hour spent trying to hitchhike the whopping eight miles back to the trailhead.

I round a corner and suddenly I am in Big Sur, so like it in color, in the grasses and trees and sky. A short time later I am transported again by the changing environment, this time to California's Lost Coast, to the steep trail Emelia and I once walked to reach the Smith Cabin from midway up the coast in the mountains, the same road I once drove in Duke late at night reckless and high on codeine with Radioman and Hippie Streudel. Those were the daze. Good times.

I stop and eat lunch. I feast for a change. I have deduced that my sluggish pace of late is due to insufficient carbo and protein intake. In Gatlinburg I stocked up big time, almost all of it free from the hiker box at the local gear supply store. Bagged "foil" tuna is a great invention. I have tuna on Stoned Wheat Thins with cream cheese. Later I wolf down a few Snickers and move through the forest, swift and agile, a wolf on the hunt.

I reach the shelter at the 10-mile mark at 6 p.m. but am determined I can make it to Tri-Corner Knob Shelter by sundown, putting me exactly halfway between today's start and tomorrow's finish, the end of the Smokies. I race on. I am in uncharted waters now. I may have to hike with my headlamp before I get there. With no knee pain today and all the nervous manic energy that made Gatlinburg difficult to bear, I burn up the trail and arrive at the shelter side trail just in time to watch the sun disappear in the west. I hike another 500 yards and step into the old stone shelter to a warm welcome from all inside. I lay out my bag on the bunk, warm my hands at the fire in the hearth, then go outside to cook. While the others inside fall fast asleep, I cook up noodles with my addition of garlic, carrots, potato flakes, and miso. I devour it, turn off my headlamp, and bask in the silent darkness. I sip hot chocolate with peppermint schnapps and stare skyward communing with constellation friends.

I did it! I knocked out 16 miles today in just 7.5 hours, a record for me. Even the boys inside were impressed when they learned how far I've come in so little time. I climbed a few steep grades, the worst at the end, of course, when my feet were screaming the loudest. They're all right when I'm moving, but the moment I stop it's as though I've tripped on a bed of nails and sunk straight through, my feet impaled by dozens of nails. This is how I imagine that would feel. Ten o'clock, a late night for me. Time to go inside and endure the snoring. The word for today: zeal. I had it today, and so did the sun. We danced together from ridgeline to ridgeline, the sun and I. With the exception of hooting across canyons with an invisible Sunset (the person), whom I knew was ahead, as he was the lone man to pass me all day, I hiked my own hike today. All my own, all done, but rich with the company of so very, very much beauty.

According to my calculations, I romped across 15.5 miles of the Smokies in six hours and 43 minutes yesterday. Today so far the sun is on the east side of the mountain and I travel the west. I walk thus through dark corridors of evergreens lit mostly by the white of the snow. They say it takes 21 days to make a habit. I suppose then as of today I am habituated to the Appalachian Trail. The thought of habituation sends my mind to one habit I wish I had developed and stuck with over the years——the saxophone. I played alto sax briefly in college and loved it, enamored of the mournful echoing sounds of one man's sax heard one night while "gone" on LSD in the redwood forest behind Humboldt.

As I traverse Hell Ridge, I am suddenly full of the devil, charged by the conviction that I must procure a sax to carry and practice here on the trail. I'd sell my soul for an alto! No, I suppose t'would have to be a soprano, for its lightness. I owned a cassette tape once that I played so many times I wore it thin until the sound was barely audible. It was Paul Winter's *Canyon* in which the sax player records deep down in the Grand Canyon. Amazing sound. Walking the ridges of the Smokies yesterday I think I yearned, unknowingly, to send such sounds out into the vast wilderness cascading downward and outward around me in all directions. But I have no such sounds to make. Maybe soon I will.

The boys of the Fab Five, the compact Christian boot camp on wheels, as I've come to perceive them, are just behind me, having been at the shelter I bypassed last night to make my mad trek to Tri-Corner Knob. They hiked those five miles while I slept in and lavishly moved slowly about this morning. When I awoke, I excitedly proclaimed to Hendrick and Mumbles, the two men still there, "YES! I wanted to be the last one outta bed and I did it!" But as I hefted my pack an hour later, the Five had caught up. While they refilled at our spring, I bounded on ahead. But now they are quick on my heels. I can hear the tick-tick of their poles just a way back. I hear a chopper approaching, hot in pursuit. It is me, making the sound with my mouth, a fast wiggle of my tongue back and forth between O-shaped lips. I imagine myself in some Hollywood-scripted mountain chase scene. I pick up the pace and hunker down against the searching chopper.

"Get down! Get down!" Now I am Richard Dreyfuss and the blonde woman clambering up the rocky skirt of Devil's Tower in *Close Encounters of the Third Kind*. The choppers are spraying sleeping formula. The fields of rocks become the poppy fields outside the Kingdom of Oz. But it's too late. Kevin "KP" can't be more than 21 years old, and he's practically running the trail. He catches me up and passes. The chopper stops chopping. My lips pucker, then pout. I stop and sit silently, for once my mind a blank.

The woods are good for that. One simply can't think too much. Your mind is always on your feet. When I stop, I make it a point to lie flat on my back and stare straight up at branches and sky. A fast AT thruhiker barely sees the forest for the trees. He sees the path ahead, almost solely.

Fifty-something Sunshine appears to be a kind of chaperone amongst the Fab Five. He catches up, and I find that I can pace him for a while. He tells about meeting Bear Behind yesterday, "a guy with a thick Connecticut accent." Sunshine says their conversation yesterday required the spelling out of several words, so disparate are their native tongues. Sunshine, from Mississippi, says last year in New Jersey he ordered a Coke at a diner and asked the waitress for "lots a aaaccce." Ice, he meant, but that's not what the ticked-off waitress heard.

Sunshine is clearly a veteran of the AT. He points out places on the trail where there are literal walls built beneath us, nearly hidden in the tall grass. He points out that "no AT volunteer did that; that was the CCC back in the Depression." FDR's boys built the stone shelters, too, I bet. Beautifully built, stout, aesthetically fantastic to behold. The Appalachian Trail is a miracle. The amount of labor invested in clearing this for "us" is apparent at every fallen tree cut by recent saw, at every crossing well signed, at every tree with the signature blaze to tell us the way. It's astonishing and, despite my occasional grievances, I feel greatly honored to be walking it, honored and grateful as hell.

SIX

Broken Keys and the Greek Ruins of Tennessee...the Little Yellow Broad in the Cage...Sylvia Plath in Remission...We're Not Famous and We're Pissed...The Old Gunfighter Trick...Enter: Baltimore Jack...Four Dead in One Year and the Wrong-headed View of Suicide...Where the Trees Get Up and Walk on Spindly Legs...Permission Granted: Shit-can the Works.

April 18. Tuned in right off this morning to Herb Alpert's Tijuana Brass. Sweet. Two hundred eighty-two miles in thirty days. Then some lousy jazz takes over, and I change the station. Yes, that's right. Henry David has gone to ear buds and Appalachian stereo. Johnny Cash is bound for the Promised Land. Me, I'm fast closing in on a town called Erwin where a new keyboard awaits to replace this poor old plastic magic gadget upon which I have wailed poetic for two years now. Until then, the words will be few, I'm afraid. [All D's, E's, and W's have been meticulously added in by hand with the stylus today.] Until then, here is a list I have compiled over the past weeks of trail names I have heard spoken or have read in shelter registers. You've got to love the imagination that's gone into these trail names.

Captain Hook, Fuman Chu, Biscuit, Fireass, Long Shot, Toe-ritis, Poppins, Squirrel, Squirrel Master, Hog Walker, James the Wandering Nun, Tinder, Shortcake, Sir Fix-a-lot, Hoplite, Mississippi Mule, Marzipan, Krispy Kritter, Eagle Eye, Blue Bell from Texas, Sweet Leaf, Ashtray, Dirtnap, Dingle, Skirt, Sarge, Little Engine, Mockingbird, Solarman, No Dog and No Beard (couple), Big Horn Wanderer, Breathless and Speed (couple), Crash Bang, Maine Sail, Circuit Rider, KP, Sherlock, Dark Cloud, Sunset and Sunrise (couple), Pipesmoke, Zipcode, Slow Walker, Pucca, Wicomico Walker, Kickstand, Squish, Grits, and me, Jester Jack Peregrine the Only.

[The following is a letter to my cousin who posted 90 percent of the raw material comprising this book to my web site Jigglebox.com while I hiked.]

Dear Justin,

Happy Easter to you, too. My love to everyone in return. I wish I could have been with family today. Instead, I got to hike for my sins. Hike and hike and hike, and in the rain no less. Then I looked up at one point to spy my buddy far up ahead, and wham! Next thing I know I'm pulling my face off a flat rock splattered in blood. Tripped on a root. First thing went through my mind was, "Well, there it goes. Broke my glasses, broke my nose, game over." But my nose is okay and my glasses, miraculously unscathed. I took the full brunt of the fall with my forehead. I was still bleeding when I e-mailed you, as I had reached a mountain top and that was the next thing I was gonna do. Got right back up and kept hiking. Spent a coupla hours at a shelter being watched/interrogated by a few fellow hikers to make sure I wasn't concussed. But this is all just fodder for the writing. I just wrote to say bang-up job, thank you, glad yer mom's diggin' the words, can't wait for the cookies, dunno at moment what else to ask for, but thanks, I'll let you know. Alone in my tent in the rain...actually nice to be alone after over a week spent in shelters. Drinking hot cocoa with nip bottle of peppermint schnapps, my Easter present to myself. My big Easter meal was powdered huevos rancheros in a bag, just add water! The forest I am currently camped in could easily be right out your mom's back door, same. God bless us beasts and the children we'll always be. - Yer Gonzo Cuzn

This place is a Greek ruin. This is not a forest! We hike of late over chunks and slabs and mountains of marble-white rock, much of it appearing to have been carved, built into something, then ruined, as though the Cherokee or early white settlers had time to build and destroy their own Troy, with history recording none of it. Sweet Jackie and her man, Ry, and I struggle over it together.

Dead and downed trees hold these chunks of white stone in their roots, like gnarled old fists refusing to let go the prizes won in the crowning days of their kingdom long-crumbled. I wonder how long before my beloved America crumbles in similar fashion. This miracle of a trail reminds me how very free we still are. But freedom is fleeing from us daily in these fearful times. Yet We The People wave it off and go shopping on Orange Alert and return home with cartloads of feel-good items, all bought in trade for civil liberties lost. Ben Franklin said, "Those who would give up essential liberty to purchase a little temporary safety deserve neither liberty or safety." I digress.

Largo tells a story of the shelter we're at this morning. Says hiking the trail last year he rounded the corner coming out of the thick of the woods and in view of the shelter. "And there," he says, "bent over right beside the fire circle was a woman, shorts and underpants down around her ankles, servicing her peach." Largo said he had the next thousand miles to think about that one.

Rael is the wiry, feisty guy from South Boston, the guy with the Massachusetts accent from Hell (I can say that being Mass-born). I didn't like him first off, found him gruff, unfriendly. I figured maybe he didn't like my hat, thought I was a fag. But I was dead wrong. As far back as the Nantahala Outdoor Center, I think it was, he expressed great admiration upon seeing a postcard of my art car Duke. I believe he said, "That's the most beautiful thing I have ever seen." I was floored. Many hikers, upon being offered a card, for free, wouldn't even take one. Lark actually attributed her "no thanks" to the weight it would add to her pack. Lark: the girl who carries her Latin textbook. Sure, Honey.

Rael points at Tinkerbell, suspended from the straps on my chest and asks, "Who's the little yellow broad in the cage?" Later we discover a mutual affinity for Monty Python. He finds my word-for-word delivery of several scenes (complete with accent, of course) fascinating. He says he's never heard anyone do Python so good. On the contrary, Rael can improv in Pythonese like no one I've ever heard before. That I cannot do. I can only repeat from rote memory.

Okay. I've had it for today. This isn't hiking, this is bouldering. Except you don't boulder with a 35-pound pack on! The rumored trail magic at the top of that brutal last climb, wasn't. Worse than no trail magic at all, there hung from a tree branch a bag of empties, the rumored cooler fulla Cokes below it cleaned out. This is not my beautiful life! That is not my beautiful wife! I'm a Talking Head. That girl running close behind me today, tailing me almost as though she's got something to say but can't, that Italian beauty and southern belle all rolled into one, that's another man's woman. Jackie. Had I the gift of foresight, I would have run from them both and never looked back for all the heartache I would bring upon myself just to be near her. But if foresight was with me, I ignored it expertly. I'll suffer a lot for a good story.

I want to go to American Samoa. I want to go to my 20th high school reunion back in Del Mar, California, and see Jennifer Schramm, the high school sweetheart of mine who never knew she was. I want to find out if she's divorced or still single like me. Has she kids? Does she smoke? Does she turn into Godzilla after five whiskeys? Does she believe in an afterlife? Has she been longing all these years to marry a half-mad social miscreant poet?

The Beach Boys come on the radio blowing Aruba-Jamaica in my ears. Eat me, Beach Boys. You slack-packers that guzzled up all the sacred Coke, may you contract intestinal bugs that gnaw at your guts for days unending.

Among my zillion trail names that flashed in the pan and vanished was one I made up and rather liked: SPIR. It's an acronym for Sylvia Plath in Remission. It's heady, I know. But it says a lot. It calls depression by its proper name: a disease. Plath and I share a birthday, and I, by this hike, and by God if it kills me, am going to beat this disease. SPIR. I liked it. But the few times I said it to other hikers, it just didn't sound right. The daily explanation of its meaning would have been pure hell.

So I let this old thruhiker Sarge name me based on my hand-made hat: Jester.

Maine Sail figures we ought to be famous by now. I agree. Maine Sail says the word "fuck" a lot. He's pissed off about not being famous. Me, too. The radio, though God bless it and WIMZ Knoxville for their Skynard Fest Weekend (I'm loving it)—the radio, as I was saying, is a constant reminder that I am not famous. I hear Maynard from Tool, Paz from Perfect Circle, Martin Sheen (my would-be father-in-law, haha), David Horowitz, you name it, I've met them. They're famous, and Maine Sail and I are penniless giddy nuts, walking in the woods far past the outskirts of infinity. Jimmy Hendrix would have liked it here. The sky is an orgasm; the tree bottle rockets of joy.

I do this thing with my wrists wrapped in the straps of my poles. Throwing my fingers out in a gesture not unlike a magic trick, showing the hands are free, I then flick them inward and the cork grips of my poles snap right into place in the palms of my hands. It's fun. It reminds me of an old gunfighter trick, twirling six-shooters out of holsters and into place in hot, trigger-happy hands. I used to juggle knives and machetes and have taken up knife throwing. I'm very good with my hands. Hell, I typed all this shit lying down.

I went without my shirt for the first time today, hiking topless. Twas hot. It varies radically out here, one minute in the 80s, sometimes 90s in the sun, and then whammo! It's down in the low 30s again at night. I want to send home my 20-degree down bag. I want to send home my tent. I want to send home everything and sleep in the dirt. Not yet. Not yet.

I'm walking this stony path that looks every bit a giant chess set to which some god has taken a sledgehammer and just whaled the crap out of it. The moss is soooo green and pours down the rock to my left like a verdant waterfall or a soggy sub-sea kelp carpet on an underwater stage where crawfish dance in tiny creeks and raccoons reach in to dine.

I hear the Perfect Circle song *Judith* on the radio and think of Luci. I know that it is Paz playing bass, but I think of Luci anyway, perhaps because of how close they were, like little twins, and how much he loved her, and how there was strife between them just prior to his death. Luci, like me, had a penchant for pouring drink upon his blues and misery—good cause for his sister's disapproval. Maybe the drink is what did him in, in the end, as a trigger anyway. I love them both, Paz and Luci. I miss the latter badly. I hike with him in mind every day.

Later I'll hear the Perfect Circle song *Three Libras* and really go down for a good cry, knowing that it's Luci on viola. He received a platinum record for that. It meant so much to him that he hung it in the bathroom at knee level, just above his dog's food bowl. I don't think fame suited him.

I stop to flick a snail off the path. It is this empathic streak in me I cannot help but answer to. I love life. I cannot kill things, anything. Not even spiders, they that so disgust me.

With my disabled keyboard, I write the following in a fit of pique. (I've reinserted some of the missing e's, d's, z's, and w's for you, where even I had troubled guessing the words):

"Okay, so sh ruin my lif. I'm starting to gt that feeling. lik two years hav passd an I'm just not cluing in , just no ralizing it, just now fling angr. Th angr thta I so abhor in othrs, th reason I let Elly go. I'm angry. An alcoholic beast cast me out of my comfy world with a good woman an I just let her. Let it. No I'm.."

Got that much written after a crying fit plopped me down in a bed of leaves, where I promptly passed out.

[Note: the following dozen or so paragraphs were written without the E, D, or W keys and painstakingly reconstructed with the stylus for your reading pleasure!]

Word for the day: Tortoise, as in I am the tortoise, the last to leave each morning, but I pass many along the trail. It's 80 degrees in the sun on this April 19. Coming out of Hot Springs, I'm carrying a 45-pound pack. Insanity. But a good kind of insanity considering most of the extra weight owes to the kindness of my many care-package-sending friends: boxes from Mary, Linda, Marie, and Justin; cards from Kathleen and Pam; and the delicious home-canned relishes from Indian Gap trail angels Jane, Tom, and Pat! The significance of such signs of love out here in Appalachian Space is immeasurable!

From my new little $40 pocket radio come the words I wanna say but cannot for the sake of being on the go, that and this failing keyboard. Skynard (I think) sings of "movin' on town to town." As the strains of live bluegrass drift upward to the trail from Hot Springs below, I know it is so of me, moving on from yet another town, this one a winner, a place I could have stopped and stayed, loved it, but left, left just as the weekend festivities were getting under way. Another song comes on, the singer sings (I paraphrase): I get up in the morning once more with the blues, summon the strength and put on my walkin' shoes. I go up on the mountain and what do I see, but the whole world falling down in front of me.

In town, we naïve Modern Savages catch snippets of news, gruesome headlines of war and fear and pain. I get the feeling from up here on the mountain that indeed the whole world is falling down in front of me. I wonder, how much longer will this exist, this paramount freedom we enjoy, this miracle path through the forest of my home, my country. It makes me feel patriotic. Then I hear how we've slaughtered another hundred Iraqies and I just wanna hurl. What madness is man? Henry Miller managed to write joyfully of his time in Greece at a time when Nazi tanks were rolling into his beloved Paris. I will try my damnedest to write joyfully of freedom and beauty in this time of ignorance and fear and senseless killing. I will try, for you Henry, if for nothing else.

The hospitality and horseplay and thruhiker camaraderie of Hot Springs, North Carolina, is a good place to focus on freedom and the best in man. Between my all-comfy three-night stay at The Gentry House of Elmer, hot-tubbing with beautiful women at the springs, and closing Paddlers Pub with the legendary Baltimore Jack (who went out for a ride and never came back), it could be said my time in Hot Springs was well spent. I want to tell you all about Baltimore Jack, but for now know the man is notorious for completing seven consecutive thruhikes of the AT, and having done so with the aid of copious amounts of bourbon. I met Jack at the local outfitters where he was working a spell before moving on up trail. This is also where I met lovely Caroline, whom I did manage to ask out for dinner or beers. Alas, she was busy that night, and her request for a rain check went unfulfilled. Come on, girl! I'm a thruhiker. It's now or never, baby, every day. What was she thinking?

My face plant of a few days back had me sure my trip was over. Broken nose, broken glasses, concussion, something. Much smaller things have spelled the end of the trail for many. Amazingly, I suffered none of these. But it was that one look up and away from the trail at my feet that took me down, the very momentary lapse of attention on the path over which I have expressed so much concern. One look up and next thing I know I'm pulling my face up off a blood-splattered rock. I got lucky. Very lucky.

In drunken solidarity to my ram-skull-tough forehead, I made an encore performance in town, a 2:30 a.m. dive off an unusually steep chunk of sidewalk outside the Hot Springs Post Office, bloodying up my knees to match head and tearing a good-sized gash in my $50 high-tech mountaineering pants. These things one must do after weeks of olympic monk-like life in the woods.

> *Mr. McKinney,*
> *It has come to my attention that you have had a wee little mishap on this trial, uh, I mean, trail. We at Mutual of Omaha want to be certain that you are in the finest condition possible to continue on this ordeal, er, vacation. We are sending our finest health inspector agent out to your location for a complete physical. We at Mutual of Omaha are requiring this testing in order to assure the financial stability of your primary dependent, Duke. Dr. Ruth Westheimer should be there to meet you at your next shelter and will need to conduct many tests to determine your true well-being. She understands that you have been woman-less for a while now and believes that this could be the underlying cause of your spontaneous face plant. It is a well-known fact that men's brains cannot function properly if there is a lack of influential female presence. This must be remedied. Dr. Ruth will be interviewing potential "mates" for you as she makes her way along the trail to the shelter. Look for marks on the backpacks of all the women as you hike. She will put large check marks on the backpacks of those that she feels are appropriate and large Mr. Yuk symbols on those that*

*are not. She is an expert in her field and you must follow her
advice. Remember, baby Duke is counting on you! Thank you,
Sister Maria Margarita aka Agent Red
Department of Salvation and Copulation*

Some of the trees along the trail have wounds, folds, places where the tree
is pulling back in upon itself, collecting itself. These wounds make for funny
shapes: this one a vagina; this one a church key keyhole; this one a mouth
devouring a "Game Lands" sign nailed there decades ago, now bent and
sinking, literally being sucked into the tree, the tree's way of dealing with
such intrusions into its skin. I wonder if I leaned long enough against a tree if
it would enfold me, grow around me, make of me a burl, a bump in its
timeless growth.

A cute young blonde thruhiker girl named Indie offers me a blow pop. I
stare at her mouth agape. "A blow pop," I deadpan. I take it.

I stop at a lovely little seep and cup my hands to drink from its moss-
shrouded spring-in-the-side-of-a-hill mouth. I drink the water here unfiltered
almost solely. It is clean. It comes from the ground, smells like Heaven. I
understand that this will soon no longer be the case. The further north we
walk, the closer civilization will encroach. Then the water will need to be
nuked every time.

John Denver sings, "In my mind I'm goin' to Carolina; can't you see the
sunshine; can't you just feel the moonshine..." I am in Carolina. Back and
forth between North Carolina and Tennessee. A few miles tomorrow and I'll
have passed the 300-mile mark.

Tiny purple irises, miniatures of the sort so loved by Van Gogh, grow like
mad now along the edges of the trail. The spring air smells of cinnamon and
vanilla. My $250 down REI sleeping bag smells of me, smells of my musk. I
crawl into it now and am comforted. No tent tonight. Zippo and Bic (my trial
trail names for Ry and Jackie) and I opt not to pitch our tents. The stars are
out in full bloom. Let's hope they stay that way and rain clouds stay far a field
for tonight anyway.

As I pass the 300-mile mark on this journey I begin to ask again the
question "Why?" Why am I doing this? Of all the things I could be doing—
sailing, jumping out of airplanes, learning the saxophone, courting Ukrainian
beauties in Vinnitsa or Cherkassy, learning Italian on the streets of Sorrento—
why this? The answer comes easily: Because I can. Because I want to.
Europe, Russia, the world can wait. People travel abroad constantly, yet

there's so much of America to see, so much they will never see. Thoreau was big on this concept. But for him the necessary "world" was smaller still. All he needed was his native Concord. Ah, but Henry David! You did climb Katahdin in Maine. Gotcha!

For all the people out there without legs to walk or eyes to see, for all friends and strangers and trail angels with envious longing in their eyes that they, too, might buy the time or find the strength of will to walk a long trail themselves, I do it for you. I do this for the living and for the dead.

Then a pine needle stylus hits the slate LP and from the horn of some mighty beast hollowed out and resonant or a wild flowering plant with gramophone petals comes the earnest voice of Bowie singing, "It's the terror of knowing what this world's all about, and watching some good friend screaming, 'Let me out!'" and I realize I'm walking for depression and resultant suicide. I'm walking as much for Luciano as for me. For Luci, for David, for Nancy, for Patty, for Nick, for Dan, for Anne and Sylvia and Kurt, what the hell.

Four suicides among people I know last year alone. Cruelly perhaps, but not without just cause, I say, "Can we turn down the wailing over cancer and heart disease and strokes and all the other terminal illnesses that make loved ones look up and care but more often than not are diseases of the aged!?" What about the lonesome disease of the shotgun and the noose, the overdose and the warm tub, slashed-wrist sluice? Can we not take seriously the illness of depression, the 8th leading cause of death among males in America?

Granted, twenty times as many people die of cancer and heart disease every year in America than of suicide. Okay. Here's a related statistic for you: 100 percent of all humans DIE! If cancer and heart disease are the way-out-front contenders in the race toward death, what are cancer and heart disease, really? They ARE Death, the Catch-Alls, the Grim Reapers for those who refuse to die any other way. So, statistically, as far as I'm concerned, they're out. They are statistically incomparable to suicide.

Only TWO times as many people die yearly of Alzheimer's and pneumonia, both primarily deaths of the aged, than of Suicide (there, I capitalized it!). AIDS doesn't even make the top ten! (Although granted, many of those are likely recorded as pneumonia.) Diabetes: two and half times as many. This latter is particularly significant in that psychiatrists, therapists, and suicide counselors use diabetes to explain to their chemically depressed patients that they suffer from a disease and need to take antidepressants daily, just as a diabetic needs insulin.

I wonder when the last time a man suffering from a stroke or a heart attack called 911 and was greeted at his door by cops with guns drawn? This happened to me, and I understand it is common procedure for suicide calls. How reassuring is that? Imagine the humility it takes just to admit defeat, to call 911 when you're feeling in danger of taking your life yet lacking the courage to actually do it. Now imagine having the cops show up, guns drawn, pointed at you? Pointed at YOU! Think I'll ever call 911 again? Fat chance.

Ah, the hell with it. I digress and the day ambles on and the bugs buzz around my ears, and everything, everything in these woods is better than THAT! Better than a shotgun bathroom goodbye and all the zillion reasons why to pull that trigger. I walk this walk for you my too-soon-departed friends and for every lonely soul who takes his life every 17 minutes in America.

Ironically, this stretch of the trail is peppered with gravestones. Little Millard Haire's tiny 12-year-old skeleton sleeps sweetly by the trail, at rest since 1863.

By day's end I calculate that I have ascended a total of 2,400 feet, not counting the down hills. This has been an average day. I am the walking dead as I stumble into camp at sundown. Only the insects gather round to greet me. My God! What am I doing out here? Oh, yes. Walking. They say we all get 15 minutes of fame in our modern televised age. Few suicides want to die unnoticed, unknown, yet someone dies every 17 minutes. I suppose then I could say I am walking off my 17 minutes of fame.

Phrase for the day: Dream Big. When I say dream big, however, I am talking about goals, like this one I'm entrenched in. Hear me now Reader: YOU CAN DO BETTER THAN THIS. This was more impulse than dream for me. If I make it to Maine, it is because I am obstinate and unruly. Dream big. No one else will do it for you. In fact, few will do it for themselves.

Last night I dreamt my father was Bill Murray. The dream took place in a garish banquet hall with bad food and plastic people. I like Bill Murray, but it was not a good dream. At Mile 352, I crest Unaka Mountain, Tennessee, Elevation: 5,200 feet. I've stopped asking why, for a while anyway.

A girl named Skirt asks me to make her a hat (a silly-shaped hat made of fleece, such as the one that earned me my trail name). Skirt hiked with a boy named Dingle who allegedly has agreed to dangle, behind, that is, like Elly who went on before me. Thus, now Dingle, like Jester, is single.

Slow Walker comes from Ireland by way of 30 years in Chicago. I discover the Ireland part by commenting on his "perfectly charming accent." Charming it is. After struggling to ingest and decipher half a dozen heavy southern accents, Slow Walker's gentle Irish lilt is maple syrup on waffles to my California ears. Self-applied, Slow Walker's name is daily earned by a cautious pace meant for tender knees that pulled him off the trail in years past. He has children in college and a wife at home. How is the wife taking this journey of his? His reply is slow and thoughtful: "She's supportive but incredulous." Slow Walker will proudly leave the trail briefly next month to see his daughter graduate from college. Beyond that, I've no doubt he'll make it to Maine fine in his own slow sweet Irish time.

Have I mentioned that the Appalachian Trail passes through 14 states, eight national forests, two or three national parks, and crosses 15 major rivers? Most impressive to me was the recent discovery that we conquistadors of the first 350 miles have already climbed Mount Everest twice. According to the statistics, the 300 or so beasts among us who make it to Maine will have climbed Everest an equivalent of 17 times! SEVENTEEN! 17 x 29,000! Do the math.

I look back at my memos from the first month of the trip and find weird notes, their meaning now largely lost to me:
cosmic banditos
panic knees
wolfsong-zipzipzing-starfire
terrible wind 30 mph
one dollar
thank u 2 docents-blazes
ankle score=5 to 3 r
topography no houses
pan scrub w bark; pad Thai
pm-gnawing on own pineal gland
Jake doc ankle
9-in 4 cold sprgs

Okay, I comprehend a few things., For starters "wolfsong-zipzipzing-starfire" is memo code for the three Von Trapp kids' names. Those kids were great, singing along on the trail, all of them getting the best education I can imagine, walking to Maine. I begin to doubt now whether their intention was to thruhike, as I haven't seen hide nor starfire-hare of them since Week One. Too bad. I miss 'em. [Note: Though I never saw them again, I heard of them, still on the trail way up in New Hampshire in September. I'd bet cash they made it!]

The "thank u 2 docents-blazes" is pretty plain. The work that has gone into this trail is awesome, the white blazes on trees every few hundred feet, constantly reassuring. I thank the volunteers silently to myself every day. Them and God.

The score on my twisted ankles is now more like 6 to 8, right. Just last night I went down hard, wrenching the right and badly bending my left pole in its fight to keep me upright. If I had pocketed a dollar every time my $129 Leki poles have saved my ass, I would already have enough to buy a second pair.

In the mountains of Georgia, I didn't see house one. That illusion of a solely wooded world continued through the Smokies. Now, however, I see houses. The trail corridor narrows as it heads north. I am told that at points it is no wider than a freeway, slipping silently and likely totally unnoticed between two noxious algal blooms of suburban sprawl.

Still translating my notes:

I nightly scrub my $40 titanium pot with bark, sticks, and leaves. One night I feasted on pad Thai, a prize find from one of the ubiquitous "hiker boxes" at every hostel, bins full of goodies no doubt woefully given up by hikers with pack weight problems. This would be all of us at one time or another.

Last, with a nod to Hunter S. Thompson, sometimes at night the endorphin high is so great that I feel as though I'm gnawing on raw pineal gland, my own pineal gland, but I think I already mentioned that.

Later that day at Cherry Gap Shelter: Jackie and Ry have gone on without me. I miss them already. They left just the day before yesterday when I, forced to go the five miles into town from the hostel to mail a package, had to let them go. They're from Asheville, very close by, so this stretch of the trail is full of visits to friends and family for them. Had a wonderful couple of days running with them through the woods toward Erwin, Tennessee. Soon they'll go off trail for a week to a wedding and I'll likely lose them altogether.

This is the bane of trail friendships. They are fleeting. I miss Maine Sail, too. He zoomed off in some rush to get to New York to meet his girl, had to crank it up to 20-mile days. I can't keep up. I finally saw Tumbleweed and Underground Radio again, a week ago in Hot Springs. But they had taken a shuttle 40 miles north to come to Trail Fest, and thus had to go back to where they had left off. Kristen…er, Tumbleweed was surrounded by a bevy of boys and happy with the attention, no doubt, though surely still missing her Will. Underground Radio and I spoke of his skipping forward and joining me, but no. He had to go back.

So it's forward and backward, and I seem ever the more alone here in the empty space between this trail family and that. I hope this changes soon and I make some new friends. Not usually one to write much in the shelter journals, today I wrote:

> *Sweet night on Unaka Mountain*
> *Where the trees get up and walk*
> *On spindly legs*
> *The forest, devilishly dark,*
> *Curls you up its downy pine bed and slips*
> *Starry dreams in your evening tea.*
> *Onward. –Jester*

Finally, for those of you with guns to your head at this moment, don't shoot. I know you've heard it before: "Just change your life, disappear, easy!" I know. It's not at all easy. It is nearly impossible to see any way out when you're that far down. But take it from me, trust me, if you will, me who has had that gun to my head many a time. There is another life right here on Earth, another reality. It's close and it's accessible. You could crawl to it naked and bleeding and be lifted up and embraced and encouraged by the angels and good-hearted hikers of the AT. Many of them/us are merely well outfitted versions of you, torn up inside and seeking salvation in the woods.

If you have the conviction to gamble on the unknown variable of DEATH and leave a grieving world, then you likewise have the conviction, and I GIVE YOU PERMISSION, to shit-can the works! You are perfectly poised to burn the credit cards, let them boot your car, take your house, redline your TRW, who cares? If you can die, thus abandoning all aforementioned crap, why not try this instead?

You are a perfect candidate for a long walk in the woods. Look at Baltimore Jack who went out for a ride and never came back. His life may not be the classic societal model of success as a result of that ride, but out here, Baltimore Jack is a hero, a god. And he LIVES!

Eight years and seven thruhikes later he lives and walks. He breathes excitement and humor into the lives of thruhikers he meets as he takes temp jobs at outfitters all along the trail heading north. He follows his tribe, this year's proud sons and daughters of the AT Thruhike. I don't know Jack's real story, but I'd aver he walked that trail once and then again and again and five times again to keep from going off the edge in the cruel "real world." Just a guess, but I bet I'm close. Why else would one hike the same trail seven years in a row?

God bless you, Baltimore Jack, whoever you are.

SEVEN

Why, Epiphanius, Why?   A Savage Act Against Elephant
Kind...Snug Cabins, Old Barns, and Yippee Spinning Tolkien
Yarns in the Dark...From Bad to Worse: Gallipoli Winds to
Dreaded Elk Park...A Leap Into Virginia, Hand in Hand...My
Heart in the Blood-soaked Earth...

In one month I have walked more than 320 miles. According to the
mapmakers, an AT thruhiker upon completion of the hike will have climbed
the equivalent of Mt. Everest 17 times. I figure by now I've done Everest
twice.

My heart beats like a flushed and frightened tufted grouse.

People keep commenting on my shoelaces. I have two shoelaces, one black,
one blue, to match my broken heart.

On a hot, dry deserted woods road, I let my poles skitter behind me,
hanging limply by their wrist straps. Sometimes the forest is enchanting. At
the moment it merely is. Poetic verse forms in my head.

> *Somewhere a shredder shreds, turns*
> *Incriminating documents into paper linguini*
> *Whilst I skip 'neath clear southern skies*
> *Kicking downy dry leaves*
> *Cool breeze, mossy trees.*

Eric Clapton mumbles cocaine marbles into my fly-fettered ears. Early
spring bugs ring my sweat-wet skull like the rings of Saturn. A new kind of
snow blankets the ground as pretty little blossoms fall from limbs of spring.
Trees on spindly, rooted legs romp around the pine forest bed, and robin,
finch and monarch play.

Maynard comes on the radio again singing *Precious* straight to some
suicidal friend and I think of Luci. I start running through the forest of

standing dead sentries, witnesses to my melancholy, watchers of my escape, gray, drizzle, still no leaves on deciduous trees.

"How's the trip treating you?" I ask Epiphanius at some weird rat cage of a shelter in the pastoral path of my first 20-mile day. He sounds offended, says my question leads to why.

"WHY?! When I get to why, I can go home!" he says, indignant. I never saw Epiphanius again.

Speed, of Speed and Breathless, pisses on my parade by informing me that I have missed my one-month anniversary on the trail. In his opinion, one month from yesterday, not today, was that day. The comment bursts my little bubble of joy, and I leave them. I have practically been skipping all day through drizzle and all so happy that today, the 20th, marks one month on the trail for me. I started my hike on March 20, the first day of spring. I think he's full of shit.

A great Zeppelin song comes on the radio and the reception is good. Suddenly I'm running! Pack and all, I'm running down the gentle path and across fields singing "got to go away, baby...." and I run and run. It is my first time running! One month today! Imagine it!

I've decided I'd like to found a church. I'll call it The Church of Everyone's All Right! It'll have but one premise: that everyone who has faith in something, some deity, some higher power, the Universe, themselves, whatever, EVERYONE gets to go to Heaven. No one gets left behind, as the popular Christozealot-propaganda novel would have one believe.

There is a newlywed couple on the trail called The Honeymooners. I can't in my wildest imagination comprehend choosing this epic jaunt for one's honeymoon. This is a gauntlet run, a bone-crusher, an X-rated episode of "Survivor" (for unpalatable violence and insanity). May God be with The Honeymooners. Vaya con Dios, my friends. Forgive me my doubts.

Later, the words of the Eagles' song "Desperado" send me into a funk. Indeed, why don't I come to MY senses? If only I could remember where I left them.

Your sins are erased, they are no more, they're all out on the ocean floor…
- random gospel lyrics heard along the Tennessee/North Carolina border

Having a little radio along has really changed the tone and atmosphere of my hike. By Hot Springs, somewhere around 300 miles into the journey, I'd heard enough of the tick-ticking of my steel-tipped trekking poles impacting random rocks. I'd heard enough of my huff-puffing emphysema-esque heavy breathing up hills. I'd heard enough of the nothing sound of so much stark winter woods only occasionally riveted and pocked by the knocking of a woodpecker on some poor tree-bug's door. I'd heard enough of my own thoughts. For despite all the people supposedly on this trail and all the great people I've actually met at hostels and shelters and crossroads here and there, I still find myself hiking alone 99 percent of the time.

Why is this? Well, imagine yourself hiking with others in a dense jungle on a winding path. You stop to tie your shoe, adjust your pack, lean against a tree and wheeze, and when next you look up, you're all alone. The people you were hiking with are now well ahead, and given that you were hiking at exactly the same pace, catching up will be a very great feat indeed. Take that same example and imagine this friend leaves an hour ahead of you, and that friend is two days behind. The result: a lot of solitude and quiet, eventually too much.

So I bought a little radio for $40. It's no bigger than a tiny stack of business cards, and supplies me with a constant racket of country music, twangy-tongued preachers, hard rock, and the ever-welcome public radio fare of folk and blues and hot-sounding indie chicks on acoustic guitar. And classical! A dreamy piece by Maurice Ravel played long and lovely through dense thickets the other day, the sunlight trickling through and turning the trail into a paisley patchwork of bright swirls of sunlight and dark greens of mossy stone.

Often the stations battle in these woods, as though my walking the line between Tennessee and North Carolina makes it okay for this rap station to seize control, totally interrupting and thus blowing the endorphin-aided high of the rock classic "Feel Like Making Love." I give up when a third offender enters the scene with fiery words from the pulpit. I reach down to the cinch strap above my right breast where the radio is securely duct-taped beside the dangling Tinkerbell and Uncle Duke figurine from *Doonesbury* and swing the dial south. Now it's "Violin Concerto #1" by Sergio Prokofiev. A complement to tree, rock and sky, it comes in clear as a bell, uninterrupted by preacher or Puff Daddy. I am at peace again.

In Erwin, Tennessee, Jackie, Ry, and I gorge on pizza. From our waitress, I discover for the first time that there are two syllables in the word "left."

We borrow bicycles from Uncle Johnny's hostel, bikes splotched with orange to signify their owner, and peddle around the odd little hamlet of Erwin. We gather supplies, toothpaste, Wheat Thins, Pop Tarts, and high-calorie candy bars and wrap the white grocery bags around our necks and arms for the ride back to Uncle Johnny's. A Coors six-pack at the Erwin gas station rings up to the nice round price of $6.66.

At the local Dollar General, I find a G.I. Joe action figure proportional to my Uncle Duke figurine. For a dollar, it comes complete with guns and a commando raft. Outside the store, I tear off Joe's arms and toss him and his gear in the trash. Later with superglue, I rebuild Duke like the Bionic Man. To ensure that his arms do not come off again on this treacherous journey, I duct-tape his shoulders and chest. He is whole again.

On the ride back, we chance to meet Paul, a former city councilman. Paul recognizes the bikes and us as AT thruhikers. He explains how Erwin once had a bad rap with thruhikers and that places like Uncle Johnny's and things like the borrow-able bicycles have helped. Somewhere back in Erwin's history, the locals executed a circus elephant in retribution for the elephant's murder of its trainer. Erwin touts this event like some kind of grand moment in its history, a thing I find odd. What makes the killing significant (and apparently the reason the town embraces it) is the manner in which they dispatched the poor creature: They hung it. I later see a historical photo of the hanging, done with the aid of a crane. It gives me the fear so bad that I know, in an instant, that I will never again look favorably upon Erwin.

The wrong replacement keyboard arrives for me in Erwin via UPS. I am crestfallen to find it doesn't work with my Palm Pilot. Hostel host Hillbilly is generous with Internet time that I may solve the problem, to no avail. Furthermore, I must now repackage and send it back, a logistical problem in spread-out Erwin that sets me back half a day and sends Ry and Jackie on without me. By late afternoon of an unintended "Zero Day" (day without hiking), I give up and zero.

That night at Uncle Johnny's I share a small, two-bunk room with Sanguine from Rhode Island. I pass out mid-afternoon and awaken in the evening to her return from town. She leaves me a cold beer by my head, apologizes for waking me, and goes out again. I thank her and ask her to leave the door open, citing my need to get up. A moment later, Rael appears in the doorway. He presents me with my Nalgene drinking bottle, lost several days ago on the trail. Nalgene is a fancy brand name and is somehow better than or healthier to drink from than a used Gatorade bottle.

Go figure. I didn't buy it, but rather adopted it from Elly, who tossed it and its rainbow-colored crocheted carrying sleeve in a hiker box, for weight reasons, as always. The story of how the bottle, bereft of any markings saying it belonged to me, made its way back to me astounds me. In a nutshell, someone hiking a short distance behind me that day found it, figured it was mine, and carried it a while. She then passed it on to another hiker, giving instructions that this was Jester's Nalgene bottle and to pass it on. On and on it went, so far as I can tell through half a dozen hikers (Lightfoot tells me he was one), a shelter or two and a hostel or two, to Rael, to me. The Appalachian Trail is Oz, Never Never Land and Narnia all rolled into one. The magic bedazzles.

The miraculous return of my bottle helps my grim, no-keyboard, no-Jackie and Ry mood, but only for a little while. Rael is intent on hiking out that night. I would like to join him but have already paid for another night at the hostel. I watch with chagrin as he hikes off across the bridge and into the forest.

Uncle Johnny's is uniquely situated right smack on the trail and right beside a beautiful river. If one were smart, one would never venture into the "town" of Erwin, some five miles distant. I wish I hadn't. Dropping off the trail and onto pavement with Ry the day before, I had made a funny show of getting down on hands and knees and kissing the tar. So close is Uncle Johnny's that my act raised laughter from Sox on the nearby deck.

Now tonight I find myself crossing the bridge in the dark but starry night, beer in hand. What's that I hear? It's that mystic sound of train roaring through dark of night. I swallow my beer in one fast gulp and sprint toward the forest, past a white blaze visible in the dark, to where the AT crosses a railroad bed. A freight train arrives just as I do, all roars and rumbles. In the pounding of your heart and rattling of your cage of ribs, your feather-light frame of bones, there is a feeling that is a word, a word as powerful as love, as freedom: ALIVE! The awesome beast, its powerful presence, exhales in the dark and is gone, a phantom. Language fails such moments.

The next morning I am the first hiker on the trail at 7 a.m. I know this because I clear the path of spider webs as I walk. After not long, I feel like a well-whiskered kitty cat. I've walked through so many strands.

A breeze blows and a snow of small white petals falls on me as I walk. It is a beautiful moment, one I want to share. But there's no one else. Just me. Alone in the forest again.

Thinking back on Elly, it occurs to me that I have lost my slinky, that someone special to walk ahead whilst I trudge on behind, then switch we do, me and you, you fall back and I, I push on through. Together and apart, we inchworm down the trail. But all this reminiscing is to no avail. For I, I bade you go, that I might walk alone.

Over the radio come the words of some band called Seether, singing, "I'm broken when I'm lonesome." One should not be set to tears by the lyrics of a band named Seether. But I am.

Later, at the first shelter, I pull out Swiss Army tweezers and alcohol swabs and perform an operation on my ailing keyboard. There on the shelter picnic table, I take it completely apart, key by key, and clean the entire thing, hoping. My hopes are in vain. Two hours later it is clear that it has been more autopsy than operation. There will be no writing for the next hundred miles, at least.

Taking the time to work on the keyboard that morning cost me. Rather than being at Cherry Gap Shelter later that afternoon, I found myself far short of it and stuck in a mounting storm. In the full fury of the storm, I ditched off-trail and down forest service roads to a strange place called the Greasy Creek "Friendly" (a valiant if somewhat opaque attempt at disarming the hostile sound of "hostel"). The hosts were kind, the hostel fine (in the any-port-in-a-storm sense). But I was the lone guest of a couple of self-professed nut cases whose next-door neighbor hated them, so I was never entirely at ease. The neighbor must have been a greater lunatic than we three put together, and a dangerous one at that, waking us as he did before dawn the following morning winding out the rpm's on his chainsaw, wood-chipper, and riding lawnmower. "He's not cutting anything," my hostess assured me. "He just does this to try and drive us out."

Every morning? I asked. Every morning came the reply. I liked the couple and wished them success, though it was plain to see that with a neighbor like that they could never operate a hostel. They would need more rooms. I slept in one of only two guest beds. Their bedroom was but a paper-thin wall away. The next morning, I ascended 2,500 feet in nine miles, hungover on boxed wine, yet I lamented the hangover not a bit. For the gift of wine, shared with me, not sold as was everything else at Greasy Creek (my meals, bed, etc.), had been the highlight of a truly weird night.

Stepping out of the storm and into their mudroom, I'd been handed a fresh clean towel for the shower and, with apologies from them lest I be a teetotaler, a glass of Chablis. Later, emboldened by the Chablis, my status as lone guest, and a twinge of the indignant at my hostess' insistence that I listen attentively to a portion of her novel, I got to the point where I just pointed at my glass when ere it was empty, and she refilled it tout suite. Word of caution to the aspiring writer: never tell anyone you're a writer, especially not one with any history of success. The moment you've made a dollar as a writer, congratulate yourself, then choose from and practice one of these simple replies to the vocation question: "I sell insurance. I am a grave digger. I'm a mud sculpture artist living on an NEA grant." No, that will likely illicit annoying queries such as "Oh really? What kind of mud?" The point is to stop the conversation dead in its tracks. Try this one instead: "I'm a fecal matter analyst at a rehab clinic."

Cherry Gap Shelter journal entry, April 25:
Out of my slack morning of writing arose
Black clouds, rain and thunder to curl your toes
From Unaka Mountain to Cherry Gap did I dally in pace
Then from Iron Man Gap became it a race
Through downpour made swift I prayed not a little
The poles in my hands would not end life's great riddles
"What's next? Who's that? What is her name?"
Failed that night to reach shelter but I'm still in the game.

Now this is what I call a treat. I sleep tonight, well, I'm too enchanted to sleep at the moment, but I have slept and now lie excitedly awake to the raucous rat-tat-tat racket of one King Mother of an Appalachian rainstorm. High atop Roan Mountain on the Tennessee-North Carolina border tonight, it rains ball bearings and basmati rice (uncooked of course) and...what's that I hear? Champagne corks, as well! Popcorn and banana peels, to boot. Man, it is storming to beat the band, rainin' to drown the pain of the world. But I am safe and snug in my musky mummy schlaffsack (sleeping bag) beneath the tight tin roof of an old fire marshal's cabin.

Built in 1932 by the Civilian Conservation Corps, the Roan High Knob Shelter is another example of FDR's stroke of humanitarian genius that put purpose back into the lives of a broken people. One of the first of just five of us here tonight, thruhikers all, I gleefully grabbed myself a piece of prime shelter real estate in the up-ladder loft of the old cabin, all the better to enjoy the symphony of April showers on a tin roof. I'm talking hours! Seems like it's been storming since Christmas, lying here snug inside a log cabin of dreams, 370 miles of the AT behind me. Mmmm. Beautiful.

Yesterday evening I was caught out in the rain, and that in its way was magical too, but this night on the Appalachian Trail is a dream come true. Cozy and dry, happy and high (6,400 feet, high for the East Coast), I'm thinking of you, all of you out there fighting the good fight, living the life they say we're all supposed to be living, but one that I and most folks asleep around me here in this cabin and in shelters hundreds of miles both north and south are too broken or choked up to live anymore. So I am become Peter Pan again, not grown up but man, and as such wishing the best for my kind, my kin.

In this high mountain stormy night dream beneath old hand-milled beams and a roof that has proven its valor and played like a harp and hammer, where Mickey Mouse makes his rounds to check on us all (and our crumbs, of course), and the beveled glass window beside my head like something seen only in shops for antiques, and—okay the roof leaks just a little but only in drops here and there—I feel sleepy again; but before I bid adieu, I send a message of care and love to ALL of you, you out there, out where perhaps this rainstorm falls more to the mundane. I am thinking of you and wishing you grace, Amazing Grace, in any measure and in any way it may come to you. Goodnight, God bless.

Five weeks out, and tonight it's an old red barn they call Obermountain Shelter, and I sleep with some dozen others. If not for the cold wind blowing through fist-sized gaps in the wallboards, the place would reek of damp 'n dirty socks, boots, the works. Today's rain soaked us all. Joke going around: What's the difference between a thruhiker and a bum? Gortex. New friend Matt collected wood for a fire but fails to get it going. I step in with little chunks of chem-log and my Pocket Rocket propane stove turned on its side like a blowtorch and voila! Despite rain and wind and making Indiana Jill nervous, fire is born.

Upstairs young Yippee and Jabberwock read Tolkien to one another by headlamp, a cute couple snug in their bags in the dark barn loft at 7 p.m. Fireside, old Slow Walker from Ireland imitates an Irish country doc pushing booze on teetotaler widows, saying, "Now what you do, Mrs. Murphy, is you take just a wee capful of this whiskey here and add it to a glass, not a pint, mind you, just a glass, of Guinness. You'll sleep lovely and feel right as rain come mornin'."

> Obermountain Shelter log entry, April 27:
> *Rickety red barn, cracks thru and thru*
> *Spin me a yarn, needn't be true*
> *Of a valley green and wide as desire*
> *A dozen damp travelers, the smoke of fire*
> *A reading of Tolkien aloud in the dark*
> *Warm cluster of life from the world so stark*

Then morning and haste, the race again begun
I to join it must this story be done.
For now anyway! - Jester

"Ain't no mountain high enough," the song plays as though straight to me as I trudge another monster ascent. Here in Bumknuckle, Appalachia, between this state and that, we are forever treading the state lines of North Carolina and Tennessee. Some days it just feels like an F-ing roller coaster, a trail designed by sadists. Good thing for the trail angels who pop up at road crossings again and again. Good thing for Oreos and Mountain Dew from Queen Diva; for ham sandwiches with homemade relish from Tom and Jane in the Smokies; for the Coors beer and homemade muffins entrusted to a cooler and the honor system at some crossing by the absent angels Rambo First Blood and Skinny Cow; for angels Emma and Christian in "No Man's Land," a tiny turnout on a road smack between signs saying "Tennessee State Line" and "North Carolina State Line."

Christian is a pastor; Emma a nurse's aide. They stand there leaning against a guardrail, a full backyard-style banquet laid out before them on the ground. Apparently we are to help ourselves. I do, to cookies made with toffee, to hot dogs and brownies and soda pop and celery sprigs. Half a dozen of us sit cross-legged on the road before them and stuff ourselves, our packs tossed about us on the ground with seeming disregard, an illusion, of course. We rely on our packs with our lives. Our trekking poles pile up against a sign, sabers at the ready.

I am grateful for the grub, as always. But devilishly, I do find myself comparing, remembering the overt joy with which Smokies' angels Tom and Jane served us, refusing to make us "work" to serve ourselves. Tom and Jane made their own relish and pickles to die for! God bless all trail angels who make this monstrous trek, so often and so easily perceived as lonesome and impossibly painful, appear once again in its proper light as the Great Dream and Fulfillment of Freedom that it really is.

I rounded a tree the other day as I often do to cop a lean and a breather, often leaning hard against a tree with my forehead, talking to it, thanking it for being, asking it for a moment to reveal its secrets to me and I will to it the same. I don't have words to describe the things I have begun to see in these moments. There will be a time on down the trail when the visions will find words to fit them.

But this time was something else. On instant impulse, I placed my hand smack on a tiny crucifix, thumb-sized, exquisite, and not carved there by mortal hand, no, natural this was. Its discovery: purely accidental. I'd had no intention of "mind-melding" with this particular tree but had merely reached out for it and touched it, unknowingly. Startling! It was like the Virgin of Guadalupe sighting on a rusty old water heater in Arizona, only this one in bark.

I've decided all the trees are wonderful expressionists with their cleaved trunks, bulbous burls, and endless writhing roots. Freud would have a special room for me in his sex-distorted asylum on the hill if I told him of the vulvas I see in every tree and the swollen testicular burls, and especially this last: That the trail I daily tread fills me with dread with its sea of soiled penises, a thousand thousand phallic roots projecting from the earth, each with but one goal—to trip me and, in bringing down this beanstalk body, stop me cold, stop me from finding that one good woman who walks with me, somewhere on this trail, not yet caught up.

Damn the ubiquitous cocks on the trail! If I were a god of the ground, I would tear you from the path underfoot that I may trip no more and she may skip the faster to find me.

For anyone thinking perhaps all the world's been developed and there ain't no open space left anymore, well, t'ain't true. I used to love flying west out of the Albuquerque airport, counting five minutes, then looking out the window at all the empty open nothing that would stretch on for the next hour or so flying 600 mph. I am not just a little surprised to find that there's a motherload of nothing out here in the East, as well. Crossing a vast field in Tennessee listening to the radio, the B-52s come on, and instantly I am transported to the beach at 14th Street by the old power station in Del Mar, California, 1983.

But the field goes on and soon climbs high within reach of gale force winds. I check my thermometer hanging on a strap on my chest: 40 degrees F. At the top of Little Hump, Mile 383, several miles past Obermountain Shelter, I find myself leaning harder and harder into the wind. Tree Frog and I estimate the wind speed at 70 mph. Calculating in the wind speed with the temperature, I guesstimate it's about 20 degrees on this late April day up here on this stupid, endless, treeless mountain. I want to get off it ASAP, so I begin to run. I run downhill and uphill, too. I'm suddenly crazed by the wind. I envision myself at battle with it, and when my lungs can take it no more, I dive into a culvert and hide and heave and work at slowing my breath. A few culverts later, I am the young runner in the film *Gallipoli*, dodging a killing spray of machine gun fire. I am a dead man running. How fast? Fast as a leopard.

Atop the vast bald mountain, I am faced with a herd of longhorn bulls. One stands directly in my path, on the AT. I begin to circumnavigate this behemoth, moving around him to the east. He follows me step for step. Shit! As if the wind ain't bad enough, now I'm being pursued by a frikken bovine psychopath! I finally take off running hard and fast in a big arc. He trots after me and roars like a mutated cyborg with a longhorn hard on. I get away safe. But the thought comes to me that first thing I am going to do when I get home is write the ATC and complain to the effect: "To hell with the damn bears! I hiked 400 miles and saw not bear one. Then a frikken longhorn chases me! What's up with that?"

Writing about the Gallipoli incident, I turn to ask fellow thruhiker Tom if he'd seen *Gallipoli,* the film about the record-breaking short-distance runner who goes off to war and gets himself killed. I ask Tom if it was a leopard or a cheetah (I can't remember). Tom says, "Oh, yeah, like Pat Tillman, the football player for the Arizona Cardinals." I inquire what he means. He explains that Tillman was offered a $9 million contract but chose to join the army instead and go off to war. He was killed recently in Afghanistan. Damn war. Damn the old men who plan it and the young men who sacrifice great destinies to run off and die in it. *Gallipoli* was one of the most shocking, sad films I've ever seen. My battle with the wind on Little Hump was imaginary. What grim tidings to remind me of my own good fortune in life.

I promise myself after the hellish battle on the hill, that once I'm back down in the trees I will be joyous, whether I like it or not. The psychology works. Shortly, the path is sweet and clean of rocks, and the sun peeks out, and on the radio comes a song that sets me, suddenly, to skipping.

Skipping! I have no recollection of ever skipping in the forest with a 40-pound pack on. Ever! The song on public radio, I later learn, is called "Great God in Heaven Comin' Down" by a group called Tangle Eye from "Southern Journey Remixed." It was an amazing song, kind of gospel with a beat to make you skip your feet. Fantastic!

I catch up to Tree Frog, a sixty-something happy-go-lucky old dude from Texas. Great guy. I ask him how he got the name, and in his high-pitched Texas twang he tells me. "Well, one night I cooked something spicy for me and my buddy, and the next day on the trail I was tootin'. My buddy would ask, 'What was that?' and I told him it was them tree frogs." The name stuck.

Tree Frog goes on to tell me that Appalachian tree frogs are still quite prevalent. "Like the mice, they hang out mostly around shelters. You hear 'em at night." I fall for it, hook, line, and frog fart.

The day goes on and on. I am in hot pursuit of Jackie and Ry, a couple of **my favorite hiking partners. To catch them today, I must hike 27 miles. It is** unlikely. (Before day's end, I will fold time and space and place myself at great personal risk and still not make it.)

It is hard to believe that on the same day I battled a Tennessee-Texas longhorn through gale force winds and Gallipoli visions, I later blue-blazed a white trailer trash neighborhood and lived to tell the tale.

The highway crossing at Route 19 in Tennessee's Elk Park region is my first encounter with people inhospitable to thruhikers. Here there is no Trail Magic. What is here could be called "Trail Tragic."

"Wingnut" (as hikers call *The Thru-hiker's Handbook* author, Dan "WingFoot" Bruce) cautions thruhikers against hitchhiking where the trail meets Route 19.

What I heard (and this is no more gospel truth or fact than ANYTHING I say in these pages) is this. The ATC wanted some land or at least rights-of-way for the trail in this area. The U.S. government stepped in, offered folks market value for their homes, and the folks refused to sell. Next, apparently the government says, "Okay, give us an easement through your property and the right to buy it outright when you die." That wasn't cool with Joe Bob and kin either. So the feds just did what the feds do next in such situations and seized the land.

Needless to say, the folks in Elk Park, or maybe just a few folks, whoever lost their land to The Man, are still mighty pissed. The cascade of trash that pours down into the river there—old appliances, tires, garbage, you name it—has apparently been "maintained" steadily over the past several years. There are stories of hikers hooking themselves on fishhooks hanging from nearly invisible fishing line directly at eye and throat level along this region of the trail. It is a very strange vibe, this section of trail. It was partially this vibe that sent me, balls over brains, diving into the nest of the "enemy" for a few highly tense but fascinating miles.

What did it was the ankle twist. Coming down the trail, a graveyard in sight below me, I stepped wrong on my right ankle again and went straight to the dirt.

Admittedly, I'd already been eyeing the upcoming "stupid loop" on the map with annoyance and suspicion, wondering why, once again, my northbound trek required allegiance to this east-west bulb-shaped squiggle. Here, there was no blue blaze cutoff. But an obvious shortcut presented itself. Two, maybe three, miles of road walking would cut off 12 miles of bullshit meandering through hostile territory. So I took to the road, limping.

Up and down streets lined with trailer homes and pit bulls frothing at the mouth and junkyard-like collections of comatose cars up on blocks, I limped, and I limped quickly.

Then I heard it, the familiar whine of dirt bike engines roaring down on me from behind. Two of them, by the sound of it. I didn't look back. A couple of local hoods, I figured, come to check out the freak with the pack trespassing on their side of the tracks. An ATV pulled up alongside me. On it sat a boy of maybe 10. "Want a ride?" he asked. I replied no thanks, and off he went, his buddy, equally young, speeding along behind him on a homemade go-cart with one flat tire.

The tension in my shoulders released as visions from *Deliverance* left me, replaced by a logical question, "Why didn't you take the ride, idiot?" It was all uphill, and I was hurtin'.

A few minutes later I caught up with the boys where they'd parked by their home. They marveled at how quickly I'd walked the distance they'd just ridden. "I've walked 400 miles, so I guess I'm pretty good at it now," I said. In answer to their queries, I told them about the trail. Though it was but a mile from their house, and literally kind of looped around their general area, surrounding them in effect, they'd never heard of it.

As I walked on, I thought less of the scary trailer home dwellers with pit bulls and cars up on blocks. I thought less of my fear, to the point of chiding myself for being fearful at all. Here were a people trapped in poverty, a poverty which, despite my constant pennilessness and occasional visits to social services for help, I would never know. I would never suffer like these people. Why not? I don't know. Education, perhaps. Imagination. Freedom maintained by not fathering any children, not marrying, and the better circumstances of my own birth and upbringing. Perspective probably more than anything. My world view is vast and boundless. Those boys had no idea that a trail of 2,200 miles of freedom, of free camping, of trees and wild ponies and deer and rivers and Life! ran right past their door. Bukowski said it: Nobody suffers like the poor.

I spotted a white blaze and was back in the woods. Poof! Like magic I'd gone from Shitville to Shire. Seamless.

Every thruhiker should blue blaze such a neighborhood. We so fortunate frolicking these woods should see what lives just beyond these trees.

At sunset, I was in so much pain that I dropped and ate several codeine pills reserved for a time-bomb abscess sure to return soon to my ailing molar. I lay there, inert in the dirt, for a good hour, staring up at sky and stars thanking God for my charmed life. I rose at last, set up tent, and slept.

After a rain, the large wet leaves of rhododendrons are the wet tongue kisses of a friendly dog.

I'm back with Ry and Jackie when we come upon a tall, monument-sized grave, the grave of "Uncle Nick Grindstaff." Aside from the uncle part, it reads, "Lived alone, suffered alone, died alone." Ry says it is the most depressing epitaph he's ever read.

I catch myself dragging my poles behind me again on a long flat stretch. I am reminded of skiing as a child, a cool hotshot mogul-junkie child was I. If forced to accompany my little sister on bunnie slopes, I'd drag my poles in boredom.

On NPR, Garrison Keillor reads a poem about a two-headed calf newly born, it lying in the night pasture, dying, but seeing twice as many stars as we will ever see. The poem is a whole cow pulling on my heartstrings. I cry like a baby.

The news comes on again. It is always coming on, interrupting the soundtrack of my life. As I flick the dial away from Iraq and toward "I Ran" by Flock of Seagulls, I've got to ask, "What the fuck is a Faluja and why are young Americans fighting and dying there?"

I hear a lot of strange lyrics as my tiny pack radio jumps station-to-station, sounding like a schizophrenic songwriter. One lyric goes like this: "Spin a bottle cap, throw a shot, cough, cry, lay down, and die."

A bluegrass tune makes me think of friend Mary in Houston. "It's a Bloody Mary morning, I'm flying down to Houston giving her the nature of my mind."

The words of a contemporary rock hit make me think of our exhausted arrival at last night's shelter. "The water there is…very hard to drink!" After a 20-mile day, we learned from the guidebook that the nearest water to the shelter was half a mile away, one mile round trip. After haggling over who should go, we all went. It was straight downhill, then straight back up. Naturally loopy from exhaustion, I hammed it up. It helped.

Seems like no matter where or in whose company I am in this law-crazed Orwellian post-9/11 America, the conversation invariably turns to cops. When the second Gulf War broke out, I retreated to my former small mountain town home to get away from it all, and all I heard about was cops this and cops that and how the cops busted so-n-so for protesting. I lived in a constant state of angst and unrest. For all the talk of cops and the fear being generated in this country, I'm happy to report that in 440 miles of hiking I have seen not one cop. Not even in the Smokies with all their rules and talk of rangers, never saw a one.

Walking these wooly mammoth wet woods, I got moss growing in my head and ferns coming out of my ears.

Ry, Jackie, and I pull a second 20-plus mile day, wind up cooking right smack on the trail at dusk, then walk another mile with our headlamps to a clearing big enough to tent in. Ry makes a fire and retires to his tent. I sit up alone and think. At 5:30 a.m., I awake from a nightmare. It's the $10,000 Question, and the gist of the nightmare is that it will never be answered.

"What's the question?" Jackie and I are walking together, swapping places on the mobile, virtual psychiatrist's couch that for us is the trail. Ry hikes on ahead.

It is the one question I would like my former fiancée to answer, and I would gladly put 10 grand on the table to coax an answer. I would ask her if she understands, despite having no recollection of things said while in her altered alcoholic state, that I left her not because I wanted to, but because she told me to go. Not once but repeatedly over the course of a year, a woman who loved me by the light of day would, when drunk, express vehement hatred toward me. First the demon in the bottle asked, then it told, and finally it demanded I go, saying, "And don't believe me in the morning when I tell you otherwise."

Two and a half years later, it is a question that visits me daily on the psycho-meditation that is for me the trail.

It is drizzling. My leg pains me terribly. I inhale a bug. I try to feel the drizzle and the pain, to focus my energy on the path. I try to forget the outside world.

Jackie is a big help with this. With her bright blue pack rain cover, she is an iridescent blueberry guiding me, even when way ahead. We stop at the state line and eat tuna from flat aluminum packages. I suck the last salty remnants from her empty bag of wheat crackers. Packs back on, we look one another in the eyes, join hands and say, "Ready?"

Jackie and I enter Virginia together with a leap and a laugh.

It's the first week of May here in Damascus, Virginia. Dee-Dee interrogates me in a doorway at the Methodist hostel known as "The Place." She wants to know all about the glorious life of a freelance writer. Actually, all she asked was what I was before this. I should have just told her the truth, that I was a depressive sometimes-suicidal poet and wandering nomad on Prozac. Instead, I say, "freelance writer," also true, but a can of worms. She said that was her dream job. I remarked on her pack, all ready to go beside her. I said it was the first time I'd seen her with her pack. "Ooh, low blow," she replied. I hadn't meant it as an insult. It was true, however. I had met Dee-Dee twice on the trail, and in both instances she was headed south, sans the pack.

The worst was the day she and a few other slack-packers (thruhikers who lighten their packs and are driven to and from trailheads by angels or hostel hosts) passed me going south down Roan Mountain as I made the monstrous climb uphill with full pack. I thought I was going to be sick. My angry poles dug deeper for a while that day. But my reward was great. Aside from the cozy night that followed in the cabin, there was a moment of excellent synchronicity. Near the very top of Roan, there is a set of handsomely built stairs, hard work by some angelic trail volunteers. I remember that the moment I set foot on the first stair, "Stairway to Heaven" began to play on the radio, and played out, clear as a bell, for the duration of the climb, the song's crescendo and my final steps coinciding perfectly. Had I been back in college in northern California on LSD, I think I would have had a stroke.

Now Dee-Dee is going home to Jersey. Off the trail for good? Not for good, she says. She will do sections near her home. I'm sad for her. Her countenance is stone, but she can't be that strong. I depart without saying goodbye.

Later, my head is full of things to tell her. I would explain how freelance writing contributed to my present state of ill mental health, and that it should be avoided at all costs. I would say to her that had she been hiking in the same direction as me, north, perhaps we could have gotten to know one another better. I would have liked that.

Grizzly Dave and I agree that town stops are a lot of work, that and a terrific distraction from the trek at hand, maybe too much so. Grizzly Dave is a former state senator from Iowa. He tells me of his travels in Alaska and how he can't wait to boast of his AT triumph at his 50th high school reunion in September. He makes a run to the spring for both of us, insisting that I rest my tweaked right ankle. In return, I make him hot chocolate after dinner. He is thrilled. We are alone tonight at the first shelter northbound from Damascus. It will be a very cold night, but we are hardy souls, the senator and I.

Lately I've broken my "news fast." It's been like a two year Lenten information abstinence. No news. That was the rule after 9/11. Not knowing the details of the constant world chaos and cruelty would help keep me out of the psych ward, my doctor insisted. I think it worked for a while. But I still read books, non-fiction mostly, and that's my fault. For with a love history comes the inescapable realization of how horribly repetitious we are in lust for war, what Henry Miller called, while walking the millennia-deep bone pile that is Mycenae, "an endless chain of assassinations."

Now plugged in to my little radio and happily tromping along the trail that Edward Abbey referred to as "one of those outdoor dream-adventures we all dream and very few have the nerve to realize," I hear this month's death toll of our soldiers in Iraq: 160 dead, as many as were killed during the actual "war" this month last year. So much for reverie.

Auuurgh! I want to tear out my heart and shove it in the ground, that in its passionate beating it may boil the earth beneath our feet to make men everywhere drop their guns and leap into the trees. I want to paint every white blaze I pass with the red blood of my veins in protest of the impossible ugliness of war. The ghost of Henry Miller walks in ancient Greece, the very cradle of civilization but also here beside me today.

> *It is glorious to offer one's life for a cause, but dead men accomplish nothing. Life demands that we offer something more – spirit, soul, intelligence, good-will. Nature is ever ready to repair the gaps caused by death, but nature cannot supply the intelligence the will, the imagination to conquer the forces of death... It is man's task to eradicate the homicidal instinct...*

I feel for every soldier stuck over there now on extended stays, stuck to die. I want to send the soldiers chunks of dripping moss from Appalachian rocks and UPS trucks loaded to the hilt with American soil to smear on their faces and be cooled by it and know they are loved and thought of.

I think to myself, what a bafflingly brilliant and frighteningly stupid species we are. "Yes," says Henry, and on we walk a-talking of life until a day hiker comes around the bend toward us. Embarrassed, I clam up. When I call out to him a moment later, Henry has gone. Perhaps he found the day hiker more interesting. She was cute.

Later, on "Prairie Home Companion," Garrison Keillor tells a story about how when he was a boy, a bear walked into his kitchen one day and he fed it peanut butter and jelly sandwiches and taught it to say big words like "loquacious," and in return the bear introduced him to credit cards. I laugh quietly to myself and shake my head. The poor bear likely would have buried himself in $10,000 or so of high-interest debt like me and every other credit slave in the world. Alas, there are no bears out here anyway.

Sometimes when not plugged in to the radio, I walk and talk to myself in Gollum tones. "They left us, they did. Maine Sail and Doug and Elly and Mockingbird and No Beard and No Dog, nasty hobbitses!" Then Smoegel chimes in: "But Maine Sail is our friend!" Then Gollum: "You don't have any friends!"

I walk down a canyon where radio reception is at an all-time low. But through the fuzz I hear the familiar strains of Pink Floyd. As over the static roar of a rushing river, a vestigial "Dark Side of The Moon" comes through. It occurs to me that I have heard it so many times that my mind is likely producing most of the sound, words, and music absent in the sea of radio fuzz.

Came up behind a raccoon today, followed him a while, he unaware of me as I crept stealthily along, finally sighted, and away he hopped. Still haven't seen hide nor Linda lip of a bear ("Linda lip" is a term my mother coined in reference to my pouty cousin Linda). I mix it up here with one of my favorite images, that of late animal actor Bart the Bear jutting out his lower lip angrily at Alec Baldwin and Anthony Hopkins in the film *The Edge.*

My means of water purification is amazing. Called the Mountain Safety Research MIOX Purifier, it employs not a filter but an electrical current (via batteries) and a bit of rock salt to create oxidized water. This tiny sample of brine is then added to one's water wherein its "excited" ions tear through the water killing everything unhealthy to the human tummy. With high school chemistry now 20 years behind me, I honestly have no idea how it works. It worked for our soldier boys over in Iraq, I'm told. By golly, that's good enough for me!

Sister Margarita sent me Crown Royal whiskey in the mail. God bless her. It helps, a little nip at the end of the day, often in hot cocoa. She wouldn't believe me if I told her how long it has lasted, still lasts.

I know I recently wrote about wanting to start my own church, something like the Church of Everybody Is Okay. But some e-mails were lost recently, several lengthy chunks of my writing were lost. That bit may have been among the fatalities. Anyway, I just heard a lyric I like, in a country song of all places. "I like to believe that Heaven waits for more than those who congregate." Nice.

Somebody asks me what I write, and I mention the screenplays. Every day somebody asks what I write about. I never give the same answer. I don't know the answer. Sometimes the conversation will go far enough along that I'll mention my brush with David Fincher.

I wonder what ever happened to that connection. "That connection" being this: Fincher, director of *Fight Club,* read a proposal I wrote for a friend based on her script idea. Apparently he liked it. My friend then parlayed this interest into production money to pay me to write the script in its entirety. I always assumed the finished script would, as with the proposal, end up in Fincher's hands. If it ever did, I never heard about it. But the end result is, for me, the same. In a roundabout way, I wrote a script for David Fincher, director of *Fight Club*, hands-down one of my favorite films of all time.

There are many pockets in my space-age pants, enough to hold one hundred rants (rambunctious ones at that!). In one pocket the ever-present TP, ziplocked, of course. In the other pocket are the map, a photo of my nephews, and today's mileage page, torn from *The Thru-hiker's Handbook.* These are also bagged. Everything is bagged against the threat of rain, of which the forest world is now a-doused, keeping me here where I landed last night.

Thruhikers drop their packs anywhere and everywhere. No one safeguards their belongings. There is no danger of theft when anything stolen would have to be carried. Theft equals too much weight.

On my second night in Damascus, I shirk restaurant food. I open a label-less can from the hiker box, discover peaches, eat 'em. Later I wander over to The Place and eat fried Spam with Tinker.

EIGHT

Sidetracked in Southern Virginia with an Angry Cuban...Trail Nudity and The Moral Chalkboard...Ever North! Krispy, Trail Widow and the Trash Bag Slack...Suicide, Narcissism and Other Unconscionable Acts...The Woods are no Escape from the Tentacles of World Horror...Trail Daze and the Mystery Courier...From a Bland Metaphor to a Dismal Flood...No Rain, No Pain, No Maine!

"And then, depression set in." Bill Murray said this. I can't remember in what film or context. The phrase, the sentiment, is, however, the first thing that comes to mind this morning as the black sedan containing my friends pulls away from the curb here in Damascus bound for points south. My journey is north. Ever north. Every morning I rise with the sun and, despite the maelstrom of mental crap which daily rises with me, I need heed but one call: Walk north.

Vanishing in the "trail-alien" automotive spacecraft are Obermeister Ry and Lady Bic Jackie (names I tried and failed to stick on them), my trail companions on and off since Day One, but especially recently. I had gone to great lengths in recent days to stay on-track with their trek. I had committed a number of trail sins to keep up with them, sins for which I ought no doubt to be in church this very moment, this Sunday morning in Damascus.

Church in Damascus. Seems a moral imperative of sorts, a kind of ironic play on words, a biblical theme ride that must, for the sake of the story, be ridden. But no. Instead I sit in my church, Our Lady of Pre-noon Hefe-Weizen, drinking my favorite beer and stroking the keys of my new Palm keyboard as one would the softest parts of a woman, touching them with a love and reverence only a writer could understand. The keys respond to my touch like bare nipples in the wind.

I have hiked the last 200 miles with an ever-diminishing capacity to write, my old keyboard stricken with a crippling combination of Alzheimer's, palsy, and just plain old age. In the end, when I pressed the W key I would get a Q.

When I pressed many other keys I would get nothing, and many more, still working, would come accompanied by a mysterious S. It made filling in the gaps with the Palm touch-pad exceedingly difficult until at last I gave up altogether.

During this time I ran into Ry and Jackie again, not them personally but their names in trail shelter registers calling out to me, "Jester, where are you?" After a weekend off-trail with their parents, they assumed me to be ahead of them. They raced forward. I was, in fact, behind them. But trail news travels fast. It is uncanny how news makes it far ahead when it would seem its only modus the journals be. I busted ass to catch them.

But all this is pointless. Though I eventually caught up with them and we hiked together three days into Damascus, Jackie and Ry are gone now. Just like Lark. Just like Maine Sail. Just like No Beard and No Dog. Just like Doug from Jersey and dozens of others who've gone on far ahead. Jackie and Ry, however, are now officially off-trail for a friend's wedding, not due back for nearly two weeks. The chances of my hiking with them again are slim to none. Depression sets in on a gray day in Damascus.

A squashed lemon wedge sits awkward at the bottom of my empty pint glass here at the Sidetrack Café, awkward as an unwanted opinion expressed and non-retractable. Boo-Boo whines across the cafe, continually mentioning my name in connection with pissing off the cook last night with my comment that "Cuban food and Mexican food are hardly different." Death by Cotton, the tie-dyed-shirt-wearing cook, was serving up so-called Cuban food. I waited for the fried plantains, ready to be proven wrong. The boiled chicken and rice and beans didn't go far toward changing my opinion. I left before dessert, disappointed, exhausted, bloated with beer and Mexicuban food.

It is a sore spot for Boo-Boo, apparently of Cuban lineage. I don't hear an accent. Boo-Boo is likely as Cuban as I am Irish. But no matter. Perhaps Boo-Boo's just pissed that I forgot who he was, despite having roomed with him one night in Hot Springs. As I recall, it had been a multi-beer night, and he'd been "moved in" to replace my departing friend, Maine Sail. Good friends leave big empty spaces. Back in my room now at Dave's Hostel, Jackie and Ry have gone. I stand in their absence like an empty and winter-wasted Iowa cornfield. Alone, I type. Later, I will cry myself to sleep.

In contrast to my comment earlier about seeing more houses sprinkled through the wilderness, this Cinco de Mayo finds me immersed once again in deep woods. Virginia brings us into the Cumberland Gap, the passage Daniel Boone scoped out in his day as the only way to hump wobbly wagons and trunk loads of dreams through the great wall of Appalachians into the "West," this at a time when Kentucky was as far west as the imagination yet ventured. The Cherokee and other Indians had learned of it long ago by following the buffalo. Daniel Boone was a cool dude, however, so we'll give him his due.

So it was trees all day today. Blossoming and blooming trees at last! Stepped through a buttery cream-scented dream, a grove of trees with flowers tiny white and a perfumed presence radiant as the sky. Were I a wiser man, I would have lain in that cream-scented dream and inhaled deeply through my nose all day. No such luck. Wish I knew their name. Later picked lilacs for Jill from Indiana as she, her hiking companion, Matt, and I met up by chance and settled on a tranquil field for dinner and sleep.

With me also today in my otherwise lonesome trek was the rushing music of water moving in tidal waves through the canyon below. Then the river came louder still as the AT dropped down and joined the Virginia Creeper Trail, an old steam railroad bed now made trail for hiking and bicycling.

I purse my lips like duck bills and, conjuring images of big black engines huffing along through the past, I make steam train sounds with my mouth as I make my way over a long wooden trestle, an antique sky bridge of aged wood taking me high above the river and far, far back in time. Breaking my time trip for just a second, I peer over the edge and the spell of suicide is on me like a fast demon. A Nordic breeze spirals the narrow tunnels of vessel and bone, and I shiver head to toe. It's a long way down, and the lure of escape intoxicates. To fly, to slough off this mortal coil, escape this troubled mind. There isn't a high bridge or cliff that doesn't lure me so.

But I feel the dirt beneath my shoes, and the bridge ends and with it the reveries of trains and final flights to the Afterlife. Then things get really strange. The trail veers off the old rail bed and back into the woods, and suddenly I am plagued by demons both physical and mental. First it starts with my right calf, my "calf gone bad," as I'm calling it. The result of the worst of many twisted ankles in the past month, the strained calf muscles are screaming at me lately, but I cannot simply stop. So I talk to them. "White light to the right," goes my silly white suburban voodoo chant with healing intent.

Then my mind starts playing tricks with me. The evergreens across the canyon cast shadows darker than chicory coffee and suddenly spookier than that dribbling nose scene in *The Blair Witch Project.*

Huh? It's the middle of the afternoon under bright sunny skies! Yet what do I see but shadowy movement in the trees all about me, ghostly in nature. I stop to rest a moment, check to see if for some reason I am dizzy, find that I am not. I decide to test myself, to see if this isn't some sort of psychosomatic trick of my mind, both the pain in my calf and the eerie visions. I pop a Klonipin, 2 milligrams, my Valium-like salvation reserved for major freakouts. But then I blow the validity of the test by also popping an 800-milligram ibuprofen for the pain. Oh, well. In either case, I should feel better soon.

Moments later, however, I arrive at Lost Mountain Shelter. The name is fitting. Besides Jill and Matt, there is an older couple unknown to me and queer somehow, perhaps for no other reason than that I'm having a panic attack and they don't jump up to introduce themselves.

The feng shui of the place is wrong. The privy is positioned straight ahead of the shelter instead of behind, a kind of "display privy," for those boring afternoons when there's nothing better to do but monitor your friends' bowel movements. There is a scary silence about the place that just doesn't mix well with where my head is at. Jill and Matt are a mixed bag for me. Either I feel a connection with them or I feel shut out, like they're a private club of two, with some kind of Indiana voodoo to seal the deal. But, as I say, I'm enduring a heavy bout of temporary insanity at the moment, so who knows what's real. Anyone who's experienced this knows well that it's scary as hell.

The drugs are not kicking in fast enough. I'm not there two minutes when I heft my pack and bail. I'm limping and wondering if the real cause of all this freakiness is a subconscious fear that this newest injury could be the death of me, could spell the End of the Trail. Last time I felt like that was in Neel's Gap, Georgia, when my knees felt ready to collapse and it seemed sure to call a quick end to things. I was wrong then. I hope I am wrong again.

I keep track of my mileage with my stopwatch. Exactly 9 minutes and 34 seconds after leaving the shelter, I round a corner to a wild and cheeringly funny sight. It is Superman with a pack and a white and balding dome. Well, not really, but the tired old man standing before me looks every bit Superman at first glance in blue tights, blue shorts of a slightly darker hue, and blue skin-tight shirt of yet another blue. The Super-cue is his bright red fleece hat hanging around his neck and positioned dead center on his chest. I give him the cheery news that his shelter is but nine minutes away.

Half a mile later, the trail intersects Route 58. I have a choice. Tendering my bum leg, I could hitchhike from here straight back into Damascus, set myself up in a $4/night bunk at The Place, and rest. I take self-portraits with my Nikon digital camera, one with thumb up (hitchhiking pose) and one with thumb down and a frown. I choose the latter and forge on instead.

I am the real Superman. Or am I a ghost who died unknowingly years ago? It is a theme I toy with now and again, nervously. It would explain the demonic woods immediately following the bridge crossing, in a *Jacob's Ladder* sort of way (for anyone who's seen the film). It would explain my dizzying urge to jump from deathly high places, to return to Heaven, where I certainly feel I'd be happier and less afraid. For now, however, I have nowhere to go but north.

Not a mile past Thomas Mountain Shelter with its wild ponies and attic loft and all that *Sound of Music* scenery, I land wrong again on my right ankle and let out a scream. After a minute, I am able to walk on it again, barely. I come to a fork just up ahead and meet Ed and two female thruhikers I haven't met before.

Sixty-something Ed is pointing the girls toward the white-blazed route that will swing them far to the east into a national park. I have studied the map and know that the blue blaze route he is guiding them away from is, in fact, the old AT route. As the girls sidle toward the blue-blazed route, Ed says, "You don't want to go that way; there's much better views this way."

It's weird, his being here, now, at this very moment. It's like he's some manifestation of my conscience, or the devil at the crossroads. "Will you be true and avoid the blue? Or will you slight the white and take the shortcut path?" I'm thinking, hey, buddy, I just twisted my ankle for the 14th time. I'm in hellacious pain, I see a line on the map heading straight north, just five miles long, and it's looking a whole lot nicer than your 15-mile reroute.

As though reading my mind, Ed butts in on my thoughts, asks me my name and where I'm headed. His silent response to my stated trail name tells me either he dislikes it or he's half-senile. He asks a few other questions. I don't like it. I don't like this guy in semi-authoritarian garb grilling me whilst standing in the way of my plotted blue blaze.

Thinking of *Breakfast Club,* I ask (thick with Judd Nelson sarcasm), "And what are you doing out here today, Ed?" He babbles something, departs, and I take my shortcut. I'm calling it an Earl Schaeffer Shortcut. Earl, first to hike the trail in the late '40s, most definitely walked the shorter route I walk today.

Few lines on a map are random. They are usually political in origin, and have been fought over by clawing, axe-wielding men for centuries. In this case, I later discover that in my pain and obstinacy I had deprived myself of one of the most beautiful sections of trail, a pastoral fairy tale of Celtic landscapes, stunning vistas and many, many more wild ponies.

One of the girl hikers' names is Miranda. I meet her later again at Damascus and find that she is leaving the trail that very day. I feel sad for her, and for me for not following her through pony land. She was cute.

Sitting sentry at the other end of the blue blaze, a kind of second witness to my AT impurity, sits Gray Fox, a tall skinny guy of 21. I sneer at him psychically, feeling caught in my shortcut and still rabid with the pain in my ankle. We walk and he tells me the story of how he came to dream of someday hiking the AT.

As his story goes, at age 11 he was hiking through this very section of trail as a young Boy Scout. They'd been hiking perhaps three days in the rain when they finally retreated, arriving at a parking lot just off the trail. There young Gray Fox and his Scout buddies saw a dog. "There was this huge dog running around loose with a pack on. We watched as the dog went over and started sniffing around some garbage at the edge of the lot. Not wanting him to get into the trash and spread it about, we went to get it. Just then, a hand reaches out of garbage and pets the dog! Turns out it was two thruhikers covered in trash bags to keep out of the rain! And it was their dog! It was right then that I decided that someday I would thruhike the trail myself!"

Earlier, Gray Fox had asked me why I was hiking the trail and suggested that perhaps I'd been dropped on my head as a baby. After hearing his story, I could see why he'd think that.

Sarcasm aside, I liked Fox and his story. I especially liked hearing of the passion he had for his fiancée, "or not quite fiancée yet as we can't afford a ring." So in love with her is he that he's going to sell his 1967 Ford Galaxy to buy her a ring. Trouble is, he lives locally and has been finding it hard to stay on the trail for very long, what with her waiting near at hand. So far, he's taken a whole month off, he said. Today is May 6.

I've hardly been ON the trail a month! Ahh, love is a many-splendor'dthing. He'll never make it out of Virginia.

Filth and Roadie show up at Partnership Shelter in southern Virginia and hand me a Sierra Nevada Pale Ale. "We're the ghosts of thruhikers past," says Filth. They're delivering late night trail beer magic. I've just gotten off the phone with Justin, my mad hatter cousin, my master Web Master bar none. He is really the only person I call anymore. He and the Swami. Otherwise, phones have become very alien to me. I get into towns and barely have time to drink, be hungover, receive and repack packages from the P.O., and get back on the trail. It's madness. I am finding that there's no such thing as a day off the trail. No Zero Days for me. Well, they ain't zero, anyway. They're work. Too much work.

LL Fluffy and Star Gazer are my new amigos, two crazy girls with degrees in outdoor fun, something I should have thought of way back in the day when I stupidly made up my mind to follow Hunter Thompson in gonzo journalism. Idiot, I. They hadn't invented gonzo journalism yet at Humboldt State. They probably still haven't. It has long been a dream of mine to make it big somehow, some way, and donate back a large sum of grant money to be given only to the student most likely to use it in the most aberrant fashion, to tweak the norms of journalism as far as possible. Naturally, I would choose the recipient.

LL Fuzzy strikes my fancy in a fun-lovin' curly-haired, petite powerhouse way. Star Gazer intrigues me, too. Hell, all female energy out here is GOOD energy. There's too little of it.

Sox and Sanguine have been great female energy for me, great hiking and/or just kicking around hostels kind of companions. Sox is this freaky ex-rancher's wife from Montana or somewhere, half-Japanese, tough as nails, smokes like a chimney, up all night or at least the first up in the morning, very, very interesting character whom I am always glad to see in this ever-in-flux family of hikers, many now ahead, many behind. Seeing her tonight at Partnership was a real thrill. I hope I keep running with her for the duration. Good woman.

Same with Sanguine. Teacher, been to Africa and taught there, tough gal with a big pack and a big heart and some indefatigable quality about her that tells me she just may well make it the whole frikken way. She too has been good to the Jester. We've shared tea, meals, readings of Henry Miller. Sox does my laundry every time I turn around. Which is nice.

Christ, there must be 30 of us at Partnership Shelter tonight, a high-class log cabin with two levels, a hot shower, and a phone from which pizza can be ordered. I tell you what, there sure as shit wouldn't be half these amenities on the PCT. The AT, for all its grubbiness and hard-core hiking and pained feet, is a high-class gig. There are people ready to help you everywhere. Just today I came off the trail at Dickey Gap and had to hitch three miles into some one-horse town to get my "bounce box" (a box of food I sent myself a week ago from Damascus). I wasn't having much luck getting a ride, and then a miracle happened. Ranger Jim and parents arrived to drop thruhiker Jim off at the trailhead. I introduced myself and asked about their going back in the direction of Troutdale; but, no, they were going the other way. I bade them adieu, gave thanks, and headed back to the road to resume my hitch. Seconds later, Ranger Jim had convinced his dad to take me back into Troutdale. Groovy!

Bill, a retired NYC firefighter, was everything cool in a sixty-something guy. He drove me into town, and town looked pretty sad. I'd heard there was a hostel there, some Baptist Mission or something; and there appeared to be a store, but man, that was it. As Bill pulled into the parking lot of the post office, I made a snap decision and said, "Bill, would you mind just hanging here a moment while I get my package? I have no business in this town and really ought to just get my food and get back on the trail."

Bam! I'm back at the trailhead. Bam-bam! I've hiked 15 miles to some shelter that's rumored to be soooo nice that it's pictured in a postcard that I bought in Damascus and sent to my nephews. They probably got the card today. Here I am now, sleeping here tonight, up in the loft, well fed on delivery pizza, drunk on Molson Canadian, buzzed on all the cool social contact with Kelly and Kris from Michigan and Sox and Sanguine and Ranger and Tree Frog, and on and on and on, oh, and the aforementioned girls...er, women.

I love women. I just can't help myself. Perhaps it's because I grew up with women. I just NEED their energy. I feed off it, and complement it, I think. Thank God for women. Please, God, let there be more women on this trail that I may find THE ONE. If not, this journey is to little avail. I think of Frankie back in Idyllwild. Frank knows women. He's got himself a good one. I think of Lori and Frank, of Frank and his ex-wife Suzanne's beautiful children Michael and Blythe. I think of my own desire to have children. I think of the one who asked me to marry her then went home to sleep with her boyfriend that night and every night. I had so wanted to say yes to her, but told her instead to ask me again a year after she'd left her boyfriend. Had she quit him that day, she wouldn't have had to wait a year. I'd have melted 'neath her charms in a week. But there's no point in these thoughts. She hasn't left him, likely never will. Time to sleep.

Dropping down out of the mountains in the late afternoon, my feet scream, "Stop! Stop! You heartless masochistic swine. Stop or we will bring you down like a broke-dick dog!" The sky is a temper tantrum waiting to happen, all black behind me and closing in, thunder and the electricity of a pending storm licking the back of my neck, all threadbare wiring snapping in the breeze and ready to burst into flame. On the urging of Leap Frog and Old Gray Goose, two women hikers at the last shelter, I do 4.5 miles in 90 minutes, half-running most of the time to get out of the mountains and to the Relax Inn and rumored Dairy Queen.

It is ironic, this. More and more, I feel I am running through forests at top speed, unable to see much around me by dint of extreme concentration on the ground below me, only to arrive at some outpost of civilization to buy caramel sundaes, Snickers, Corona beers, and clean sheets.

I pass an old schoolhouse, circa 1894, door open, desks all in rows with books tucked inside every desk, even writing on the chalkboard. It is part of a museum of some sort, one utterly bereft of attendants. Alone, I step out of the field and off the trail a moment to peek inside. On the chalkboard in cursive letters is written, over and over in the style of one kept after school as punishment for something: "I will not hike the AT naked. I will not hike the AT naked."

Just out of the woods, I drop down into stunning green grass fields stretching onward to forever, dotted here and there by a white farmhouse or some flattened old barn. I pass a sapling not much taller than me with a tiny gray woven bird's nest sitting gingerly on a branch. I could reach out and touch it, but I leave it be.

The thunderheads lingering overhead, I pass into a power line easement and beneath mammoth power lines buzzing dangerously as though about to pull down the fury of God from the sky and burn a hole the size of football stadium right where I stand. I duck and run beneath them and back into the cover of another small stretch of trees.

As civilization approaches, I am again reminded of the pure genius, the engineering, the determination, and the magic that have gone into creating this uninterrupted "corridor" through all lands from Georgia to Maine for nearly 2,200 miles. Down close to towns and roads like this, the AT might only be a thin green easement on the map, but there it is. A passageway. Like a modern Underground Railroad wherein capitalism is the master and we are all of us slaves, the AT provides safe passage through the consumer world, safe and free.

The white blazes never fail. Onward and onward I go, 535 miles now, and always they are there to greet me. If not on trees, then painted on guardrails, telephone poles, sidewalks, random rocks. A docent at Springer Mountain called it "the largest volunteer effort in history, the pyramids notwithstanding, as they were not likely built by volunteers."

Earlier in the day, Dingle passed me going "sobo" or southbound. Dingle, then Van Gogh (spitting image of his namesake), Ludicrous, and one other. I asked Dingle where was his Skirt? (Skirt, another thruhiker, appeared to be his mate when I first met them both in Gatlinburg). Skirt, it seems, is northbound still. Hmm. A cooling-off period, perhaps. No matter. In just a few days, EVERYONE will descend on Damascus for the three-day orgy of trail excitement called "Trail Days," alleged attendance 30,000. I can't picture it. Damascus is a tiny hamlet, a handful of churches, maybe two bars, a few gas stations. Where the hell do they put everyone? At Burning Man, I have seen 30,000 people. There, they are spread out across a vast dry lakebed. It is an awesome sight.

I am still debating whether or not to hitchhike back with hordes of others like me who are now some 100 miles north of Damascus. At 37 years old, I have spent much of my life living like a trust fund baby (sans the trust fund) but very much with the nose for a party, anywhere, everywhere, and making one up where it didn't exist. I have always tried to live well, to adventure, to eat, drink, and be merry, to suck deep of the marrow of life, as Thoreau suggests. But I have all the while lived in poverty, making it no small wonder that I'm half out of my mind by now. Poverty will do that to you. I've been writing when I ought to have been working some shit job to earn money to eat or pay that damn bear's credit bills. Anyway, I feel I will see nothing new at Trail Days. New Hampshire beckons. Then Katahdin, the pinnacle endpoint in Maine.

The next day, I embark on a new strategy in AT thruhiking. Thanks to Krispy Kritter and his visiting wife, Trail Widow I will do my first "slack-packing." A slack-packer empties his pack into a trash bag, tosses it into someone's truck, and "day hikes" ultralight to some predetermined meeting point. Today we will hike just 11 miles to some road where Trail Widow will pick us up and ferry us to a free hostel. We will do this for five days, increasing mileage daily and staying thus every night in the same hostel. Thanks to the miracle of the automobile, however, we will make 100 miles in just five days, all with very little weight on our backs. I have blue-blazed (taking short-cut trails) due to injury or foul weather. I have cursed southbound slack-packers as they passed me running down some heinous mountain that I was killing myself climbing up, a mountain over which runs a road by which one can be delivered by car. I call that smarty-pants hiking, not stupid, just a bit unfair to those of us other northbounders actually hiking NORTH up every mountain. It pissed me off enough that I swore I would not go sobo. Slack, okay. But NOT sobo. So here I go. A slacker at last.

First slack-pack day. It's Bear Trax and River Queen and Scholar and Krispy Kritter, his lady, Trail Widow, and me. I dub us "The Slack-pack Six-pack" on account of the six-pack of beer Bear Trax is carrying in lieu of his heavy pack.

We witness a garter snake eating a shiny black salamander, and later a fat centipede wrapped around a stick. Bear Trax tells me about how in Madagascar lemurs have been seen to catch big poisonous centipedes in their mouths and then bite them, but only just enough to make the vermin emit its defensive toxin. The toxin gets the lemurs high, says Trax, so they do it repeatedly. He says they've been seen to just fall out of trees, drunk on bug toxin. Where did he learn all this, I ask? *National Geographic.* I like Bear Trax. He's simple in a way I am simple.

Everyone crowds 'round to watch the snake eat the salamander. I can't watch and so move on down the trail. For a nonmilitary person who doesn't work as an EMT or a veterinarian tech, I have witnessed violent deaths of both humans and animals. If I had to choose which left a bigger scar, I'd say the animals. It's their innocence that kills me. I have no defense against the pain of watching innocents die. I say that, and yet the violent suicide of my friend Luci left me equally traumatized. Ah! Perhaps it is because in my eyes Luci was an innocent, so soft-spoken, so gentle, natural, like a small animal incapable of preying on anything. If I were to fall prey to a grizzly or a mountain lion, I would consider it a great death, although I'd prefer to do a Thelma and Louise off the rim of the Grand Canyon any day. Full tank of gas, maybe a trunk-load of full propane canisters. Really go out with a soaring freefall and a final bang. To heck with the park rangers and naturalists who would curse me for damaging the ecosystem. We're all walking pollutants to this planet. Altering that great Roald Dahl line mouthed by Willy Wonka about us being the dream makers and dreamers of dreams, I say "We are the garbage makers and we are the taker-outers of trash."

While lunching at the local shelter, the topic of "aqua-blazing" comes up. My ears perk right up at the very sound of it. Aqua-blazing! Doing a stretch of the AT on water! River rafting! Now that sounds like my kind of cheatin'! Apparently I'll get my chance come Shenandoah. I can hardly wait.

When you 51/50, as they call attempted suicide, the on-duty shrink automatically adds "acute narcissism" to your diagnosis, this apparently because you really have to love yourself a lot to hate yourself enough to want to do yourself in. Make sense? No. Not to me either. But then again, it does when looked at differently, more narcissistically. I love myself. I hate living in the world. I love myself enough to "help" myself out of this situation I hate. Suicide: the ultimate act of self-love. That's why it is illegal. God forbid anyone should be free enough to exercise such total control over his or her own life.

Narcissism. Empathy. I cannot watch little creatures eat one another. The salamander, unlike me, has lost its element of choice. Thus, I am a complete failure in the killing department. I can't kill anything, not even kill spiders, a species I generally loathe. There's one exception to this rule: scorpions. In a court of law, it would fall somewhere between temporary insanity and self-defense. If one fell on me or I pulled back the sheets to find one in my bed, I would kill it with a level of vengeance known only to God.

Despite a lighter pack, the day is still long and my body screams at me from various directions. Early on, I forget my age and ailments and go charging up no-switchback straight vertical ascents. At the tops, I am heaving like an elephant with emphysema. But I do it anyway. Mid-afternoon with the temperature sticking in the mid-80s, I am dying. The water from my hydration system tastes like powder. Food doesn't satisfy. I begin to wonder if I'm not dehydrated or ill somehow. At a stream crossing in a cool and shady rhododendron grove, we all find needed rest and cool water. I linger there a little longer than most.

Descending the final descent (ascertained by studying the topographic profile on my map), I pick up the pace, almost running again. I know, also from the map, that a river is just ahead, and I have every intention of jumping in it. I can feel it drawing me forth. I am an Iraqi prisoner on the river's leash, being tugged downward and humiliated by some young siren soldier on the riverbank, just following orders. Yes, even out here in the sticks, bad news bleeds through. Saw the photo on the cover of *USA Today* this morning. NPR slips it in, too.

After a jolting town supply run in which I saw news of the first of the new trend of war-instigated beheadings, I crumple to the earth in the woods of mid-afternoon and write:

Starlife and night in all of this. A footpath of stone and sand and mud, framed in purple iris and ghostly white Indian pipe. I am telescoped a million times down from curious worlds above, lain here, stretched out on sacred ground, that indescribable sweet scent of soil. Earth. God shed His grace on thee. The mother wails in Iraq, "Why?" The Michigan soldier's mother wails, "Why?" Terror lands on us like bird shit from the sky and I ask, "Why?" Yet these trees have no interest in answers. This Earth will not entertain our queries. The cicadas have gone deathly still. Just try. Scream your WHY far out across a wide vista. Yank the hanging kudzu vines. Shake the canopy for answers! Curl up in the limbs of a tree three centuries old and cry. Surrender.

Just when I was beginning to heal again! All this oxygenated air exhaled by trees that know no sadness. Streams that sing one to sleep at night. The simplicity of the mission: walk north. I cannot worry my head again! I cannot! I will not! For what? For my foolish race? My race, sick with envy. Know you what you envy, man? Equilibrium. You envy equilibrium, and you don't even know it. You chart a course of chaos and so will never find it. It is here, however, here in little things. Here in the white flesh of Indian pipe, as frail and translucent as the soft skin of my grandmother's hands. It is the faerie in Keffer's periphery in gray-green buzzing air of growling storm a-brewing. But go on, fools. Keep up your death dance, your angry face, your hate. No matter. The Mother loves. And God is bulletproof.

The other day, I was so upset by the number of soldiers killed in Iraq in the past month that I wrote feverishly about wanting to tear my heart out and paint the white blazes on every tree red, that every soldier dead or walking around "a marked man," marked by death, his days numbered, might know that back home there is a place where peace reigns, flowers are blooming, green leaves are growing and none of that war shit matters. Would that the blood of my heart could blaze a new trail to guide them homeward. I would give of that blood. I would give up my heart, my beating life, were it that my death mattered to more than a few, to see an end to this oil war and bring our troops home.

I have heard it said, "Never underestimate the power of celebrity in America." Would that I had the celebrity of an A-list American actor, I would fly my jet right into Baghdad and offer my head up to the nearest gang of butchers that the shock value of said act might end this senseless diversion of the collective American consciousness. No. It would only trigger a redoubling of our efforts and an exponential increase in deaths on both sides. What do I know about war? I am a poet, and as such genetically predisposed against it, vehemently.

Saying this, I might be accused of not appreciating what my soldier brethren are doing for me, for freedom. I do appreciate it. What I disagree with are fundamental issues far above the foot soldiers' decision-making capabilities in the military chain of command. The Commander in Chief knows the truth: Osama beat us. His war against us began and ended the same day. Aside from beating the living shit out of everyone in his family until the coward stepped forward (instead of flying them OUT of the country on secret jets when all other commercial air traffic was halted), we should have begun immediately to build our defenses at home, not pack 'em all up and send them to a country that had nothing to do with 9/11.

God, what a waste. But the foot soldiers, Henry reminds me, are neither ignorant nor entirely innocent. They had to know what they were going to be asked to do with that gun, that tank, when they were taught to use it.

> *Each one individually must revolt against a way of life which is not his own. The revolt, to be effective, must be continuous and relentless. It is not enough to overthrow governments, masters, tyrants: one must overthrow his own preconceived ideas of right and wrong, good and bad, just and unjust. A billion men seeking peace cannot be enslaved.*

I look back at the snake and the black salamander writhing in his mouth and think, "What the hell. You're lucky, both of you, victim and prey. You know no politics. You simply live to eat and copulate and sun yourselves on the trail for us to trip over."

Turned the damn ankle again. Always the right. For a while I was keeping score: 5 right, 7 left, etc. By now I'm quite sure this is about the 12th time for the right. Turned it, not doing anything foolish, like running (which I had been doing just moments before), but just walking, slowly following Trax and Scholar and Krispy and bamm! down I went. Fruck! Krispy, a retired fireman from Florida, came to my aid, offered a cold pack, ibuprofen, arnica. I took the arnica, an old Indian remedy, and got right back on it. I refuse to let it stop me.

This whole week of slack-packing was intended to give the ankle, the calf, the quads, the groin (the entire progression of the pain making its way up my leg in weeks past) a needed rest without actually zeroing. I can't afford Zero Days, neither financially nor spiritually. Town days suck me back into the world of banality and anxiety (if ever the two could have been said to coexist!). So I refuse to take them, not more than one a week tops. I've been out here seven weeks, hiked 580 miles, and have taken just six such days. I'm due one, I suppose.

But should it be tomorrow? CAN it be tomorrow? If it is, they'll want to take me to the local hospital. The nurses will at most take an X-ray. The doctor will find no broken bones and so tell me I've suffered tissue damage and stay off it for six weeks. Forget that. "Pardon me, Doc, but I don't think you understand who you are talking to. I have a threshold for pain you wouldn't believe."

For weeks I hiked on screaming knees and have steadily made progress on feet driven through with rusty iron spikes and charbroiled on the backyard barbecue of some queer-ass Appalachian Cannibal Cookout. Then the ankles. Twisted again and again until I lost track of how many times, I seem to have done sufficient damage to one that it now pains me constantly. I rub the foot, I stretch the muscles, I tender it. Then whammo! It twists again. Or maybe it sprains or re-sprains. Do these diagnostic terms really matter? I think not.

I think my plight, as with so many of my brethren hikers, can be easily summed up in the words of the late Grandma Gatewood, AT thruhiker in her seventies and eighties. She said, "Most people are candy asses."

Tomorrow this Candy Ass will likely take his candy sitting down. I will very likely Zero. But I'm not going to the doctor. Krispy's wife, Trail Widow, does Reiki. I will let her work her Reiki magic, and tomorrow I will sleep at Tilly's old homestead hostel of chestnut beams and Virginia backwoods hospitality just south of Pearisburg, Virginia. The following day, if I'm up to it, I will hike the last 13 planned miles of this grand, group-oriented, pizza and fried chicken and beer-filled slack-pack adventure week, an idea hatched in Atkins at the Dairy Queen and carried forth with all the pomp and circumstance of any candy-coated clusterhump for four or five days now. We've made good miles, and I have made great new friends.

Krispy Kritter is a man of humor and seriousness, admirable qualities in good, clean, and balanced American proportions. Trail Widow, his classy carrot-top beauty of a wife, has handled well her newly begotten role as trail angel to us all, showing up at day's end with a cooler fulla beers on ice and surprise snacks and lodging arrangements for us, the lightly packed yet still bedraggled hikers dribbling down the trail like Gerber mush from the chin of a dissenting, high chair-bound toddler.

Praise be to all trail angels, newly christened angel Trail Widow not the least of them. They feed us and sate our thirst and drive us hither and yon and on and on.

Many a time in the past two weeks I have contemplated a speedy hitchhike return to Damascus to rest and heal my ankle. But it would mean a rest of several days blending into the festival of Trail Days for a total of two weeks off. I have limped, stumbled, groaned and moaned, but I am now 120 miles further north. "No rain, no pain, no Maine," they say.

Got to eat crow the other day. Locked in to the schedule of the Slack-pack Six-pack, I wound up being driven up a mountain and dropped at what was supposed to have been the tail end of the day's hike. Result: a sobo day. Grrrr! I swore I would never hike southbound! But it was mob rule. All of us in the back of the truck all the way up some winding mountain road to find the end to show Trail Widow where to pick us up; and, hell, once there, why not just get out here and sobo? Group decision.

So I hiked sobo past Switchback, Zippy, and the girls, Beatbox, Sox, you name it, all with mud on my face after bitchin' at sobo'ers in the past. Oh, well. The fantastic hospitality, assistance, and trail magic administered by Trail Widow and Krispy made for a great week. I think I'll live.

Happy Birthday, Ranger Jim. The maniac from New York is hiking 37 miles today, one for every year of his life

Heard a lot of music by the Carter Family on the radio down here, something to do with the 75th anniversary of the music's recording, or something crazy like that. Love the stuff.

Okay, this is some fun X-file, conspiracy theory stuff I think you'll all enjoy!

I have decided that nerdy little Danny Ashman from Massachusetts is really Bill Gates's son in disguise. There could be celebrities among us. How would we know? No one uses his or her real name. Except: Aha! Danny Ashman, who insists on using his "real name." Which is what leads me to believe that his "real" name is a false name and he isn't who he says he is.

Pirate is another suspect character. I long ago decided that Pirate is really Slugworth (another Willy Wonka reference). The aging, portly, bearded old sailor who, to watch his gait, appears to move as much sideways with each step as forward, and who, to swallow whole his shanty tales of trail life, has been wandering the AT for some 14 years now, is not the roving rebel he purports to be but is in fact an agent for the Other Side.

Over the course of many miles and hours of trail delirium, I have deduced that there exists a secret Appalachian Trail Organization that, until we discover its true name, we will call the ATCIA. In this organization, there are many cells, and subcells, and tangential wandering arms and bodies, but important for our story here is that Pirate is ONE OF THEM. Pirate wears a black tee-shirt with a blue blaze down the middle, quite proudly proclaiming himself a "blue blazer," or one who takes blue-blazed shortcuts whenever possible. Blue blazing, to the purist AT thruhiker, is akin to stealing the

Everlasting Gobstopper from Willy Wonka and giving it to Slugworth for free, just to spite Wonka.

If my theory holds true, Slugworth...er, Pirate is an agent out on the trail, much like a narc, to wrongly encourage blue blazing and report back to headquarters in Harper's Ferry with a list of those who do. A kind of Pied Piper of Blue Blazing, Pirate lures us with his encyclopedic knowledge of the trail into taking the easy route to Maine. But just you wait, Blue Blazers! Just you wait until you apply for your Official AT Thruhike Patch at year's end! Forget it! In the words of Willy Wonka, "YOU GET NOTHING!"

I expect to be branded a slacker, caught in the act. I really could care less. As much as I've accomplished and as far as I've come, I can live with that.

> One night at Tilly Wood's "Wood's Hole" Shelter, a lovely old
> house and hostel of chestnut and oak deep in the woods, I write:

> I am a machine.
> Cut and pull back the Gortex
> Skin of my arm and
> See only Snickers, granola, and REI gear.
> I am a Twinkie assembly line
> A porcupine
> A crab with titanium pinchers.
> I am a devourer of roots, rocks, moss, and pine
> Terminator of the AT
> I will not stop, ever!
> Until you, Sarah Connor, are dead!
> (er...I mean, until I reach Maine)
> The end.

Trail Daze has begun. Truth to tell, I hitched south from Bland, Virginia (great name, eh?), about 120 trail miles north of here yesterday, Wednesday the 12th. Wednesday night at the Sidetrack Cafe was a bender. Awoke the next morning with a 30-pack of Old Milwaukee by my tent and zero desire to drink any of it.

To make something of the day, I go check out a film someone made on a previous year's trek. The film is showing in the auditorium of the Damascus "Rock School," literally a whole school, maybe even a high school, made of stone. In the audience are Dingle and Skirt and Kickstand, to name a few. The last I haven't seen since Hot Springs, or was it Nantahala? Great personality, Kickstand. Big, jovial, generous, a constant smile on his face.

The film starts out depressing and stays that way, focusing on the probable failure of just about every one of its subjects. The highlight of the film (up to the point where I walked out) was this pissed-off dog that refused to let its owner put one of those "doggy saddle" packs on him. He'd growl and bare his teeth and snap at anyone who tried. Otherwise, whatever year they were filming must have sucked for all present. The scenes were full of rain and misery.

I've no doubt that in a better mood, I might have sat the whole thing out. But spiritually hungover and wrestling enough with my own doubts about finishing the trail, the film was not what I needed. I retreated to the Sidetrack for a beer, the Dollar General store for a clean towel and a cheap floor mat to sit on outside my tent whilst here at this mud fest of 30,000 so-called hikers I've never seen on the trail, then back to the tent where I sat out the drizzly day in my tent.

Next morning felt much improved. Walked the 8/10ths of a mile into town from the alleged former "Superfund site" where they've got all us hikers camped out. Walked in for the breakfast at the fire station. Last night there was a free dinner sponsored by the Baptist Church that I missed for lack of a ticket (never did learn where to procure a ticket). I figured maybe the firemen were being charitable, too. But at $4 for an ice cream scoop of scrambled eggs, biscuits and gravy, and some dried up sausage, it warn't no charity, as the hicks say.

Walked from there to the vendor area in town where all the makers of backpacks and sleeping bags and hiking shoes are hawking their wares. I went to the Lowa hiking shoe/boot tent to show them the travesty their $95 shoes had become in 600 miles, in hopes they might cut me a deal on something stronger, perhaps with better ankle support. The rep, named Casey, assured me that the baling wire repairs and failed seams at every vent point were normal wear and tear for that many miles. She suggested I write the company and, pointing to the www address on a brochure said, "Just write them." I asked her repeatedly to whom I should address such a letter (since e-mail requires a name and the @ symbol preceding the URL) and got nothing but a polite smile and a hint of consternation. Shocked, I realized the girl had so little understanding of the basics of the Web that my query was pointless.

I then made my way down to the makers of Smart Wool socks and long johns and such. Here I explained that a $50 pair of their long johns had torn right down the leg after being worn only three times, and only to bed, at that.

Here I got a little more help, sort of. I was introduced to Jim, another re   ⌐⌐
suggested I write the company and actually gave me his card with an e-mail
address. Looking at the card, I noticed he was a rep from Lowa, the boot
company! Well, how about that. Again, I repeated my tale to no avail. These
were salespeople, after all. I'd heard stories of Trail Daze being full of reps
from various outfitters tripping over themselves to repair or replace gear so as
to maintain a good name on the heavily trafficked AT. So much for the facts,
Bronco!

But my morning meanderings were not totally in vain. At the MSR booth in
the campground, assistant Steve went right to work trying to tighten the tines
on my cool little Pocket Rocket stove. I love the stove and was consequently
quite chagrined when the tines, or arms that spread and hold the pot above the
flame, started to loosen. Steve went right to work with a mammoth ball peen
hammer and a stone, a fix-it method I found rather frightening. But perhaps
this savage and impossible cure was a blessing in disguise, for he quickly
gave up and gave me a replacement set of tines, tearing apart a new stove to
do it. Groovy. Thank you, Steve and Mountain Safety Research, for being the
only company here at Trail Days that has thus far shown me they give a
damn.

Having said this, I would like to retroactively thank Leki poles. They have a
fix-it booth here, replacing all busted and bent parts for free. But I was
already covered in that department. Thanks to Leki's solid guarantee policy,
the outfitters here in Damascus replaced my bent Leki parts last week, totally
gratis. So, in addition to MSR, a special thank you to Leki! MSR, whose
Pocket Rocket stove was the coolest thing I've bought myself since saving my
allowance for model airplanes to build and throw off the roof of our house in
flames; and Leki, whose poles became extensions of my arms and by Maine
would serve so many different purposes as to be worth their weight in gold.

*Dear M: The allure of this place, of this pub/eatery called The
Sidetrack Cafe here in Damascus is evil, what with its Web
terminals and 75-cent Mickey's big mouth beers. I keep trying
to go to town to buy toilet paper or ramen noodles or other
important errands, and always I get sucked into this place, and
down I go into that fat green bottle, a reluctant genie returning
to the lamp. Well, it's 3:15 p.m. here on Friday, and the Trail
Days Festival has kicked into high gear. I have some sort of
mystery guest arriving at 5. I should heft my laundry back to
camp, some 7/10ths of a mile away, and hang the still-damp*

sleeping bag from the nearest poison ivy vine. Then I can jump in the river, beside which (almost on top of which) I erected my tent, fully intent on being as far out in the woods and away from the mainstream crowd and noise as possible. At night I go to sleep to the sound of the river, rushing, falling, swirling. For a toxic waste dump, it's not bad. I will bathe and be the glowing me I've always hoped for and be back here by 5.
                                          -Lord Duke Jester the Only

My mystery guest arrived on time at 5 p.m. on that Friday in Damascus. My friend Bruce the Swami had been sending cryptic e-mails for some time about some mystery delivery person who would be arriving from California or transporting something to me from California. I was to name a time and a place I'd be on Friday, May 14. To whit: "Project some approximate locations for your position May 14 or 15. I want to send a special emissary with a top secret delivery chained to his wrist . . .FOR YOUR EYES ONLY."

Then a week later: "The secret mission is on for about May 14... This is very Top Secret Black Ops stuff...Hush Hush, Chop Chop, and stuff."

Out here in Appalachian Space, Bruce is my Mission Control. He is a great friend and as reliable as a guy could hope for on such a long journey as this with need of ample ground support. Bruce sends me my pre-packed resupply boxes, my prescription meds, my whatever I need. He's the man.

So who could this mystery courier be? Anyone with less talent than I for willful suspension of disbelief might immediately have suspected Bruce himself. But I like a good surprise and so kept any suspicions hush-hush in my head. Bruce has family all over the East, especially around here, it seems. As it is, I almost took a day off from the trail to be hosted by his cousin in North Carolina. So I really thought it might be a family member of his. It couldn't be him. How the hell, and why, would Bruce come all the way here to see me?

At 5 o'clock in line at the Sidetrack Cafe waiting to buy a beer, I turned around and there he was. Bruce Endres. Alias The Swami. Alias Bruce the Moose. Damn near no hair (he pledged to shave his head that my knees might heal earlier on the trail - he did and so did they), but it was he. I couldn't believe it. I hugged him tight to my chest, my mad faithful friend from the west.

Turned out Bruce had bought a used Mercedes on eBay from someone in Maryland and had taken Amtrak out to pick it up. It was parked out front. Almost immediately, I learned that he had to leave again in five hours to drive to Memphis to interview the owner of Sun Records. I was crushed. But I got over it, and a great visit ensued.

And that was that. Aside from garbled notes, the above letter, and one posting written from my tent on Thursday, the first day of Trail Days, I recorded nothing else of the madness of the festival. I was too busy having fun and unwinding from two months of grinding over mountains to write anything else. Such is the fate of what-makes-it-down-on-paper and what doesn't in the life of this writer. Very often the best living doesn't get a word, because I am too busy living it.

From my notes I can ascertain a few things. I had fun swimming in the creek with Heidi and Holly Hobbit, twin sisters from Vermont. Then some people set up tents right beside mine and crowded me in, pissing me off. The town center and the camping area were too far apart, and I did a lot of hitching rides. Seven-time AT thruhiker Baltimore Jack gave me several tips on people to visit in towns along the way. I lost my handmade Jester hat in Dot's Bar & Grill on the outskirts of town the night Bruce visited (got a little drunk). And, finally, I met a cute girl whose trail name is I Need A Hug. When I hugged her too long, her boyfriend appeared outta nowhere and put a stop to it.

Trail Days ended for me on Saturday with the grand water balloon fight-of-a-parade down Main Street, a street that in Damascus is an actual part of the Appalachian Trail. I've never seen so many water balloons fly. The citizens of Damascus took it rather well.

Sitting in Dairy Queen in Bland stuffing myself on a FlameThrower burger and mocha malt, I try and prepare for my next step north along the AT. But I can't shake the sense of being inside a metaphor. Bland. It is nearly 2 p.m. on Sunday the 16th, almost time for the talent show back in Damascus. But I'm not in Damascus. I, am in Bland.

Feeling uninspired, drunk, depressed and/or ecstatic these past four days, I opted not to write my short, mock-Monty Python script and skip town a little early instead. Also, the performance would have required Rael from Boston, my partner in perfect Python improv, and he was not to be found.

Took just two hitches to get here, one right from the corner of the 91 by Cowboy's and the Damascus Dairy "King" from a woman named Cantaloupe and her son, Bags, section hikers up from Florida just for the Daze. They dropped me at the intersection of I-81 and I-77, where I sat a good half-hour or more slowly losing faith in any possibility of a ride. I finally hefted my pack and was headed to the nearest truck stop to solicit truckers when Bonnie, a cleaning staff person at the nearby Super 8, yelled down to me, asking if I was trying to get to the AT. Whoosh, off we went, on her break I guess. With Bonnie in the driver's seat and April beside her, it was a fast, fun 12 miles of cranked-up big bass rap and R&B with the cleaning girls dancing in their seats, not a care in the world. I could not but smile, a wry smile, grateful and highly amused.

I look at my watch and realize that this time yesterday I was walking the streets of Damascus with a thousand other hikers, me garbed up in rubber ducky slippers and a crazy purple-n-green patterned bathrobe, a child's green beach sand bucket on my head, plastic shovel 'round the handle at my chin, and a mop found in someone's trash, mock "mopping up" after my fellow paraders as water balloons burst by the dozen every minute of the parade walk. Without my art car, Duke, I couldn't have done a better job of hamming it up with the local audience and having a blast myself.

Out front of the DQ, I can't figure out where to start walking. I look for white blazes, expecting to see them painted on guardrails or power lines or something. After all, when the Slacking Seven stopped here last week, we saw lots of hikers.

Later that night I'm in my Hennessy Hammock, a hammock tent with bug netting sewed right to it and a rainfly taut overhead, floating above the slanted forest floor. I need a root canal very soon. This could be bad for my progress down trail. I'm half awake amidst the song of raindrops on the hammock's rainfly overhead. It is a lullaby, and soon I'm a goner. I fall asleep contented, happy to have made it back to the trail.

Next morning, I awake to terrible toothache pain. The abscess is back in all its fury. I've endured yet another rough night of sleep in the hammock. The jury is still out on this one. Sent my tent and sleeping bag two weeks or so ahead, with the Priority Mail option to bounce it to New Hampshire and my cousin's for storage till the fall. But the way things are going in this thing, I may be picking it up in Waynesboro. Aurgh. Could be just the toothache. Running outta codeine and Klonipin. Scary time. Damp time in the woods. I'm definitely the first hiker on this stretch of trail this morning, clearing all the webs with my face. At least I'm not stuck working in a Dairy Queen in Bland. I think of that poor bastard yesterday, my age, and all the noise in that place. I take another step toward Maine. The birds sing on. In the words of the little boy in Reidar Jonsson's *My Life as a Dog,* "Sometimes you just have to compare."

I walk in the rain for hours. It is warm enough on this mid-May day that I wear no rain jacket. I don't even own one, come to think of it, just a lousy windbreaker I got at a thrift store for a buck. I put this on over a synthetic turtleneck if it's a cold rain, and though I'm soaked, I'm warm. Today it's just a nylon tee-shirt and my one and only and oh-so-wonderful synthetic pants that zipper off to become shorts. Shoes soaked. Socks soaked. Backpack soaked beneath a worthless pack cover. But, no, not everything IN the pack is soaked. That could be very dangerous out here. Hypothermia bad.

No. Instead of a new, high-tech waterproof backpack, I have two very good, very expensive "dry bags," one for my bedding, one for my dry change of clothes. When you're hiking 2,000 miles, you don't carry much of a wardrobe. Mine consists of the aforementioned one pair of pants, two nylon tees, one synthetic long sleeve, one light wool sweater, one set of synthetic long johns, three pairs of socks, one pair of shoes. Oh, and the nonsensical combination of the dollar windbreaker and $50 pair of rain pants. That's it.

Sometimes the rain is coming down so hard it is like pushing through a waterfall. Then voila! I arrive at the beautiful yet poorly named waterfall called Dismal Falls. As I round the corner and come in sight of the cascade, the rain stops and the sun peeks out. Everything is glistening green, wet and shiny. I am a sticky, damp, chilled, squishy-shoed walking machine.

Across the river there appear two familiar faces smiling to see me. It's Franko and Bennie, two really cool guys my age from Indiana hiking together, childhood friends, I guess. There's no chance of conversation over the roar of the falls, so they rock-hop across the rather wide river to chat with me. I'm glad to see them and pleased as hell with the beautiful scene that will be my home for the night.

The boys cross the river and we chat. I'm so sticky, soaked and gross from rain and sweat, I swim beneath the falls to clean off, despite the cool air and no sun.

I start to hang my hammock tent from a couple of trees downstream. I look up and watch as two fishermen, formerly standing mid-stream on the same exposed rocks the boys had crossed over on a short time ago, suddenly jump and run for the shore. Huh? My eyes travel to the falls themselves. Handsome at last glance, the falls are suddenly gargantuan and floodwater-brown. Two, three, perhaps 10 times the volume of water is coming over Dismal Falls. I yank down the tent and head for higher ground just as the flood plain I was standing in becomes one with the roaring torrent of swollen river.

Must have been the rain. Across the river stand Franko and Bennie, looking at the river and me, bewildered. "Oh, shit. They're marooned," I realize aloud to myself. They were to come over later with whiskey. We were going to make a fire, have some laughs.

They never made it over that night. The next morning, the waters calm again, I jump off the high falls, first alone, then with Jabberwock, showing off for his lovely girlfriend, Yippee. As with many others who stop a moment to regard the falls, Yippee and Jabberwock hike on. Wet rats Franko and Bennie finally arrive soaked up to their armpits, having slept not a wink the previous night searching for a safe crossing and not finding one til morning. Even then they had to carry their packs over their heads through deep water. They, too, are gone within minutes. I sit back in my hammock and write a while. I don't strike camp and set off hiking until early afternoon. Such is the slowed pace of the hiker writing, the pace and the price. I fall behind. I believe that in the end, however, my added labors will set me far ahead.

It has been a night and a day of adventure, respite, reflection and what I'll call "rural luxury" on the AT. For what are a waterfall and its deep swimming hole but luxuries unknown in urban hours? Replicated yes, but the same?

Never.

NINE

Party Girl, Ducky Slippers, Tooth Drugs, and Rattlers...the Smoegel in Me...Why Jesus Didn't Need Prozac...a Strong Whiff of the Band-Aid Ghost...the One Nude Woman Wonder... Leaping Stags in a Magic Light...The Keffer Oak and the Quantum Field...

Time to count our blessings on this May 19, 2004.

Blessing #1: Despite our current dental problems, we did have the money to pay the dentist to write the scrips to get the drugs to nail the pain to kill the infection to stave off the inevitable root canal by a few months. Bottom line, we're still on the trail at Mile 622.

Blessing #2: Virginia is bursting out in green all over the place. The robins are out, the air fragrant with flowering azalea and rhododendron. Every cell in my body leaps forward with spring. We are a part of all of this, from molecules to handshakes and trail angels. Welcome guests are we, and the trail goes on and on.

Blessing #3: We don't have diabetes and swollen feet and the demeaning fate of a four- hour wait, unattended, at the local ER, as was the case with Gatorman. Bottom line, there's always somebody who has it worse than you; and in this case, in my case, in OUR case, that of all thruhikers here on the AT, we have it very, very good.

Okay, enough with the blessings. Today I had to go off-trail temporarily to see a dentist, get some drugs, kill this rip-roaring pain in my mouth. Other hikers here at the Catholic charity hiker hostel in Pearisburg want to know if I'm going to go back up into the mountains to make up the 10 miles I missed today when Miss Tilley and friends insisted on driving me into town to get help immediately. Won't I feel guilty for missing 10 miles? Good question. Here's the best answer I can come up with presently, with a head still full of pain and recovering from a medical pit stop and the shellshock of two trips to Wal-Mart.

No.

I know this about myself: If there's one principle etched into my person that will overrule any guilt at miles lost to a medical emergency, it is that I loathe retrograde motion. "What is behind me is not important!" I won't go backwards. Think how often we return to old habits, failed partnerships, places of which we'd grown weary, people of whom we'd grown wary. In the Quantum Physics "create your own reality" sense, by its very definition retrograde motion (going backwards) is just a hair short of insanity. Retrograde: the worsening or returning to an earlier worse condition. I won't do it.

What I'll tell them when I am done: Yes, I walked from Georgia to Maine. I took a few shortcuts. I rode a few miles in cars when walking wasn't working. No, I am not a purist. Yes, I walked the Appalachian Trail from end to end.

The original trail was 2,000 miles long. It has been expanded to encompass 2,174 miles. I figure that gives me 174-mile buffer zone to fudge it here and there and still be a "2,000 Miler." Setting out, I said I'd be happy if I made it one-tenth of the way. One week from today, I will have completed fully one-third of it. Guilt? Screw guilt. I'm a frikken Olympian.

Next morning and I'm a groggy Olympian from the 1300 milligrams of Percocet it took to keep me from screaming my head off last night in Toothache Hell. Lying awake last night to a chorus of snores, male and female from the bunks all around me, I decided I'd ask Bill, the attendant here, to take me back up the otherwise desolate winding dirt roads to Wood's Hole so I could make up the miles I sacrificed yesterday to suffer a dentist.

Well, Bill just came by and said, "Sure, I'll take you up. Twenty bucks for the shuttle." I hem and haw. A man of decision, conviction, impatience, one or all three, Bill walks off saying, "Well, you haven't made up your mind." Now he's gone. Big Bill with his profiteering and his red truck and weensie cat-sized dog.

Out here on the trail, on foot, we hikers are at the mercy of people with cars. Many would say I'm wrong here. Okay. It depends on the situation and your perspective, I guess. But here's one clear case where I'm kind of screwed. The hostel where I now stand is 3.5 miles off the trail. Wood's Hole, where I left off, is 15 miles or so away up-mountain. I just blew $120 on medico bullshit yesterday, leaving me $50 in my pocket to last the next 10 days. Twenty bucks has suddenly become a fortune. Does this sound like a cheap rationalization of a little AT white blaze lie? Well, I guess it is. What did I miss? Twelve miles? Groovy. Twelve is what percentage of 2,174? Not much.

Whereas $20 is 40 percent of my cash on hand. Sorry, guilt, you evil manmade poison. I walk north.

Some walking through horrid suburbs and a few hitches, and I stand at a crossroads. Right where the AT enters and exits Pearisburg, Virginia. I could back-hike 12 miles going southbound and bank on getting another ride out of the woods. Or doing as I decided at the hostel, I can say adios and not look back.

I leave it to the flip of a coin. A nickel, my favorite American coin. If it comes up heads, I'll go with my head, where I believe guilt resides, a learned emotion not at all genetic or instinctual, and go south. If it's tails, I get my tail back on the trail in the RIGHT direction and go north. I flip.

It's tails. I heft my bag with a smile and disappear into the dense undergrowth. I have found the coin flip to be a sure-fire way, when indecisive, of finding out what I really want, every time. I'm pleased with the decision of the Fates. Just a few feet into the trees, I feel triumphant in my escape from Pearisburg, a queer little town in Virginia where the people are nice but the vibe is weird. Don't ask me to be objective about Pearisburg. My experience of it was dental pain and Wal-Mart, a consumer tomb lit like the bright light at the end of the tunnel of life (and likely just as dangerous to the not-yet dead). Mostly for reasons I cannot explain, Wal-Mart is a repository of deep spiritual angst for me.

All was not bad in Pearisburg. There was Party Girl, after all. Party Girl: restaurant manager from some tiny New Hampshire hamlet near Concord, Conookanook, or some such thing; Party Girl resting her ankle from some injury and due to be back on the trail in five days, having already missed a week (oh, Jeezus, I would go nuts!); Party Girl, early twenties, sleeping outside the hostel on the picnic table. One hot number. The Beastie Boys sing, "Phone is ringing, oh my God."

Tall, tanned, talkative, funny, a Greek goddess in proportion, lain out banquet-style on a picnic table, and at a Catholic charity hostel! Wonderful. There is a God, and today He wears the devil's grin.

Party Girl shares her photos from Trail Daze in Damascus last weekend. Every other one is of her doing a beer bong. Incredible. She looks at the photos with the same incredulous wonder that I viewed photos of Burning Man 1999. Photos are about the only memory I have of that year's gathering in the Nevada desert. I'm told (and I recall the general sense) that I had a LOT of fun. I was never without beer in hand, and I was popping Klonipins the whole time. Result: memory wipe. Party Girl's recollection of Damascus appears similar.

"I was the guy with the neon green beach sand bucket on my head, rubber ducky slippers, crazy patterned green and purple bathrobe, mop in hand, yeah, the guy pretend-mopping up the streets after all the water balloons."

I watch as delight dances across her face and her eyes light up with lost-memory recalled. "Oh, my gawd! That was you? I remember! That was great!"

We laugh and swap stories of New Orleans, realizing we both lived there for the same brief period in 2001. She's an Amazon, a goddess, a credit to her name, and a nut. I cannot but adore her.

I was a fool to leave, of course. We got along well. She wasn't going anywhere. Maybe? No. I'm a freak, a hot-footed sketch-case currently with toothache, freaked out by Wal-Mart and the location of the hostel (deep in some suburban neighborhood several miles from the trail), second day, mid-afternoon, I've got to go.

Away I went. But not before she thrust a pen and pad in my hand and demanded my e-mail address. I hope I hear from her. We could have a blast when I hit New Hampshire.

I say "I" and not we, because she's not only five days behind me now, but several hundred miles before that, as well, having hitchhiked forward to Pearisburg for some reason. Whatever. I wish her well, a great hike. No matter how "complete" or incomplete a thruhike it is, Party Girl, just have a blast. You deserve it! This is YOUR great adventure.

On the outskirts of Pearisburg, the AT passes right by a manufacturer of Celanese acetate, whatever that is. The plant is depressing to look at, dismal really. Right out of *Joe Versus the Volcano*. A sign over the entrance (or was it on the smokestack?) says "Our People Make the Difference." Man, if ever there was a frightening, banal, meaningless statement of corporate pride, that's it.

Even up in the trees away from the factory, the air smells bad. I cross a creek with an orange cast to it. Not that I would have drunk from it with that queer color, but a sign says, "This stream has naturally occurring bacteria and should not be consumed," or some such horse shit. Naturally occurring, eh? Just like that factory back there and their waste dump upstream that I passed awhile back. Hmm. Yes, very natural. As I ascend the mountain out of town, clouds of tiny flies blur my vision. I almost step right on a giant black snake sunning itself in the trail. Eek! Get me outta here!

Franko and Bennie hail from Indiana. They are shorter and stockier than I. Knowing they both cashed out savings and quit jobs to do this hike, I ask Franko if he doesn't sometimes wish he'd blown his wad on a trip to the Bahamas rather than trudging in the bug-infested woods. "No," he replies, "because I'd be home now and broke." Good point.

Bennie, the bigger of the two, seems always to be following Franko. Now I'm ahead, talking to myself in Smoegel tones and coughing from pollen. The cough forms a word: "Gollum! Gollum!" Franko is Frodo, and Bennie, Sam. I turn and beckon them forth with a wide swing of my arm. "This way, hobbitses." I cannot but make the connection. Physiologically, given their height, and in my case psychologically (alone, auto-conversant), we are the last hope for the world of men. I hope Franko still has the ring. I have the oxycodone. Bennie has bank. I caught him checking his stock profile online the other day at a cyber café. I was shocked. Wow! Stocky stoner bearded Bennie is a stockbroker! We make a good trio. I promise not to lead them into the lair of any big spiders.

Saying this, I remember today, the REAL today. I feel pangs of guilt. I should have done something to warn them. I was far out ahead but knew they would be next to encounter the monster. I almost stepped on it myself—a mammoth rattler, whatever brand of rattler broods in the grasses of Virginia. It lay straight across the trail, tail hidden in the grass on one side, head hidden on the other. It might be a log with uncommon fractals color and pattern. Step over it and see. Not.

It is the second baseball bat-fat snake I've seen in 24 hours. Seen and almost stepped on. Yesterday's was black as night, a giant negro phallus underfoot, another Freudian slip, a cock of a root to trip you up and take you down harder than usual.

The rattler doesn't move. I back away to a safe distance and lob a stick at it. Nothing. Another stick nearly hits its tail. Not a flinch. I am Indiana Jones. Don't like snakes, even the ones behind thick plates of glass. There is no glass between Mr. Snake and me. Snakes, I'm told, are capable of speeds hard to imagine from something lacking legs.

What can Smoegel do? How can we warn master and the fat one? Maybe it's dead. Yes, we convince us, it must be dead. No movement. No rattle. Case closed. Giving it a wide berth, I pass and move on.

What was Smoegel thinking?!! Gollum! A short coughing fit later, and I am myself again. Ah, peaceful woods. Back in the Shire again.

At the next shelter, I nervously prepare lunch. I await Frodo Franko and Bennie Sam's arrival. "Hobbitses taking too long! Oh, no. What has Smoegel done?"

They arrive at last, intact, with a digital photo no less, of the snake coiled.

In the evening, we make camp amidst the ferns. We drink whiskey and smoke cigarillos far afield of the crowded shelter. Smoegel takes his whiskey in tiny sippy sips and tries not to cough. "Don't you think Bennie looks like Gimley? You know, the dwarf?" Franko asks.

"Yes, master!" says us.

I heard cicadas for the first time today, the 22nd of May. The flies arrived on the 20th, on my two-month anniversary. One minute there were none, and then whammo! They were a plague. The big ones buzzed my ears in that super-annoying round-yer-head 100 times fashion, and there appeared an ever-present crowd of tiny ones just in my field of vision. Madness. I feel like an Ethiopian child or a water buffalo just covered in them, doing nothing to shoo them away.

Audioslave sings, "Take it out on me" as I take it out on myself, straight up a hellish incline, 2,000 feet in one mile. The trail is crowded now here in the mid-600s. I remember many days when I would walk all day and see no one. Now we are bunched up. Puca and Eagle Eye, Franko and Bennie, Pilot and Krispy Kritter and Little Chicken and Beat Box and Pita Man and Palm Tree and on and on.

Beat Box earns his name as I hike with him. For a while when we run out of water he is quiet. We find a stream and resupply. Now he is going again, doing raps, singing songs from *Aladdin* at the top of his lungs, telling tales of his time spent working at Disney World. When not talking, he walks and makes sounds like a "beat box," all percussive sounds from his mouth. He's a trip.

Hikers are so intent on the trail they never look sideways. You pull off a bit and disappear. You and your lover could be buck naked banging back to nature just 30 or 40 feet from the trail in plain view and, so long as you remained quiet as the next thruhiker passed by, go entirely unseen.

Flowers. Okay, we have flies, but we have flowers now, too! Tons! Orange fire azaleas burn against the green forest backdrop. I learn the names of some of the other flowers: pipsissawa, wintergreen, pyrola, toothwort, chickweed, and stonecrop. Naming things in nature has meant little to me in the past, but lately I crave names as I marvel at the beauty and variety.

I pull 20 feet off the trail and set up my keyboard on a flat high rock. There are not many desks in the forest, but here is one. My blotter is dense green moss. My feather pen and inkwell: a cluster of grass growing out of the moss. Puca and Eagle Eye pass me, totally unaware of me, absorbed in the trail and each other. Not even Puca's dog, Zack, sees or senses me. Astounding.

You can always be alone out here, if you want to be. A little to the right or the left of the trail and you vanish amidst oak, hickory, hemlock, and maple.

I pop another oxycodone. I don't like taking them during the day while hiking, but the pressure, the intense strain on all the muscles in my body as I pull up a mountain, this has set my tooth to aching again.

I immerse either full-body or as much as I can in every stream, every creek, and the occasional bonus deep river. Ry and Jackie are close on my tail. Even after taking 10 days off the trail for a wedding, they are catching up to me. I can feel them gaining on me. They are very close now.

All clustered together, we finish a heinous ascent to find that a trail angel has left two large coolers full of sodas for thruhikers. Yes! I drink one, turn and see cars on a road nearby. To my half-dozen fellow thruhikers I proclaim with indignant surprise, "What? You can drive here?" It's difficult to describe the feeling you get when you scale a mountain by foot, only to find cars at the top. It is a sense of injustice, but one that fades quickly when you come to understand all that you in your hike have gained, benefits day hikers in cars will never know.

The profile map lays it out for us every day. The topo map shows the bird's-eye view of the lines nicely dancing northward through the Appalachians. But the profile, with its look of the polygraph test of a terrible liar, gives the heavy news, tells it to you straight. "Son, you gonna CLIMB today, straight up, and then straight down again. Ooh! Look, another 2,000-foot climb before dinner!"

I begin to see a pattern in all of this trail shit. It is this: The only wilderness left anymore is in the high country, mountains too high and steep for lazy-ass humans to build upon and develop. Aha. How about that. Big mystery, right? So "doing the trail" means daily going where no man has any desire to go. Up. Straight up. Then straight down again. Whippeee!

The other day in dense jungle-like forest, I saw a stone wall about knee high going straight up a 45-degree grade on a mountainside. Hmm. Our forefathers in this area certainly weren't lazy. Stupid perhaps. No, silly me. They had slaves!

I feel utterly tapped this morning, an empty keg, and somebody stole the pump, to boot. The thrill is gone. Not a shred of yesterday's zoom is in me. But the usual parade of early-risers had already made up the five miles I gained on them last night and passed me in irksome procession as I contemplated making coffee.

"It's not a race," I hear my gentle self say. But it pisses me off. Their movement makes my non-movement look bad. There's just no way around it. It's not a race, but we fall into these social groups, and whether you like the crowd you're in or hate 'em, you feel compelled to move at a similar pace. I hear myself ask that Christian question: WWJD? Well, what would Jesus do? Jesus wasn't depressive like me, was he? No. He got righteously pissed and tossed the tables of the moneylenders. Getting pissed is a good thing. It's therapeutic. If depression is anger turned inwards, well, Jesus homey, you were safe from the suicidal blues. Homey Jesus didn't internalize nuthin.

People often ask me about Tinkerbell and Uncle Duke, my two steadfast, never-annoying companions on this walk in the woods. The figurine of Uncle Duke from *Doonesbury* and little Tinkerbell in her tiny red lamp both hang from the chest cinch straps on my pack, so right out front. I am reminded of what I told some woman the other day about the two. "They're like the little devil and the little angel on my shoulders. Tink speaks good sense and gentleness and understanding. Duke is there to maintain obstinate forward propulsion, at any cost. He is the enforcer, the bully." She looked at me as though I'd offered her a banana from my underpants in trade for the peach in her panties. I'm still laughing at the recollection of her bug-eyed expression.

Walking along the crest of some major bump on the profile map, the one that tormented my listless body this morning, I turn to look over my shoulders and have the queer sensation that I'm seeing the forest through one of those helmet cams. You know what I mean? That kind of floaty, sometimes bumpy, disembodied camera work used by climbers, explorers, whatever. Looking through my eyes this morning is a trip. Things are a wee bit strange.

A local radio station called "The Bear" plays a long "Tool set," as it were. It helps my energy level immensely. I walk and sing to the trees and piled stones, "I am just a worthless liar, I am just an imbecile, I will only complicate you, trust me, trust me!" Of course, I really wail out the chorus.

The piles of stone are increasing in number here atop Braisers Knob somewhere south of Catawba. Flat stones all, they are piled sometimes higgledy-piggledy, sometimes as to make a fireplace or a wall. They are everywhere, and as I walk amidst them, I shake my head amazed, wondering how they got there, up on a mountaintop in lush jungle-like overgrowth. Very strange. Tool sings to solve the puzzle. "I know the pieces fit!"

Suddenly in the forest today I smelled Band-aid smell, that special smell that only comes from Band-aids. You know the one. My senses heightened by all this nature, I wonder if what I smell is the lingering scent of the very spot where one of my comrades stopped to redress their wronged and beaten feet?

Up ahead I meet Polar and Hot Rock and their golden retriever, Jake. Bear Trax backtracks to warn us of a snake on the trail (as I, er, Gollum should have done for the hobbitses). Sure enough, there it is. Another rattler. The third I've seen in four days. I taunt it a bit to make it rattle for me. It looks at me with boredom in its snake eyes and only flicks its tongue.

Speaking of taunting, I have been taunting, or testing, the bear myth. Last night, too tired to bother, I simply hung my food at eye level on a broken tree branch. Screw it, I think. There are no bears! Sure enough, no bear comes. Not 10 hours later, Krispy Kritter walks by and regales me with the tale of his morning bear sighting. Bastard!

Arriving at Niday Shelter, I heard feminine laughter coming from the creek below, dropped my pack, and headed down for water and whatever fun was going on down there. I rounded a corner to find Pilot, twenty-something, pretty, currently nude, bathing in the stream. Surprised at the sight of me, she proclaims the obvious. "I'm totally naked, just so you know." Oh, really.

I told her that was fine with me, and she seemed much relieved at that. I'm the same way. I could give a rip about stripping down and hopping in. My only source of concern, and even this seems dumb out here, is the potential discomfort of others. Following that experience, Pilot definitely moved up a few notches in my estimation. It might also have had something to do with her, well, her ample, um…her body. Very nice. A few nights later with Trax, Krispy, Franko and Bennie, I would retell the tale, musing at where my sex drive had lately gone, and how Pilot's little visual treat had returned it fully restored. Sitting around a fire, the boys sure enjoyed hearing about it, though there wasn't much to report. Just the fact that she'd skinny-dipped and I'd been witness was enough. You would have thought I'd witnessed an orgy, so excited were the guys to hear every detail.

But after participating in the Burning Man gathering annually since 1995 where nudity is accepted and liberally practiced, and given my circle of circus freak unabashed free spirit friends, one nude girl on the trail hardly blew my mind. The trail held another surprise for me that day, however, one that I imagined would blow my mind if only I could get there in time.

It occurred the evening of the day that Krispy saw his bear. If it weren't for my getting in a huff about that and the general crowded state of the trail, I might not have walked so far and pushed so hard this day. But I did. Leaving the thruhiker cluster far behind (passing them in fact where the nattering sheep had herded together at a late afternoon shelter), I dashed out of the safety of the forest alone. I ran far out across open fields beneath blackening thunderhead skies onward and onward exhausted but driven, by God, to reach and sleep beneath a rumored gigantic 300-year old oak tree. As like a digital photo with the contrast cranked all the way up, the atmosphere all around me lit up with fierce golden sunlight beaming horizontally across the earth beneath the boiling black mantle of storm sky. As I navigated the prairie, the tall grass around me sprang to life with stags leaping, their hoof impacts drumming in frantic retreat, startled no doubt by my own late and frantic dash for the cover of the next copse of trees. A small gathering of buildings sat nestled in the distance, a white church, a red barn, a handful of graying old skeletal houses, once homes where families gathered around the hearth, worked this field perhaps. But not a human soul was out and about. I must have been quite the sight, had anyone been watching. To the hidden observer, I might have resembled the Arctic scientist in Farley Mowat's *Never Cry Wolf* running naked across the tundra, a wolf-frightened herd of caribou splaying out ahead of me at top speed.

It just got better. If I weren't a strong believer in quantum theory and basically all the magic and mysterious unexplainable goodies that go with it, I may not have been privy even to what I'd seen so far. But in the woods ahead, greater magic lay in wait.

Into those woods I ran, the darkest woods imaginable considering the sun had yet to set. Dark, electric, haunting was the trail. Not a few centuries ago, no sane man ever would have dared enter such a forest. He would have been eaten alive, if only by superstition. But onward I ran. I just knew that giant oak had to be somewhere up ahead.

Then the shift came. The insects disappeared and the air directly in front of my face turned a pea soup green. If I'd had a tuning fork it would have been singing a bone chilling shrill song of warning. Final warning: Lightning strikes and rain imminent. So I stopped.

I stopped and went right into emergency tent setup mode. I wasn't happy with the setting, and of course, I hadn't made it to my intended mark, the Keffer Oak. But it felt as though I didn't have a second to spare. No time to even scan the area for a better spot. I tore off my pack, eviscerated its contents like a bare clawing out a honey comb under heavy attack by bees, found my tent, tied one end to the nearest tree (for I was using the hammock tent at the time), rushed to another tree sufficient distance from the first, and tied off that end. Not until I had attached and anchored down the rain fly did I breathe my first breath of faint relief. And that's when I saw it.

It had been there all along, but I'd been too focused on the task at hand to catch it in my peripheral vision. The Keffer Oak. Not only had I made it to the tree of legend, so large and far reaching were its limbs that I had indeed set up my tent beneath it as had been my wish. It struck me so dumb I fell right over on my ass and stared agog at its magnificence. At its base, it was big as a house. Okay, a small house. Thoreau's cabin perhaps. But huge by tree standards. And reaching out from it in a hundred directions, some directly over my head, protruded its multitude of arms, each branch as thick around as any tree in the forest!

Sprawled out on the ground, it occurred to me that the deluge had not come. Not yet anyway. But it didn't seem likely now. Just like that, the atmosphere had softened, the green cast gone out of the air. Thunder grumbled and lightning still flashed but nary a strike. It just flashed, as if to say, "I'm still here, watch out!"

But we knew better, the tree and I. For by now I had risen and covered the distance to the wooly mammoth and stood touching it, my right hand palm open against it feeling its life force. I closed my eyes and focused all my mind's attention on catching information coming in through my hand, if any. So much history, so much time. This tree had witnessed America's entire history as a nation and then some. "What stories you could tell," I spoke aloud as I crossed to a tall stanchion that served as both a ladder over a cattle fence and, in this case, a platform by which to more closely admire the Keffer Oak. "How little and insignificant I must seem to you," I said. "In your perception of space-time, my night's visit will seem but a fleeting millisecond flash."

Standing atop the stanchion, I embraced the tree with all the reach possible of my puny arms. I hugged it and spoke at length with it of many things. Beyond the fence there stretched a small field of grass. Beyond the grass: more forest. I invited all those who have gone before me to join me there and sit in the arms of this oh-so-stunning giant. I gazed up and pictured them positioned throughout its branches, smiling at me, their legs swinging like children: Chris O'Connor, Glenn Smith, Luciano Lenchantin, Uncle David, Aunt Nancy, both my grandfathers and sweet angel Grandma Selena, and many, many more. My pets, too: Lucy, Sketch, Gator and Matilda. My eyes delivered then what the storm had not, and I slumped to a sitting position and howled like a wolf as grief blew out of me like steam filling field and forest alike.

Lightning flashed, less frequent, less threatening. But no rain came. I chanced to notice that the mosquitoes had not returned. Not a single insect hung in the air.

Standing there hugging this ancient giant, my right cheek against its soft skin of bark now wet with tears, my body stoned on its own adrenaline, my mind open to the whole field of possibilities in this infinite universe of which we are an infinitesimally small part, there in that state of mind I saw her. My faerie. Clear as a diamond held up for inspection in the bright flicker of a Zippo's flame, there hung in the periphery of my left eye's vision the most lovely little feminine creature I've ever seen, the only I've ever seen. She smiled at me and, before I could lift my cheek from the tree to see her better, was gone.

Then and there, while wonder lingered in my mind and before disappointment at her sudden disappearance could dim the shine of my bedazzled face, night finally came and with it a million fireflies to light the Keffer Oak and me and the field of grass beyond. Despite my general disenchantment with the hammock tent and many a night of poor sleep, that night I slept the sweetest sleep. I believe my soul slept in Heaven that night. I really do.

TEN

The Dragon's Tooth, Catawba Chaos, and a Galaxy of Earthbound Stars...a Bodhisattva in its Frightful Aspect...Mama and Papa O: Southern Hospitality Defined...Hush Puppies and Seashell Babies...Borders-ing on Madness in Shopping Ville...

It was bound to happen eventually. Last night, May 25, 2004, will no doubt be remembered by many an '04 thruhiker as the night all hell broke loose in Catawba, Virginia. The whole of the post-Trail Days bottlenecked trail population all descended at once on the Catawba hostel, Mile 688, someone's garage generously opened up for hikers to kick it, have a shower, play horseshoes. A note in *The Thru-hiker's Handbook* warns the solace-seeker against stopping here for a quiet night's rest. Today, the day after a wild and bawdy hostel experience that nearly put the "i" back in host-el, two dozen pissed-off thruhikers stomp the forest, most of them over fifty, all apparently having missed the guidebook's warning.

I came upon the place utterly spent after one hardcore day of heinous ascents and descents that culminated, without any warning from the guidebook, in the Dragon's Tooth, a seven-mile departure from our northern tack. By the time you realize you've been duped, this ingenious and ingenuous reroute nails you with incredibly arduous bouldering. This is stuff I would normally consider fun but not with a pack on, no way. There were places where one could easily have fallen to their death and not likely have been found for some time, not until the dragon's breath stench of their rotting corpse made its way up-rock to passing hikers. I kid you not. The whole hump out to the "Tooth," a gigantic pile of rocks with a grand overlook, was more like scaling up and down the ridges of a dragon's tail than its teeth. Once reached, the overlook held little interest for me. I was too tired to scale the towering final rocks to take in the view. Anticipating my normal pace of about 25 minutes/mile, I'd run out of water halfway when the seven-mile jaunt turned into a seven-hour jaunt.

Needless to say, when I hit the hostel, or garage, whatever it was, I was thirsty, spent, and mad as hell at the trail engineers who'd made the Dragon not a blue blaze option but a must-do white blaze section of the AT. [Note: Had I been a day hiker out for some rock climbing, the Tooth would have been great, but it was an inappropriate finale for a thruhiker's day.]

Cyberdine handed me a beer. Heaven. I grabbed a cot in the Red Cross-esque garage shelter and headed to the local quickie mart in the back of a truck driven by Joe, the 16-year-old son of the host. We beer-and grub-seekers held on for dear life in the bed of that truck while Joe made the one-mile trip at 80 mph around hairpin curves.

Before long there was something like six cases of beer floating around the crowded garage. Pilot, cute but unworldly, snapped pictures of the men all sprawled about in front of the garage drinking beer. At that point in the evening, she still found it funny.

It didn't take long to cure that. So many hikers had clogged up this section of trail in central Virginia that before long not only was the garage full but a tent city had sprung up on this guy's several-acre property. By dusk, it was "damn everything but the circus!" With some three-dozen thruhikers as his captive audience, young Joe gave it his 16-year- old all, popping wheelies and roaring across the resident acreage at top throttle on his dirt bike. Much like his Marmaduke-sized dog that stood barking incessantly at us just his side of a buried electric doggie fence, Joe rode that dirt bike as fast and hard as he could within the confines of the football field-sized yard. We, the ragged and masticated victims of the Dragon's Tooth, whooped and hollered in fine redneck style, guzzling beer and trying to out-shout the family dog.

No longer content even with that, Joe began weaving in and out of the tents in the yard behind the garage. But he was a good sport. He'd stop every once in a while to drive the newest arrivals to the local store for beer and grub. By dusk we were all getting hammered, young and old, male and female, but mostly male, as is the demographic here on the All-Testosterone AT. As I begin this tale, what happened next was just a matter of course.

A drinking game sprang up out front of the garage. Beat Box, with his Robin Williams-like facility for machine gun humor, banter, and outright insanity, seized the helm and around we went in a circle naming celebrities by the last letter of the preceding star's name. When a player failed to deliver an immediate answer, the penalty was drink until you think of one. As night fell, a lot of hikers did what they do every night out in the woods at nightfall, they went to bed. We were just getting rolling.

Before long, Pilot came out and asked us to keep it down for the benefit of those trying to sleep. Jesus-lovin' Beat Box was on her like a Hail Mary on sin. Immediately, he grabbed his Wingfoot guidebook and read aloud the passage in the manual warning against expectations of any quiet at this shelter. A defeated Pilot went back inside.

Okay, so the book warned them. But should we rub their noses in it? I asked myself, impressed by Box's performance but feeling bad for poor Pilot nonetheless. I moved that we relocate the game 50 yards away at a picnic table on the lawn. After some grumbling, the gang agreed and we moved. But faster than you can say Linda Lovelace licks long lollipops, the topic of the wordplay game sank from celebrities to porn stars, real or imagined. To the credit of the group, some incredibly creative porn star names were created around that table that night. However, with this new topic and increasing inebriation, the decibel level rose dramatically. To those trying to sleep in the garage, it likely sounded not as though we'd moved the party away, but that we'd crawled into bed with them and snuggled up to howl drunkenly in their ears.

I believe I was the first to retire. Quite contentedly anesthetized from my day's pains on the Dragon Tooth, I sauntered into the garage and plopped down on my cot. I was half asleep when something strange began to happen all around me. Silhouetted hikers seemed to be moving all around the garage, their halogen headlamps dancing in the dark like some hallucination of alien visitation.

It took a while, but I finally caught on, laying there watching them stuffing bags with dark objects. The drinking game had ended and seven hardcore men had decided to pack up and hike out, right then and there.

Naturally, I joined them. They had to wait for me as I stumbled around in the dark. Krispy Kritter took a group photo of all the boys packed and ready to go, and off we swaggered.

Pack thrown together out of rote habit developed over two months (with no real clue as to what I might be leaving behind in that garage), I hoofed it down the driveway and onto the empty highway for the 3/10-mile walk back to the trailhead. Back to that tiny hole in the forest wall we walked, a hole no wider than a household doorway, two holes actually, one on either side of the rural highway, where hikers of the Appalachian Trail enter and exit the Real World all the time, likely most often entirely unnoticed by passing automotive traffic. We are Alice when she's 10 feet tall.

I had never hiked drunk before. I don't recall having done much if any hiking in the dark. So it was a double adventure. I found very quickly that I had a problem with the normal positioning of my headlamp. When pointed low enough to see the ground, the light's beam lit up my glasses, making it hard to gauge depth. (This was not merely a function of the beer. I have since tried it sober.) So I just shut it off. Closely following the person in front of me, I availed myself of the brain's aptitude for instant recall, recalling thus what it saw a moment ago in the light ahead. My performance rather impressed me, in a rum-addled pirate-high-in-the-rigging kind of way. I never once fell.

The going was easy, the terrain smooth. After a short distance in the woods, during which Beat Box, perhaps the drunkest of us all, rattled off every crass dead baby and paraplegic joke I'd ever heard as a teenager in one unending monologue, we hit a meadow.

My breath and body halted in astonishment. Fireflies, a galaxy of earthbound stars, danced in the air, popping like ten thousand tiny flashbulbs over the grass. Yellow-orange, they fluttered brilliant against the dark backdrop of the forest beyond: pure magic to my liquid yet lucid brain. With my headlamp off, I got all the benefit of their brilliance. I've not yet witnessed the Northern Lights. I've seen plenty of manmade light and laser shows, but this beat all.

We walked for some time in tall grass, and the magic of the fireflies made the night! A line of Appalachia's rounded mountains, perhaps some of which we'd climbed the day before or would climb tomorrow, could be seen clearly outlined, backlit by the distant city lights of Roanoke.

It was a beautiful night, one well worth the pain suffered later in the morning upon sobering up. We, the warriors of the long trek north blew off some steam, shared a lot of laughs, and witnessed a kind of low-flying aurora borealis in a pasture in west-central Virginia. Fireflies!! May they live forever, never succumbing to man's proclivity for nudging species into extinction.

When walking amongst so many fireflies, you have the illusion of a meteor shower unfolding in the sky. For every time a firefly goes buzzing by overhead, in the dark without depth perception, you can't differentiate between the lightning bug and a shooting star.

Earlier that day, well before the tortures of the Dragon's Tooth but after a morning of hard climbing, I'd made this note to myself to develop later: "Creek. Falls. Foot massage. Fishies. It is enough."

I'd arrived at a fair flowing stream, and while a few other hikers splashed their faces at the footbridge and quickly scurried on, I'd gone downstream, found a small waterfall, stripped off pack and emptied pockets, and jumped right in. It was Heaven on Earth after the morning's labor in dense, humid heat. In a pool deep as a claw foot tub, I had flip-flopped from dunking my head under the falls to turning, lying back in the pool and letting the falls massage my feet. In that position I watched the fish swim around beside me in crystal clear water. It was indeed enough. I could live out the remainder of my life in sedentary repose and be happy in the recollection of that moment alone. The beer and fireflies and Seven Dwarf-like camaraderie of the night hikers later that day just added to it all. Another day on the Appalachian Trail. It is enough. It is more than enough.

Chazzan!! Like lightning popping off right near you and that crash of sound, instant, thunder, boom! Or the zip-zap miracle of instant information transfer from a little device in your hand standing deep in the woods, baffled by it all, then whoosh! With the alacrity of an e-mail reached, read, and returned, zang! I'm out of the woods and in the passenger seat of a next-year's model BMW beside a pretty, wild-spirited 19-year-old chauffeuring her brother, his girl, and me far, far away from the relentless and intrepid AT, spiriting us away like some angelic elf out of the dark forest, taking us to…The Beach!

Wow. I am Kerouac's Japhy Ryder on this May 27th, or Kerouac himself as Ray in *Dharma Bums*, whisked away on the rails or an easy Zen hitch fast out of one glorious exultant moment straight into another, totally different, always exciting. Japhy in his logger shirts and rucksack stepping out the mountains yodeling and into the way of Ray, hitching, tramping, back into the perpetual motion that was me with too many cars and endless Zen patience for the drive.

Now observing Ry's little sister, Karen-O, as she maneuvers the stealth German road machine down interstates and out of Virginia and Mile 714 of the AT parallel universe, changing the volume of the stereo pumping out Smashing Pumpkins without so much as a glance at the console, all done with covert controls hidden on the wheel itself, a techno-wonder I've never seen; and the car flying, erasing in minutes what just took me all morning to hike, in hours what took me a month, back south paralleling, the AT to Charlotte, North Carolina. Whoosh. Effortless. Going to the coast to dive in the ocean, to revel in the holiday weekend, to seize the day memorial, to celebrate with my brother America when he celebrates. On schedule with the western world and the workingman, I bust out a last batch of "work" on Thursday morning and clock out at noon, leave early and to hell with Friday.

Zero Day? How about a Zero Week? Adios, AT and all your ankle-twisting snaking phallic roots and REAL snakes, the venomous and rattling kind that have popped up underfoot EVERYWHERE in the past week of Virginia heat, coiling up and into the forest experience, a new, added sense of danger and sinister slithering freakiness. Adios, AT nobo peligroso. I'm taking a week. Off.

How did all this come about? Miraculously, of course. It all started in Damascus weeks ago, or maybe as far back as Day One when I first met Ry and Jackie just north of Springer Mountain, Georgia. Nothing special that first day or the next, but memorable as our first meeting, all of us launching north in what could be called the Great Eastern States Social Trek of Aught Four. When I tell people I hail from a hamlet just off the Pacific Crest Trail in southern California, always the question of why not the PCT first, and always I answer easily that I chose the AT for its social life. To undertake the 2,600-mile PCT alone as my first and actually only big trek of its kind would have been a lonesome and thus perhaps unsuccessful endeavor.

Jackie, Ry, and I became fast friends in the weeks that followed Springer, especially after the Smokies and moving on into Virginia. In Damascus we sadly parted ways when they had to go off-trail for 10 days for a wedding. By my reckoning, it would be 250 miles at a lowball average of 10 miles a day before we'd meet again. Thanks to a couple of e-mails and notes in shelter registers from me forward in time to them, arriving at said shelter a week or more later, they knew where I was, and I knew they were moving fast to catch me, skipping as they did the big thruhiker beer bash in Damascus so as to make up time.

Just as they were closing the gap between us, however, I slipped into some kind of possessed overdrive, driven forward at a juiced-up pace in a race to escape a crowded knot of thruhikers with whom I felt I had nothing in common and wanted to lose in the woods. It took a week and several heavy beatings at the hands of sandstone upthrusts and mean, anything-but-northbound jags for me to realize that the only solution, the only real way to lose them, was to stop.

Stop I finally did with monumental mental effort on the Wednesday leading up to Memorial Day weekend. At first I just slept in, a not-uncommon practice of mine, utterly incomprehensible to hardcore big milers who rise with the sun and roar across the dank morning landscape, only to poop out at

3 or 4 and witness (with a snarl) as I pass them in the magic light of late afternoon. Once up, I sat at the campsite picnic table in Lambert's "Meadow," a meadow when named, now long since a dense forest. A table not directly fronting a shelter is a real luxury outside of national park sections of the trail. It's hard to convey the how and why of how hard it was watching without following as one after another of my fellow thruhikers passed me by. For perhaps the first time in 700 miles on the trail, I felt the familiar jones of the unmedicated junkie, not for drugs or alcohol or sex for a change, but for the hike.

I bet if I were to return to Lambert's Meadow and to that site, I would discover deep indentations in the wood beneath my picnic table seat where I dug my fingers in straining against nine weeks of conditioning toward habitual movement: get up with the sun, pack it up, wolf down a Pop Tart, hit the trail. Every day a different place. Every day movement northward along the thin licorice whip line of the AT to a new forest, a new mountain, a new shelter, a new spring or stream to draw water to drink and eat. Go back I doubt I ever will, however. That is the nature of such a long, straight trajectory as this. Everything seen is seen for the first and last time. Every morning you awake miles from that flower, that tree, that section of trail you hiked just yesterday, never to be seen again. It is a metaphor of life's fleeting essence, a reminder of how each day MUST be lived as if it were the last.

I succeeded in fighting the urge to move on. I rose late, around 10, and set up shop at the campsite picnic table, laying out the makings of breakfast, lunch, dinner, leaving my hammock tent suspended in the trees behind me, and simply sitting there, a receptionist at his desk in the forest a few feet from the main corridor of AT traffic. It was a scene right out of Monty Python sketch. All I lacked was a flat bell to slap "Ding!" with every passing customer.

They came. One after another of my brethren and sister thruhikers came walking, tromping, zooming, some hobbling down the trail, but all right past my imaginary reception desk. Some said hello. Others ignored me. Most that I knew stopped for a moment to inquire if all was well and why I wasn't on the move. Town, you see, was just nine miles away. Town! A hotel, laundry, an outfitter, and a buffet-style restaurant waiting to be gorged upon like Romans at the dedication ceremony for the new vomitorium. Shoney's! Shoney's! I heard the name repeated, almost sing-song spoken with reverence and awe again and again as they passed. How could I miss out on Shoney's? They didn't understand.

Neither did I, for that matter. I knew only that I was tired of the lot of them, and that my ass refused to move, and that maybe, just maybe, my friends Ry and Jackie would at last catch up with me, rounding the same corner down to the creek where I sat in my forest cubicle typing away, typing, nibbling on granola and dried mango and candied ginger. Somehow I resisted all the force of the peak-bagging jones and just sat there. I smiled, entertained their complaints and lobbying efforts, and sent them on their way. I felt like the guard in the film Life of Brian, saying over and over: "Crucifixion? Ye-ess. First door on the right, one cross each. Crucifixion? Ye-es. First door on the right."

If I myself and severe depressives everywhere could view all life as a Monty Python sketch, seriousness would be lost and with it, much of the power that pulls the trigger, that eats the pills that kill.

I spent the whole day catching up on writing and watching Franko and Bennie and a few others I didn't wish to lose, pass on with those I did. I checked my e-mail. Which was odd because I was deep in the woods and felt sure I wouldn't have signal. But I did. Surprise, there was a message! It was from Ry and Jackie, by way of Jackie's mother, dictated over the phone from some remote motel in some backwater Virginia Appalachian town where they'd conked out and off the trail the day before. "We're going to the beach and want you to come along. Call us at our motel before 9:30 tonight if you get this message." They told me later they thought there was a one in fifty chance they'd hear back from me in time.

I hadn't checked my e-mail in days. Miraculously, I did that day. I wrote them back immediately. I couldn't possibly hike the nine miles out to the nearest phone in time. So I just sat back in my hammock that evening and waited as a monsoon deluge rain dropped from the lightning strobe-lit sky and thunder crashed through the forest like a herd of wolf-bitten caribou. At nine o'clock that night, I had my reply. I was on my way to the beach!

Now it's sun and surf mellow as a bay and the warm southern coastal Carolina waters off Ocean Isle, and showers, as many as you can take, and cake and wine and fresh-squeezed lemonade and southern special sweet tea. It's three meals a day, every day something different, and stories by chef Terry of how hush puppies got their name and what makes a grit a grit.

Been three or four daze of absolute, luxuriant beach living here in a rental cottage smack on the sand courtesy of Terry and Linda, my trail friend Ry's delightfully cool parents.

"She talks to angels," come the lyrics into my ears. "Says they all know her name." I, too, have conversed with angels, but thus far they haven't talked me into Heaven. Most days on the trail now, I feel sure this is a good thing. I haven't always been sure. In *Dharma Bums,* I read about Rosie jumping off the roof, chased by imagined demons and cops and think of Luciano. I read about John Muir and think of Luciano, choosing to exit this world in the bathroom of a friend, ironically the great or great-great-grandson of the famed naturalist.

I get an e-mail telling me the spec script I wrote for David Fincher has sold for twenty grand and that Luci's mother wants to pay me my half, and I don't think of Luci at all. I don't mix up thoughts of Luciano with cerebral wrangling with his mother and my protracted muddy working relationship with her. All the mess and confusion that has come of it is sad and stupid. When I get the news, I feel excitement for about a minute before the terror sets in. I wrestle with the fear of dealing with her on a business level again. A whole 24 hours passes before I find Terry's phone in my hand, the number ringing.

For 10 minutes she talks about some nebulous unnamed investor, a group, she explains, interested in all her projects. Like the title of the script itself, *The Bridge*, this is a refrain I have heard before. In 10 minutes she says nothing about any twenty grand, nothing about the script actually selling. In pregnant pauses, I listen to the Carolina beach waves chortling on shore and try to make sense of what she's telling me. As best I can gather, she's telling me she wants to buy me out. But also I'm hearing what sounds like a pitch of some sort, half pitch, half ultimatum. She's got two weeks to "fix" the script.

What am I supposed to do? I'm walking the Appalachian Trail. A few years back, while being paid to write a film script based on her concept and *Fight Club* director David Fincher's interest (by way of her rock star daughter Paz of Perfect Circle), the money to pay me had dried up during the second act of a three-act play, as it were. After I finished the script on my own time the following fall, Luci's mama and I shook on a 50/50 split of the final sale to compensate me my extra time. It's been years since then and nothing. Nothing, that is, but the occasional rumblings of some potential buyer that invariably end in... nothing.

Today I am sad. I feel like some half-psychotic bad-dream arm of gangly monster reality has reached out across the country and touched my pure white Appalachian quest with oozing, disease-ridden hands. Using false good news to lure me, some beast has sucked me back in. Not Luci's mother, per se. Just the energy, the entropy, the chaos surrounding any and all attempts to work with her, or she with me, in the recent past.

Worse, I shared this good news with Ry and Jackie and family, all without really knowing the truth. No, even worse is that I still don't know the truth. Has the script sold? It doesn't sound like it. But if someone wants it and they want to buy me out of it, isn't that good news? Maybe. I just don't know. The cell phone lost signal at some point in the very unclear haze of her story. I dialed her again, only to have the signal dropped shortly after saying hello. I didn't call back. The surf rumbles and churns across a warm evening breeze. I wonder if there are tiger sharks out there and if a few knife swipes across my arms might interest them in an evening snack. David Fincher. A Perfect Circle. Shit. I don't know what to think. I decide not to think at all.

So back to the trail. Yes. Except we can't go back, not yet anyway. Ry told me when he picked me up it would be a week. What a glorious sun-drenched and salt airy dream week of beach life it has been, gourmet meals and all. Shrimp Creole last night. Fresh locally grown beans and corn and potatoes daily. Chicken and sausage gumbo. Up at dawn (because after weeks on the trail rising with the sun it is hard to change) for pancakes chock full of freshly picked blueberries and glazed in pure Vermont maple. Out to dinner one night at a fried fish joint so popular that folks stand in line for hours to get in, and once inside and seated, no beer for thirsty me but "hush puppies" and southern sweet tea and later the story from Papa O (Ry's dad, Terry) about the origin of the name hush puppy. Hanging out for a week solid with Grandma and sister Karen O and Mama O and Cousin Molly and Aunt Trina, all of us comfortably ensconced in this four-bedroom house smack on the dunes, sound of surf, two big beds in every room, AC and ceiling fans, and a widow's walk high atop the roof for sunset viewing, terrific in Monday evening's electrical storm.

I sit here in a white porch rocker, one of six on the deck, each with a towel drying on its back, and acting thus like little wind-filled sails rocking each chair in the wind, a ghost of some Atlantic sailor's sea-gazing widow in every one. I stare out at that immortal sea, that sea that connects me with my youth, my father, my Uncle David drowned off Acadia far north in Maine, my destination. I stare and the pelicans perform for me in constant show, flying, flying over the sea in front of me all day and dropping, one every 30 seconds or so, dropping from the sky like mortally wounded bombers straight down and into the sea with an inaudible splash. Watch them long enough as they fish from 30 feet or so above the waves and you can almost hear the snap of salt-encrusted synapse as they hone in, commit, tuck wing, and drop like stones onto unsuspecting fish.

Only the constant rhythmic whirring and scraping of the sea and the tink-tinkle high- pitched chirps of people on the beach reach me up here. Through all this I read Kerouac and wonder and "Wow" at his 50-year-old words, at simple thoughts parceled out to me across time and space from a brother now dust and legend. I relate too strongly perhaps and too word-for-word with his struggles, but it's a good thing after years of being told that I sound like him, that my writing rings of his, and having never read him, ever, not even *On the Road,* although I've often fibbed and said I had to save face among literary brethren. I've never been a fast reader, and my pen far outpaces my digestion of books.

Ry talks to the neighbor about the trail, says he was considering quitting, that he felt "the tug of the real world, get a job, you know." I can't help myself and chime in immediately, not looking up from my work but saying, "That ain't no tug." It's true. I don't feel it to be that at all. But Ry, he's younger, eager to meet the world eye-to-eye, to show it his stuff. Me, I am jaded at 37. I interviewed the parents of the morning's dead and made front-page news in New York for my journalistic sins. I rode with the King to see Amtrak from the eye of the engineer only to witness as the train ate a human and spit out her bones with teeth on glass gnashing sounds, impossible. I have seen enough with their paycheck-chasing eyes, walked enough with the skin of their jobman on me, and I have turned away from all of that. It was turn or be turned, zapped into a pillar of stone, die.

Mama O is interested in my "career," such as it is. She points me to an article in the May 31 *New Yorker* (page 30) titled, "A Book in You." It's about a young assistant at International Creative Management in NYC named Kate Lee whose job is to turn Internet "bloggers" (or Web loggers) into writers with book contracts. Even out here in Appalachia, trying hard as hell to ignore that world, I confess I am intrigued. How do I get this Kate Lee to read *Jigglebox*? I don't think if she went Googling for "blogs" for a hundred years she'd ever find me. I never refer to my work as blogging. What I call ranting long preceded the net-invention of the former. Will she ever go Googling for "rants?" We can dream.

Ry's sis, Karen O, turned 20 here at the beach this week. She is looking for a cause to embrace, around which to wrap her obvious gift for lobbyist gab. She speaks of going to Washington perhaps, to intern for the campaign to save the penguins of Antarctica. She has a voracious appetite for books that impresses me. I suggest, only half-jokingly, that she ought to intern for some big New York literary agent, then turn her appetite for books toward the cause of struggling writers everywhere, starting with her brother and me. We are a cause worth fighting for. I, for one, will be dead one day, perhaps having never enjoyed the fruits of my work. The penguins of Antarctica will be dancing on my bones long after we are all dead and gone. Oh, well. Kate Lee is 27, my lucky number. There's that, anyway.

Thursday and the day of our return to Appalachia approacheth. I wake with a start (as always lately, too comfy in big beds), and this morning like no other find the strength and focus to pilot my dozy-dream-and-dropped-egg-awakened body out the glass door onto the porch and straight to the sand, drop towel, run, and splash! Into the Atlantic I go, christened and baptized and doused full-body in the salty warm waters, calm now but surely later in the season the stuff of hurricane floods and the sucking and slamming away of all this sand, this manmade beauty strip beach of dredged offshore sand where normally no beach exists.

Thus begins another day on Ocean Isle, a tiny island separated from the mainland only by the wide channel of the Intercoastal Waterway, a community of beach houses old and new, the elder sporting names like Crusty Cottage and Driftwood Den and Salt Box Special and Last Dime. To get booze here on Ocean Isle or anywhere in North Carolina, one must visit the ABC store, or, as Ry calls it, "The Alphabet." I drag Ry and Jackie inside where they stand like a couple of deer in the headlights while old man drunkard I, suddenly feeling like a big lush for buying a case of PBR beer and five liters of boxed sangria within the past 48 hours, my contribution to the beach house fridge fillins, buy tequila and triple sec, standard margarita fixins. Then I take 'em next door to a water's edge shanty bar and order up three margis to celebrate the alleged sale of *The Bridge,* my script written with Luci's mother. Oh, well. One can never have too many causes for celebration, even if they do turn up bogus.

Couple of days later, and I am the only one who has had a margarita. It was a good one, too. Got Ry to hand-squeeze half a dozen lemons for lemonade, some sugar to sweeten, and a slice of lime, mmmm! Best margarita I've had in recent memory. But I'm the only taker. So it appears I'll be heading back into the woods with a couple of 12-ounce Coke bottles full of booze. Groovy. The beer, however, is already gone. To soothe my drunkard's guilt, Ry and Jackie fess up to putting a major dent in that case of PBR.

Papa O has a story for every type of beer or food. So sure enough, when Ry and I return from the store with the PBR, he's got a story. His is about how

Pabst lost the loyalty of Milwaukee drinkers and how they're just lately making a comeback. In the car, I had just told Ry my Pabst story. So Ry jumps on his father's story and insists that I tell mine. I do. I tell about how in my last summer before high school graduation I was taken to Colorado with friend Rudy O'Meara and his mom and sis for a family trip to their grandparents' home in Aspen. Arriving there, I was stunned to pass through an archway and gates and continue driving for what seemed miles past stables and barns and various other outbuildings obviously attendant to some grand estate, to arrive sure enough at a log cabin mansion easily as grand as the palatial inn atop the North Rim of the Grand Canyon. This was Rudy's grandparents' "home." Rudy's mother's maiden name, as you may by now have guessed: Pabst.

In another strange flicker of small world irony, last night Ry's sister is working through a crossword puzzle when she asks aloud for a five-letter city in Utah staring with O. Without so much as a thought, my mouth blurts out "Ogden." Bingo. It's a good 30 seconds or so before my brain catches up and reminds me of the sad story behind my knowledge of this obscure piece of Utah geography. Ogden was home to my first publisher, the crooked swine of Northwest Publishing, Inc., who accepted my first novel in 1994, sat on it for a year, then went bankrupt, taking my innocence, my naïveté, and my vanity press investment of $2,000 with them, first to Vegas and the Bahamas, then later to prison in one of the largest and ugliest cases of vanity press fraud on record. I still feel the sting of this, and its scars are easily visible in my life, the most obvious being the stacks of manuscript beneath my bed, never final edited, never published. But beyond my scars, I think of all the other writers who likewise took it in the ass from the pirates of Ogden, 1,400 of them in all, or so the legal documents said.

Out here in Appalachia, 700 miles along and now on brief hiatus at the beach and soon to stomp another 400 miles of AT terra before I break again for Independence Day in New Hampshire, out here I feel only pity for the scum suckers and tricksters of the world. I read Kerouac and feel a dharma bum-kind of peace wash over me as I forgive them all and laugh a happy Buddha laugh and heft my 35-pound rucksack full of all I need in the world to walk and live and breathe and feel truly free.

For the first time in a long time there is a twinkle in my eye. It is the smile of God. It is the knowledge that out here on the perimeter, on the other perimeter, the opposite perimeter from where Jim Morrison saw no stars, there are a zillion stars and infinite possibilities and joys, and there is no death, no need of early exit, no fear of that monster emptiness of which

Bukowski said, "It's not death, but dying will solve its power." I have but just begun to breathe and see again. There are many, many miles to go before I sleep the sleep of Kerouac and Morrison and Luci, too. I love you all, and now leave you to the joys of Heaven. I will get there soon enough.

So on the last full day here at the beach to fully "be me" in every sense and feel me and breathe me and drink me, I nudge Ry into driving me to a thrift store and then to Home Depot where I buy a couple of baby dolls, a caulking gun, and an 11-ounce tube of silicon glue. On return to the beach, I hunt down the pile of beach detritus I've been gathering for days and set to work gluing colorful shells to the bare plastic skin of dolls. Jackie's first reaction is typical, and thus forgivable. She finds it "strange" and "weird" and probes me for answers or reassurance. I give her both, and at once, neither. What's the point of telling her that a doll makes a cool canvas? A doll carries with it so much inbred subconscious "meaning" and "significance" and elicits such personal feelings that, well, they make the perfect template upon which to glue a Freudian id's wortha junk. These words are mine, but the inspiration belongs to Phillip Estrada, an Arizona artist and friend who works a lot in doll sculpture.

By dusk I am the proud father of two bouncing baby boys. Both sport natty gray hair down to their bare butts, courtesy of the local brand of Spanish moss heretofore hanging from some Carolina coastal jungle tree. They are armed. Or armored, I should say. Each sports a calcium carbonate equivalent of Kevlar, a bulletproof vest of oyster and every other imaginable seashell. My boys are seashell mosaic and wild-haired beasts. They are my creations, and soon they will be with my nephews Matty and Jake. May they love them, and be loved.

The moon rises tonight dark as a wet dagger's shine. It sits a moment not two fingers-width above the horizon at arm's length. She is a lone blood orange in a Parisian black market night sky begging for the memory of Benedict Emerieu, my lost lover and friend. She is the moon, and Pierre de Joinville is the ink on my hipbone, and ever I can only guess that they are lost. Not even Google has unearthed these long lost French friends of mine, and thus said, this is my greatest fear, that somewhere, mon frere du tatouage est mort. Bad French notwithstanding, I want all my friends accounted for. I want them here with me again, wherever I am. Alas, the last beach night wanes, and I grow tired. I had so much more to say. C'est la Vie. C'est la Vie.

Back in the Charleston kitchen of the O family home, I crack open my pint of Franziskaner Hefe-Weisse, a gift from Ry, pour, and taste. Ah. There are few finer tastes in the world. I can think of but one. But every source of that sweet sodden-panty wine has left me, or I her, leaving me out here in the Appalachian parallel world of abstinence, cock roots, poison ivy vines, and vaginal-wounded trees, celibate by default, and thirsty by God.

Today was "waste-a-day" day whilst we wait for Ry's pop to pilot us back to the very dirt doorstep where we got off-trail, some obscure roadside portal in Troutville, Virginia. From there it will be back through the magic wardrobe and into the forests of Aslan again. Aslan, poor old Jesus-freak lion, I hope he'll forgive us our departure from our regal duties in that land. The beach called, and I, hungry water dog and lover of forward flips into waves and diving pelicans and faceplants in the sand just because I can and salt on my lips and in my nose and full moon's rising o'er the Atlantic, mmm, I couldn't resist.

Did the full immersion into consumer reality today, just for the shock of it, just for the buzz of fear and loathing a major shopping mall sprawl affords a modern day bark-eating, Prozac-snorting, gonzo-loving Edward Abbey-esque child of capitalistic doom like me. Love it. Give me Regal Cinemas with 400 theaters and 87 bathrooms and a labyrinth of tunnels to lose my inflated ego in, to lose my mind and melt my bipolar ice caps and bring on *The Day After Tomorrow* with all its pat plot pseudo-emotions and too-fast progression to the end of the world. But Oh! Wow! What fan-frikken-tastic computer graphics, ginormous waves, and freezing people, and all that shit. Loved it. Just what I needed before stepping back into the forest to walk more every day (statistically) than the average American walks in a month to and fro car and through the aisles of Wally World, etc. Just the thing.

The real bummer came after the movie when I found myself milling through a Borders bookstore getting ever more depressed (me without my meds now for several days thanks to failings in the mailings of so much and many supplies from California), awaiting Ry and Jackie and Ry's trippy sister, Karen O (whom I've tried like hell in 10 days to get to warm up to me, to no avail). They'd gone to see the third Harry Potter film and all its dark teen-Harry villainy; and I would have gone too just to see Gary Oldman put his freak on the goofy Potter scene, but I JUST HAD TO SEE the new apocalyptic flick on the big screen and was sure it'd be gone from theaters a month or so from now when next I'd be out of the woods and in the shopping world again.

So I'm milling around a bookstore, a place that, by now in my career, should be a place of pride and celebration for writer me, but isn't. And, as usual, I need to necromance my failure-filled past, so I plug my name into the

AUTHOR search on the Border's catalogue computer and voila! There I am, author of the supposedly "out of print" novel *Catcher in the Sky*, and all because the fraudulent swine father-son team atop Northwest Publishing, my first and last publisher, did at least register my book with the Library of Congress, thank you very little.

In walk Jackie and Ry and Karen O. Jackie comes up to me first where I stand poised between the "Automotive" and "Nature" sections, both reading a book on edible plants and guarding THE BOOK, Harrod's baby, *Art Cars: The Cars, the Artists, the Obsession, the Craft,* which I was quite pleased to find in stock here at Borders Books, Wherever Suburb, Charlotte, North Carolina, thank you very much. I had mentioned to J & R that should they wish to see me in a book, this is where they might look.

Cut to me in the passenger seat of Ry's car, Ry driving, girls in the back. We're driving back to the O Family Estate at Aero Plantation, a ginormous brick castle, modest, homey, a little museumy in the front rooms but full of love and damn nice people, his parents. Aero Plantation, the one and only upscale community development I've ever walked around with leg muscles to spare, wild eyes, and cranked-up racehorse-on-speed kind of energy, walking and shaking my head in amazement as I pass home after regal home with, not only garages, but HANGERS! Every house a little airplane hanger with airplanes ready to go!

Smash Cut. Smash my ego and squish it on the floor. Radiohead on the CD player, their song "How to Disappear," singing "...this is not happening," the song I made love to Alice to as it played on random repeat again and again for hours as we rocked that rickety old Idyllwild house for one glorious night last summer. It was the crescendo of a week or month, whatever, of pure good lovin' (some of the only lovin' I've had in years), a prime memory locked inside a fine song. But now I'm sittin' in a car just shaking my head (internally, of course, so as not to worry the others with suspicious head-bobbling), sad, sad as the greatest dreamer at the death of another dream. It's all about the art car book, I'm ashamed to say. I just expected more.

I mean, If you were my friend, even a new friend, and you'd pulled me aside in a bookstore and said, "Hey, check it out. This is me in this book. See?" Even if I was totally unimpressed and unenthralled and the book was about plumbing or dental extractions or rectal sores, I STILL would have made a big show of saying, "WOW! That's YOU in that book! That's far out!" Excepting the subject of rectal sores, I would have called people from all around, called over the name-tag-wearin' wanna-be writer bookstore employee types and gloated at my protégée, saying, "Look! This guy's IN THIS BOOK!" I mean, come on. How many people are IN books? How many people in that store that day could pull a book off the shelf and say, "This is me! These are my friends!" Zzz-ERO! Or in the words of Ace Ventura: Pet Detective, "La-hoo, saa-her!"

Not so for Jackie and Ry and Karen O. If they were even a modicum impressed, they sure hid it well. For the sum total of her reaction, KO may as well have just been informed she'd been impregnated by aliens, flipped a mental circuit breaker, and gone straight into denial.

Oh, dammit! I know it's wrong to expect ANYTHING from ANYONE, but ugh ugh ugh! It was sure as hell depressing. My first feeling: I hate my life. Next up: Kill me now. Finally, (a smidgeon more sane and recently employed toward laudable self-adjustment): Get me back to the F$%#-ing Trail! I mean, forget for a second that I'm wearing this self-sewn cloak of shame and am chock full of irony over the fact that after 15 years of writing books and plays and essays and poems, my car has an agent and I STILL DON'T. Forget that J & R & KO didn't know any of that. My display of the art car book by Lark Press and the ever-magical Mr. Harrod Blank still went over like the proverbial fart in church.

Hell with it.

Oh, and starting today, no more Jack Kerouac. I mean, I love the guy, but dammit dammit dammit, I just don't want to be like him. I don't want to live like him, and I don't want to die like him. But whammo bingo! I read *Dharma Bums* this week and what do you know? His path reads like a roadmap of my own half-mad wanderings, his words and poems and spiritual meanderings a mirror to my own. I love him. I hate him. But if I hate him, it's not really him I hate but the righteous comparisons made between him and me. The same could be said of Bukowski and Hunter S. How often I have been asked if I would like to meet the latter and always my answer is no. Yet I have emulated his lifestyle to an oft times dangerous degree. Be wary, Dear Reader, whom you choose for heroes.

I want to be Old Money rich fat and happy and have the problems of the rich to deal with instead of mine. I don't cherish this golden yoke of freedom called poverty and nothing-left-to-lose. I hate it. I despise my obscurity in a world where fame is everything, and yet I don't NEED fame. I need the financial security that fame might-oughta bring, but whatever. I love you, Jack. But don't, as I bade S. Plath, don't put your dead poet juju on me. You are gone and I yet live. I want to live a long life. "Longevity," said the King, "has its place."

If I could fly, I just might this night walk down the street and commandeer one of the neighbors' little planes and fly out of here. I am antsy for the trail. My whole countenance this past few days has been one of extreme self-control, waiting, waiting for the ride back to my beloved trail. I loved the beach. I reveled in Papa O's delicious gourmet meals day in and day out, for daze and sunny salt-sprayed sand and surf and wine and re-lax-ation daze, but I am ready now. Were my BMW here and not far away in California, or had I the money for bus or the guts to hitch a hundred small hitches outta the burbs and upstate into Virginia and to the Trail, I would be gone now. Ten days is half a dozen days too many to be removed from that parallel reality that is the Appalachian Trail.

But I knew this (if only subconsciously) when I climbed into Ry's sister's car. I knew it might be a sketchy-sketch too long, but I signed on for the whole trip. It was glorious. But I'm pounding the beers now to drown my fears, and there's that last dram of Crown Royal from Mary to whack down so I can fill the jug with denatured alcohol for my new catfood can stove. I drink alone, and I dissipate evermore by the hour. God Almighty, please get me back to the woods. Amen. - Yayzeus Christoos Jester Jalopy, once a Lord and a Duke

[Author's note: Special thanks to Mama and Papa O in Charlotte, North Carolina, for their kindness and fantastic southern hospitality. My last entry was a maniacal half-drunken ramble that had everything to do with my own personal discomfort with extended stays with ANYONE, and nothing to do with them. I've been such a loner for so long, I did well to last 10 days with one family. They were fantastic to put up with me.]

A funny thought occurred to me just now, upon finishing this rant, this blog, this post, whatever. I have come across several passages in *Dharma Bums* that I wanted to quote in these pages, but likely never will, because tomorrow I'll be back on the trail and not at all hip to lugging another x-amount of ounces of book pages with me in my carefully calculated, algorithmically postulated and desegregated, slimmed down and vastly lightened backpack. So just READ THE BOOK YOURSELF! I highly recommend it, though it be ever-so-full of hard-to-fathom hopeful Buddhist happy smack, it has its merits, and they are many. Read it. Until then, there's one passage that pressed my irony button most pleasantly.

Kerouac is at a party. There is a poet tacking off a list of all the great poets of their time, all the Beats, where they are, what they are doing, and what he reckons are their chances for success and immortality. He places himself high in the ranking for the latter. When he finishes his list, someone asks about Kerouac, in the character of Ray Smith:

> *"What about Smith?"*
> *"Well I guess he's a bodhisattva in its frightful aspect, that's about all I can say." (Aside sneering: "He's too drrrronk all the time.")*

Think "Beat Generation?" What poet comes first to mind? Kerouac, and, perhaps for many, only Kerouac.

I rest my case, all 24 bottles.

ELEVEN

The Little Engine that Might Have Been? Jersey Doug, Maine Sail and other MIAs...Moose Killer and the 1,800-pound Freight Train Standoff...Camp DuPont and Angel Gravy...Trading Poles for Oars and Getting Stoned to the Gills... Spider Island & Rope Swings Forever...Another Head for Vengeance ...The Snuggle-bug Warm-Biscuit Groovy Goose Feather Cocoon.

Back on the trail with a vengeance. Feeling somewhat retarded both in my pace and in my brain after 10 Zero Days on Carolina beaches, I hit the Appalachians hard on Sunday, cranking out 40 miles in the first 48 hours of my return. It is now Wednesday. On Sunday, I was looking at 130 miles to Waynesboro, Virginia, my next mail and supply stop and the southern portal to the Shenandoahs. On Monday morning, I had delusions of making it to Waynesboro by Saturday morning before the post office closed at 11 a.m. After a humbling day of grueling ascents yesterday, fully 5,400 feet in total spread out over an insane 21.7 miles, I am no longer delusional. Just dead on my feet. At least now I've entered the 700s.

Despite all the ascension and "big miles," I'm not sleeping at night. Three nights now, I lie awake most of the night. I joked to Jackie and Ry that I had just gotten used to sleeping in a hammock tent when they abducted me and made me sleep in plush comfy beds for over a week. But it's no joke. I do recall nearly acclimating to the odd sleep of the hammock two weeks ago, and now I hate the thing. If I had Mr. Hennessy handy, I'd make him eat his invention, as Werner Herzog ate his own shoe.

Today at John's Hollow Shelter somewhere near Glasgow, Virginia, I saw Sarge, the cool old black dude who dubbed me Jester one night over beers in the Nantahala Outdoor Center, what feels a lifetime ago (just two months). I inquired after Little Engine, and to my surprise he said she was still on the trail. "Oh, yeah, she's slack-packin' down around Daleville. She's got problems with her back, I think. But she's got money, her family's got money.

166

She could walk the entire trail without carrying a pack, if she wanted." Sarge went on to tell me that Little Engine inquires after me once in a while, but denies any interest in me. I like hearing that (a dead giveaway). Too bad she smokes like a chimney and is way behind me. A fine looking woman, she. But it sounds like she needs to marry a sherpa.

Seeing Sarge got me thinking about Jersey Doug. I wonder how he's doing. I wonder if he's still hammering down the trail, stabbing the ground beneath his feet with his poles like he was mad at the earth. I miss Doug. Hell, I miss a lot of people. So many, many people I've met on the trail are now well ahead of me. Many are behind. Sarge says he's getting off soon and is going to bus it up to Vermont, then flip south. Listening to the reasoning of a man who has done the whole trail once and continues to do chunks of it every year, I begin to think that might be the thing for me.

The Flip-Flop. Hike north to Harper's Ferry (roughly the halfway point), then catch a ride or bus north to Maine, do Mt. Katahdin in July instead of October, then hike south through the summer. This eliminates the dangers of hitting early winter storms in northern New England, gets you out of hot Pennsylvania and New York in the dead heat of summer, and ensures that you don't miss getting to climb Katahdin. The "deadline" for a northbound hike is October 15, when they close Katahdin for the winter. Sarge says last year there was ice on the rock-faced mountain in late September, and a lot of people went home disappointed when the rangers called an early close to the season.

I'll be cutting it close now if I try and stick to my northbound course. Very close. But if I flip, I get to walk through Maine and my beloved New Hampshire in summer, allowing family and friends there to join me for a section if they like in good weather. One other thing, and here's the reason Sarge likes flipping: to see all the friends he made on the trail that year, friends he has since fallen far behind. Great idea! I can see Maine Sail again! Elly, too, for better or worse.

Last night wide awake at 4 a.m., I decided it was high time to break into my coveted stash of Klonipin, all of ONE 2-milligram pill I have left. I ran out of my daily Prozac a week or so ago, the Klonipin even further back. I squirreled away one K, for dire emergency, for that moment when it's nearly nuthatch time, when it feels like a dose of knockoff Valium is the only thing standing between you and a straight jacket. Both the 'zac and the K are supposed to be mailed to me monthly from Houston Ground Control to keep me from spinning out of orbit and into deep space. "Houston, we have a problem."

Prozac is for depression in case you've been asleep for the past decade. The K is for anxiety, taken on occasion, as one takes an aspirin for a headache. But you, my loyal readers, already know I'm on crazy meds. You probably know I'm a fan of pharmaceuticals in general. Love 'em. Give me a whack of heavy doctor dope (in the form of a little yellow horse pill called oxycodone - think Rush Limbaugh) over a joint any day. What's good for the Big Fat Talk Radio Goose is good for the Jester.

I made it! I can't believe it, but I did it again: another big mile day, this one 19 miles, and most of it in the afternoon and early evening. After not getting going this a.m. until 10:30, then stopping and shooting the shit for half an hour with Sarge when I ran into him down by the James River, then typing for another hour at some other shelter, I hiked till dusk! I was inspired by a rumor of trail magic at Mile 785. Good thing I was the last man on the trail at 8:30 p.m., because I rolled in here just in time for a couple of cheese sandwiches and two Nesteas! No matter that I missed a dinner of sausages, beans and bell peppers. I made it!

Breakfast this morning courtesy of trail angels Renegade and Tomboy. From their little outdoor kitchen setup came the biggest meal I've had in days: two eggs over medium (my favorite and without even asking), two sausage links, two sausage patties, two strips of bacon, two cups of coffee, and a juicy juice. Yum! Yeah, so Kerouac and Snyder had yabyum, and I could certainly use some of that nowadays, but yum yum works, too! Renegade tells us a tale of putting peanuts in his Coke as a boy, about how his grandma would tell his friends and him not to, so of course they would go right ahead and do it. Wild. Never heard of such a thing. This must truly be a cultural phenomenon unique to Appalachia. Where's *National Geographic* when I need them?

Fueled with a full tank, I expected to roar out of the gate this morning and rocket down the trail. Strangely, however, this was not the case. I lagged inexplicably all morning, barely putting one foot in front of the other for hours.

Came upon a beautiful swimming hole just before noon. Man, I can't pass up a swimming hole, no matter what kind of make-believe schedule or haste I have myself hooked into. So in I went, into a churning liquid pool beneath a waterfall. Not a minute in and I'm giggling silly, dancing a jig as a hundred little fishes nibble on me, probably snacking on the salt of my sweat, all four pounds of it that I carried on my skin into their pool.

Then along comes Fred, 19 years old with a 19-pound food bag and (speaking of four pounds) the gigantic 900-page Cervantes classic *Don Quixote,* just about the only two things in his otherwise near-empty pack.

On average, thruhikers carry about 10 pounds of food at a time on the AT, tops. This boy is a big eater. "Don't you carry a change of clothes, a tent, anything else?" I ask him. "Just a fleece sleeping bag," he says. He goes from shelter to shelter, relying solely on the shelter system to protect him from the elements. Okay. Fair enough. The way I'm feeling about my frikken spider's-wrap hammock tent, I just may start doing the same. Fred heads for the pool, and as I make my way on up the trail, I hear him giggling, the little fish a-nibbling.

A mile or two later, and I'm just dying. Thermometer says it's 90, but it's got to be 80 percent humidity to boot. A goddamn fly buzzes my head incessantly, one of those low-frequency dumbass buzzers that circle your head for a full minute or two, then vanish, only to return to do it again a minute later. Seems like it's the same damn fly time and again, but if so, he's been with me for four days and 70 miles.

Today in the dead zone center of the Blue Ridge Mountains, there is but one choice on the radio: country. At least in days past I was getting R&B and hip hop stations, too. Ridge walking Virginia, said music has me imaging a whole society of Crackers and Afreak-ans living together in some kind of weird harmony down in the cities below. Crackers are crackers, white people, you know. Afreak-ans, I imagine, are both black and white people, all getting their freak on to Dr. Dre and Shante and Eminem and them. Afreak-ans. Okay. Whatever.

Near the intersection of U.S. Route 60 and the Blue Ridge Parkway, I come across Moose Killer. Here is one funny old dude, older than dirt and plagued by bad knees, heart attacks, and, yeah, you guessed it, moose. Still he hikes on.

I knew I was talking to a character when I saw his hand-carved walking stick with the names of all the states on the AT, the IAT (International AT), and some other branch of the AT to the south into Alabama and Florida the initials of which I've already forgotten. Beside the name of every state he's finished sits the head of a flathead screw he's driven into the stick. How did Moose Killer get his name, I inquire?

"Attacked by a moose!" he says. "Twice! I'll never hike in Maine in September again." My mind immediately does the calculation. Yes, on my present course I will be in Maine in September. "That's when they're in rut.

They got poor eyesight, so a male moose, he'll charge anything that moves if it gets in between him and his woman." Unknowingly, Mr. Moose Killer did. The moose charged.

"You got an 1,800-pound freight train coming at you, and it'll scare the shit out of you."

"What did you do?"

"I sprayed him with pepper spray, and man, he laid down skid marks THIS long!" Was that it, I wondered? "No, he backed away, shook it off, and came at me again. This time I hid behind a tree, and thus ensued about a 15-minute standoff. The only thing I had in my favor was that his antlers were so big he couldn't get around the tree at me. I told my friends later, I got home and didn't have to shit for three days!"

Surreal romp through the fast forest of morning today stomping the terra double-time to reach a road crossing at Mile 808 and a rumored ride to town. Surreal music, that is. Or voice/music overlay. It's June 10 and suddenly Ronnie Reagan and Ray Charles are married in a weird mournful tribute montage of Ray's song and Ronnie's rockem-sockem "Don't tread on us!" rah rah America drama club champion oratory overlaid. Very strange. There ought to be an Emergency Broadcast System warning on the radio, followed by Roseanne Barr's hoarse, atonal voice howling, "Warning: Dead President Overhead!"

I'm very near D.C. now and all I can think is: Yesterday the old coot's corpse flew over my head on its way to the Rotunda in D.C., and this afternoon they're wheeling his old bones back on another armor-plated stealth jet and roar over my head again enroute to Simi Valley, Cali-Cali, and stick him in the ground just as the final green flash goes, "Fffflllppppuut!" and the Pacific goes dark and mournful forever more.

A dead president flies overhead, and old Ray Charles finally gets his sight back on the streets of Heaven, and me? I've been humping the Blue Ridge with all the gonzo conviction and masochistic foot-mashing, bone-crunching, slam-dunk drive of Attila the Hun on a rotgut homebrew binge and tear, stomping out 90 miles in just 4-1/2 days. Madness. The result? Well, hell, it was suddenly announced to be a national holy-day-of-mourning, so, why should I work? Hiking from dawn to dusk 12 hours a day for close to a whole workweek. I quit.

Morning. Awake. Shake dreams from your hair, my pretty children, my sweets, my Powder Finger, my Whiskey, my Flatbed, Yovo, Wife and Beater, and me. Whiskey of Whiskey and Flatbed, true to her namesake, brought Old Crow to the DuPont-downwind lycra-scented river bendpark here in Waynesboro, Virginia, where we all sat last night 'round the picnic table drinking, beer mostly, and swapping AT war stories in the gentle dancing light of fireflies abundant.

The local YMCA provides showers and a grassy field in which to camp. We carry passes in our pockets, call them "noble hobo visas," signed by YMCA desk personnel to prove to the cops that we are indeed of the "2,000-mile masochist" variety and not just grifter opportunists who happened by the open field between the YMCA and the DuPont factory to pop a squat a while with questionable motives. There are a few such folks out here in the field. The cops, if they came by, would not need to do a tent-by-tent check. They would need only to ask us.

Thruhikers can spot their own kind in a heartbeat, and thus spot interloping posers, too. They walk through, and no one knows them. They don't give their names or say much of anything, unless prompted. Their tents are a dead giveaway: Wal-Mart specials, huge and silly and structurally poor, they stick out amidst a dozen of our smaller stealth tents, high-tech and expensive every one. I look out across the field here by the river, and just in the dozen thruhiker tents (not counting equipment stowed inside: $200 packs, $100 MSR alpine-ready cook stoves, $200 and $300 sleeping bags, $75 Thinsulate ground pads), I see three to four thousand dollars in tents alone.

I spent my first night back in my beloved Mountain Hardware Wayfarer II tent after weeks of ugly sleep in the airborne cocoon of my Hennessy Hammock. After waiting out a heretofore nonexistent postal holiday in honor of old Ronnie Raygun, I at long last collected my tent and REI mummy bag from the Waynesboro PO, where I had mailed it ahead in time and space to myself, for possible pickup or forwarding on to New Hampshire if all had worked well with my summer bag and hammock tent. It did not.

So I picked up my so-called "bounce box" and gleefully ran back to the YMCA "Distance Hikers Only" refugee camp to bust out my warm fuzzy. Zip-zap went my knife down the packing tape seams. I lifted the folds of the box open and WHOOOOSH! A noxious wave of ammonia leapt out of the box and hit me full face, and I thought, "Oh, no." I knew immediately the source of the stench.

It seems back in Damascus in the thick of Trail Daze, I, in a drunken haze, washed and only half-dried my $300 down bag, mummy-wrapped it in Hefty garbage green, and packed it away in a tight little box. And there it sat. For damn near a month. Rotting. The horror.

Oh, and speaking of nightmares, here's a little flashback from my weekend in Waynesboro. (Incidentally, I salvaged my beloved down bag. After something like three washes, four cups of Febreze, and five hours in the Laundromat, we killed the demon stink.) I'm not sure what was worse, that or this:

I arrive exhausted at the shelter just south of Reed's Gap to an egregious, ugly vibe from the two men and their three pre-adolescent children ensconced in the shelter. I am exhausted after a 25-mile day. The sun is dropping like a duck from a buckshot-riddled sky, and this duck needs a place to call it a night. There isn't another shelter for miles, and I'm too tired to ponder a stealth camp somewhere nearby. Why should I? There's plenty of room in the shelter. But no. The vibe from these men is ugly. I try and ease the tension by telling the kids stories of my long journey. The kids dig it, but not so the men. I give the fathers a discreet once-over. A minute later, I look one of them right in the eyes. Suddenly I get it. "Holy pigs in a blanket! You're off-duty cops! You think I'm a pederast. I'd bet money it's the other way around, you creeps!" I don't say this aloud, of course, just talking in my head.

Never before had I been unwelcome in an AT shelter. The shelters are there for everyone, free and open to all. I had caught a ride that morning 50 miles south along the Blue Ridge Parkway from Waynesboro, Virginia. The plan: Make up the miles missed by jumping ahead after a big fried chicken lunch at the Dutch Haus in Montebello left me lazy and hungry for city comforts just ahead at Waynesboro. As I stood there trying to visualize sleeping in the single-car garage-sized space with these cop-vibe spooks and their kids, I looked at my maps and made a decision. I'd made half my goal, and the parkway was very close. I said sweet goodbyes to the kids, gave the men the stink eye, hefted my pack, and hoofed it another mile to the road. It took a while, as the scenic road was practically empty at dusk, but I got a ride, finally, from a guy named Dave who lived nearby. May the faeries sprinkle Dave's dick with magic dust. The guy drove me 50 miles out of his way to take me back to Camp YMCA. Oh, and you spooks? May your dicks rot off, you fear-engendering, shelter-hogging swine.

Had a great time hanging with newfound trail friends Flatbed and Whiskey tonight. We three downed a 12-pack of Yuengling Black & Tan, and I pitched the New Hampshire couple on my latest obsession: The Aqua Blaze. The idea is to raft or canoe a stretch of the Shenandoah River equidistant to the length of the Shenandoah Mountains, as the one parallels the other from the valley to the west. It was a super cool idea, but everyone I asked just wasn't interested. Well, they ARE interested and envious but all hung up on being religious about sticking to the white blazes. Fine. Not interested in doing it alone, I had all but given up.

Now it is a Sunday morning in mid-June and this is Camp Zero, Waynesboro (I spell it Waits-burro), Virginia, population I don't know but apparently the largest town we will pass through on the entire AT. It is the southern gateway to the Shenandoahs, a hundred miles of ridge during which the AT more or less parallels a commercialized section of the Blue Ridge Parkway where restaurants and tourist kiosks allegedly abound and the trail crosses the highway 42 times! I have just walked 90 miles of a pristine Blue Ridge Parkway (no shops or cafes) in 4.5 madly driven days and am not looking forward to the Shenandoahs.

I spent a large part of my weekend here at Camp YMCA stumping for someone, anyone to join me not IN the Shenandoah Mountains, but ON the Shenandoah River! Flatbed and Whiskey are game! But, sadly, they are about flat out of dough, which means not only no aqua blaze, but no more trail. I wished more than ever then that I were Hugh Hefner or Bill Gates or somebody capable of just surreptitiously sneaking them a stack of Benjamins. You know, Make a Wish Foundation for coin-dying thruhikers, visiting angels from the big cash vault in the sky, all that stuff. (I never saw Flatbed and Whiskey again after that weekend.) So here I sit, resting my mashed-potato feet and bullfrog-bloated knees. Tendering a Black & Tan hangover, I contemplate my immediate future.

Then along around noon come trail angels Gravy and Korpi. These guys just pull up to Camp Y-not-Thruhike, pull the gas grills out of the bed of their truck, and lay out a great feast of BBQ for all. They arrive and cook for us with such conviction that I never question what appears odd logic on the part of the Waynesboro AT welcoming committee or whoever it is that later that day charged us five bucks a plate for BBQ in some official AT downtown park gathering. Well, turned out Gravy and Korpi just had priceless timing. They fed us well, and for free! We later trickled into the official gathering downtown, but I didn't pay to eat. Hell no. That was just the beginning of Gravy's contribution to my AT experience.

I'd just about given up on the aqua blaze when who should arrive on Monday but Party Girl and her new beau, Spiceman. If there's one thing I can say about Party Girl, man, that girl is game for anything. She was an easy sell.

When you're feeling blue and you've lost all your dreams
there's nothing like a campfire and a can of beans. –Tom Waits

I'm sitting in the stern of a 17-foot canoe gently sliding down the
Shenandoah River with fellow AT thruhikers Spiceman and Party Girl, and
we've got it going on—our wish, our Shenandoah River Aqua Blaze! With us,
a 30-pack of Miller High Life, half a gallon of Jack Daniels, a half-gallon of
Evan Williams bourbon, a case of Coke, five gallons of drinking water, a fifth
of mescal, pharmaceuticals for emergency sedation, a quarter bag of
Spiceman's "special spice," and our brains—each so wild-eyed and googly
that it ought to be licensed as a concealed cerebral weapon in the everlasting
gonzo fight of the free and the brave.

Initially reticent about this whole river gig, Spiceman is getting into the
aqua-groove now. Granted, we're only moving at perhaps one mile an hour on
the slow-flowing Shenandoah. At about Mile 3, we need to pull out and
portage the canoe around a dam. It is the first of three dams we will conquer
on our trip. I've got poison ivy on my right arm in a kind of slice-pattern, as
though I slit my wrist laterally, the wrong way. That isn't bad. The bad spot is
on my left arm, just inside the elbow, such that every time I fold my arm, the
oily poison spreads itself. Ah, the joys of nature.

This stretch of the Shenandoah River is ideal for our little half-cocked
threesome in a canoe. Every 10 minutes or so comes a sweet little stretch of
rapids, a narrowing of the river with rocks to dodge and trees to duck. There
isn't another soul out here. Just us. We laugh like children as we take on a
rapid, zooming through, the boat jiggling up and down, water spraying over
the gunnels, Spiceman up front taking most of the splash over the bow.

We cruise along sighting out rope swings, sizing them up, comparing them.
Most are ropes tied to random trees on the river's forested edge, not a house
or cabin in sight. We pick one, a blue and white rope, strong and thick like a
climbing rope. I scale up the tree, which reaches far out over the water, in
itself a sweet diving platform. I pull the rope up and Spiceman follows,
swings, arcs far out, and drops with a splash. PG is inspired. She leaves her
throne in the center of the canoe and is in the water and up the tree. Later we
talk of how our trip would make a nice board game, each stop on the way a
mini-adventure unto itself.

Last night it was Spider Island. We had spent the late afternoon rowing in
light showers, alternately relaxed, then wired with the approach of rapids,
always on the search for the perfect isle to call home for the night. We wanted

an island because it assured us of some privacy and in all likelihood no accusation of trespassing. We found one, a long narrow isthmus that I liked but had to admit, as romantic as it looked, twas too narrow to tent on with anything but a hammock. A few fun little rapid runs later, we came upon Spider Island, a tiny jungle in the center of the river that we so named for its preponderance of arachnids. I hit the beach like a hurricane, feeling great, and in rare form took a paddle in hand and, wielding it like scythe or machete, cleared all the mad lush jungle creeper vines to reveal a nice sandy patch of beach. This would be our home for the night.

Spiceman, who had lost his little jar of herb…er, spice, earlier that day and proceeded to drown his sorrow in half a gallon of southern whiskey and a 2-milligram Klonipin donated by yours truly, did a fine job collecting stones from the shore and building a fire pit. Nay, twas more than a fire pit. It was a work of art, smallish stones piled and fit together puzzle-like into a towering well.

Upriver today, we meet our first "fellow canoers," a family or two in three canoes, mostly kids. On the river since Tuesday, we'd been totally alone for 40 miles. Several Budweisers and a shot or two of mescal in me, I spy a great jump spot, a tree jutting out over a deep section of river at less than a 45-degree angle, thus easy to clamber up, and great for jumping. At its peak, that is to say as high as one could climb amidst its branches without snapping one off, it's a 40-foot drop. We race ahead of the kids and pull up to the base of the tree. I climb out and straight up it; as always with an almost uncanny sense of balance, I am up and away and ready to plunge in no time. The kids notice. They tune in and pretty soon everyone on the river is watching.

It should have been a perfect 10, a bold and beautiful leap from great height to the amazement of all. But I'm too confident. Or was it the Budweiser? I don't know. I lower myself down and hang from the branch, increasing the tension below by putting myself in a position of "no turning back." Then I make my mistake. I start swinging. I let go on a backswing and plummet 40 feet to the stone-hard surface of the water in full belly flop posture.

Mind you, celibate for months now, I had nearly forgotten I had balls. With a blinding smack and flash of white light, I rediscover my testicles in all their fragile glory. Later, I climb and jump again to avenge myself. But it's too late. The kids are gone.

Midday Wednesday we pass beneath a new bridge and suddenly find ourselves rushing headlong into a dangerous obstruction in the form of an old bridge, sitting right at water level, left there long after it was outmoded. I try to swing the canoe far to the right of it, to what appears the easiest takeout spot. PG is shouting to go the other way. But it's too late. The canoe slams sidelong into the water-level concrete bridge. Immediately it threatens to barrelroll as a million gallons of rushing water work to suck us down beneath the sunken bridge. I leap out and with bare feet in waist-deep water employ tremendous force to keep the canoe from flipping. But I can't do much else. The pull of the current is strong. I feel something sharp slice open my left foot.

We AT thruhikers zealously pack in and out our own trash, and even now here on the river are collecting every empty beer can, every cigarette butt, every wrapper, for later disposal. But not so of the rest of the world. Every time the AT crosses a road in the forest, someplace where car campers have access, there's a mound of trash. Somehow, we three manage to raise and sidle the canoe to the edge of the river and clear the old bridge. I check my foot and find a good-sized gash. Broken bottle, likely. Nothing another day or two of water and shoeless canoe living won't cure. We move on.

We float on in the sunshine, the heat, and the doldrums of midday. Relaxed, I sprawl on my life jacket against the rear of the canoe. I daydream as we slip along, seemingly going nowhere on the glass surface of the river.

Beautiful day. Stunning. Just dreamy. Dreamy.

Then pop! I open my eyes, startled awake by the sound of rushing water. Was I asleep? Had I slept? I notice that both PG and Spiceman are also asleep. A large rock juts out of the water dead ahead. I grab my oar and jam it in. Tea for the tiller man. The boat turns just in time and the bow of the canoe misses the rock by the width of bottle cap.

"PG! Where were you?" I shout. She rolls out of a siesta haze. She is point man, after all. It was a close one, dangerous but exhilarating. I don't know how we all fell asleep at the same time.

Onshore that evening, Party Girl walks down a lonesome country road away from our camp by the river. "Hey, PG," I shout after her. "If you get in any trouble down the road, anyone try to molest ya, just squeal like a pig and we'll come running." *Deliverance* jokes abound down here.

But Virginia is beautiful, no question. Colossal castles of cumulonimbus rise up into the heavens, their bottoms blue as oceans, their tops gilded in the late afternoon sun, already set behind the mountains for us but still shining way up there. The river wends its way on and on and when we ask folks along the way where we are, no one seems to know. It's like a dream and we're all in it together, PG, Spiceman, me, the young girls swimming in the shallows, the boys swinging from the rope swing, the old dudes standing waist-deep in the water fishing, fishermen on boats as well. No one knows quite where we are.

Still, Spiceman asks the same two questions for days. To the fishermen, "Catch anything?" and always the answer is no. To everyone and anyone, "Where are we?" No one knows. The little bastions of human life come and go. Most of the time on the river we are alone. I stand up, first in the canoe and later right up on the rear plank, playing master balancer, the circus performer, showoff.

My sense of balance astounds me. Standing up as we drop into a shallow trough of rapids without falling or needing to sit, I am an Indian scout on birch bark canoe, trained for such balance since birth. I begin to hum and moan and wail like a possessed man, like a blues man, like a freed slave still bound by sharecrop servitude. I sing an old slave song at the top of my lungs. I don't even know any old slave songs. But the spirit is in me, and the river waters are thick with voices of the past. I tap into them, toss in a handful of amens, an "Oh, my Lord" and a "Jesus gonna save my soul," and it's sounding real good.

I keep it up for hours, irreverent of who's listening and oblivious to the apparent disinterest in my singing from my canoe mates. I'm having fun, and so far no one's complaining.

Walked hardly a mile today, but man o man did we have a blast. Right out of the tent and onto the river and straight into the most intense rapids we've encountered yet. Class Two? Class Three? Maybe not that high, I don't know. But I can say with some confidence that one wouldn't want to take a canoe over whitewater of any greater intensity. "Stay to the right," some guy told us a while back. "When you see the train trestle on the right, them rapids just ahead, if you're on the left, you're dead."

Train crossing the high, high trestle, iron, majestic, levitating in an open patch of forest just as the early light of dawn sets a white fire to the haze of morning river. Long, long freight train of boxcars old and authentic, like Boxcar Bertha and Kerouac and every hobo for a hundred years. I think of Thoreau and his crotchety bitchin' about the iron horse invading his natural world, and us now, in the age of cars and jet planes shouting a nostalgic "Wow!" at the sight of it roaring by, filling up the river canyon with sounds of thunder.

Those southern boys fishing off that bright blue pontoon boat, fishing quiet and we lolling by in empty beer can-loaded canoe yelling, "Hey, cow!" to some fat smelly fly-infested clan of black cows standing belly deep in the river, no doubt blowing it for those fisher boys, for the moment anyway. Passing them, Spiceman asks what they've caught and it's nothing, just little things they been tossing back. But yesterday, and now again today just up ahead, giant fish leap from the water, flash in the sun, and splash back down, which only means something bigger is chasing them. We could just hold out nets as we cruise languidly north toward Port Royal, beer in one hand, and catch us a mess.

All the time thinking 'bout where we should be, where we could be, up there walking the Blue Ridge Parkway through Shenandoah land, following the blazes from hot dog stand to vending machine. Ah, who knows? That's just what I heard about the 'doahs. Too civilized. Too many cars and road crossings.

Out here on the green green river there is forest aplenty but parted for us like Moses parts the Red Sea, a wide path of golden sun on churning water, choppy, now calm, but always moving, making rowing an easy thing. Started Tuesday night when we put in near Elkton to Mike's wide-eyed amazement and childlike enthusiasm and spun the canoe, immediately plunging backwards into our first small rapid with Mike passing by up on the bridge waving and honking and no doubt getting one hootin' good laugh out of that.

Tuesday night about five river miles, easy, and camping drunk and stoned at dark in some field. Wednesday another 25 miles perhaps and a stop in some hamlet, a ride to the store with two scary looking but ultimately harmless white boys all muscle and big tattoos and drunker than us on any day. Me staying with the canoe in the rain, PG and a very stoned Spiceman going with and returning unharmed and bearing a case of PBR and three "special beers," tall pint-sized Yuengling lagers, a beer that claims to be the oldest in America.

Then Spider Island that night and hacking out our place in the jungle, searching out dry timber in the bug- and spider-infested underbellies of fallen tree roots and under logs where the day's rain hasn't reached. Big fire that night. On the river, great blue herons, turtles plop-plop-plopping from every exposed stone and branch sticking out. And we three cooking like lobsters and loving it after the dense and shady woods of AT ridges where, in point of fact, the shade is gratefully enjoyed on heavy romps in 90- degree heat and high humidity, trekking hard and fast with Maine in the periscope spyglass of our downcast eyes, our trail-focused minds. Run through the jungle, down the Green Tunnel.

After another 25 miles or so yesterday and a dozen now on Friday, we'll likely finish today In Bentonville. Yesterday weird with widened river going shallow and lots of rocks beating out a jangling jungle beat on canoe bottom, and all of us hot and PG hotheaded, not wanting any special treatment from Spice or me, and finally just dropping overboard like an Eskimo suicide and splashing in and feeling better, all of us feeling better with every swim and dip and swing from rope or drop from high tree branch into water. Water water water. At base, what more is there to life than water?

Sacred water of life, even given that we wouldn't drink it to save our lives, with cows swimming in it and all that agricultural runoff, none of it appealing, but water, sweet cooling water. We jump in and it doesn't matter. It cools and the whiskey shines, flashing caramel brown going down with knock-off cheap brand Cokes; the whiskey shines and smiles and we are all high on the river, making miles and saving our poor beaten feet. Now it's shoulder pain and sunburns but all of it beautiful and soaked through with the magic of Shenandoah, the river, the floating trail where Spiceman, PG, and I became fast friends.

I'm asleep face down in a field by the river, my nose and cheeks pressed against a laminated Virginia state map, laid out to keep the grass and bugs from tickling my face whilst I sleep. I'm hot and tired and happy as a bovine up to her teats in cool flowing river water. I awake with a start and Spiceman hands me a cool Coke, a big smile on his face.

Yesterday, far downriver from Spider Island, he discovered his trekking poles missing. One hundred forty dollar Black Diamond poles, M.I.A., left on Comatose Beach after a night bleary of memory from a full day of whiskey and pills and sun and fun and beer. Comatose Beach, our gonzo given name for our 8x12 patch of sand on Spider Island. Spiceman recalls little of the night, including failed attempts to erect his Beta Light tent, a tarp-like tent that uses a hiker's trekking poles as tent poles. The next morning in the pale light of new day dawn and spider-bite hangovers and the ever-pressing junkie-like urge to move Onward! The poles easily escaped a lackadaisical inventory of the beach and were left behind forever.

When you're hiking the trail, you know very quickly if you've forgotten your poles. Not so out here on the river. Ten miles or so later, their absence was at last noted. I don't know how. For by then we were drunk again.

Poor Spiceman, I thought. First he loses his special spice, a baby food jar full of green bud left in some field the first morning. Then his poles. I don't deal in spice: can't handle the paranoia. So I don't know which loss was more costly. Probably the poles.

So now up comes Spiceman with a big grin and a couple of Cokes and he's got through on the phone at Down River Rafting, the only phone for miles, kindly provided by owner John whilst his prick competitor across the highway told us, with phone in hand, that we'd have to hike several miles to the state park for a phone. Anyway, Spiceman got through to Garret at Black Diamond to see about replacement poles. I'm just dying to hear what story he gave the company rep.

"I told him I'm off the trail, doing a little aqua blazing, giving the feet a rest, brought my poles along to set up my Beta Light tent (also a Black Diamond product - hear the smooth pitch?), and well, there was bourbon involved and a lot of beer, and then Garret says, 'You lost them.' I say yeah."

Spiceman told the truth. Now Black Diamond, via their rep with a good rap, Garret, is Fed Exing Spiceman a brand new set of poles. Unbelievable.

I guess it's true what I've heard along the trail. The gear companies really are eager to please the long-distance hikers. They know how word travels on the trail, and a bad rap, well, they don't want it.

But wow, man! To replace a guy's poles when he comes right out and honestly admits losing them in some gonzo mad river re-enactment of Fear and Loathing in Vegas! Olympian thruhiker's poles lost in an off-trail drunken haze! You've got to love it! God bless America, and Black Diamond, too.

We're back on the river and near the end now. Looks like some Class Two rapids up ahead. Better pack up the keyboard and Palm Pilot, slap 'em in their little triple-thick Ziplocs and throw 'em in the dry bag, as I have done a hundred times in the past days. Gonzo journalism on the water. Hunter S. would be proud!

[Postscript: Almost all of the preceding Shenandoah River chapters were in fact written while under way, in my lap, on the water in a heavy-laden canoe full of booze and 450 pounds of hard hiker meat (we three) whilst bedeviled on all sides by splashing crashing waves, diving turtles, and swooping pterodactyl-like blue herons, all moving at incredible speed downstream in the good, God-fearing, backwards-ass antigravity and illogical direction of NORTH! Yes, folks, we're still headed to Maine. We were just coloring outside the lines a bit and loving it! It was ecstasy every league, every liter, every mad gonzo mile of the aqua blaze!]

Now it's The Center City Motel, a slightly seedy siesta joint in Front Royal, Virginia, courtyard-style with a fifties neon sign announcing in blinking pink and green, "Yes! We have air conditioning!" Here in Room Four, Spiceman and PG and I have all the trimmings, the unintentional M.C. Escher-esque pattern bedspreads and damn-near burlap towels and spackle patches in the wallboard where some one or another punched through and the Pakistani management has yet to catch up with beige semi-gloss paint. Altogether not a bad place for a ragged-out hiker in need of a wall plug to charge digital camera batteries and to lie on the floor typing, feeling every bit a beached whale with PBR in easy reach and all naked but for silk SpongeBob Squarepants boxer shorts. But not a whale anymore. No! A man unrecognizable to himself, a "ripped" man, a model of wiry male musculature like some found object sculpture, a man of wound wire and a head of rigid, razorback hog hair. Who is that man in the mirror?

PG on the phone to New Hampshire tells folks at home how she's thinking about hiring someone to carry her pack for her the rest of the trail. "A little Incan warrior, perhaps," she says. Me on the bed writing incessantly, trying to crank out this story before the next chapter begins, I chime in singing, altering a popular INXS tune, "Your own, personal, sherpa! Someone to heft your pack, someone to smack!" Party Girl ignores me and continues her phone call. I keep forgetting that probably half my cultural references are lost on PG and Spiceman, as both were in diapers whilst Duran Duran and The Bangles were blinding adolescent me with science and strange eighties synth-pop tuneage fish.

Out here on the AT we are all ancient and immature, all sages and silly punch-drunk saints, all lost boys and lovers and angels and outcasts, all growing and stumbling and trying, trying, trying, some dying on their feet, most dying to beat the if-nots and no-ways and good-luck-you'll-never-make-its heaped upon us by a world of underachievers, a culture of doubt and fear. Young and old, we, the trekkers of this and other long-distance pathways in America and across the globe, are ageless giants, unsung heroes in our time.

Though few of the general population have any idea the AT even exists, and even fewer Wal-Mart shoppers will ever know that Spiceman or PG or Maine Sail, Mockingbird, Sox, Flatbed or Whiskey or I once stood upon the cold stone pinnacle of Katahdin and said, "I did it!" it just doesn't matter. I now know after three months of constant proximity with vagabond giants that I, too, am a giant and the most regal of vagabonds. No house, no matter how palatial, will ever compare to this 2,000-mile star-roofed home we walk through and sleep in every day. Not ever. Not in this price range.

Philosophy aside, I've a few facts I would like to impart, for the record:

Yours truly got it in his head (after hearing the term from another thruhiker weeks ago) that "aqua blazing," if for no other reason than it's such a cool-sounding word, that aqua blazing the Shenandoah Mountains (rather than hiking them) would be really, really cool. He, that is to say, I, got it so firmly in his head that he quizzed and queried and lobbied every hiker within 50 miles of the Waynesboro YMCA in hopes that someone or ones would be interested in joining him on said adventure.

Trail Angel Mike "Gravy" Brubaker (after first serving up a killer pro-bono hiker BBQ with his friend, Korpi, last Sunday) bent over backwards and forwards and performed logistical contortions of a superhuman kind to help me realize my river-blazing dream. Mike is a trail angel of the highest order, one who not only comes out for a day and gives of his food and time to hungry hikers, but goes far beyond that. Mike drove all over hell and back to get us a canoe and get us on the river and ferry us around for ample supplies and pick us up 75 river miles later and deliver us to Fort Royal, leaving us at last with beer and Gatorade and grapes and bananas and Pringles chips. His parting words to me: "Doing things like this, keeping up with you guys on the trail, it helps build the anticipation for my trip two years from now. It's like it allows me to do the hike from work."

Spiceman would like it known that he was lured entirely against his will into this mad aqua-blazing act of piracy. Any and all blame for his apparent misconduct and gross divergence from the strict AT white blaze code of honor should fall on Osama bin Laden, since said terrorist got off entirely too easily when all the blame for his actions was suddenly and quite ironically foisted upon the Butcher of Baghdad and, with the aid of massive doses of reality television and aquifer-introduced Valium and soma, 280 million Americans were made to forget him altogether. Bad Osama! How dare you make Spiceman aqua blaze with us! Bad, evil Osama!

Now it's pancakes and scrapple and coffee, coffee, coffee at L Dee's Pancake House here in Front Royal. Lovely night of motel comfort last night courtesy of PG who said, "Jester, it's my treat. If it weren't for you, I wouldn't have had this excellent aqua blaze adventure!" Works for me. Forking out the dough for motels gives me a real pain in the groin, as it were. It inflames years of ingrained poverty consciousness. With so many free hostels and campgrounds and the entire free forest, I'd rather spend what little dough I have on good food and beer.

So last night PG and Spiceman went out to shop and resupply and PG took with her a short list of stuffs I needed and took my laundry (all one pair of shorts, a shirt, and socks) and washed them with theirs and brought me back McD's burgers to boot and all the while I wrote and wrote and wrote trying to wrap up this story; and when it came down to turning the TV on, good girl PG was even kind enough to abstain so's to allow me to concentrate and into bed they crawled, and I doused the lights and typed then in the dark by the thin beam of my headlamp and the reassuring whir of the air conditioner.

Somewhere across the world, agro pissed off towelheads take another American head, and I think, thank God for the woods and the blissful ignorance of us, rowing, trekking free, and full of beans high through the mountains of the East, oblivious. But not oblivious, of course. There's just no escaping the news.

I think of Linda back in Idyllwild who sent me a box of "blondie" brownies that I never received. I haven't heard from her since, as she no doubt thought me ungrateful. Poor Linda. But the postal workers of Appalachia are bogged down with thruhiker packages piled high like Christmas, and open thus to error, scanning the shelves full of General Delivery packages and missing one or two, figuring they've found them all. So now I need to find out what town them blondies are sitting in and get 'em forwarded to me and eat 'em up, yum yum. I hope she sent them Priority. Postal lady this morning told me with Priority shipping the USPS will forward them, unopened, as often as needed.

Then there's Mr. Strick.net, in my mind these last few days when I noticed a surplus in my PayPal account and discovered he'd sent another donation to the cause. God bless him. I can count my *Jigglebox* supporters over the years on one, well, two hands, I guess. God bless every one of you who believe in the Holy Grailesque Quest of this Gonzo Author. You are the few, and must count yourselves the proud.

Thoughts of Dad this morning with Father's Day just tomorrow and me all spun out on river dreams and trail magic and town-stop resupplying, but wow! So happy happy full of fat Buddha joy to hear Dad on the phone from New Hampshire the other day praising and raving 'bout the writing, loving my AT journal, his voice all full of pride, and me, not knowing I did, needing to hear that pride, big time. "The way you describe your hike, I feel like I'm right there with you. I can see the roots, the rocks, the sky, fantastic." Something like that. I love my Jesus-lovin' Dad and am pleased as punch that he's enjoying my not-altogether pious or God-fearing gonzo ramblings. Happy Father's Day, Dad.

I sit here watching peripherally as PG and Spiceman chow down breakfast while I slurp coffee and type maniacally, knowing that soon I'll be back in the Blue Ridge and out of the service area. I need to zap these words out now, out into the ether amidst the invisible gridlock of cell phone conversations and radio waves and TV waves, microwaves, gnarly rip-curl waves, you name it! Spiceman with his jawbone beard and goatee and curly hair looks every bit Bob Dylan at age 21. He chomps a banana, and I thank God he's still with us after our mad rockface scrambling a few days ago on the river, sans rope and stoned above the river. All seemed well as Spiceman fingered his way up that face like a pro, doing finger jams and hard reaches and always dangling high out over the river. I followed but got not nearly so far up as he, when, feeling stuck, I let go and launched backwards through space to the safety of deep water 20 feet below.

But soon Spiceman was damn near outta sight some 60 feet up and in the midst of loosely rooted cliff-dweller plant life. Then we heard the raking sound of a lost footing, and the tiny trees fluttered and rocks cascaded down to the river as Spiceman slipped and barely caught himself. He gave us a good scare. For unlike my fall from flat rock face to river straight below, the debris falling from Spiceman's perch hit a lower shelf before ricocheting into the water below. Had Spiceman fallen, this consequent happy tale of river fun would have been anything but. Unless, of course, Spiceman is a Bumble and didn't tell us! For as you may recall from animated Christmas tales of years past, Bumbles bounce!

From the little yellow box in my pocket on this humid Virginia daydream morning Aerosmith sings "Sweet Emotion," and I'm feeling all that on this June 20, 2004, my Three-Month Anniversary on the AT! A scout troop 30 boys camped all around us half-dozen thruhikers last night. We were holed up in the Molly and Jim Denton Shelter, under siege by a teen scout tent city. Not really, but last night around 10-ish when sleep seemed like a good idea, there was no having it for the boys. I hopped up, had a cold dunk beneath the spring-fed gravity shower, and, having no towel availed myself of the scouts' fire to dry off.

When they discovered I was hiking from Georgia to Maine, they asked many questions. I answered, feeling suddenly heroic and grand and Buddha-like in that Massachusetts-born, baked-bean-eating, port-swigging hobo Kerouac kind of way. Their eyes were full of young wonder and wowness as they tried to imagine a trail so long. Once dry, I said my goodnights, returned to my loft bed in the swanky-built Denton Shelter (the first heading north outta Port Royal), popped a few Excedrin PM, plugged into Skynard's "Freebird" at peak volume, and passed clean out, Party Girl and Spice snuggling tight in the bed beneath me.

I awoke snug and warm and hearing the complaints of all those who froze in their summer bags in the 40-degree night. Ha! After so many sleepless nights cold and uncomfortable in my summer fleece and that damn hammock tent, I made the wise choice to keep reclaim my 20-degree REI bag from the post office (and wash it four times!) and pack off the hammock tent and, grudgingly (but a must due to weight concerns), my Mountain Hardware sil-nylon tent as well, keeping only the hammock's rainfly and the stakes, an adequate shelter weighing less than a pound instead of the four-pound tent.

BUT I KEPT THE BAG! YEA! Not to celebrate the frozen-ness of my compadres this past night, but thank God I kept my warm bag. This bodhisattva sleeps cold, baby, and I need the snuggle-bug warm biscuit groovy gravy goosedown of my REI bag. Amen.

TWELVE

The Hilltop Hotel Lounge Lizards...Nayber, The McCleary Clan and Conscious Inaction...My Ankle Needs a Beer...Beth Who? Weird Phone Call to a Lost Cousin...Antietem and the "Froag" Girl Little Princess of Innocence...Losing Heart with Pennsyltuckey Coming Up...James Spader's Twin and the Dudes & Dykes Misconception...Powder Finger, a Tragic Loss...The Drunk Cannon Marathon and The Doyle At Last!

Chef massages the upright piano in the barroom of the historic Hilltop Hotel here on a ridge high in Harper's Ferry, high above the confluence of the Shenandoah and Potomac Rivers where all this crazy Civil War shit went down, cannon fire, death, betrayal of brothers, mayhem, madness, and what's that? Archaeopteryx is a walking Civil War encyclopedia. He tells of the South taking siege of the Union armory RIGHT HERE!
Chef takes siege of the hotel bar, empty but for us, takes over the piano and has us all groovin' to his gentle Zen talent suddenly unleashed (there aren't many pianos on the trail); and Party Girl and Spiceman sitting here and all of us drinking beers bought at the local drug store and poured into bar glasses (procured by me from behind the unmanned bar) and used for the purpose of pleasing the management who won't (naturally) allow us to supply our own alcohol but will turn a blind eye if it looks legit. Obviously not under the best management, the slack nature of the Hilltop scene is greatly to our advantage. I mean, picture the scene: a handful of thruhiker bums sitting in the lap of luxury in an regal old setting with 180 degrees of million-dollar view.

Harper's Ferry marks nearly the midway point on the trail at 1,000 miles! It is home to the Appalachian Trail Conference, the Foundation that coordinates all trail maintenance and events, and records thruhikes. Here we have all signed our names, been photographed, and become part of Appalachian Trail history.

Now the alleged bartender is in, though he has no customers. He's trying to explain the hotel policy, and manages to get one of our group to pay for a drink, but otherwise my "grab your own glass" deal is working. In now walk Don't Matter, Don't Mind, and their nephew, Don't Bother. Funny group of names.

The Shining. That's the comparison everyone is making to the place as we sit in our historic hotel with Chef on piano, and then Chef stops; and I say, "Hey, Chef, don't stop, man, we got something going here!" But it's hard to translate to these guys the absolute anarchic beauty of this golden sunlit clifftop hotel moment that any poet would relish and say "Keep it going!" The bartender, who looks suspiciously like Joe Pesci, keeps coming in and diddling around behind the dead bar and saying how we need to buy our drinks and that if the owner comes by we're all going to be kicked out of the place, but who cares!

This is Harper's Ferry and every one of us has walked a thousand miles to get here, and wow! We ought to all be proud as tidal waves and typhoons and peanut butter tycoons, every one of us. But, of course, neuroses abound, starting with Party Girl, who isn't feeling too great cause she thinks she didn't do the right thing, didn't walk the last 12 miles into town because of a few bad blisters on her feet, and had to be driven into town by the New Hampshire-ite caretakers of the Blackburn Trail Center, Bill and Sue, who last night fed us a giant spaghetti dinner with green beans and free sodas all around and bread pudding dessert and then let us sleep on the grand screened-in porch—wow!

I go up to the bar and ask the woman now inventorying the booze and locking up cupboards what her name is, and think I hear Genita. I ask Genita how she is, and she says, "No, my name is Lenay." So I say, "Okay, Lenay, what do you think of this? You got yourself a free piano player, it's too bad you have no patrons." Lenay says she was trying to say, "Do ya need a bartender?" Genita-Lenay says she'll be back in a minute.

When she returns, Chef has quit the piano for the fifth or sixth time. Joe Pesci returns, and I talk him up a while, feeling kind of bad for him, apparently sent to babysit us, and wanting to include him in our little scene, a kind of way of thanking him for putting up with us. I marvel at the view and the location and the old historic building in general and ask if he knows what the last selling price for this place was. Pesci says $3.5 million. Wow! You have to see this place to understand. I would buy this place at a loss. It sits atop a pinnacle hill far out and far above everything here in the eastern tip of West Virginia, the Shenandoah River churning by in shallow water far, far below in golden sunlight late afternoon, all of 7:30 p.m. now on this 22nd of June. I would buy this place for the view. I would buy this place to glue

Chef's ass to the piano seat and make him play for eternity whilst I type endlessly on my portable keyboard to everyone's annoyance. "All work and no play make Jester a dull boy."

Now it's pushups and talk of muscles and Chef is excited because he finally has an ass, and Spiceman says he has to admit that he admires his calf muscles a lot nowadays. Me too. It's me doing the pushups. Hell, I'm 37, and it's kind of novel to be able to DO pushups and to be able to RUN down or up trails like a madman, down especially fun using my Leki poles to vault three and four feet at a time. I practically leapt into Harper's Ferry at two this afternoon. I have to get the V-shape upper torso thing going to match my monster thighs!

As though in payment for the sin of bringing up that scary movie, I am now transported to some weird frikken sports bar with giant screen TV sporting horse races and video games of golf, all the usual bad and tacky MGD and Bud sports mirrors. On the big screen we have scores for "Tank Grrrl" and "Midway Girl" and I'm thinking, man, if we could unleash the lioness in PG, it'd be Party Girl all the way winning 1000-to-1! Here in this bad-taste bar or back in that great old historic bar, either way, we are all one thousand to one. Each of us, to a man or woman, has stomped on the terra, in the sense that Lord Buckley meant it, I am sure, and far, far beyond that. We have all walked a thousand miles, and I remain alone a man, a man alone on the testosterone trail, and Elly discovered today so very, very far ahead of me. Tonight in our hotel room, PG will curse me, jealous perhaps of my long call, such fun sharing my joy with Mary in Texas! I should be the jealous one as they two, PG and Spice, will be together tonight, and I will rise in morning sick in the wake of a manic high and leave them both and go.

Go! "Go roll your bones, alone!" Kerouac said. It is nonetheless a grand occasion I will never forget.

> *Dear Elly,*
>
> *Remember me? I wanted to write and express how very pleased I was to arrive at Harper's Ferry and discover that you had not quit the trail. And wow! Not only had you not quit, but you've made incredible time. Number 100! I'm so very proud of you, and happy for you, and have no doubt you're nearly in NH now and will surely finish. I regret that I lacked the patience and/or understanding to cope with your intensity. Unlike you, my melancholia has robbed me of righteous indignation and left me rather cowardly. I did enjoy*

your company, your laughter when you laughed, your smile, your intelligence, and learning all about your life at Twin Oaks. I meant all the nice things I said, and despite what may have looked like ease, I was anything but comfortable with saying goodbye. I had really hoped that we could merely hike along and be friendly. But I'm sure you did the right thing for you. I, alas, passed through Harper's Ferry Thruhiker #410! Quite the difference. I'm having serious doubts of finishing. You really helped launch my hike on a pleasant foot. I don't know if you've any fond memories of me, but I am sure glad our break didn't cause you to quit. Please forgive me if I hurt you, Elly. I wish you only the best. – Rick, a.k.a. "Jester"

Early in the day I write: "I'm halfway thru Maryland, 'charging the light brigade' to get over the state line into Pennsylvania by tonight. I'm hating the trail right now, but sssshhh. Don't tell anyone, including me. I'm doing my best to fool myself. This is feeling more and more like a job and no fun. I hump it over rocks all day, pushpushpush, stare at my watch anxious for lunch break."

Following 19-year-old Big Stick through the darkening evening woods of Pennsylvania, it occurs to me that I've been humping it over every boulder and jamming along at the tireless gait of a 19-year-old for days now. Martin Sheen's voice as Willard comes to me from *Apocalypse Now*, as he reads through Kurtz's top-secret file, about Kurtz dropping out of the brass and applying for a transfer to airborne, back to boot camp basically, and Willard saying, "They must have thought he was some far-out old man humpin' it over that course. The next youngest guy in his platoon was half his age."

On this late-June night, I am that far-out old man as Stick, with energy to spare, strums his guitar and the molten gold light of last sun sets fire to the tops of trees to the east and all the world is north to us. Ever and always north.

Pulled a 23-mile day yesterday, 18 to make it out of Maryland into Pennsylvania by the 27th, my lucky number, and another five miles to get to the next nearest shelter. Day before that was another 19 or so, to about the middle of Maryland and some shitty shelter in the rain, half a mile from a roaring freeway. Major drag. Looking back one day further to Thursday, spent the day varnishing ancient windows in some historic building on the Potomac, a building with cannon thunder in the cellular memory of its bicentennial beams of ancient wood, no doubt. I evicted spiders as I went, slathering toxic varnish on their egg sacks and remnant webs. Seems like my days are filled with spiders out here on the trail midway to Maine. Seven hours painting, then, pack hefted, I set out across the footbridge over the river, out of West Virginia and into Maryland for a whopping seven miles in the early evening.

That night was Deer Lick Shelters, beautiful wooded abodes amidst wonderful company. Which was a damn good thing because I needed it. Foul mood. Lonesome. Bad foot pain from continually hiking on my now 1,000-mile-old shoes, light distance runners not meant for such endurance. Met Nayber, Phlegm, El Paso, and a Mark that night. All but Mark are former thruhikers, from two years ago, I think they said. Nice guys. They came loaded with groovy foodstuffs from Trader Joe's, a West Coast-founded exotic food store whose brands I never expected to see in the East. Some was for their personal consumption that night, but most was earmarked as thruhiker booty to be distributed to whatever thruhikers they met on their one-night "angel hike" out. Well, guess who was their only thruhiking customer?

Man, those guys were happy to see me. Nayber busted out a little bottle of Cuervo and we toasted to present, past, and future hikes. Perhaps thanks to all the residual varnish fumes, I was high as a kite in no time. Mark, a section hiker from Annapolis, either arrived after or was already there when I arrived, I can't recall. But in either case, not being a thruhiker, the poor guy didn't get the goodies like I did. Nor the adulation. Unfortunately, the day's labors had sapped my energy, and I crashed fast, crawling up into the Swiss alpine lodge-like loft of the ginormous-beamed log cabin shelter. I must have slept like the dead, because they made a fire and Phlegm played flute, and I never heard a single blue note.

I left Friday morning with a promise from Nayber of replacement shoes that he said he'd send me to my next mail drop. I told him I couldn't accept a gift of new shoes (trail running shoes run $100 or more), but he assured me he had tons of used hiking shoes. If I never hear from him, twas at least a sweet gesture. My poor zapatos are destroyed.

I called Lowa shoes damn near two months after talking to the Lowa sales rep at Trail Daze, my procrastination owing entirely to the way the Lowa rep dissed me that day. So now on the phone beside some famous Civil War battlefield that I don't know dick about but can just feel the death of the place, the sadness, the smell of the blood in the soil, a disembodied voice tells me this call will be recorded. I've got one hand on my Palm Pilot and I'm thinking, "You bet your ass it will," when a guy named Mike comes on and gives me the brush-off, saying, "We get thousands of AT hikers calling us every year. We KNOW what YOU guys DO to our shoes out there on the trail." What? "Mike," I said, in an honest, Charlie Bucket, the-meek-shall-inherit-shit tone, all I did to your shoes was walk in them."

It's "The Bluegrass Show" on 107.7 Great Country Radio here at Quarry Gap Shelter, Pennsylvania, June 27, 2004! It's Big Stick and Austin and Mousebait and White Patch and Dutch and me around a little fire with the light fading in the western sky and the forest a neon green all around, rhododendron blossoms perfuming the air and a spring popping water right out of the ground and trickling through this Japanese garden-like landscape out front the shelter and me on a park bench writing on my little pack pillow and drinking a Bud and remarking how closely the radio station's call numbers match this milepost on the trail: Mile 1070. No, this ISN'T a normal shelter environment. It's like some kind of country club version of the typical run-down spider-infested lean-tos we sleep in. I lift the little red, white, and blue can of beer skyward and thank God for the McCleary Clan, all 20 or so of 'em down there in Caledonia State Park. How we came to meet Grandma and Grandpa McCleary and their kin went something like this.

This morning around 11, I twisted my ankle bad. In seconds, my pace dropped from about Mach 5 to zero. I was screaming. But I had it coming. I thought to myself, "Now see, there you go! Thinking about your troubles 3,000 miles away and loves-long-lost and other worries far, far away from the here and now," and whammo! My body says, "Well, here, wanna worry about shit that don't matter? Let me twist your ankle and drop you like a stone and voila! You're present now, aren't you? Think about this for a while!"

I thought about it all right. I thought about my ankle for hours thereafter, grimacing with every step yet sending healing power to the ankle and leg that had given me so much trouble back before Trail Daze but had been so good to me since. I walked chanting, "White light to the right," a sort of quantum tool drawn from some cellular depths and spoken over and over on a subliminal level. On a more audible level, one might have heard me from a mile away as I shouted, "MY ANKLE NEEDS A BEER!"

Ask and you shall receive. I tell you, I have seen that adage evidenced more out here on the Appalachian Trail than ever before in my life. Most often I don't even have to ask. I just think it. Or it comes, as though the AT in its entirety were one long phonic wonder, a vortex of sound and intention wherein a whisper uttered on Springer Mountain, Georgia, can be heard clear as a bell on Katahdin, a thousand-mile crow flight away in Maine.

Big Stick is not your typical 19-year-old. He listens. He seems genuinely interested in my views on life and art and following one's passion and the books I've read and films I like. As we hike together, he stays with me and listens to everything I say. I feel as though I sound like a crackpot. But still he listens.

I can't swap movie dialogue with him, like Python skits or damn near anything in my vast mental archive of trivia, as he has missed 18 years of my life. Even contemporary references fail, leading me to believe he's lived in a sort of cultural vacuum his entire 19 years. But perhaps it's me. No television for 20 years will do that. Despite our lack of common culture, Stick and I get on fine. Now and again, he'll chime in with something brilliant. Like wu-wei.

Wu-wei, says Big Stick, is conscious inaction. It's about being an observer of life right up to the point where your role is needed or wanted. Like timing. I suppose perhaps it's having perfect timing, and knowing that good will prevail. It's not butting in or forcing things.

Well, when Big Stick and I made our mid-afternoon arrival at Caledonia amidst all the picnic splendor of a Sunday summer in America, we were hungry and tired and dirty and thirsty. By now my whole right leg was screaming at me to stop. It really needed a beer, but I didn't see any trail angels and wu-wei was far from my mind.

Now there's this talent in thruhiker circles for improving one's diet via social interaction with picnickers called "yogi-ing." Wingfoot's thruhiker handbook defines Yogi-ing as the "good-natured art of letting food be offered cheerfully by strangers without actually asking them directly." Wingnut adds, "If you ask, it's begging." No, duh, Wingnut.

Now whether this term comes from Yogi the Bear or yogis and Sufis and dharma bums and such, I don't know. But I do recall that when I first came across the idea in Robert Rubin's tale of the AT, it terrified me. I feared that no matter how I might yogi, I would feel like one of the homeless beggars I daily encountered on the streets of Berkeley. Had I given it more thought, pulled back the focus a bit, I would have seen the truth behind my terror. For 20 years, I had persevered as an impoverished poet, all without begging. The idea that perhaps I was already a master yogi, just too proud to admit such, hadn't occurred to me. Thanks to so many, many trail angels in the past three months and 1,100 miles, I haven't had to yogi.

In fact I've never felt less like a beggar and more like the baby Jesus. I have been fed and beered and supplied and transported and gifted and graced befitting a Lord of the Royal Court, a Duke, not a jester. We thruhikers have been so kindly treated. We are all become Lords and Ladies and through the grace afforded us on our journeys north; we should all reach the end new women and men enlightened, philanthropists, benefactors, altruists, and future angels all.

Ah, yes. The McCleary Clan.

Big Stick and I parked near them on accident. Sort of. I mean, we followed the white blazes through the maze of picnic benches and people, keeping our eyes on the trees. When we came to the last free picnic tables before the trail disappeared back into the woods, we plopped down and resolved to rest a while. Me, I slung my pack up on the table, climbed up on the table myself, lay back, and placed my feet atop my pack, at rest above my heart. Big Stick just sat. We were pooped.

Big Stick pulled out the companion book and noted that there was a concession stand across the park by the pool. "Do you want to go there?" he asked. "Is it far?" I asked. "Looks like it." "Then hell, no," I concluded. My ankle was killing. There appeared to be no angels in Pennsylvania. I was more tired and in pain than hungry. Was I thinking about yogi-ing? Sure. But I wasn't movin'. Far as I was concerned, I didn't have it in me to yogi, and now with my leg killing me, I was doubly excused from duty. In truth, however, I had positioned us with undeniable intent in a state of conscious inaction. It took a while, but the wu-wei worked. From the large family gathered at the set of picnic tables 20 feet from us to the north, there came Shooter with the magic question. "Are you guys thirsty?"

Shooter isn't his real name. I wish I could recall his name, but it was soon lost in a sea of names. For suddenly, Stick and I were introduced to the whole family. My head became so full of names that I just lost them all. Except one. Grandpa McCleary's granddaughter, the nurse. Wow. It was love at first sight for me. Then I heard the boyfriend word and remembered where I was and who I was and how far I had to go, and my heart sank straight down to my aching feet.

No matter, for the wu-wei had worked its magic. We didn't do a thing, and the McCleary's came to us. First, Shooter (I call him this because he talked incessantly of hunting) supplied us with a couple of Cokes on ice, real nice. We thanked him, sipped our drinks, and continued our entirely unplanned regimen of wu-wei. Then, sure enough, one of the sweet ladies of the McCleary clan boldly stepped through the invisible stargate and into our parallel reality with an offer of food. "Well, all right," said I. "We surely wouldn't turn that down. Thank you!"

The McClearys were good people, and they fed not only Big Stick and me, but half a dozen of our smelly cohorts as one by one they trickled in. As each hiker came down the white-blazed path behind us, they were fed.

I'll never forget the looks of astonishment as I, suddenly turned teacher, pointed out to the ladies the white blazes on the trees just to the north and south of them. I showed them how their chosen picnic site was in fact right on the famed thruhiker highway. To me, the blazes were clear as day. But not so to the untrained eye. It was a perfect example of how we only see what we want to see. They had picnicked in the same spot for years and never seen the blazes. When they finally did see the blazes, and understood me when I explained that such marks ran all the way from Georgia to Maine and were how we found our way, they were amazed. All the while, White Patch, Austin, Mousebait, and the others were devouring the McCleary picnic offerings. The McClearys happily handed over all the goods.

At last, we said our goodbyes and thank yous and headed off into the woods again. But not without a little treat for later: a six-pack of beer. I packed it out for medicinal purposes, of course, for my ankle, on ice, inside my dry bag in my pack. But we were a group now, and so, painfully but with a smile, I shared with all my friends that night. Thus, the one beer I got, under the circumstances, tasted better than pussy.

Much to my surprise this evening, I realized that today, June 28, is my 100th day. One hundred days of living in the forest. Big deal? Yeah, I think so. It feels, in a sense, even more remarkable than passing the 1,000-mile mark last week. What with aqua blazing the Shenandoah and a dozen or so miles lost to car rides for dental and mental emergencies, it's hard to say exactly how many miles I have hiked. I can say with assurance, however, that when I finish this "round" in Duncannon, Pennsylvania, on Thursday at the Doyle Hotel, I will most certainly have hiked 1,000 miles, as I will then be at mile mark 1,133. But today, tonight rather, is Day 100. Pretty exciting, really. What a strange day it was, too.

I figure I've got Noah and his ark licked. How long was it Jesus wandered in the desert eating peyote and kicking the devil's ass? Couldn't have been more than a couple of months. A hundred days, baby. A hundred days.

Awaking this morning to the loud and monotone jabber-jabber of a female hiker who shall remain nameless. She's nice, but for my tastes she talks too much. Grumpy thus, I set out on addled right ankle into a morning of exponentially increasing pain, worse with every step. Today I'll hike 20 miles, or roughly 40,000 steps. Gnaw on that one ye couch potatoes. Can you say OUCH?!

Then the shorn-head gang-banger-looking guy with the cool Japanese letters inked into his neck gives me four 800-milligram ibuprofens, a godsend as I hobbled near tears at noon. The pain only slightly reduced, I flew in and out of Birch Run Shelter, losing Big Stick, who wanted to stay a while and wait out the coming rain. I was in too much pain. Short of a hotel bed, a morphine drip, and dark curtains drawn, I could see no benefit in stopping. So, as would happen often on my trek, I took off alone just wanting to "get there," wherever there was.

Today "there" was Pine Grove Furnace, some old historic site with an institutional-looking International Youth Hostel that had "tight sphincter" written all over its austere façade, and a state park with more rules than there are words in the Book of Proverbs. I don't exaggerate at all when I say they were posted, every frikken word, in agate type tiny print on giant posters slapped all over the park. It had been my intention to overnight there. But standing there, I felt the vibe, and it was all wrong. I watched with mild amusement (and an itch of impatience) as three of my fellow thruhikers made themselves sick on Hershey's ice cream whilst engaged in the "Half-gallon Challenge," a long-standing AT tradition that for some reason takes place right there, at the tiny general store at Pine Grove Furnace. In a rule-crazed state park, the rules for the "challenge" are simple enough: Show up, buy ice cream, eat it all and voila! You're a winner! You're dead dog sick tonight, too, I'm betting.

While my dairy-sickened friends ambled aimlessly around, zombies ill afoot in a kind of ice cream-induced Thorazine shuffle, a cop car pulled up and parked. Out of the black & white and into the store goose-stepped a gigantic constipated-faced dyke cop with a gun and the posture of a string puppet being pulled upward by its nipples.

I had to get out of there. I made a hard and fast study of Austin's topo map, ascertained that the anal-ass state park and its creepy police force ended a mile up-trail. Freedom! Just 20 minutes away at a good clip. After that, I knew, would be forest, forest, and more forest. Unpoliced, unpopulated. Walk in and vanish. I love the forest for that! So, much to the disbelief of the bloated ice cream champions and late comer Big Stick, who knew I was walking in a world of pain, I said adios and hobbled off. Amazingly, at 6:30 in the evening with the evil ice cream empire behind me and freedom ahead, I no longer felt any pain.

Not for a while anyway. Just to be safely out of reach of Ruleville, I walked a good two or three miles as the sun settled down in the west. Some crazy over-passionate Italian opera filled my ears from the local public radio station as I mounted a long, steady slope of a hill through low shrubs and oak and hickory and hemlock and fir. It was during the opera as I half danced up the trail, forgetting my sprain and feeling good again, that I thought of the date and did the math and realized how far I'd come. I crested a hill and rounded a corner to a lovely cleared flat spot. I dropped my pack and surveyed my night's home.

Several little toads hopped about in the leaves beneath my feet. I walked over and sat on a nice mossy green cushion at the foot of a tree and cooked up a batch of dehydrated lasagna homemade by river angel Mike. Man, was that good! I lay out my army poncho ground cloth, and using my Leki trekking poles, erected a tiny lean-to rain shelter using only the sil-nylon rainfly from that dastardly hammock I so hated, threw down my bag and Thinsulate air mattress, and voila! I was home. Then I sat down and wrote these words.

Called a West Virginia cousin that I haven't seen in 14 years from the pay phone at Penn-Mar Park, a little patch of grass and picnic tables marking the border between Maryland and Pennsylvania. Despite my best intentions, I intuited the moment Renee answered that it would be a weird conversation. Too much distance. I never have been very close to anyone on my mother's side of the family. But I remembered her as being kind of cool, a little older than me, so looked up to in a way, and pretty with long blonde hair.

She had no idea who I was. It took me about a minute to explain. "Beth's son," I said. "Beth who?" I rattled off my mother (her aunt)'s various last names from her maiden name to my father's to her current husband's name. Then my given name. When we finally got through all that, I explained what occasioned this call out of the blue, that I was hiking the AT. As soon as she heard the words Appalachian Trail, she said, "Oh, my brother Rick did that a few years ago."

"Really?" I was stunned. I remembered my cousin Rick as being halfway cool. But as far as I knew, no one in the wide array of both my paternal and maternal relatives had ever done anything terribly extraordinary. Why had I never heard about this? Even as distant as our families are, surely I would have heard of a cousin successfully thruhiking the Appalachian Trail. "So, you taking a week or so to do that?" she asked. Suddenly I wondered just how much of the trail cousin Rick had done. When my estranged cousin Renee found out I was doing the trail alone, she was beside herself. "You know, people get murdered on that trail a lot, just so you know."

Uhuh.

We chatted a bit more, and as the seconds ticked by I could feel my interest in this awkward reach into the past waning exponentially fast. Then she hit me an uppercut. "So is this a midlife crisis thing for you? That's what it was for Rick." Then she came out with this ignorant generality, a statement both sexist and, in this case, entirely erroneous: "All you guys do something like that."

I was speechless.

It had always seemed to me that midlife crises were for guys on the corporate, family path who at fifty or so found themselves missing the freedoms of their youth. I wanted to tell the blood stranger on the other end of the line that this was just another adventure for me in one long string of adventures called My Extraordinary Life. But I said nothing of the sort to Renee. Why bother. My energy would have been better spent explaining God to a goldfish.

In the back of my mind, I could hear Mickey Rourke as Bukowski in *Barfly* whispering "There's no reality here!" Indeed, there wasn't a pebble-sized piece of common ground from which to speak anymore. In Renee's words I heard her mother's voice. I had never much liked her parents. From my scant memories of him and family gossip, her father (although I'm sure a very nice man deep down) was a jackass, a bigot, and a wife-beater. Her mother treated me well on occasion but mostly followed her husband's cue on how to deal with children. In Renee's pessimistic summations of my journey, I heard traces of all my maternal aunts, all much older than my mother and condescending to her and her children.

There in Penn-Mar Park with Mousebait and White Patch and Big Stick, all of us fully halfway along one of the longest unbroken trails in the world feeling powerful and proud and me eager to reach out to a blood relative in the area, I was instead snared by the ugly past and an ignorance of the forest I found both sad and incomprehensible. I was suddenly 10 years old again, a tiny boy Cinderella with three evil stepsister aunts, and proudly showing one of them my pet gerbil and her one-upping me about her pet squirrel that was "much more special" (as though an adult ever need one-up a child).

I said, "Goodbye, Renee," and she said, "Goodbye, Scott."

I hung up the phone and chuckled at her error. Scott is my father's name.

***

We pass right by Antietem Park and shelter, a place infamous for being home to the greatest single loss of life in the Civil War. We don't even stop to sign the shelter log, even though two trail volunteers working on a log bridge implore us do so. A darling little girl of maybe 5 or 6 with a cute southern accent catches a "froag" and holds him frog-hostage in a 12-pack Mountain Dew box. She says he "hopes." That she stands on the blood-soaked soil of Antietem means nothing to her, so I decide it shall mean nothing to me. I feel sorry for all the death and pain man inflicts upon man, but I turn my face from it and walk north.

At the next shelter, a guy sits reading *Wildlife* and *Nature* magazines. From a distance up the road, we saw him hop off his motorcycle and run up the trail. He gives me the creeps. But Big Stick wants to stop for snacks. There are two small shelters here, each with a gigantic pile of stones-around-a-truck-wheel-well fire pit out front. One shelter is labeled "Snoring," the other "Non-Snoring." After 100 days out here on the trail, I understand this joke very well.

Setting out this morning, I got well ahead of Big Stick in a short space of time. We've been walking together for a few days now and I'm surprised when he comments on my quick pace. It is the pace I always walk at now, with the exception of impossibly steep inclines. It is as fast as you could walk on a flat sidewalk without breaking into a run. It is almost a trot. Perhaps he's right, though. My pack grows lighter as I deplete my food supply, and the effect of one less pound is amazing. This is how Flyin' Brian makes 35-mile days. No tent, just a half-pound sil-nylon tarp. No change of clothes. Three days' food tops.

Back at Antietem, the workers said something that irked me. They asked our "numbers," that is to say what number thruhiker we are/were when we passed the halfway point at Harper's Ferry and joined the registry of hikers. When we both answer in the early 400s, one man shakes his head and says, "Hmm, getting up there." I'm thinking, looking at this pot-bellied wanna-be hiker weekend ditch-digger, thinking, "Screw you." This is not a race!

Suddenly I feel as though I am at the end of the pack, and it isn't a great feeling. Man, I just can't go on. I've come 1,100 miles now, and I just can't take it anymore. S'FRIGGIN POINTLESS! I miss SEX, goddammit! Nature without sex is, is UNNATURAL! It's goddamn boring after a thousand miles let me tell ya. I don't know whether Thoreau was a celibate or what. A castrato? Gawd! Banish the thought. A man with no balls! Even my favorite women writers have balls, of a sort. No favorite writer of mine could possibly be sexless.

I sit here by the side of some road in southern Pennsyltuckey and I just want to get up off this frikken rock, heft my pack, stow my poles, and stick out my thumb. This isn't fun anymore! I gauge my progress every day by how far I am from the nearest mattress, the nearest beer, the nearest decent Zero Day town. Ugh. Where is the zeal that got me out here? Where is the love? Where is the sweet woman companion to warm my nights and make the miles fly by with talk of everything and nothing? This is ridiculous.

I've got just 33 miles to go to get to Duncannon and the historic Doyle Hotel where I'm going to check in for three nights at $17.50/night and drink dollar drafts with bawdy women and randy local men and sit in my room and write glowingly of the AT and my adventures this past week. But all I want to do on this Tuesday morning is quit. Aauurgh! I'll get back to you later. I got to walk.

Feeling better here at The Boiling Springs Tavern. Muuuuch better. Locally brewed Stoudt's Pale Ale in hand, another 10 miles, one two-hundredth of the trail behind me. My feet are killing me still, no doubt about that. But I'm happier. Dropped dead at the last shelter after five hours of solid truckin' down the trail. To my amazement, I went undisturbed for a full 45 minutes of total blackout nap, flat out on the shelter floor with nothing but my hand towel rolled up for a pillow. It was bliss. I remember having such a vivid image of some lovely female handing me something that I sprang awake a moment, catching myself in the act of reaching out...for whatever it was. Then I was dead out again.

When I awoke, I tanked up at the nearest spring and hit the trail running. I was in Boiling Springs in just over an hour, some four miles away. Now I'm in a bar, a tavern I should say. Tres chic. Reminds me of the haughty atmosphere of the country club in *Caddyshack,* the kind of place where young people, most of them likely not even nearly-rich, have to act rich and stuffy to make it with the clientele. If I had the sarcastic class and dry wit of Chevy Chase or the pure crass and brazen carefree balls of Rodney Dangerfield, I'd have made some noise in here. But I have neither. I'm just glad to have a beer, and to have made it to Mile 1,107 on my northbound conquest of the Appalachian Trail.

Bartender Mike is James Spader in the eighties rat pack flick *Less Than Zero,* sophisticated, cool bordering on chilly, but then suddenly (also like Spader) friendly like a brother and impressed with me and/or my little technological wonder upon which I type these words. Though I'm unshaven a good week or so, and hiding natty hair beneath my AT insignia ball cap, and I probably smell bad, he keeps the beers coming. I donned my dark blue wool Crew sweater to get in here, on the advice of mammoth thruhiker Caterpillar, who said they wouldn't let him in without sleeves. The high bar and dim tavern lighting hide my mud-smudged shoes and the ubiquitous stains of my one-week-unwashed shorts. I figure if I just keep flashing them ATM-spewn Andrew Jacksons, I can close this place, no problem.

Now Jeff, the owner, comes in and we chitchat and I tell them about Party Girl and Powder Finger, proof positive (in my mind) that the trail is not all "dudes and dykes" as Jeff put it. "You've likely got a few beauties to look forward to in the coming days," I assure them. Jeff and Mike joke about how little I must get laid on the trail, and evidence the fact that I'm sitting in their tavern typing alone and not drinking with one of the aforementioned girls. You got me there, fellas.

What the guys wouldn't get was the good fortune of so much as a glance at Powder Finger.

I later learned, much to my chagrin, that Powder Finger had gone off-trail in Front Royal. Such a soft and lovely countenance I've rarely seen, soft yet solid, confident, Powder Finger looked you right in the eye seeming to say, "Here I am open and free with nothing to hide." I would claim to know Powder Finger not at all but sure I am that from what little I saw that there is mystery and mischief aplenty behind those doe eyes. Had I known I would never see Powder Finger again, I would have proposed to her on the spot in Front Royal, supported her on the trail, married her if she'd let me, carried her to Katahdin if need be.

Okay, three (or was it four?) beers in now, and it is likely time to go find that campground outside of town. Shit toast. I have to backtrack a full mile. I ain't gonna dig that. But there's no camping in town and nowhere for the next 14 miles as the trail dwindles into a series of narrow easements through farmland. So the options are: Hike another eight miles and pay big money at the Super 8, or hike the full 14 miles to the next shelter. It's six p.m. I'm not going anywhere.

Now it's nearly midnight and I'm chuckling to myself as another freight train approaches. Just as it seems ready to crash right through our little "thruhiker camp" clearing in the cornfields outside of town, it roars and crashes and pummels and blares on by just yards from my tent. That makes me giggle. But what's even funnier is Mousebait snoring in her tent a few feet from me. Hell, I'm not sleeping with these trains storming by, so I figure no one else is either. Wrong. Nipply Mousebait is a snoring locomotive. (I said to her earlier in a Russian accent, "Twas your happy nipples what got you in tavern in naught but tank top when all men must wear long sleeved shirt.) Ha. Ha. Ha.

THIRTEEN

...The Doyle and the Dreams of the Ones Who've Slept There ...
a Flight with the Pegasus, Brief but Sweet ... Hitchin' a Ride
with a Ghost ... Independence Day in Parallel Dimension, NH ...
Jesus is a Pita, I'm the Prodigal Son, and the Walrus Ate the Mad
Hatter, Too ... Who's Going to Heaven and Who's Not: the Final
Revised List Revealed ...

On the last day of June, we arrived at last in Drunk Cannon, Pennsylvania,
and landed, blissfully, in the barfly arms of the 100-year-old decrepit Doyle
Hotel, long a haven for AT thruhikers, located as it is smack on the trail at
mile 1,134. I'm on the fourth floor of the old firetrap in a room that, I swear to
God, is the spitting image of the final location shots in the film *Drugstore
Cowboy*, a seedy old hotel where Matt Dillon and William Burroughs eat
methadone and swap war stories of the heroin junkie life. Great flick, one of
the few DVDs I own. In the film, Matt's character, Bob, has been a junkie all
his life, robbing drug stores, finally cleans up, and in the end gets shot and
wounded by some punk kid, and as they wheel him off to the hospital, his
closing line is, "The irony was brilliant. The chickenshit cops were giving me
an escort to the fattest pharmacy in town."
    I loved that. I just loooooove irony.
    Been at the Doyle just 24 hours and already things are getting way out of
hand. The bartender, my love, my life, my future wife Sara, has just admitted
to me that she wants Pegasus in the worst way, that she likes to lure girls off
the trail and take advantage of them. Sara's mother, Sue, strums her guitar and
sings, wrapping the present of an evening bar scene in the ribbons and bows
of acoustic blues, beautiful. Here in the bar in the downstairs of the Doyle
Hotel, Duncannon, Pennsylvania, it's poetry. It is the poetry of peeling paint
and corkboard ceilings bowed by rain, of leaking roof of varicose veins, and
athletes with blisters and barflies listing, gravity tugging them sideways into
the jukebox music of their shiny youthful past, of love that didn't last but will

always be with them, in them somewhere, a caesura or a cancer, and sawdust on the floor soaks up beer, blood, upchuck, anything.

This place a favorite of thruhikers for years now and years to go, I'm sure, with rooms reasonable like thrift store prices and a clientele rife with all the usual vices and tap-tapered 16-ounce cures of all the ills of the sad modern world of terror and cruel, cruel poverty. Pegasus tells me how she likes brutal honesty, so I finally, after an hour or so of build-up, come out with: "I'd like to take you upstairs right now and get nekked, you know, no expectations, I can't promise you much, been drinkin' all day and all, but I'd just like to get naked with you, just be. It's been a long time since I've so much as touched a woman."

Well, Pegasus took it rather well. But she didn't bite. We sit here still an hour or so later listening to the harmonica and guitar riffs and wailing....

[The preceding passage was never finished due to the author being swept away in the clutches of a winged horse and dropped onto a squeaky metal bed and um....]

We apologize for the abrupt cessation of the previous passage, but Net Nanny has censored said explanation. Thank you and good night.

I pulled my longest day yesterday, 26.4 miles from Boiling Springs to Duncannon in one shot, Mousebait, White Patch, and me. A true marathon, much of it over heinous rock fields, miles and miles up and down over toaster- to TV-sized stones. Insane. As such, arrived here early for my Saturday flight. No problem, I thought. I'll write. And write. And write some more. Oh, and drink vast quantities of beer, since I'm basically now living above a bar. Single room: $17.50/night, 22-ounce PBR draft: $1.95.

Heaven.

Owner Vickie took a shine to me immediately. Wouldn't let me go to bed last night without a hug. Bathroom down the hall, pull-string overhead lighting, lottsa caulked holes in the walls, old wooden six-pane windows that threaten to launch out into the night with every touch. Sturdy fire escape right outside my door though. Paradise.

July 3. Mary Parry is a trail angel. She drives hikers the 15 or so miles from remote Duncannon to neighboring big city Harrisburg for trips to the outfitter or perhaps even to the airport. Mary makes it very clear that she doesn't do it to profit from the hikers and will take only gas money. Unfortunately, Mary wasn't available this morning.

Heather, the cook at the Doyle, offered me a ride to the airport two days ago. Heather does profit from hikers. No problem, I say. Just be clear that this is a fee ride, not an act of kindness. Heather, however, neglected to tell me that it would cost me $20 until late yesterday. I slept on it.

After three nights at the Doyle at $17.50/night, meals in the bar, and two good nights of swilling Pabst Blue Ribbon, I just don't feel like forking over $20 for a 15-mile ride. I decide to hike it, or hitch, or both. What the hell. I hike 20 miles a day now! I'm a machine. I've got all day to do it. My flight isn't until 7:30 p.m.

I heft my pack alongside my weekend romance, Miss Pegasus, and together we walk north out of Duncannon and over the bridges of the Susquehanna River. There, the trail is once again a portal, half-invisible, in the vaulting forest canopy beyond the freeway and the railroad tracks. I watch Pegasus disappear into the AT. I turn then and face my day's adventure. It isn't looking good. To my right, the river. To my left, the forest. The only passageways heading southwest toward Harrisburg are the unwalkable freeway and the illegal but navigable railway easement. I walk the tracks.

It's hard walking railroad tracks with the roar of a nearby freeway and a giant pack on your back that blocks your peripheral vision, making a glance over your shoulder a full torso-swing thing. I walk about a mile to the nearest hamlet and a widening of the heretofore thin corridor between forested mountain and river. Here at least there are exit and entry ramps for the freeway. I don't stand long at the onramp before the absolute lack of traffic reminds me that I could be standing here a long time waiting for Grandma or Grandpa hamlet dweller to come out of the house and hit the freeway for their monthly pilgrimage to Wal-Mart. I begin walking a frontage road instead, fairly sure that it will soon end and I'll be forced back onto the train tracks. At this point, I'm walking on pure faith.

I am quickly rewarded. Jumping ahead a moment in the story, let me tell you this. Just north of here on the AT a few miles further than I have yet traveled, there are buried the ashes of a man who long dreamt of hiking the AT from end to end. He managed to section hike parts of it, but fate cut his life short before the fruition of that thruhike dream. Where Mark Noel's ashes rest, there now grow wildflowers from seeds planted along the trail by his brother, Richard.

I know all this because the one car, the only car, to stop (and at this point I didn't even have my thumb out) and inquire if I needed assistance, was a car carrying Richard and his son, Andy. I know this because Richard picked me up.

"It was Mark who picked you up," said Richard. "I haven't picked anyone up in 30 years. But you had that AT hiker look."

Richard introduced himself and his son, and told the story of his late brother, Mark, as he, or Mark, one or the other brother, drove me straight to the airport. "Hiking the whole AT was a lifelong dream of Mark's. This is Mark's doing," Richard insisted, repeating his sense of his brother's intervention in what might have been an impossible airport walk. Looking out the car window at Pennsylvania's capital city as we cross freeways and navigate interchanges and endless city blocks, I must agree with the impossible part and thank Mark for stepping in.

Saying my goodbyes and stepping out into the airport world, I have a wide smile on my face as I shake my head with wonder. On a journey full of seemingly endless favors and kindness and hospitality and graces and trail magic and angels, this one was truly unique. I'd been helped out in time of need by many a trail angel, but real angel Mark beat all.

Thank you, Mark Noel, wherever you are.

Then ding! With the jingle and the brief jostle of an elevator ride, I was in New Hampshire. What name would the Namers of All-Things-AT give to flying a section of trail, skipping ahead, as it were, via Flugzeug? (I've always loved the German word for airplane. Oh, and Hubschrouber, that's another good one, for helicopter.) The sky is blue, but blue blaze is already taken. Perhaps jet blaze! Yeah, I like that. Ding! I jet blazed to New Hampshire.

The intention had been that I would, by early July, have hiked sufficiently close to New Hampshire that my cousin could just zip down and pluck me off the trail in Connecticut or so. But I had only made it to very southern Pennsylvania, so fly I did, my father most generously throwing down for the plane ticket. Most of the week or so spent there is a happy blur, seen only in retrospect, as I was way too busy having fun and truly vacationing from the trail to write a word the entire time. Independence Day was, like every other weekend day or holiday in New England that summer, damp. It rained, but did Cousin Justin let the rain spoil his vision of a wild weekend of pool party and margarita debauchery? Heck no.

[Warning: the following account of one very busy week in New Hampshire was written well after the fact and the author admits to being under the influence of an entire trunk load of Fear and Loathing and other Hunter Thompson literary paraphernalia whilst recalling its events. Open your mind. Remember that truth is stranger than fiction, and endurance more important than truth (Bukowski).]

As I recall, we were somewhere around Tilton on the edge of...well, Tilton in central New Hampshire's lakes region when the drugs began to take hold. I remember asking Justin just what was IN the MSR hydration bladder he'd gone to an outfitter and bought just to make hiker-me feel "at home while drinking." He had suddenly taken on an unearthly, airplane-toilet chemical blue glow. I flipped down the passenger side mirror to get a look at his girlfriend, Jess, in the back seat and sure enough, same glow. When my cousin turned to respond to me, his eyes had gone alien black, and he grinned a wide grin with multilayered, sharklike teeth. Oh, Jeezus, I recall thinking. This is going to be one helluva ride.

Justin had spent a small fortune on fireworks; his mother (my aunt), Mary, a small fortune on booze. Apparently, I'd specially requested top-shelf tequila, fresh lemons and limes, and Grand Marnier instead of standard triple sec. Justin squeezed lemons, and I whipped up some five-star margaritas, and, with drinks in one hand and roman candles in the other, Justin, Jess, Mary, her husband, Chris, myself, and Justin's amigo, Dennis, all ran screaming around their farm in the dark blasting one another with fireballs. Mind you, this came directly on the heels of a long soak in the redwood hot tub in the barn and was performed in the drizzling rain, so there was no danger of immolation involved.

Everyone wore eye protection. Those without prescription glasses wore welding goggles or welding hats with protective face shields scrounged from Chris's metal shop. Afterwards, and before a scrumptious prime rib on the grill dinner prepared by Mary, we took turns running through the rows while those in the driveway unloaded several gross of bottle rockets into the cornfield. It was good clean American fun, and everyone treated themselves to a double dose of Prozac to celebrate our freedom to wage war on anyone we want all around the globe. Gosh, it felt good to be an American that night.

We later drove over to Justin's friend Shawn's house on the lake and got completely twisted. All I remember through the haze of Jack Daniels is standing at the helm of Shawn's parents' speedboat, ripping across Lake Winnepesauki at Mach 5 and Justin screaming at me over the wind, something about larceny and "We're dead!" upon which he returned to his fit of giggles, nailed as he was to the back of the boat by the tremendous G-forces. "I'm not dead!" I howled. "I'm more alive than ever!" I had no idea what he was talking about.

I remember we did a lot of tooling around in my Aunt Mary's new bumblebee yellow and black Jeep. Mary's the greatest, truly the antithesis of all my maternal aunts, although, to the credit of the latter, I never spent a lot of time with mom's much older sisters. But I'm pretty sure that's a good thing. Mary reads like a fiend and is no doubt responsible for Justin being the extremely literate news aficionado that he is. Perhaps because she reads, Mary more than anyone in my family appreciates what I do and how hard I've struggled to keep at it when the world wanted me to get a job. A job! Can you imagine such a thing? Atrocious. An abomination.

Anyway, Aunt Mary and Cousin Justin delivered the goods. All inheritors of depressive genes, we share a love of self-medication via "ye ole cocktail." We put a good dent in the New Hampshire state liquor store that week, let me tell ya. Every morning, Mary whipped up a batch of her famous bloody namesake to kill the irksome ache of last night and lay the groundwork for another day of liquid summer fun. Although Justin's lovely redheaded, sharp-witted and barely-out-of-her-teens girlfriend, Jess, never hooked me up with one of her hottie young friends as I begged her, we did manage to squeeze a lot of fun into that Fourth of July week, including waterskiing, wave-hopping with tear-ass jet skis, pole-vaulting over livestock, rope-swinging and jumping off the train trestle into the river, and, of course, 18 holes of golf with New Hampshire native Adam Sandler, in town to visit his folks.

Jenna Whatsherface from the first episode of "Survivor" is from Justin's hometown of Franklin. She must have been home to visit her parents, too, because we ran into her at this seafood joint on the lake with a dock and boat fueling area out back where my grandpa used to take me to fuel up the boat. Justin's brother's best friend's cousin's sister went to high school with Jenna Survivor, and I was apparently sufficiently intoxicated that night to draw a six degrees of separation connection out of all that, bringing it down to one degree as I sidled up next to her at the bar.

I don't remember saying anything to her, kind of like you don't remember the moments leading up to a major car crash you were in. But according to Jess, who smelled trouble and followed me chaperone-like from our booth to the bar, I laid that line on her from the comedy film *Joe Dirt*, you know, the one with the girl at the fair: "If I told ya you had a nice body, would you hold it against me?" It's that whole useless celebrity thing I was talking about, I guess. I didn't really want her. I guess I just wanted to piss her off. Apparently, I succeeded. The next morning Aunt Mary served up not only a bloody but an ice pack for my right eye. That Jenna Whatsherface apparently has a mean left hook.

Just so you don't think my family and I are a bunch of complete miscreants, we did do something altruistic and selfless that week. We did trail magic! That's right. You see, I wasn't the only AT thruhiker playing hooky from the trail that week. Party Girl was in Contooquack or Loonville or whatever the name of that town she's from in New Hampshire. Big Stick was in the Granite State, too, somewhere on Lake Winnepesauki with his family. We weren't able to contact Stick in time, so he missed out. But Party Girl, Jess, Justin, and I headed up to where the AT crosses some isolated highway just south of the White Mountains with a cooler loaded with hot dogs, sodas, and beer. Oh, and a big jug of whatever insane cocktail had turned my cousin into the Great Black-Eyed Alien Shark back on the ride home from the airport. This was for late-evening consumption, after we'd established camp and spent the day feeding hikers, just in case things got boring.

Well, it was boring all right. Right from the get-go. Why? Because we didn't have one damn thruhiker customer in the two nights spent out there. All I can figure: location, location, location! We were just too far north for the AT in early July, and no one, not even speedy Elly, had yet made it that far north. Sure, we saw hikers and fed or watered a few. But these were all just day or weekend hikers. I'm sorry, but after a thousand miles, I was already a hiker snob. Day hikers just weren't up to snuff. I gave them sodas but sat on the beer cooler with zipped lips until and only after hikers had proven their salt. If they were cool, we gave 'em the works. If they were dorks, they went hungry. We were savage and cruel by the afternoon of our second day. I had wanted to show Justin and Jess REAL thruhikers, and I was sorely disappointed and took out my disgust on every ill-equipped day-hiking dork.

No, wait. I remember what it was that really chapped my ass and had me bad-mouthing hikers just out of earshot. It was that whole "don't talk to strangers" fear thing adults instill in their children. Okay. There are monsters out there, and sometimes children get eaten. This is horrid, but it is nothing new. Look at poor toaster muffins Hansel and Gretel from centuries-old folklore. But after all the beauty and kindness and trail magic of the South, I'd forgotten to fear strangers in the forest. Everyone in the South was an angel. So I was unprepared to be treated like a potential monster by fearful parents out hiking with their kids. But that's exactly how we were treated.

Think what you want, but it had nothing to do with us. The beer we had for beer-thirsty thruhikers was, as I said, hidden from view. So then was the beer we consumed, poured from cans into our Nalgene bottles or plastic cups. Both Party Girl and Jess are extremely attractive women, and Justin and myself are at the very least non-threatening in appearance. But the fear-addled parental units had never seen trail magic and apparently had no idea why we were sitting there trailside handing out sodas and cooking hot dogs. The children, thirsty from a long hike, would dive for our sodas, but the Units would intervene and tell the children, "No, you're NOT thirsty. You can wait until we reach the car."

Yeah. That was it. That was what turned me mean by day's end. I'm disgusted by war. I'm disgusted by television. I'm disgusted that every other show on TV is about cops and lawyers busting people. But what really disgusts me, what I'll go so far as to say I hate, is fear.

Funny. All these years I've been repeating Hunter Thompson's famous phrase "fear and loathing," taking it at face value and enjoying its linguistic weight in describing some general state of darkness surrounding all good and honest pursuits. But you are what you eat, as they say. And the heart listens; the cells listen. Fear has undercut everything in my life; and the loathing, denied expression in the form of healthy anger, has no doubt added to my downfall.

But philosophical bullshit aside, I would rephrase Thompson and call what I felt there in the woods trying to be an angel but being regarded as a threat, "loathing of fear." It pissed me off something royal.

So at day's end, we gave up and retreated to our camp not far from the trail and drank the devil's punch. When in Rome, you know the rest. I wasn't the only one who felt smudged by the largely ill reception of our good deed. So we drank. And out came the politics: abortion, capital punishment, you name it. I learned that night that Party Girl, like Jester, was a misnomer of a trail name. Party Girl was actually a fairly serious, sometimes-contemplative, sometimes-hot-headed woman with stone-set conservative values. If she was the life of the party that night, it was only because her every political stance was so absolutely 180 degrees from those held by my cousin, and to a lesser degree (because I'm about as fond of polarized political parlance as I am of TV), me.

The party, then, was largely a joust between P.G. (as she would later call herself, trying, like me, to shake her given trail name) and Justin, with occasional shouts, screeches, guffaws, and camel-spitting by Jess and myself. I would say it was a drunken joust, and often enough jocular, but there were a few explosive moments, and I recall P.G. claiming she was sober. Anyway, as far as I recall (and this was probably intentional on my part), the debate and all else that night degraded into madness as I took to speaking, nay, shouting in tongues and dancing around and occasionally into the fire like an insane native whose spirit animal is the moth. In the morning, there was rain. A deluge. We packed out and went our separate ways.

Then it was off to Hampton on Friday for an all-family barbecue at Dad's house by the sea. Love my Dad though I do, I wasn't looking forward to a weekend in his wife's house (that's what he calls it). With her daughters grown and moved away and my sister and I gone 23 years ago after our parents' divorce settled, the house is like a little museum of New England-flavored…whatever. Everything is very neat and clean, and one hesitates to besmirch with one's presence. Ever since I arrived fresh off a cross-country train trip years ago, and, upon being shown my room by my father's wife, was told I stank, well, I just feel dirty when I'm there. Not welcome. The refrigerator in my stepmother's house, like most refrigerators in America, has pictures all over it. But there's something decidedly different about her fridge. One, all the pictures are arranged in a neat square, dead center of the fridge door; and two, every member of our extended families way out to distant cousins is represented except one. Guess who?

As a joke, Mary and Justin bought the prodigal son a milk advert knockoff tee-shirt, black with white lettering that said, "Got Jesus?" Oh, how I wanted to wear it. But going to my stepmother's house meant sobering up. Not out of etiquette, but angst. There's nothing worse than being emotionally hungover in a house where the ill-repute is you. With the copious cocktails of the past week, so went my nerve. Thus, no shirt. I mean, I didn't wear it in front of them anyway. Besides, it would have been a conversation starter. The last thing I wanted to talk about after 1,000 miles of walking off the death of a not-likely-religious buddy who blasted his way into Heaven with a double-barrel shotgun, was Jesus.

Not long into the barbecue, Mary and Justin and Jess drove off in Mary's bumblebee Jeep and left me. The sting was almost unbearable. A drive to the beach and some time spent with my lovely stepsister helped a lot. The next day, when my stepmother made a shockingly uncharacteristic laundry blunder and shrank my favorite wool sweater, she sent my Dad and me shopping for a replacement. That done, Dad took me to his old watering hole, a fish and cocktail joint off some ocean tributary in Portsmouth. I watched the sun set over the water and all the pretty boats at dock, and Dad had a few drinks with me (he doesn't drink around his wife) and eased into himself, into a more comfortable version of himself as the father of a nearly 40-year-old man, a man who had inherited all his father's insecurities and proclivity for depression but was this very summer climbing Mt. Everest 17 times. In the golden light of the magic hour my father joked with the waitress and here and there announced my great undertaking to people around us in the bar, and it was good. It made up for the erasure of me from his wife's fridge. In the morning before he took me to the airport, we attended service at his church, and some woman he knew well stared wide-eyed upon meeting me, having never heard he had a son. In retrospect, our sunset moment in the Portsmouth pub makes up for that, too.

So now Jesus is a pita here at the Rye Bethany Church, and the pastor says he will come like a thief in the night. And steal what? I wonder. All our bread? The pita and the rye. Ha-ha hodeeho. (Until today, I'd never seen a communion where the Body of Christ was finely chopped pita bread.) Let him come. Me, I'm gone. Been here, done the family thing, and determined, perhaps once and for all, that discussion of politics or the news or religion is pointless with my father. God bless him. The banquet has been laid out, and he will have his place at the table. Me, I'll return to the pure, unquestioning Christianity of my youth when all Christians everywhere open their arms and say all who believe in a supreme being will be welcome in Heaven, religious affiliation aside.

For now, however, the Jews are out, and forget about the Mormons, the Muslims, and the Buddhists. "Don't get hung up on that," my father says. "Don't get stuck on that issue or you'll never come to know the good things about Jesus." Don't get stuck? Does that mean don't think? Turn a blind eye? Pay no attention to those people being loaded onto boxcars. They're not going to Heaven, anyway. They're not Christians!

I am stuck, thus, at the exclusivity clause. I will probably always be stuck here. Stuck in the Hades between Heaven and Earth. Stuck between the zealous likes of my father and all my independent, intellectual, artistic, and thoroughly anarchistic agnostic or atheistic friends who believe in a different god or no god and find my hopeful belief in Heaven an absurdity.

In my father's church this morning I met a pretty woman named Katie. Very lovely, tall, intelligent, no doubt believes in Heaven. I doubt she smokes, probably my "ideal" match. We chatted briefly.

Katie: "So you're hiking the trail. What do you do for work that allows you so much time off?"
Me: "I do nothing, actually." (My father standing by, horrified)
Katie: "Where do you live?"

211

RICK McKINNEY

Me: "I live in the woods, going on four months now."

I left the church sad this morning, sure that no such woman would ever embrace the likes of me, a broken and hobbling Christian summer camp refugee-gone gonzo drug-addled devourer of earthly life. Despite all the walking, all the depression-busting levity, all the fun where might have run the blood of suicide, at times like this, I feel less the athlete, less the accomplished writer and more the Mad Hatter in an oyster-sucking contest with the Walrus. The Walrus is winning. After 10 days off the trail, I am forgetting. When the oysters are gone, the Walrus is going to eat me, my hiking boots, this book, and yikes! If you don't let go now, he'll probably even eat YOU!

It's July 11 here at the Manchester Airport bar as I await the flight that will return me to Duncannon and the Appalachian Trail, and I'm cogitating.

Where am I? What's it all mean? Will I, when I crest that cold rock far up in New England where Maine juts hard into Canada, will I have written something worth reading, worth publishing? Will I have stomped the American terra and told the tale well enough and with enough pride and gratitude in my American freedoms to please a nation of fear junkies and, maybe, even the poor battle-crazed soldiers in Iraq?

Will I?

Shark fish turbine with whirl of deadly spinning whiskers walks me, effortless, through cumulous sky seas high into the blue July of coming night. Now it's Pittsburgh below like a bad memory fading, and funny it is that God would drop me here as well on this epic journey, after dragging me through Albuquerque and Chicago and all those other memory-laden towns full of failures and faded, jaded faeries, and here I thought Pittsburgh was far enough west of the AT that I would never pass that way and have to think of her.

No matter now! Dancing in the white cotton mountains of pure magical moist air and, thanks to seatmate Linda who switched with me in the last minute before takeoff, her noticing my fascination with the spinning blades outside her window, we're nose to the glass now, in love with the magic of flight. Now high, high! Old Jack hitching everywhere never had it so good! For this day I thank my father, not the heavenly one but the slipping-into-silver salesman dad who bore me into this world; and, with all his faults and follies and mistakes and beauty, he is a good man.

And good his wife, forgiven now for whatever angered me about her years ago in my mad, anxious head of San Francisco 1999 living in the art car Duke and crying and rising every morning to death thoughts, to which tree in the Berkeley woods I would hang from, madness. Me just wanting Daddy, just wanting him but being denied, yes! That was it, though first I dropped the bomb on the wife, holding the grudge as I had for harsh words already old...whatever. Was I forgiven my words and anger and angst? So much pain and ill communication.

But now a new sweater, Patagonia! To replace the shrunken one, and new shoes and new reasons to stomp on the terra and all this heavenly beauty out my window, the window of this Dash 8 doing the tightrope, no, the slack-line over Appalachia. Walking through and over cauliflower mushrooms and explosive milk-white dreams and mountains, peaks no man will ever ascend and should he try, would fall right through, ethereal. The plane, the puddle jumper, as Linda calls it, rocks and shimmies and I just laugh, fearless, not wishing ill on my fellow travelers, but fearless myself, intoxicated by cloud heavens and not caring if I die tonight, for I have seen and felt the rapture of God's best work! Clouds as seen from Heaven.

Which makes me again think of all that hogwash about how only Christians and those who come to know Jesus will get into the Kingdom of Heaven. I don't care if it is written in the Bible, I don't believe it. I love all creatures and see something of myself in Everyman, even he who, should the worst happen, looks me in the eye and guns me down or cuts off my head in the name of his god. His god, my god, your god, it is all one God.

Who has flown who could doubt the existence of Heaven or Grace Eternal? Who could question Heaven who has tickled the tops of snow-white floating worlds of weather brewing? Up here it is azure blue and no earthly mountain, none high enough in the East, peeks through. I want to live up here. I must learn to fly, and soon. I would rise up and never come down. If I knew how, I would fly and never again return to leaden earth. I'd sooner fly into the sun.

[Afterthought on the Afterlife: He would know me, and know my meaning; and my place at the banquet would be set, for there is a place in Heaven for poets and dreamers, a place the scriptures may have missed but which exists. Sure as Jesus was a Jew, and shame on you for believing that a Jew would have any less chance than you, of eternal salvation. We all on this Earth bleed and die and hope and try. We are all going to Heaven.]

FOURTEEN

Pixies with Chiggers and Sweet Gordy Sings...Brewhikers, Purons, and Pink Blazers...Out of the World of Lies Came I...Tampon and Condiment Art...One Night in a Pennsyltuckey Jail...a Thousand Frogs Melted Together, Their Eyes on You Always...My Lyme Tick-Bitten Madman Friend...

Just now recovering from a couple of nights of torrential rains and howling winds from a tornado that literally missed us by a mile or so here in Lancaster County, Pennsylvania. Were I in a car, the odometer would read 1,150 miles now, maybe more.

Sleepytime tea in this old lodge-like shelter, all the makings of a two-story loft lodge minus the one exterior wall. And me on the nod, zonking out in the dark upright at the picnic table, eyes closed, and others all in bed, slipped into their bags and snug, and food hung, and me sniffing my new sweater for signs of burn. No burn. I got lucky.

While cooking the night's dinner over my cat food can stove with denatured alcohol, I accidentally left the butane lighter too close to the stove's heat shield. The red-hot metal melted a hole in the lighter and whooosh! The butane lighter turned into a tiny flamethrower and together with the burning alcohol sent a fireball up into my face. The explosion sure excited the gang! But I was all right. Quite a night, this after hobbling in here with Jackie and her Aunt Chris, the worst ankle sprain I've felt yet.

From e-mail sent out the following day: "Rain rain rain. Ugh. And gorillas on your end! The world is coming to an end. The sky is falling. My feet are rotting from three days of soaked shoes. Tornado in Pennsylvania! An F3 the experts are saying. Tore up a stretch of land seven miles long, winds 200 mph. Really! Happened right nearby yesterday, same county I'm in, whilst I on the mountaintop hunkered down in the trees squat beneath my poncho like Frodo 'neath his invisibility cape. I became a rock and waited out the deluge and powerful winds, impervious. Odd, but what saved us from the tornado was the

214

Appalachian ridge and our comparative elevation. We were literally right in the tornado's path but above its reach. Crazy weather.

Brief sweet moment last night, however, in crowded shelter thus tight up against pretty young Gordy, the wood nymph. She pulled out her guitar and sang angelic, a siren benign without her rocky shoals yet powerful enough in song to pull us all in, every ear in the crowded shelter that night attuned, listening.

I nursed her on my fifth of mescal by candlelight while a dozen guys and a girl or two looked on in the dark, gaga. "Too bad she's southbound," I thought to myself. "I'll likely never see her again." Another ghost, another angel!

Gordy is a ski lift operator in the other world. Her bare legs are long cat scratch posts, all scrapes and mud and bug bites and long gouges and dried blood. Suddenly I am Tarzan, and they're beautiful in a Jane kind of way. I ask about the gouges. "Chiggers," she says. How do you kill chiggers? "Nail polish. You suffocate 'em. They die beneath your skin." Then what? I don't want to know.

Wild girl Gordy strums her guitar, a narrow thing lute-like, and sings sweetly from a handful of damp and dog-eared lyrics somebody printed off the Web and carried, triple-folded in rain-soaked pockets. Now it's the Dead and "I Know You Rider," and Arms, the quiet giant, has joined in on his guitar, peeling off the bubblewrap and tape with which he carefully protected it from the rain. Beat Box, ever the man to reappear in my hike no matter how much time I take off or fall behind or climb ahead, he's there. Heappears here tonight phantom-like, the genie from the bottle, his ever-singing spirit Aladdin. Loquacious and never at a loss for quoted words or lyrics, he seems to stumble in the face of true love. "Gordy, if you were a guitar, you are the one I'd pick," he says.

Now Beat Box has bowed out, gone back to his journal. Gordy sings "No Expectations" and Arms play along here in the loft of the William Penn Shelter. A friend writes and describes swimming with dolphins and though I can only imagine, I feel I can relate after this day of so much rain like walking through waterfalls. Gordy, the siren, the mermaid, gives us music, a higher intelligence than these dull and static words. Tonight, I too swam with dolphins.

My sister, three years my junior, blew the Santa Claus myth for me when I was nine, and I've never recovered. I insisted for years that all myths were truth and still persist in conjuring faeries taking flight in my mind to places of beauty and eternal late-afternoon summer sunlight. But I began to understand eventually that quite the opposite was true of this world. Indeed, most truths I have ever been told by peers and family or sold by crafty advertisers are myth. My father asked me the other day what it was about the "real world" that made me anxious, panicky, paranoid. "Advertisements," I replied, feeling at a loss for answers but hitting it damn close to the bull's eye. "To know that I live in a world of lies."

Back here in the woods of Pennsylvania, there are no lies flashing in my face. Even corporate logos are kept to a minimum as diehard thruhikers strip their gear of labels and most of the small towns we hit lack the usual glut of chain stores. No lies, only rocks. And rain yesterday in buckets and soaking showers. On my first day back out on the trail after this latest break for major resupplying and family visits in New England and the consumption of vast quantities of beer, on my first day back I rolled my right ankle again. Twice. The first not so bad; the second, crippling. I slept and rested it well, taking it slow today.

As I walk I speak this mantra, this prayer: Please let me continue hiking. Please don't send me back into the world of lies. I can think of nowhere safe for me out there anymore, nowhere save a secure lodging, and a room of my own within it, shades drawn against the false night sun of pink-orange streetlights, phone unplugged against greed and collection. I would have access to music and film but ones without advertisements. From such a safe haven, I would surface aplenty, but never long enough to let the sadness of the world creep into me.

Crazy days. Rolling my bones alone, again. Twenty-two miles today, just four days back on the trail after a decadent 10 days off drinking beers and eating and getting zip for exercise. Nada. Then whammo! Twelve miles Monday, twisting my ankle late in the day. Then 17 miles Tuesday. Twenty yesterday. And I thought when I twisted my ankle this time I was finished. It hurt that bad. But I talked to it, and massaged it, and took it slow each day until, as usual, by mid-afternoon and into evening, my pack and I were back at it, dancing across the stone fields of frikken Pennsyltuckey, a ballerina with a hump (the backpack). Now tomorrow just six miles into Port Clinton where I'll pick up my first of a new string of resupply boxes, grab a hamburger somewhere, a shower if that comes along, and then back on the trail for at least a 14 tomorrow. I've decided I want OUT of Pennsylvania by Tuesday night. Today is Thursday, the 15th of July. I have nearly 90 miles to cover. I can do it. [I made it out by Wednesday.]

Now on the mp3 player I discover Lamb. I'd never heard of Lamb, a band whose music came to me and my mp3 as part of a huge, 60-gig bundle of music from cyberfreak friends, audiophiles with a pirate radio station in northern California. I recognized the female singer's voice immediately, that of the vocalist from Portishead, whose name escapes me, if I ever knew it at all.

But then I take breaks from the mp3 to conserve on battery power. The batteries are rechargeable, but out here in the woods wall plugs are few and far between. I tune into radio instead, my little credit card-sized radio that I've had duct-taped to my pack for months now. On comes a real throwback from the seventies, a veritable soul hoo-rah for women called "It's rainin' men!" Cyberdine says it's the Pointer Sisters.

I recently set up thruhiker friend Ry with a Palm VII and keyboard, my ancient-but-effective wireless means of reaching YOU and the world in general. An hour ago I got an e-mail from Ry, he and girlfriend Jackie and her Aunt Chris just behind me (I thought) saying that they were off the trail as of midday due to auntie's bad boots and the rain. Damn.

Now I want to write Ry and tell him that when he rejoins the trail to just skip this frikken section, four miles of solid swamp. I'm just a few miles from hitting the 1,200-mile mark and it's nothing but bog. The swamp trail! Then sure enough, along comes a portly family of day hikers, Ma, Pa, and Jr. Whopper, headed straight for the swamp! I'm like, "What are you people, nuts?" It's not the first time I've seen Pennsyltuckeyians out thrashing merrily over their state's evil rock-infested forest trail and I wonder. I mean, I'm doing this because I'M NUTS! This is just one part of a long trail for me, one on which there are many nicer parts. These people ought to move to Virginia or Georgia.

I'm thinking of a title to name the book that must surely come out of all this gibberish. One idea: *The Fantastic Possibilities: Or How I Walked Through Your Yard Unnoticed This Summer While RPGs Whizzed Across Your TV Screen.* It's wordy, I know.

Speaking of wordy, here's some new terminology for *Wikipedia.com*:

- Pink Blazer - a guy who adjusts his pace to hike with a woman
- Blaze Licker - an AT white blaze zealot overly concerned with passing and/or touching every white blaze
- Puron - same as above, derived from "purist" and "moron"

- Brewhiker - a thruhiker who utilizes beer as a means of motivation to get from town to town; since one cannot possibly hike with beer, let alone cold beer, one must keep going to get to the next beer (Yes, it's true, this was the driving force behind my thruhike.)
- Green blazer - one who uses that other (absurdly illegal but conveniently light) form of motivation to get down the trail
- Superpower privy - a lightning-fast bowel movement technique perfected to get in and out of a stinky privy in one hard-held breath

I try to get ahead. I really do. But the inherent flaw in any attempt at gonZo journalism is that life is ALWAYS happening. Now, perhaps there are those people out there in the world who can BE gonZo AND take time out to rest and WRITE about the experiences they just had. Me, I don't have that luxury. Especially not now, moving as I am at 20 miles a day across the stony eastern seaboard. Pennsylvania, anyway: stony as a kidney preparing to avalanche down some poor bastard's urethra. Piss on Pennsylvania. Sodom. Gomorra. Pennsylvania. Transylvania. It bleeds me, giving me naught but fields of stone over which to stumble and curse.

Here at the town pavilion of Port Clinton, Pennsylvania, Cyberdine paints with found paint, a broken ink pen of black, and a tampon. Not the applicator, the tampon. The tampon itself is fuzzy, you know, like a brush: very handy in a use-what-you-have situation. Word on the trail is he's been bit. Lyme disease. As I watch his tampon art, I'm a little concerned for him, but mostly I'm amused.

Cyberdine is an artist and computer genius, who, thanks to the latter talent, has made a fine living in the new world order of LANs and WANs and other wireless Web networks simply by employing his vast knowledge to locate and point out holes in corporate security systems. Amazing, really. To hear him tell tales of his past life is to be inside the Matrix, to be Neo hearing it for the first time from Morpheus that the world he thinks he lives in IS NOT THE REAL WORLD.

I knew this wasn't the real world, this trail world I'm in. I've given plenty of thought to how grossly unreal is that other world, the "desert of the real."

Cyberdine paints now with ketchup and mustard. They are the only things left here at the pavilion with any color to them in the wake of some grand mid-trail gathering called Billville, missed by yours truly but heard about aplenty. Beck plays on a tiny pocket pc, a thing no bigger than my Palm Pilot but 20 times the price with 20 times the upgrades. Its power comes from the sun, channeled through another Cyberdine miracle toy, the Brunton SolarRoll 14, a four-foot roll out mat of solar energy cells sealed in flexible plastic. Wow.

Cyberdine finishes his masterpiece with a liberal sprinkling of sea salt. His license plate- sized canvas features rolling hills, clouds, a hiker, and a bunny rabbit, all under a swirling sky of sea salt smelling strongly of McDonald's. If it sounds like I'm being sarcastic, I'm not. I do in fact think it brilliant. Here is an artist and thruhiker like myself, working with nothing and making art. It is the best sort of art. Call it outsider folk art. Call it tasty. Call it smelly. (Just give it a few days.) He titles his piece, "I saw a bunny." Yep. He's been bit.

"I have to say, this is the first time I've ever painted with a tampon," Cyberdine remarks. We drink quarts of Yuengling Premium, a beer I've only ever seen in Pennsylvania. Cars roar by on Route 61, and the sirens squeal off in pursuit every six minutes or so, a speed trap to end all speed traps. Must be a major thruway, but it drops to 35 mph right around the sharp corner into town, and the boys are reeling them in today. Sitting in the bar at the Port Clinton Hotel, it sounded like there was a fire every five minutes. What a country. Most folks speed now and again. Some people suffer with speed. Some people benefit by it. Me, I hear the sirens and am damn glad I'm walking for a change. I've walked twelve hundred miles as of today.

Out front of the pavilion stand two centurion-like castle columns. They look like stone sentries drawn by Maurice Sendak and brought to life by the surreal ketchup-painted landscape of Cyberdine's tick-bitten bunnies and too much Yuengling on an empty stomach.

Cyberdine and I sit here at Port Clinton's public crash pad like vendors awaiting customers. At last one arrives. Boo-Boo.

"Mountain Hardware sent me the wrong gaiters!" he says to us, a cell phone at his ear awaiting customer service. It takes Boo-Boo a while to say hello. He's just come from the local outfitter and he's fit to be tied.

Oh, Jesus. Cyberdine has taken up with ketchup and mustard again. It's a good thing this pavilion is huge, plenty of air space. The McDonald's stink is everywhere, and I'm about out of beer. With no desire to paint, I seize the life-sized two-dimensional cardboard Yuengling promo girl and take her on a wild tango tour of the lawn.

But as I was saying, I try to get ahead. The miles are flying. Then there was New Hampshire, seven days or so of major beer consumption with my cousin Justin. Then church with Dad. God. Beer. Major distractions from…um?

From the woods! Yes, this was about the forest, wasn't it? Anymore, it feels as though I hike with naught but the towns in sight. Descending into Harper's

Ferry, Chef said: "Funny how after six days out on the trail, we equate the sounds of traffic with beer and food."

So true. And showers. Amidst the siren scream of some young buck cop with a hard on for speeders, I walk into the Port Clinton Peanut Store and pull four Andrew Jacksons out of the ATM. The mini-ATM company makes its two bucks off me. PayPal already took their percentage on the front end.

I am grateful for the $80, although I'd expected $100. Whatever. There's no denying the pure magic of standing thousands of miles from home, snapping your finger, and yanking a handful of Jacksons out of R2D2's mouth. God bless capitalism. God bless America.

I drop a twenty at the Port Clinton Hotel Bar. It's worth it. I order a hamburger and set about to charging my mp3 batteries from a wall socket by the bar. The woman bartender eyes me suspiciously, and I flash her a toothy Cheshire Cat smile. In here earlier with Cyberdine, I laughed aloud when she bitched about our body odor. "You hikers stink!" she sneered. But the beers kept coming, and she snapped up our sizable tips like the best of Henry Miller's back alley whores. In the future, perhaps the hotel would be wise to offer free showers to purchasers of more than ten dollars of beer and/or food. Offer it up front, like, "Open a ten dollar tab and go straight to the showers and freshen up!" Then everybody would be happy: the itchy and oft self-conscious hikers who know they stink, and the poor, put-upon nasally offended bartenders.

Spent last night in jail. I should have seen it coming. All that talk about computer hacking with Cyberdine and me giving him pills because he said was really stressed. Hell, they're MY prescription drugs! Once they're mine, it's legal to give them away if I want, isn't it? Apparently not.

Anyway, I left Port Clinton kind of hungover and creeped out, the latter for no logical reason I could discern just the usual post-drunk day-after psychosis typically quelled by some member of the benzodiazepine family. At not quite 7 a.m., I was up, packed, and out of town, vaporizing back into the magical forest as though I'd never set foot in Port Clinton.

Except in the 1200 block, the forest isn't so magical anymore. Here in Pennsylvania, God said let there be rocks, and there are rocks. Big and small, from fields of rocks to scramble over to endless foot-torturing pathways of smaller stones. The whole state is rocks. Then there's the "green tunnel" effect, the cloistering cave-like claustrophobia of the Appalachian Trail in full summer deciduous jungle-like growth. Views are scarce, especially now.

But I've become quite proficient at rock hopping and I like the color green, so I suppose I'll live. Gifted with a keen sense of balance, I dance along the fields of bigger boulders. And so that July 19 I danced and danced and damn near ran in rare moments when the path was clear, until very late in the day, dark in fact, I stumbled like a drunkard exhausted into a campsite. I checked my mileage: 28 miles in one day. It was a record day.

As you might imagine I could barely walk yesterday. But I did. I got up, deservedly late at 9 a.m., and broke camp in the rain. I rock hopped and hobbled and stumbled another 12 miles to a shelter where I met a man. His name was Jim. Jim said he was the caretaker of that particular shelter, but I wondered. He looked more like a plain-clothes cop or a bounty hunter than an AT volunteer, and it was as though he'd been awaiting my arrival. Just me, a wet rat coming in out of the storm. There was no one else in the shelter.

Jim gave me a handful of smallish apricots and offered me a ride to town. "To Slaterton?" I asked. "Nah, don't go into Slaterton. You don't wanna go there. You wanna come to Palmerton. We like hikers there, and we've got a place for you to stay, for free!" That got my hackles up. It was all feeling very creepy: the fruit, his hunter garb and weird vibe, and now this queer invitation. But after 7 days and 110 miles on the trail without a shower or laundry, I needed town, bad. The other town would be a long hike, or a miserable hitch in the rain. My only other choice was to stay put.

Into Jim's truck I climbed and off we went, but not before I noticed the objects in the bed of the truck, among them a shovel, a pickaxe, some rope and some tarpaulin, things one might use to bury a body in the woods. Who was this guy? Something just didn't feel right. But then, I hadn't felt quite "right" since Port Clinton. Not long after I'd pulled $80 out of the ATM, $50 of it mysteriously vanished. I had stayed overnight though, against my better judgment, in the damp and highway-noisy pavilion. Worst of all, though, had been seeing Cyberdine go from jovial to grim to kind of psychotic looking, even after I'd fed him 4 milligrams of Klonipin, enough Valium to calm a werewolf.

Now here I was riding into some unknown town with a probable serial killer or plain- clothes cop. Then it happened, sure enough. Jim drove right up to the police station and said, "Here we are."

Oh, Jeezus. They've finally caught me! The net has descended at last. FBI. CIA. Whoever. They'd take me into custody quietly here in Podunk and I'd disappear, end up imprisoned in a shipping container somewhere overseas. It wouldn't matter to them that I'd committed no crime. They'd find something.

RICK McKINNEY

This was the Patriot Act at work, I just knew it. Homeland Security had deemed me a National Threat. I was fucked.

But my paranoid fit was all for naught. In the tiny old mining town of Palmerton, Pennsylvania, the city generously allows thruhikers to overnight for free in its historic "old jail." Jim was actually a really nice guy, and the "jail hostel" was fine and cozy and full of my fellow thruhikers, most of who had been there since the night before, waiting out the horrendous and relentless rain storm I'd been hiking in for 40 miles. I was out of my mind.

Thank you, Palmerton, for a night of rest and forgive my psychotic musings.

When you're hiking 15 to 20 miles a day over every imaginable obstacle and falling down at dark into smelly hiker-filled shelters that vibrate at night with the nocturnal roaring bass of snores, and your every day off is a frantic run around some unknown town from Laundromat to grocery store to church hostel or motel (or jail!) to bar to bed, written record of said days is choppy at best. Forgive me then for short-shrifting town stops.

Pennsyltuckey wasn't all bad.

In Duncannon, I discovered that I liked open-fist boxing thanks to hottie lesbian bartender Sara who, after inviting Pegasus and me to her house undoubtedly with the intent of getting Pegasus to stay, decided to beat up on me. My willingness to hit and be hit by this girl caught me totally by surprise.

Just months ago, I would shy from any major roughhousing with my small nephews Jacob and Matthew. I felt frail. I felt old. Not anymore. Now I'm hand-wrought bronze and forged steel. My legs, without flexing, constantly look as though I'm flexing muscles. Even my upper torso has taken on a lean, V-shape. In response, I have taken to pushups, at first in camp and now, of late, along the trail whenever the urge strikes me, pack on and everything. You get fewer pushups wearing a 30-pound pack, but they're satisfying, all 15 or 20 of them.

Nayber! Alumni thruhiker and trail angel Nayber came through with his promise of shoes! The guy saw how messed up my Lowas were and sent me a pair of Adidas! Used, but in great shape (I wouldn't accept a new pair, I told him). Thank you, Nayber! I'm banging out the miles in them, roaring out of Pennsylvania and through Jersey now.

On the radio comes the song "Born to Run" by Bruce Springsteen, I think, a song that always gets me pumped up and all misty-eyed and full of passion. I charge up a rock pile singing at the top of my lungs, "I wanna die with you, Wendy, on the street tonight in an everlasting kiss!"

222

There are two songs that I will forever associate with my hike of the Appalachian Trail, as they've been burned into my brain by Clear Channel Radio, the corporate destroyers of originality in radio. One is that damn ballad by Hooba Stank where the guy lamely apologizes for breaking his girl's heart and though he's lost her now, he'll always be a better man. Crap. Crap, crap, crap! The other is that song "Fifteen" by, who is that? Dave Matthews? I don't know. Burn them both.

Climbed up out of Palmerton the other day into a probable Superfund site that made our Damascus Tent City location look like Eden. It was a horrid toxic nightmare world full of gnarled dead trees and mutant fungal plant life with eyes that watched you as you went, like a thousand frogs melted together and stuck in a puddle of goo. The wasted hilltop is all apparently the product of air pollution from past local industry, ground leached and bleached by mineral-hungry men with no concern for the world they had left behind for their children.

But later that same day, miles away in a healthy forest, I ran my hands through dewy blades of grass to wash off the stickiness of a Snickers bar. I saw a turtle and a groundhog, a black snake slithering across the trail, and one of those brilliant orange little newts, called efts. Every day I see deer, sweet, silent, skittish, brazen, playful, close at hand. I have yet to see an East Coast bear.

FIFTEEN

Pain Bad Enough to Make You Piss Yourself...the Politics of the White Blaze...a Distant Angel and the Gift of Motel Bliss...Rooster, Ski Bum and the Great New Jersey Deluge...Jester's Magic Raincoat...Nature: the Great Equalizer...the Vernon Burger King and Yes, I am a Car...Derek Jeter Who? Walt Whitman in a Forlorn Old Zoo Full of Black Children Singing Jesus Songs...

So I hit a wall. Anxious to get out of Pennsylvania, I charged headlong past a sprained ankle, through a nasty stomach virus (or bad water, not sure) that had me swaggering dizzily for three days, and over far too many miles for my poor feet with nothing but the rest of night. Some nights I was still hiking an hour or so after dark. So not even night could protect my feet from my madcap zeal.

At last the miles got to me. Here I had planned to rip through 50-mile New Jersey in just two days, and on the second day at 25 miles in, I nearly pissed my pants coming down a steep slope, so all-consuming was the pain in my feet with every step. I had pushed my high tolerance for pain to the limit.

I e-mailed friend Mike Strickland of my situation, of how close I'd come to quitting earlier that day, and he booked me a room for two nights at the Forest Motel. Mike has a vested interest in my successful thruhike. My success will be his success. In a letter that I carried the whole length of the trail, he wrote:

> *Your writing continues to captivate me, to touch the free spirit*
> *chained inside me...I thank you for keeping the words coming.*
> *They fill black-and-white lives with dazzling color.*

Big Chief Paisley Feather sits here basking in the air conditioning and off his feet for a solid day tomorrow thanks to one of a dying breed of old friends, perhaps my second oldest friend in terms of going back in time. For only the second time on this 1,300-mile, four-month journey, I pressed the Panic Button today and a friend answered the call.

Thanks to my old high school amigo Mike, I am comfortably ensconced in Room #3 of the Forest Motel just off Highway 206 here in Branchville, New Jersey. Big Chief sits squat on the bed, a happy man and proud, my hair full of colorful feathers I've been collecting along the trail, proud yet humble as any true wise man seated before the Great Wood chipper in the Sky, and typing, of course, and plugged hard into Massive Attack, "Teardrop" at the moment, a powerful song for a powerful man, a powerful day, a day full of pain and rain and ticks and filth and grace and wide, wide open space, and a sweet ninth inning rescue from failure, defeat, retreat.

At noon today, I found myself roadside at Culver's Gap, one of the many places where the AT encounters the real world and we are forced to dodge traffic or walk through fenced-in bridge overpasses or through tunnels beneath the traffic. I've crossed a zillion roads and freeways by now it seems, but today was different. I was looking at this rather rural road as the Beginning of the End. I wanted to quit the trail today, and I was but a hitch away.

Such constant and extreme physical rigor I have never known before in my life. I was never been much into sports in my school years, and as life went on into my 20s and 30s, I never exercised. Well, rarely. I didn't need to. I had a high metabolism and a natural slimness about me, and I was plenty active. Not athletic, but wiry, manic, frantic. Now suddenly, driven on by haste and a desire to match the kind of pace Elly (already in Maine) had set, I've been running a marathon nearly every day.

I was sick of the trail. I am sick of the trail. I am sick of the rocks, of which there were about 200 miles in Pennsylvania. I am sick of checking my legs, my balls, my ass crack for microscopic bloodsucking ticks which, if undiscovered, could make of me a more physically and mentally deranged person than I already am (I pull one off me every few days). I'm sick of EVERYONE on the trail, from the worst fuddy-duddy dorkos and jerks to people I really dig. But of course what this really means is I'm sick of myself and all the work of interacting with ANYBODY, EVERYBODY on the trail.

There are still a lot of us. To hear the statistics, you'd think there'd be nobody left way back here at the ass-end of the pack but me and about three other circus freaks with twiggy arms and Popeye calves. Nope. There's a buttload of freaks. This could be a record year for successful freak thruhikes.

But what I'm MOST sick of is the politics of white blazing versus just plain walking north. What is it about humans that no matter how kind and gentle and soft and fluffy and eco-tickly and lovey-dovey you get, an elitist spirit is spawned in the minds of some or many or even just one, and suddenly a hierarchy is born and with it all the divisive and derisive bullshit of a Hitler youth brigade?

I almost hitchhiked off-trail this morning (who knows maybe a full Kerouac-hitch to California), not because my feet were hamburger after ten 20-mile days in a row (a very good reason to stop, if not quit) but because the two cool young guys I'd recently hooked up with turned out to be serious Believers in the whole Neo-Nazi Arian Blaze Race bullshit.

But the problem, as usual, was mine, not theirs. I don't believe in absolutes. I don't believe in going backwards, for anything. So when Catherine at the AMC Mohican outdoor center said this morning, "Hey, you guys don't need to backtrack, you can just go up this trail over here and be back on the AT in no time," I said "All right!" The boys were not in accord. They would back-hike to the spot we'd left the "White Blaze Inquisition" and begin again from there. Ugh.

I like these guys and respect their zeal. There are worse cases, hikers who insist on physically touching every white blaze on every tree from Georgia to Maine.

I loathe perfection. I embrace chaos, as does Nature, I'll remind you. Nature loathes perfection, as we humans define it. Nature IS chaos. Heading north, I took the logical "shortcut" back to the trail. The result, sociologically? I am alone again. George Thorogood, if I may? "I hike alone, yeah, with nobody else."

I walk north. I walk north until I hurt all over. I walk north for no good goddamn reason at all. I walk north for me. I walk north because I feel that I've never really had a triumph in my life, nothing to call a total success. I will succeed, but I will not fuss over every single white blaze, not even every frikken mile of this ever-expanding trail. Two thousand miles afoot and the Katahdin summit will sit just fine with me, thanks. I'll make it with the love and support of many at home, Mike, not the least of the bunch. Bruce, and Justin, and Timmy, and Mary, and Marie, Linda, and Kathleen Pearson, the latter on whose postcards and letters I can ABSOLUTELY count on at EVERY mail drop. Wow. No one tops Kate for consistency. Thank you all.

Now it's tomorrow. July 22, to be exact. I awoke this morning groggy from painkillers and beer, the former a necessity just to get me off the mountain yesterday, so bad was the pain with every step. The latter serving a necessary medicinal function, that of calming my frantic wound-up speed freak Greyhound dog-on-the-run mind, which couldn't quite grasp WHY we were stopping. Hell, we'd done 180 miles in less than 10 days, two of them measly 10-milers due to a sprained ankle. Which boils down to 160 miles in 7 days, 88 of them in just the last four. Insane, by any standard.

When I hooked up with Rooster and Ski Bum the other day, I expressed my gratitude and appreciation for being able to simply walk between them, to follow their pace. "Me, when I walk alone I just go and go. I have no governor, no shut-off valve, no throttle and no basis for comparison. So I hike fast and hard and kill myself in the doing." They nodded understandingly. Rooster moves at the ultimate cool pace. His whole demeanor is cool, unhurried. Here's a guy whose feathers would be very hard to ruffle. "I think subconsciously I'm trying to catch up to Elly, the girl I started this hike with four months ago who is now already far into Maine," I tell them.

Sadly, this is true. I have no delusions about "catching" Elly, nor would I want to try. But her electric pace shamed me horribly when I arrived in Harper's Ferry, West Virginia, to find that she'd been through there over a month ago. That she was #100 on the march to my #410? Augh. Shameful.

I lie here in this bed in some funky motel where the satellite cable doesn't work and the shower doesn't drain and thus floods the room with the tide of my long, luxurious showers, and there's no phone in the room, but I'm happy as a pig in shit to be here. I lie here because I tried hard to catch Elly, conceptually anyway, although my bruised feet might argue that point. It is an impossible task. Oh, by the way, don't ever stay at the Forest Motel in Branchville, New Jersey. It sucks. I mean, to me, in my condition, it's Paradise. But it basically sucks.

I treat myself to some HBO while I rest my feet. It's the only channel that's working. It's a film called *Lone Star* with a tolerable cameo-like sprinkling of Matthew McConaughey and a whole lot of Chris Cooper, one of my favorite actors since he popped up in *American Beauty*. I like the film's setting, desert-urban like Tucson or El Paso, some border town out West. I recognize the palm trees painted white up to shoulder height and that dry light of the Rio Grande, the bottles of Lone Star and Negro Modelo. These things feel like home to me. Film scenes of crossing over the bridge into Juarez send me back to that Christmas years ago, Dave and I driven south and over the border by friend Miguel "Gallo" Silva to the Mexican bus station for our long ride to Mazatlan.

In the film, a Mexican character says, "In Mexico we invented recycling," and I laugh. It's so very true.

There's something I love about Texas, too. She's always been good to me, Davey Crockett's birthplace, Ozona, for instance. Such good people.

But there's that whole shiftiness to the border world, a friendly yet atavistic realm, a queer, gun-toting Mafioso "family" of corrupt small-town politicians, Texas rangers, and white hat-wearing drug lords with helicopters and gold teeth.

Later, after a few phone calls to the West, I cry myself into an afternoon nap, lonesome for the desert dust of Arizona, Mexico, California, the dust and ocean sunsets that long ago crept into the marrow of my Boston-born bones and stuck there. I cry for Jacob and Matthew, for Colby and Brina, for Mom and Sis and Bruce and Timmy, for Mary in Texas and Kathleen in Bisbee, for Dave and for Harrod, sweet whale-hearted Harrod, and many more who will make it very hard to leave Hotel California, if I ever do, to give it up for a return to my eastern roots. Exhausted, I cry out this journey, yearning for family, and most of all desperate to feel love again. "I am the luckiest man alive," I cry into my pillow. "I am the luckiest man alive!" The luckiest and the loneliest.

"What's the best thing you've ever done?" asked Rooster yesterday. "I wrote a novel," I said. But I quickly followed with this: "For me. That was the best thing I did for me, but as for doing things for others?" Whatchoo do, Rooster and Ski Bum wanna know. "Cared for the mentally retarded, was a friend to old people, lived and worked as a guide to a blind man." That was that, my proclamation of having lived a grand life. Rooster, Ski Bum and I seated atop Jacob's Ladder high above the Delaware River in New Jersey, all of us soaked to the bone from a half-hour of torrential rain that made a river of the trail. "If I dropped dead tomorrow I would die a happy man, a full man." My belief in Heaven and God would carry me through to where Luci's gone, and Chris and Grandma, too. Later I'm reminded why I was never a very good journalist: I never did ask the boys what comprised their greatest gifts to the world.

Mashipacong Shelter, Mile 1,316, some New Jersey refuge with an unpronounceable name in the rain. Beautiful. Soft wind plays surf and sand sounds through reeds of birch, maple, oak.

Awakened by the slight discomfort of summer nights turned cooler than I like, I slip on my long johns and socks and fleece sweater, my cozy Patagonia on this 23rd of July. I set about to playing my own music, that silent song of keyboard and fingers in the dark. It is most always a lonesome song. But tonight I don't mind, or I should say I don't feel lonesome. The old walls of stone and stout wood beams of this shelter are companion enough. And Spare Pocket and Rooney Tunes are here this night, my two newly met and quite congenial shelter mates (you just never know who you are going to get, a point which of late has kept me out of shelters). They are nice enough, and their soft snoring now cuts the lonesome song of my typing, makes it ring practical, even poetic.

Charles Bukowski said, "Endurance is more important than truth." Now more than ever with all this shit about the pure thruhiker, I feel its meaning. I have always been a truthful person, often to my own detriment, so for me the truth part just kind of goes without saying. But endurance, in this case is to endure healthily, to lug along on a super-extended timeline, to endure the repetition of four months afoot yet also the constant change of surroundings and curve balls thrown at you by Nature.

Nature: the great equalizer. Out here, we are all just hobo mountaineers, a smelly bum nobility that move almost unseen through a vast narrow tunnel of green light, fireflies, wind, rain, and rocks and pain, the latter endured quietly, endlessly, yet soothed by friends aplenty. One cannot walk 20 miles in a day every day without pain.

So it was two days off my feet, two days without pain, then there's me yesterday, my motel tenure up, the rain coming down, and it's cold but no poncho. Lost it a few days back. But onto the highway I stepped and walked, and facing an uphill climb of several miles through construction and fast cars that I doubted (in Jersey) would ever stop for me, I walked, but I stuck out my thumb anyway, almost lazily, my back to the oncoming cars. And whammo. Within seconds I had a ride, a young guy, thick Jersey accent, no idea what or where the AT was but said he'd take me. I got out at Gyps Tavern near the trailhead and went inside, the lone customer, and Genie whipped me up a burger and a birch beer for the "road." I wolfed down my burger and root beer and we talked and outside it began to pour like a Texas flood. Shit, I thought. No poncho. "Dammit! How could I lose my poncho?"

I'd been learning to endure long walks in the rain. You get wet no matter what. But the poncho makes for a little mobile tent, reserving for its occupant a warm damp space in which to dwell, either on the move or at rest, folded up inside of it like a giant green Hershey's kiss by the side of the trail, waiting out the worst of the thunder or deluge. Then there's its other function: my ground cloth. Without it, I'm like a guy with half a tent.

I seize upon a break in the rain and make for the door. But in the time taken to pay the check and double check the dry bag and Ziplocs for the safety of my change of clothes and my electronics, the rain has begun again in earnest. What can I do? Sit and wait it out in the tavern all day? The forecast is for rain all weekend. There are miles to be made. Maine will not come to me.

Outside the tavern a man running a summer school in the woods is about to go get his students from up trail. He offers a ride to the next shelter. I decline gratefully, but I do accept two turkey sandwiches and some chips after assurances that they have enough to feed the kids. Rain is dripping down my nose. I need to get moving. I thank him and cross the street and dash into the relative cover of the forest canopy. Thanks to thirsty trees, it's always raining a little less in the woods.

Not a hundred feet into the forest, just far enough that passersby on the streets won't see, sits a yellow delivery newspaper sleeve, full of something, with the following words written on it in bold black Sharpie pen: "This poncho belongs to Duke, aka Lord Duke aka Jester aka Peregrine Jack. Hope you get it. It sure will be wet w/o it. - Rooster"

Rooster just leapt up the roster of my all-time AT heroes. Two days it sat there, two rainy days. Many hikers had passed. No one had taken it. That's AT magic!

[Afterthought: When a hiker named Paradox saw me and expressed relief that he'd "caught up with someone," and others in the group here tonight expressed surprise that I was not far ahead of them by now, I responded with a wry smile. "Well, you see, the ATC got hold of me and arranged for me to stay in a motel for two nights, drop back as it were, so that all of you could enjoy the morale boost of 'catching up' to a big miler like me." The boos were unanimous, but mixed with laughter, too.]

Now it's Vernon, New Jersey, and Burger King fries and Budweiser from the can, always from the can out here on the trail, you see, because cans are crushable and light and more easily packed out, should one be crazy enough to pack beer "in." Some town called Vernon, another dart throw at the American map anomaly, a place I never would have encountered in a zillion years were it not for this trail, were it not that the Appalachian corridor slips right through here like the second coming of Jesus, like a thief in the night.

"Take me to the Episcopal Church, please," I said to the elder Romanian couple just off the trail from a day hike and climbing into their SUV when I arrived at the road. The church basement felt like, well, a church basement. It was stuffy and reeked of rules, REALLY reeked of hiker stink, and of course didn't allow drinking. The clincher for me was the TV, on and babbling incessant and insane. Television: my nemesis. I grab Rooney just as he arrives and lead him over to the town pavilion, where I've heard hikers are welcome to sleep beneath the giant metal roof that keeps the rain off 50-some picnic tables used in town gatherings.

And, of course, we buy beer. Or, I should say, I buy beer, since Rooney is puny, if you get my gist. Lots of beer. The sun goes down and there we are sitting drinking beer right out in the middle of everything that is downtown Vernon when a cruiser pulls up. "Oh, shit. Here it comes," I think. Supplying a minor with beer, tickets for vagrancy, who knows. Instead, the kindly sounding officer merely leans out the window of his cruiser, asks how we're doing, takes us on our word that we are indeed thruhikers, wishes us well on our journey, and drives away. Astounding. Now I'm hungry.

I stroll over to Burger King just before their stated 11 p.m. closing, a Spiderman winning hamburger ticket in hand from a visit earlier that day. The door, however, is locked. The girl inside gesticulates wildly and makes some statement in a Jersey-esque tongue further complicated by several inches of glass. "Ovemadkermitayog," she says. "Okay, you want me to go order at the drive-thru," I pantomime in response with a thumbs up and a smile. "Fine." I walk over to the rather busy drive-thru and, embarrassed, immediately assume the stance of a waiting automobile. I think to myself, "Be the automobile." I stand before the ordering kiosk and talk to it. "Hello. Hello, I'd like a hamburger."

No one answers. I savvy the problem.

Turning, I summon the car behind me to pull up and touch off whatever ground weight-sensor or laser-operated summoning system they've got at the Vernon Burger King, and voila. It works. The response from inside is immediate. Good for me the two guys in the car are young and silly, like me. They're hip to my gig and, judging by their expressions, getting a big kick out of it. I talk into the speakerphone, throw down my order, and close the deal. I then instruct the dudes in the car to back up and pull forward again, to reignite the grill fires of Burger King's attention. They do as bidden, and give me the thumbs up as I walk off toward Window #1.

When I reach the window, I say, "Hi, I'm a car." I get the feeling they don't believe me. The window girl is mystified. "How did you fool our high-tech system?" her eyes inquire. Where is your car? "You can't come through the drive-thru without a car," she says. "I am hiking the Appalachian Trail," I

231

explain to her, "which, by the way, goes right through your town, so I don't have a car."

"The Appa-what? How come you don't have a car?" I explain in further detail, adding that surely if I had a car, I would have driven it. This does not compute. With an air of spite, Window Girl thrusts my burger at me and slams shut her little fast food window on the world. I accept it with a smile, pantomime a shift into Drive, and roll off the lot, burger fuel for the tank in hand and a secret in my bones, a secret no one at Burger King Vernon or any Burger King or Mickey D's or Taco Smell or Wal-Mart will likely ever comprehend. Keep moving. Keep moving, stay weird, live every day as though 'twere your last, and if you see an Einstein-Rosen Bridge, take it.

I know, aside from jumping into manmade wormholes, the first three are not new ideas. But trust me, there are plenty of good old ideas that get conveniently lost in the censored teachings of each new generation. Jesus said, "The Kingdom of Heaven is within You," and, yea, the forgetting was swift. And there was much rejoicing.

Rooney Tunes is my new friend on the trail. As I implied, he is not quite of drinking age, just a few months away, a point that got us kicked out of the local pub and stuck down here drinking at the pavilion. He hails from my native Massachusetts and has a good mind and gentle demeanor. I share my burger and the last of a 12-pack of Bud with him, and rather than becoming stupid, he seems to become wiser with every beer.

But now the beer is gone. All the other thruhikers chose to stay and sleep at the Episcopal Church amidst a chorus of horrid snoring and evil, three-day rained-on sock stink. We chose instead to come here, to the big picnic pavilion beside the fire station, where we swapped many stories and drank many a beer. Naturally, I told him the story of my alcoholi-schizo ex-girlfriend. After we've snuggled into our bags for a night of sleep and picnic table dreams and all has been quiet for a good ten minutes, I suddenly shout out, "Get off the trail, you pre-pubescent dweeb! Nobody wants you. When I wake tomorrow sober and say, 'Hey, Pal, let's hike together!' don't believe me." The poor bastard flopped around in his mummy bag like a hooked marlin before he caught the reference and understood I was playing *her*. He settled down to sleep, eventually.

Two days later, I'm trudging the northern end of the Abram S. Hewitt State Forest on the New York/New Jersey state line, my energy zapped. Ski Bum, Rooster, Rooney, everybody passed me. The view was nice. Too nice. The whole time you're walking along a stony ridge high above a luscious body of water that I believe is called Lake Sterling, but no matter. All I could think of was swimming. Immersion. Wetness. Coolness. It was a hot day.

So, as day approached night with the next shelter waaaay off and the trail wrenching absurdly west, stupid-looping away from the jewel of water far below, I did what any self-respecting gonzo journalist would do, and said "Dang, this is a great story, but me thinks I smell a better one down thay-a!" Just like that I cut right on a blue blaze straight down the ridge toward the water. I never did make it to the lake, but I did find Main Street in the town of Greenwood, New York. There on the main drag, I looked left, I looked right. I spied a bar. Shazamm!

I was hesitant at first: a lone thruhiker off the beaten path in an obvious locals only kind of bar. But then I met Joe, a fixture at Murphy's Pub and a damn nice guy. I bought him a beer, and in so doing broke the silence of my status as stranger. Never sure from one place to the next what the protocol is with packs, I had left my pack outside. But it began to rain, and when Joe savvied, the little guy got off his stool and went out and dragged the damn thing inside for me. Then an unexpected change came over everyone in the bar.

My first indication that something had changed was the fresh beer that appeared in front of me. Rose, the motherly bartender, said, "That one's on me, Honey. God bless you in your hike." So it went. In very short order, I went from stranger to celebrity and the rest of the night it was, "Let me buy you a beer," and me regaling the locals of Greenwood with tales from the trail.

By closing time, I hadn't given any thought to where I was staying. I just figured I would crawl back into the woods and make camp on the ridge from whence I'd come. But then I offered old Joe a last whiskey and he offered me a place to crash for the night, and as he made me cheese sandwiches in his tiny efficiency apartment, he told me of a couple he'd once had over, "thruhikers like you," he said. "They took down my address and thanked me and promised to send a photo from the summit, but I never heard from them again, nuttin." Naturally, we'd bought another 18-pack of Bud to go with the white bread and cheese, so, needless to say, I was pretty messed up the next morning.

For added color, here are my Palm notes from that night:

> *crashed toinight aon Oe's ofloor. Joe drinks at the local bar,*
> *urphy's Pub, which couldn't have been more accessible for*

gy like me,, no, not one-legged, but certaiinly of onemind,
justin thinkging about beer after an initial NY covearage of
maybe fifteen miles. I just rerouted the tril today fofr my own
porowewllI'do[nt ikonw whereMiekke wsas when I was
romoanccing full blown dyke bullll mooowe oin the
2hite.... 'qne wo thenei iteeqthere eof for

I think I was channeling some ancient form of Swedish.

I made a point to take Joe's address, and unless he moved, he's got a picture of me on Katahdin to show his cronies and Rose back at Murphy's. I'll never forget Joe nudging me as we stumbled home from the bar and saying, "You know who that was throwing you the free beers, don't you? That was Derek Jeter's Aunt Rose, and that's her bar." He must have caught my quizzical look. I speak about as much sports as I do Russian. "You know, THE Derek Jeter of the New York Yankees?" I know now, though at the time I hadn't a clue.

Horrible weather up here on Bear Mountain in New York. Bad weather but bay-ootiful friends. I am OUT of the rain now by a mere six feet or so, just enough, snug against the back wall of an old stone shelter with a good metal roof. I'm looking out at the weather, sticking my tongue out at it, and all it can do to me now is make fog of my breath.

Fog-breath on July 27th. Now that's some weird weather, all right.

My beautiful friends are not with me, not in the flesh anyway. No one is with me tonight. Driven here by relentless rains, I made an exception to the rule and traveled an entire 6/10ths of a mile off the trail to get to a shelter. Typically AT thruhikers scoff at any shelter more than a few hundred feet from the trail. No sense adding extra mileage to your 2,200-mile trip. On that note, I say no sense taking a white-blazed stupid loop when your map clearly displays the old trail (now blue-blazed but heading due north). Ah! But we've had this argument, yes?

Anyway, tonight I had no choice. It was rainy and cold and fast becoming night with no other shelter in sight. By now I was down to a thin summer sleeping bag and no tent. As I approached, I had a sense it would be nice. For the aforementioned 6/10s of a mile reason and it being a weekday and miserable out, I would likely have the shelter to myself. I was right. At roughly 7 p.m. I came running in here at top speed, the extra effort employed not out of haste but fear. I could feel the temperature dropping rapidly and I was soaked. I had stopped only briefly for a rest and could literally feel my body temperature dropping with every few passing seconds. Can you say hypothermia?

I was so motivated by fear of hypothermia that I made the last half-mile here in under 10 minutes and in so doing generated enough body heat to sustain me whilst I stripped naked, toweled off, and got into warm dry clothes, literally putting on every dry article of clothing I had in my scant reserves.

I now sit wrapped in my thin summer sleeping bag drinking Sleepytime tea with Crown Royal on the side. Mary Forbes, you spoil me! I'm about to plow into the Mountain House brand Pasta Primavera Mary sent me, too. Today was a good day at the post office. I have some very fine friends indeed. Not lonesome tonight, no, no. Cozy, warm, charmed by the stonework and old wood of this ancient mountain dwelling I'm in, and eating and drinking the love of my friends. It was kind of like breaking bread with Jesus, his body, his blood, all that, but with absentee earthly friends instead.

I've got a new friend today, too! Cynthia of San Diego, who are you? You goddess, YOU! Cynthia sent me Paul Newman Oreos and a frikken pound of Gummi Bears and a pound of dried mango and jasmine green tea and the book *Immortality* by Milan Kundera, all with a sweet little note that lent no clue as to who Cynthia is. "She certainly knows what you like!" I said to myself. "I wonder how she knew so well? Then, answering myself, "Well, duh, you do write about your damn self all the time. You probably wrote that you liked Gummi Bears."

Marie, Mary, Nayber, Kate with her never-miss postcards, Mike with his care package and the gift of a motel, my Sis and nephews, Linda, Tank Girl, Chris Stock, Colleena, Justin and Jess, Cynthia. I truly am a very lucky guy.

Dinner eaten, I am now, however, a meat Popsicle. I'm done for. Exhausted. I wanna write a few e-mails, read some Kundera, expand on some thoughts I had today on the trail, but I can't. I twisted an ankle today. The balls of my feet are perma-bruised, and I'm wiped out. Took every ounce of energy to get me another 12 or 14 miles along the trail today in the pouring rain. I can do no more. It's 10 p.m., well past hiker midnight. Gonzo. Goodnight.

The next day, July 28, I crossed the Hudson River, famed channel of so much history. As I stared down from the bridge at the gray and choppy water, I tried to imagine how far I had come. But all I could think of was the poor broken-down animals in the zoo just behind me, of that ginormous otter doing endless loopdi-loops in his tiny tank, of the bobcats pacing, and the couch potato bears, and of how very far I had yet to go. Sometimes you can try real hard to feel grateful and all that comes out of your heart is sadness. I imagine it doesn't take suffering from severe depression to have moments like this. If it's any consolation, I never gave any thought to jumping.

Good thing, too. Because had I jumped, I probably would have landed square on the guy swimming the Hudson River from its trickling mountain source all the way to the sea. Unbeknownst to me at the time, my friend Hunter Mann was somewhere down below in that river filming a documentary on the Hudson swimmer from a boat running alongside him. Funny old life. The swimmer probably would have broken my fall and I'd have lived and been busted for two counts: attempted suicide and involuntary manslaughter.

Mowed field of early morning grass wet and bejeweled, diamonds of dawn as golden sun not seen in days rises powerful over eastern forest. Yesterday I met Walt Whitman in a forlorn old zoo full of black children singing Jesus songs and howling to make the caged coyotes howl. Walt standing there eternal, eternal as bronze anyway, tall majestic there at the lowest elevation point on the AT saying, in essence, you can have your cities, your stress, your Turtle Wax and toenail polish...give me the trees, the rocks, the long open road across America. Ah, hell, why put words in the man's mouth when he said it best himself.

> *I tramp a perpetual journey*
> *My signs are a rain-proof coat and good shoes*
>   *and a staff cut form the woods;*
> *No friend of mine takes his ease in my chair,*
> *I have no chair, nor church nor philosophy;*
> *I lead no man to a dinner-table or library or exchange,*
> *But each man and each woman of you I lead upon a knoll,*
> *My left hand hooks you round the waist,*
> *My right hand points to landscapes of continents,*
>   *and a plain public road.*
> *Not I, not anyone else can travel that road for you,*
> *You must travel it for yourself.*

I think again of those tired looking bears, not old, just tired or maybe just content, I don't know. I turned to an attendant there at the Bear Mountain Wildlife Center, a haven for animals that can't survive in the wild and said, "In 1,400 miles, those bears are the first I've seen on the trail!" Her response was a non-response. A blah human reflection of the bored-to-death look of the caged bears. My words meant nothing to her. Fine. I crossed the Hudson River and disappeared back into the forest. But not for long.

Six miles later I arrived at this place, The Graymoor Friary, an old monastery whose brothers have been taking in thruhikers for decades. Got here just in time for the 5:30 dinner of spaghetti, heaps of it, and salad fantastic, and bread and butter and Jell-o and three-bean soup and iced tea. Wow! I even managed to squeeze in a 48-second shower to peel off a layer of sweat before dinner down here at the sports pavilion's ice-cold cedar shower house. Invigorating!

Rain last night, again, but again I beat it, warm and snug under cover of the friar's soccer field pavilion in my bag and long johns and fleece sweater stretched out atop a table. Wonderful. Twenty miles ahead today but with no pack! A kind angel named Gene is going to run our packs ahead, Michael, Nitro and me. Then tomorrow one more twenty to the Appalachian Trail Train Station and boom! Outa New York State.

Smash cut to the RPH shelter about 20 miles from the Connecticut state line. All present go in on nearly a full case of Heineken. But Ursa Minor is on antibiotics and can't drink and neither Nitro nor Michael drink much, leaving it all to Swan and me. I did my best.

Late night now and me out of the shelter to pee in the bushes and noticing that the sky is still blue and all the forest a silhouette and whoa! Day has surrendered to night, the former saying nothing of my 19-mile day, the latter only proclaiming again her name, NIGHT! "Oh, Day! Speak up, already!" Day says nothing, and Night, predictably, "Nighty night, Dukey."

Night suffers my lids to close in mid-sentence here at the *Like Water for Chocolate* picnic table 'neath the overhang here in the New York state garden of Appalachian comfort, such as it is, and my cat food can stove burns a small alcohol flame to hold the day, to stave off night for me to have something, to say. But no sooner said than "poof," flame out and all thruhikers with beers in their bellies to bed in their snug tents, crickets singing irreverent in the brambles, Radiohead singing irreverent in my ears, "far away, far from pain, so you aim toward the sky...." I am interrupted from my reverie to brush a daddy longlegs from my ankle, about the third in as many minutes.

Suddenly Cynthia's Gummi Bears take center stage over the remnants of damn near a case of Heineken beer slapped together from some interstate Sunoco gas station, trail angel Gene's generous driving, a few bucks from me and the others and a twenty spot Swan kicked down.

Cynthia! Who are you? Lovin' the Gummi Bears, even tho' they don't mix well with Dutch beer drunk from an MSR titanium cook pot. Who knew?

So get this! Michael (of Nitro and Michael - don't know why he doesn't have a trail name and she does) and I go into S& J Deli somewhere between the Taconic forests of New York and the 'burbs, and counter girl Angie says, "What do you want?" and I say, "Italian sub, please, and can we fill our water bottles?" Michael says something about how we're hiking, and Angie asks, "The Appalachian?" and BOOM! Just like in old Aunt Jeter's bar, the atmosphere changes from diffidence to damn near reverence. Suddenly Angie and Richie behind the counter want to know all about it. Angie says she's a California girl and is more interested, it seems, in how close I live to Ontario, California, where she's got family, than the trail, but the truth comes out that Michael and I and all our time-neighboring freak brethren have indeed walked 1,400-some miles to get here, here in the neighborhood of the S&J Deli Superette, a place with a strong, family-owned feeling. Water bottles filled, I go to the counter to pay up and Richie puts his hand on the sub, slides it toward me, and together they say, "Have a safe hike." Huh? Big Italian Richie is like, "You walked 1,400 miles and you're gonna try and pay me? Fah-get about it."

Back in the car, Gene says, "Yeah, New Yorkers are pretty soft-hearted."

Now it's past hiker midnight and I'm about to puke on Gummi Bears and Heineken, and everybody else has been asleep an hour or more. The chocolate-covered espresso beans I ate just to keep me from face-planting on the picnic table are about to wear off. Got to go. Goodnight and Godzilla.

I've had a recent revelation! It concerns pack weight. The day trail angel Gene slack-packed us 19 miles from the Friary to RPH, my foot pain and ankle sketchiness disappeared as I soared, comparatively weightless, at speeds in excess of three miles an hour.

"That's it!" I decided. "I'm tossing my pack and everything in it and keeping only my sleeping bag! No more fuel, no more stove, no more hot meals, no more first aid kit, no more too-much food. I'll grab a mesh laundry sack at the next town and go ultra-light like Grandma Gatewood.

Weight is the killer, my killer, even though mine is a relatively light pack. I subsequently did this very thing, mailing off a full eight pounds of lord-knows-what, but opting out of the mesh sack as it looked absurd; I kept the pack for one reason: the appearance of legitimacy. The pack is the signature of the thruhiker, the identifying mark that separates us from vagrancy, or rather shows us for what we are: the nobility among vagrants. I decided I would need the pack to catch rides and to keeps cops off my ass.

The result: I did move faster, felt better. In fact, I roared across New York, Connecticut, and Massachusetts. But I quickly reclaimed my Thinsulate pad, as the ground and/or floors of shelters were just too damn hard without it. Then in the Berkshires of Massachusetts, I began to freeze my ass off, in August!

As fall approaches, it won't be long. I'll be adding back a lot of the weight. I will continue to miss, however, my mp3 player, which was far too heavy with batteries and charger to lug "thru" to Maine.

Summer sounds come to me through the woods, sounds of children laughing and playing. I have crossed hundreds of empty dirt roads on this journey. But today I came across a dirt road deep in the woods that made me do a double take, jammed as it was with SUVs going somewhere. I'd been hearing sounds of what seemed like a radio in the woods at first, and then walking on realized it was bigger, maybe a parade in a nearby town. It was Sunday. Now here were all these cars cued up and moving at a snail's pace through the woods. As I crossed their path, I asked a driver what was up. "Parents' day at summer camp." Ah, fine memories of summer camp so long ago, of Susan and Melissa, so young and sweet. Mine was a Christian summer camp! My God, I was going to be a minister! You've got to love it.

My days are full of blueberries now. I eat them from trailside bushes as I walk. Blackberries and raspberries, too. It's nice.

What is it about daddy long leg spiders that they run exactly back toward you when you shoosh them away? I mean exactly! I flick 'em away and they retrace their steps perfectly. Weird.

I am a mass of bug bites and patches of poison ivy. I itch constantly but am very Zen about not scratching.

.The other day I summited Bear Mountain in the fog and went looking for the water fountain promised in my guidebook. This close to major cities, Appalachia's mountain tops often come with visitor centers and public bathrooms. In this case, both were closed, and the spigots yielded nada. But, heh! Look what we have here high on a mountain without a consumer, uh, I mean human, in sight! A Dasani water-dispensing machine!! Just $1.50! I "make" more water in one zap with my MIOX purifier than this machine can supply me for a buck and a half. What a laugh. I head down the mountain, find a spring, and roll my eyes at the absurdity of it all. I do mean: IT ALL!

Down at Bear Mountain Park, Mama Rooney feeds us. Rooney Tunes's mom drove down from Massachusetts with chicken and deviled eggs and pickles and macaroni salad. It is a nice treat. Then that night, after the zoo of broken-down animals and Walt Whitman and all, I'm fed a full meal by monks! What a world.

One day in New York State, I'm running at top speed through the forest, thunder rumbling overhead, rain imminent. The midday sky has darkened, the forest lit only by occasional flashes of heat lightning, yet no rain comes. I'm plugged into my mp3 player and running, transfixed by Radiohead's *Pyramid Song* playing over and over, the player set to repeat, and it's a dream. In the span of what seems like an hour running at speed, I cross a set of railroad tracks so wrapped up in the music, with the "black-eyed angels swam with me" that I never even looked to see a train coming. If I did look, it was with imperceptible awareness, some sixth sense. I am a wildcat deafened by the music but fully attuned in all other senses and on the move in a waking dream of the animal.

Toward the end of the storm that never came, the strange light still aglow, I surface from the forest and step into an open grassy field with an old iron arch where once must have been a road. No graveyard, no house nor sign of life save one: In rusted iron on the ancient arch are the words "Gate of Heaven." Tempted I am, not just a little, to walk through that gate. Just see where it takes me.

SIXTEEN

Off the Map in the Big Apple…Dinner with a 911 Firefighter for Whom God Definitely Had Other Plans…the Backpack as Potential Conveyance of Terror, or Why I Never Got to See the Big Apple from the Empire State…the Invisible Guest at Alice's Brooklyn Tea Party…Yab-Yuck and One Piss Poor Ambassador of Buddhism…Connecticut and Massachusetts Lost in a Blur of da Vincian Circles of Forward Motion…A Wild Horse with a Crepe Paper Heart…Wind Sock & Dave's Mattress Flight School…Mandi and Me in Our Crystal Palace Birch Tree Heaven.

Jesus! New York, what a clusterfuck. Beautiful, mind you. But still. One needs a local guide for this town. Haven't had much luck myself since NYFD Fire Chief Dennis dropped me in the Bronx and I hopped a subway to Times Square. OK. I've had plenty of "fun," doing the same thing I do every day on the trail, walking with pack on and taking in the world around me. But here in New York City, there are no roots to trip me, so I walk now with craned neck staring skyward at the vaulting, incomprehensible monoliths to man's vast ego.

Unfortunately, thanks to Ahmed Al-Ghambi & Co., there's this thing about backpacks in NYC that I never thought of. They don't like them. I tried to get up into the Empire State Building along with a jillion other tourists on this Saturday in July. Yeah, right. That went over like a fart in church. "Backpack! Oh, my God, Harry, he's got a backpack!" How was I to know I'd walk out of the woods and into the Big Apple and suddenly be viewed as a dangerous criminal, a walking thermonuclear weapon bound on blowing myself and a jillion fat tourists sky-high for no good reason at all. Without a hint of sarcasm and a heartfelt nod of solidarity to my brothers of color, I say thank God I'm white and have a disarming smile.

Okay, I admit I did think about it a little, the pack I mean. I actually looped back to Grand Central from Times Square to ditch my pack full of smelly socks and melted deformed Snickers bars and hand-carved tent stakes and granola (all dangerous items, I'm sure) in one of the many lockers I'd seen in movies for time eternal. But guess what? No lockers in Grand Central since 9/11. Well, fuck me! Excuse my gutter vernacular, but fuck those fuckin' jihad bastards who knocked a whole lot of lockers and loved ones out of the sky that heinous, surreal nightmare day three years ago. Thanks to them, I can't go up high and get a bird's-eye of the greatest city in America, the most famous city, a mythical Camelot known to me only in film and books until today. Thanks to Osama and carnage and orange alerts and paranoia and hell, probably even the war on drugs, I can't see the city from the sky.

Not that I'm complaining. I'll live, whereas many are sadly long gone. Seated here in Don Vito's pizzeria in Little Italy drinking a Peroni and wolfing down a slice of genuine NYC pizza, all floppy and fold-up-able and dripping cheese, and the waitress cute and not afraid to get close to me, breaking the two- (or is it three-) foot barrier of personal space held by most Americans, putting her face right close to mine as she suggests broccoli instead of pepperoni on my pizza. "You're absolutely right," I said. "I need vegetable matter. The forest is turning me into a junk food and dried-pasta mutant." For a moment, I wonder if her suggestion isn't a Tyler Durden thing, if members of Project Mayhem are right now back in the kitchen performing foul and ungodly acts on the pepperoni.

But let's talk about good food and the good people I stayed with last night. I had the honor yesterday of meeting Fire Chief Dennis Munnelly and his lovely family. After meeting them on the trail, I hiked some 18 miles to their town of Pawley, New York, whereupon they took me in, fed me dinner, got me showered and laundered and tucked into the couch bed of their guest room. After a day of running to meet them by dinnertime, I passed out fast and slept deep. Before bed, however, during dinner, I found out Dennis had been a Manhattan fireman in 2001. I had to ask.

Stories? Yeah, he had a story. It was short and bittersweet. "Those were my men. I would have been killed if I had been there. My entire unit was wiped out." He went on to say he'd been called away to Vermont the day before, something about coming to his wife's aid. A fluke. An anomaly. Jesus. What a thing to survive. God bless you, Dennis Munnelly.

Did I mention that I invited myself to dinner with the Munnellys? Oh, yeah. Met them on the trail yesterday morning when they were ending their morning hike and readying to drive back to Pawling. Did I want a ride, they asked? "Well, no, thanks," I said. "That would kind of defeat the purpose of my journey."

But there was a connection between us, strong I felt. This might have had something to do with Cristelle, their daughter, a girl so lovely that a braver man than I would have dropped to his knees and begged her hand in marriage right then and there amidst the wildflowers and the bees pollinating in the sun and her mother's lovely sing-song French accent. It didn't seem right to just say goodbye there and never see them again, especially since I was heading straight for their town and we could maybe visit and I could get better acquainted with Cristelle before our betrothal. So I just came out with it. "Why don't you invite me to dinner? I could tent in your yard?" That did it. Mother Muriel was all about it.

Cristelle just smiled all sweet, and all agreed that, yes, I would come to dinner and should sleep on their couch. Dennis was sitting in the car and, I think, more or less got roped into the deal by his friendly French-American wife. Hey, whatever brings people together. If not for sensual blossom Cristelle, honeybee me might not have had the honor and pleasure of meeting her mom and dad.

I see myself in their shower, my feet actually, ringed in dirt circles and all busted up like a couple of old fishing boats tossed ashore in a hurricane and circumscribed, slowly, by receding waters and mud. I see the hot steam of the shower and the cleansing waters hitting my champion feet and all that dirt swirling down the drain and hear myself whispering, "Thank you, God. Thank you, Buddha. I am so blessed."

Then came dinner and brief conversation, me all doped as though on Valium but really just stoned on fatigue, good food, and rest from all my running. Then sweet sleep. Then poof! I'm in Brooklyn, seated on Alice's couch. Alice from Wonderland. Alice from Idyllweird. We're rapping, catching up. Her puppy eats my shoes. She drinks coffee. I drink Foster's. We nap. Life is good.

Strange rhythms in Brooklyn. The evening with Alice unwound like sped-up time, the spring of a sprung clock in the arms of a hasty rabbit. I enjoyed about an hour alone with Alice before she tired of me. Or so it seemed. We were both tired so went down for a little nap at 3, slept damn near an hour before her friend Jamie showed up. Suddenly it was all about the girls, and Alice, for reasons I'll never know, ceased eye contact with me altogether. It was weird. Almost as though I'd disappeared. Maybe I had! Maybe I was the Cheshire Cat now, and naught but vapors and glistening teeth.

Alice and I, the recently self-titled "Your Madnessty" (to add to my long string of given trail names—Jester, Jack, Gadget, Malcovich—to name a few), have a long-running relationship with the Wonderland idiom. Actually, Alice has a VERY long-running relationship with Alice of Wonderland. I simply toy with the language of the story when relating to her. For Alice (not her real name) is in fact the fifth-generation granddaughter of the little girl Lewis Carroll took such a fancy to, both in his photography and opiate dream-filled fanciful tales of life in a netherworld of backwardses, upsidedowns and folks not-quite-right in the head.

Alice's friend Jamie is cute and speaks of interesting things, so I endeavor to get her to make eye contact, but meet with little success. She is in fact looking at everything but me, and I begin to follow her gaze, looking for faces in the smattering of inanimate objects to which she speaks. I am drinking beer. Have been since hitting Little Italy around noon all dizzy with the city and needing a beer to right myself in the unright world of dizzying heights and crushing crowds. Jamie and Alice are watching the idiomatic clock and telling disparaging tales of times past when they'd have to drink a bottle of vodka just to leave the house. Both are in their early 20s. I'm 37. I say nothing, drink my beer, and wait.

At last, apparently, the magical hour arrives and out come the blue glasses with ice, tonic water, and vodka. I hold the vodka bottle up and turn it around, sure that if I stare hard enough I'll see the words "Drink Me." Suddenly, there is laughter and connection between us, and a funny shift occurs. Although Alice continues to avoid my gaze, Jamie comes around and suddenly is talking TO me directly rather than to the walls and the furniture and such, none of whom, I dare say, were half as fond of her comely looks, blanched white skin, and auburn hair as I. (You notice this kind of shit when you've got nothing better to do but watch people. On such occasions, I notice a lot. Perhaps too much.)

Now Eleanor arrives and after a brief introduction in which I introduce myself in my Werner Herzog accent, she talks a blue streak in Germanlish. I'm thrilled to finally connect with someone. She's hilarious. A dancer and a big girl, she bounds about the Brooklyn flat like a wide-winged pelican yet graceful as a swan. Flinging open the fridge door, she curtsies then throws her legs high, first one then the other, arcing over the fridge door as though it were a footstool. My mouth forms the word "Wow."

But it's well-past hiker midnight now and though I don't make an issue of it nor do I even openly admit fatigue, I am caught yawning, caught closing my eyes. It feels like something of a sin in New York City to be nodding (without the aid of opiates) at some pre-midnight hour, but here I go. Out of sync with

244

the world again. Never quite on the up and up with the Laws of Time and rarely in line with the world of men.

Another guest shows up, and then another. One is "The Jackie," so referred to because of all the stories I have heard about her and the photos I've seen. Alice is a photographer and Jackie her best model. Jackie is the one person I was truly looking forward to meeting tonight. Alice told me Jackie really wanted to meet me, too, to check out this character who moved about the rigid paths of men like a silverfish or hawk, sliding, gliding, and outlining the irony of it all in sweeping ink scribbles and shark tooth keystrokes of his pocket computer.

Jackie, however, hardly says hello. No, in fact she doesn't even say that. I say something like, "So, you are The Jackie," going on to say that I'd heard lots about her. But that's it. No conversation. Jackie, Jamie, and Alice become a block of impenetrable female energy. Jackie follows suit instantly with the no-eye-contact thing.

On the one hand, it's endearing, watching these three soul sisters unite and share such obvious camaraderie and love. But it's also sad. Very quickly I have gone from "featured guest" to invisible man, a second-rate Cheshire Cat forced into invisibility by majority vote.

I keep my composure. I keep my eyes on them all, looking and listening for a way "in" to the conversation, an "in" that never comes. Eleanor either notices my painful waning visibility or relates to it or something. She keeps saying that I need to go to bed. Finally, I do just that, shrinking down behind the couch like the mythical Alice when she was just small.

So it was that smack in the middle of the party in a one-room railcar-shaped flat in Brooklyn, New York, I conducted the ritual of my 134 nights of life in the forest. I lay out sleeping pad and bag, unfurled my fleece pillow, hit the floor behind the couch, and promptly passed out. I remember being half-conscious of folks leaving not long after. I never met Alice's boyfriend, who returned home sometime later that night. In the morning, I packed with thruhiker efficiency and stealth, my own self-taught method of silent packing, so done usually out of consideration for others still sleeping in the close-knit quarters of trail shelters. I thus disturbed no one, not even the sleeping dog. I swiped my leftover slice of New York pizza and oil can of Foster's from the fridge and eased out the heavy metal door, out into morning, down a hole in the streets of Brooklyn, through a series of tunnels and trains, and back to the safe forest world.

I felt small in New York, and Alice's Brooklyn tea party did little to help that. She did, in fact, make it worse. But no matter. We had our fun last summer. Out here in the forest I am a giant again. I am Alice when she's 10 feet tall. Hell, I've come 1,500 miles between March 20 and today, the 2nd of August. The book says I'm on Schaghticoke Indian lands now. I regret that the only image I can muster in my mind of an Indian running is that of *The Last of the Mohicans* actor Daniel Day Lewis playing an Indian. With apologies to real Native Americans, I have to say I feel an awful lot like that Indian lately, like the Last Survivor of some once-great tribe, my legs and arms and poles (spears?) drawing blurred circles beside me like the pistons and armatures on old steam train wheels. Machine, Indian, White man-I stop at a stream and splash down, cool off. Exhausted, I drop onto the footbridge and rest a moment. Looking up, I see steam coming off my body, mist rising skyward and waves of my heat warping the trees and sky above me.

I'm up and moving again, a little slower, when around the bend comes this shirtless day hiker with hairy chest and folds of fat hanging over his pack waist-belt. If I'm the last of the Mohicans, he's Boss Hogg on an ill-conceived weight-loss kick. Hogg stops and starts making conversation with me through my headphone music-busied ears. I oblige him by pressing PAUSE, and he asks me what I'm listening to. "Morphine," I respond. Suddenly his eyes are giant shiny eight-balls as he says, all accusatory-like, "You're shooting morphine?" I look at him like he's grown a third head and reply, "You asked me what I was listening to, Sir," the word *sir* snapping off my tongue with a thick dose of sarcasm as I smell cop all over him. "Do you think if I were shooting morphine I would have made it fourteen hundred and (a quick glance at my watch as I do the math) forty-nine miles from Georgia to here in four months? Music, man. The name of the band is Morphine."

I decided Boss Hogg was either a cop or a moron. Either way, his intrusion upon my bliss was over. I spun round on my poles and flew down the path at speed, an endorphin-stoned laughing squid climbing out of the sea and taking up land travel with a shit-eating grin and legs to spare.

Last night it was cowboy camping here by this trickling little brook, a tub-sized pool all my own, and me on my rain poncho spread out over a sweet soft bed of green, green moss, no tent, just the sil-nylon tarp staked in on three corners and ready to be pulled full over me in case of rain. No rain came. Cold dinner of sweet granola and dried fruit, powdered milk, then out like a light with the last light of day, worn out from an early morning rise in Brooklyn, the commuter train back to the trail, and the ensuing 16-mile hike out of New York state and into Connecticut. That's right! I said Connecticut.

This severe depressive head case on crazy meds just entered his 10th state in a 14-state run from the illness of inertia. Look out, Everest, here I come!

Now just three miles from Kent where I will intercept a package of food and very possibly stick my whole heavy pack and everything but the "bear necessities, the simple bear necessities" in a box and ship it off, off my back, off my sore dying feet, then RUN! Run fast as a leopard across Connecticut and Massachusetts and into Vermont where at last I'll feel the Cherry Garcia ice cream buzz of the sweet, sweet finish line not far ahead, and noble granite New Hampshire full of family and then Maine, Maine, Maine! Beautiful! Get me there, feetzes! Get me there, Jesus! Get me there, Jehovah and Buddha and Allah and all my friends and pets long dead or not so long, Luci in the sky with Matilda. Get me there! I love you! I love you all, and I walk now to kill time, grandiose, to hasten this journey back to you.

Awoke this morning to the pleasant sound of rain outside, drops plopping on large leaves of garden plants, dripping from tree branches, lovely. Just what I needed to hear at 6:45 a.m., still wrung out from a week of solid big mile days capped off by the past two nights of horrid survival sleep, first in a rain of daddy longlegs and next in a real downpour that flooded the ground beneath my tarp.

I rise from comfy futon and visit the commode. I contemplate the connection between the words "commode" and "accommodation." Perhaps it simply means that an accommodation is a place to stay where there's a commode?

The accommodations here are just dandy. Peg Leg and I had been picked up at a road crossing by a woman I'll call Switch. Switch introduced herself as a devout Buddhist and said we could stay the night at her place in a nearby small Connecticut town, hinting that it would be nice if we made a donation to the erection of a large Buddha statue she was building to adorn her front lawn. Sure, why not. It was cheaper than a motel by far and included laundry and a shower.

Back at her house, things went smoothly enough save one detail: the transfer of money. You can tell a lot about a person by how they ask for and/or receive money. Switch was not what you might call at ease with the transaction, and her uneasy tone of voice struck a brief odd chord in my first impressions of this otherwise pleasant woman. I was so exhausted at this point, however, that Switch could have been Satan himself in female form, and for the love of a bed I would have seen only an angel, a shower, and a pillow.

247

This morning then, my musings complete, I returned to bed toute suite. Feeling a bit of a headache, I took a few ibuprofen and went back to sleep. Ah, it was a divine sleep. It had been all night, starting from around 7 p.m. when I first hit the pillow. All told I slept about 14 hours. Wonderful. I'd needed it badly.

Then WHAM! Like the crash of unfriendly thunder, reality slams into my sleep with locomotive force. "No! No, this can't be!" a voice is shouting. My eyes snap open and I roll over to face the shouting.

What I see is gruesome. The third eye Switch had been telling us about just the night before had flared and swollen, grown pustulant and mean and twitchy. Downright cannibalistic, it had eaten her two normal eyes making of her the first Buddhist Cyclops I've ever seen.

"No this isn't right! You must be out of here at once! This is the only time I have to clean the room! No! You have 15 minutes to clear out! Dammit!"

With the slam of the door it was gone. It, she, whatever that was. It wasn't the kindly calm Buddhist woman we'd met the night before. No, this was no bodhisattva, but a beast, a monster with bloated head and gaunt body, an hysterical jabbering thing, a bipolar version of the Switch we'd recently known but not at all the same.

Just the night before, whilst drifting off to sleep, I had thanked Kerouac for working his dharma bum magic for me and landing me this sweet haven of rest. As Peg Leg and I hurriedly pack our bags to go, I half revoke that gratitude. So much for yab-yum and the sweet loving girls of the Buddhist beat revolution. Homegirl's yab-yum days were over. Switch had clearly slipped a gear out of sync with dharma and straight into yab-yuck, the culture of fear and angst and worry, an ugly zone where true full-hearted altruism (of which I have seen so much in my AT travels) is clearly an impossible dream.

To think the night before I had arrived at a possible name for my book on the trail: *Faith in Humanity Restored.* Oh, well. It was boring and pat anyway. I still have the faith, however. But I won't be using that title now, it having come to me in the wrong place at the wrong time, in the angst-ridden morning realm of Switch the schizoid Buddhist.

A few days later, I arrived in Massachusetts and noted that a thruhiker-friendly and quite reasonably priced place to stay the night was, of all things, a Buddhist retreat. Like a child fallen from his bicycle just days after the training wheels came off, I forced myself to get back on the bike and give it another try.

That evening, the retreat proved itself a fine place, and I was grateful. However, I awoke late that night plagued by a horrid dream, a dream that time had tricked me, that in my race to cross the mid-Atlantic states with impossible speed, I myself had jumped gears in Time and Space and, in fact, Here was really There, and in the morning I would be rudely awakened by a psycho woman, a dream-loop of yab-yuck infinitum. Had it been Massachusetts and not Connecticut that we'd met Switch? Had I dreamt the past few days of hiking? Was the retreat the real home of Miss Yab Yuck?

Decompressing now after a charge of the light brigade, three utterly mad days of racing across Connecticut, trekking poles like lobster claws hungrily snapping at rocks, my legs and arms furiously spinning in da Vincian circles of forward motion as I ate up mile after mountainous mile of 54 miles of Connecticut in two days. I wanted to step over the state line into my birth state REALLY bad. I had set the goal to arrive in Massachusetts in time for my cousin's birthday.

Reason? None but that I was born in Massachusetts, and for 1,500 miles I've felt I was "walking home." My favorite cousin, Justin, was also born in Massachusetts, his father's family going way back in Malden. Anyway, I worked for it. Today I pay in spades. I am the Energizer Bunny towing freight cars.

I hate to say anything disparaging about the guy who wrote the trail guidebook that 3,000 hikers spent $16 a pop on, but here goes. Wingfoot, you screwed me! For months I had been planning carefully to "return home" to my birth state of Massachusetts after decades away in California, the AT as my ticket home. I had planned to burn through Connecticut in two days and cross the line into Massachusetts before midnight on Justin's birthday, just to say I had.

I fell a little behind this week, so had to pull a 27-mile day to make it last night on time. I even gave up an invitation from several other hikers to join them in hefting cases of beer up a mountain out of Kent, Connecticut, for a party at a shelter a few miles shy of Massachusetts. No way was I going to miss my goal.

Well, I made it! I crested a mountain and in descending saw a sign with arrows that said Connecticut this way, Massachusetts that way. Wingfoot's book breaks the trail down into increments of a tenth of a mile, and after coming this far, I knew exactly where I was based on the length and speed of my step measured against my stopwatch. The only variable was Wingfoot's coordinates. Thus said, the sign was right where the book said it should be, so I took it as the state line sign. I was so pleased. Then I got up this morning, hiked half a mile downstream, and arrived at a big sign in the woods saying

"Welcome to Massachusetts!" What? Now either the Commonwealth of Massachusetts just recently moved its state line, or Wingfoot's guidebook is WRONG! So much for the facts, Bronco!

Thanks to the man everyone on the trail calls Wingnut, I had failed in my mission. Crestfallen, I began a long grueling ascent up the first of many mountains ahead of me here in the Berkshires of Massachusetts. My depression hit me like a flash flood, triggered by my failed goal. I was so wrecked I could barely speak. As one after another spider web or silkworm strand or whatever the hell they were struck me in the face, I became angry. I tripped over my poles. I slipped on wet rocks. And I shouted. A lot. "Dammit, dammit!"

Then, it hit me: I'm angry. I'm angry! Suddenly I was skipping down the path, pleased to be expressing anger for a change. I've heard it said by many a shrink: depression is suppressed anger. It felt good to express anger, a thing I rarely do.

I hear my father's voice in my head, telling me for the Nth time that I wouldn't be depressed if only I had Jesus in my heart. "Dad," I say, "God and Jesus are in me, all around me. But I will never embrace a religion that claims it has a lock on the path to God and Heaven."

Then he says it, his voice up an octave, a mix of frustration and accusation, the line I've been hearing forever: "Son, don't get so DEFENSIVE!" And wham! It's a lock. I've got the core of the Death Star in my sights. I've found Neo's location in the prison outside the Matrix. The key fits.

I know now why I never get angry: Because Daddy didn't let me. Father made anger, in this case healthy anger, an instinctual self-defense mechanism as old as DNA, a thing to be ashamed of long before my memory was memory.

Depression, thou hast a new name. It is suppression.

On a lighter note, I hitched a ride out of Kent back to the trail with a stunning woman roughly my age or younger named Athenade. I wanted to marry her right then and there. Was she married? I couldn't tell. Her ring finger was hidden by her grip on the steering wheel and she was late for her goddaughter's birthday party and had to run. But she liked me, this I know. Despite my own wealth of athletic smells, I picked up on her pheromones immediately. If I could go back in time and change one thing from the AT journey, I'd be right back in her car, my hand on hers and, ring or no ring, I'd seize the pheromone day and grant Athenade her Tarzan fantasy so convincingly, so completely, with such masculine power and sensuality, she'd totally forget she had a god-daughter.

Every day I walk now hard and fast and always thoughts in my head and always I think, "When I get to my destination, I will write at length on these thoughts." But always it is the same. I arrive exhausted from 20-some miles and a 3,000-, 4,000-, 5,000-foot elevation gain over the course of the day and write nothing, falling asleep in my bunk or beneath the sky, keyboard splayed out on my belly, tiny input screen as dark as I am drunk with fatigue.

Now on the dock here on Goose Pond, that perfect golden light of late afternoon, 7:30 p.m. on this August night in the Berkshires, lights up the green corset of full rich forest surrounding the pond, flawless, uninterrupted. Such light is the most fleeting of gifts. It is given, and then gone in an instant.

I have bathed in the pond and washed my sweaty body, toweling dry with a pack-sized towel most people refer to as a washcloth. I eat Fig Newtons and toss crumbs to the fish milling around my still-screaming-in-pain feet now soaking in the icy water. The fish eat the crumbs and get greedy. A big one nips at my toe, and when I jerk away in surprise, I scare away the lot of them.

I came earlier to a bridge over the pond's outlet. I was happy to have arrived at Goose Pond. But punch drunk from fatigue, I nearly pitched sideways off the little bridge and into the brook. These words came to me then: Tippy tippy topsy turvey, spent and bent and a little scurvy.

Not a hundred meters later I came to a sign in the woods announcing that the cabin was still another mile off. I couldn't believe it. I mean, there was the frikken pond, right beside me. How could it be another mile? I sat down hard on a mossy rock and began to cry. I am new to the game of extreme physical fitness, and I push myself too hard. My endurance grows and grows, but my feet, and often my ankles, are not keeping pace with my muscular and respiratory health.

I cry because for the past hour I have had that recurring sense that with the next step or the next I will piss myself, my bladder control somehow connected to my pain threshold. I don't know. It's all new to me. But I had to push. I had to push out of stony Pennsylvania and through New Jersey and New York and Connecticut, too. I've been pushed, too, by increasingly unfriendly townsfolk, by hostile hosts, by ghosts of my New England past, and by one truly creepy stretch of Blair Witch-like woods in Connecticut. Now I'm halfway through Massachusetts in just two days. It's madness, but I've had to do it to keep from quitting altogether. It's psychological. I had to achieve New England, and once in, get to Vermont as soon as possible. Why?

Perhaps because I grew to the age of 13 here and watched my parents tear each other to shreds here. Perhaps it is because they broke me here. Like a wild horse with a crepe paper heart, I was broken, and in the breaking, a part of me died here. Now, like some ghost on parole, the little dead me is bound by law to Massachusetts, stuck here waiting for the rest of me to die that it may join the whole and be free at last.

But it can't follow me into Vermont, oh no! Because hungry lover Vermont spoons my beloved New Hampshire. They're like bosom buddies on the map. New Hampshire will soon follow Vermont. Then there's nothing left but Maine. I want this victory in my life. I need this finish. I want this badge called Katahdin. I want to have finished something for once in my life. So my feet will just have to carry me there. Somehow. But wait.

Have I finished nothing in my life? I must have finished something. But what?

Don't remember. There beside Goose Pond my hands fly up to my ears to cover them. I see my reflection in the water. I'm a boy of maybe 12 with giant azure blue eyes shining, stunned with betrayal. Now the boy is bald, his eyes in sunken sockets. "Not listening. Not listening! Smeogel not listening!"

Stunning blue sky today on October Mountain, clear and bright and cold. The temperature in the forest shade hovers in the 50s. I froze last night in my thin summer bag with all my clothes on, cursing myself for shipping off my thermals in my last weight-reduction frenzy a few days back. How was I to know it would be near freezing at night in the Berkshires on August 6?

But pancakes this morning at Goose Pond cabin, blueberries and tasting fine, and fresh coffee, too, even though I couldn't seem to connect with any of the seven or so people present. Only Jolan-Jolan did I click with, and thus walked out with him this morning. His name is something picked up in Indonesian travels meaning "walking, walking." Nice enough guy. Short and bearded and bespectacled, he begs to be called Tyler, the scientist character in one of my all time favorite films, *Never Cry Wolf*.

We walked together a while until nature called. I answered the call, and I haven't seen him since. Expected to see him lunching at this shelter midday, but nope. As Thompson said, "We move in fast strange ways." Indeed, I would see Jolan-Jolan again only once, and not for several days at that.

Been encountering a lot of southbound thruhikers now. Meeting them is a mixed bag. On the one hand, it's nice to think, "Hey, this guy's got 1,500 miles ahead of him, and I've got fewer than 700." On the other hand, it is socially awkward. Both "he" and I are moving at breakneck pace through the forest and neither really wants to stop and chat but you do anyway out of politeness. There are exceptions to the "duty bound by protocol stop," and it's all in the eyes. Sometimes you just see it in someone's eyes and know "I must meet this person."

I met a sobo the other day who had just a week ago been picked up by my buddy Dave in Vermont. Dave was hauling mattresses to a storage place or something and picked up a guy hitching named Wind Sock. Apparently Dave gets talking excitedly about his friend who's doing the trail northbound and blah blah blah and, says Wind Sock, Dave's foot is going down harder on the accelerator to match his enthusiasm and suddenly whooosh! Off the roof of the truck come two big mattresses flying off into traffic. Wind Sock says it was a miracle no one was killed. I can see the headline: Death by Sealy Posturepedic.

So I get the names but little else: Charlie the Tuna (my favorite), Hemingway, Skins, Tumblelina, Four Winds. Doctor Jones, meet Lord Duke. So it goes.

I've long kicked Jester, by the way. Started kicking the name 900 miles ago but no one would accept a replacement. It took two 10-day zero chunks to displace me enough in the AT space-time continuum to where I could introduce Duke to a new crowd. But I'm not happy with just Duke, either. I was Duke in the other world. I want an original trail name, one that sparks a story, as so many do. But it's hopeless, too late in the game. When I use Lord Duke instead of just Duke, I get these incredulous looks, mostly from women, like, "Well, don't we think we're special." Which sucks. Would they like me better if I were Peasant Duke?

I met a guy named Jersey the other day who says he hiked last year, almost the whole trail, then quit in Maine. Andover, Maine! That's sooo close! Why? Said he wasn't going to make it by October 15, when the park service closes the icy rock mountain of Katahdin. So the guy turns around and goes home. What a nut! He's doing it all over again this year. You see a lot of that out here.

You won't see it from me. I'm of a mind that life's too short to repeat anything anymore. I want to do everything, and do it once. There's too much to see and do, and life's short. May as well do something different next time, every time.

Deep in the dark forests of the Berkshires, a tiny pornographic little wood nymph walked alongside me a spell and told me stories to keep my mind off my screaming feet. Here is one of his stories, told to me in his thick Scottish brogue.

Hansel and Gretel were out back doin' it doggy style in the woodshed when suddenly out of the shadows came a giant weasel who bit off Hansel's head, and tearing off the boy's cock ring said, "With this, Gretel, do I thee wed."

I swear, that really happened. Or was it the pain meds talking? I'm losing it.

Today whilst walking through a "select-cut" harvested chunk of Berkshire forest (very odd, I thought that they would harvest right on the AT, and recently), I had a sudden urge to hear Neil Diamond, and to see again the film *The Jazz Singer*. Why? I remember it as a tale of triumph over old ideas and traditions, a triumph for one's personal mission, deeply felt by old Neil. Why not.

The forest has changed as I move into New England. Mostly pine and birch forest now. Birch fall and break apart like candy cane, sections, chunks spread all about the woods like so many scrolls of parchment strewn about in the wake of some ancient library bombing. If there is any one natural symbol of New England in my mind, it is the birch tree. We had birch in our yard in Melrose, Massachusetts when I was 10. In winter, a freezing rain and snow would bend the birch straight over until it formed a crystal palace through which my sister Mandi and I would wander, dazed angels in a newly renovated Heaven.

I don't want much from this life. I just want that. I just want that Birch Tree Heaven again. I want icicles warm to the touch. I want no death, or a world wherein death is definite, de-fined, divined to end in bliss. I want everyone to get to go to Heaven. I want everyone to believe that everyone gets into Heaven. Given that knowledge and security, I want everyone to start living life in the Here and Now as though there is no Heaven, as though there is no tomorrow. I want an end to fear and judgment and guilt. I want love. Is that too much to ask?

SEVENTEEN

A Bland and Half-Hearted Ode by Thoreau...Swimming for Beer and the Amusement of Beavers...Slower Than a Half-Stomped Slug...PATTS: a Support Group for Sufferers of Post-AT Traumatic Syndrome...Ten Lovely Days in a Bromley Dave Haze...Still Frank, Woo-Hoo and Tullamore Dew...Tinker the Trail Angel and Cannibalism at Sundown...

Strange night. All alone here in the bunkhouse behind Bascom Lodge high atop Mt. Greylock, AT Mile 1,571.5 and the highest point in Massachusetts. The Bascom, a lovely old lodge with breathtaking views to the south and west, provides bunks, blankets and pillows, and access to the lodge's showers for ten bucks, a lot less than the cost of a room in the lodge itself. But down here in the bunkhouse tonight I am the lone thruhiker, and as I walk from lodge to bunks in the growing dark and cold, the clouds settle on the mountain and caress you with their damp embrace, the whole eerie place a labyrinth of low hedges reminiscent of the film *The Shining*. I am stunned at the winterlike conditions of the past week here in the Berkshires. It's the first week of August! It can't be in the 40s! But it is tonight, and the other day whilst hiking I donned my fleece for the first time since the Smoky Mountains, wearing it while hiking, that is.

Now to add to the creepy *Shining* theme, a flashlight beam searches in the window of the bunkhouse long after I've climbed into bed and someone jiggles the lock. I have bolted the door. Why not? I'm the only one here, and it's frikken spooky out there so...so...so there!

But suddenly it occurs to me that it may be a late-arriving thruhiker, very late indeed. I remove the keyboard from my lap, climb out from beneath a mountain of blankets, and go to the door. Opening it, I see only the spirits swirling 'round in the dark cloaked under the cover of low-flying clouds like pickpockets in a crowded piazza. There is no one there.

But I am not entirely alone. A bold little mouse came out to inspect my food cache a while back when I still had the light on. I found a five-gallon paint bucket with a firm lid and locked up my food for the night. Sorry, Little Friend.

No frills, someone called it. It was a lodge like this one somewhere a ways back and offered, in addition to their normal high-price rooms, "no frills" rooms for thruhikers. Which is funny. Because for those of us who have laid face to the grass or upon wood slats in drafty half-cabins full of mice and spiders for four months, our "frill-o-meters" are quite skewed toward the simplest of comforts. A roof is a frill, a bunk a frill, a bath a thrill!

It seems to me I have stayed in nearly a hundred funky places like this in the past four and a half months. Last night in Dalton, Massachusetts, I showed up at the Shell station in town and, on a tip from other thruhikers (one not published in the guidebook), I got hooked up with Rob, a local musician and friend to thruhikers. There I found Jolan-Jolan, Skins, Hemingway, and a few others all flopped out watching *Jurassic Park* on TV. When I first came into the house, I went to sit on the couch in the living room and was stopped in mid-sit by Rob, who said, "Nope, sorry, son. Out on the porch until you've showered." I'd bought a giant jug of some locally brewed IPA, and was already sipping on it and pouring cups for the boys, so I took it in stride. "I'll be out here in the quarantine area enjoying my beer," I said, fully willing to take a shower but having to wait til it was unoccupied.

I've slept on floors, on rooftops, in basements, in an old jail, in stone huts built by men of the Depression, and in sweet old log cabins atop mountains, and on the edge of long prairies and ponds. I've had a few motel nights, not many. I've slept out under the stars and through torrential rains. I've slept side by side with other thruhikers in dozens of shelters, cabins of the three-walled variety. But I have rarely been alone in a structure or hostel of any kind. Rooney Tunes and I even slept on those picnic tables in that small-town pavilion where the locals of Vernon, New Jersey, gather for barbecues. Now that was a helluva night.

Tonight, however, is unique to my experience thus far. I noticed in the lodge ledger that I have just about caught Mousebait and White Patch. I am glad. I caught up to Kris and his girl, Kelly. But Kris and Kelly fell behind me just as fast, and Rooney Tunes, too. Jackie and Ry have never caught up. Strong of body and driven by the prize, I can't stop to let them catch up. I'm like a junky, my body addicted to its new 20-mile/day regimen. I remain thus alone.

I could have zeroed in Dalton. Could have had Rob drive me the 10 miles to Cheshire to get my food drop at the local P.O. this Saturday morning. But I chose to rise, hungover as hell from half a dozen Budweisers atop my jug of local brew, and hike out. Damn near running, I made Cheshire just before the P.O. closed for the weekend, then humped it, slower than a half-stomped slug, sick as suicidal salmonella, up the highest mountain in Massachusetts. Can you say dumb ass?

Dumb Masshole? Funny, but I heard that term used by a lot of nobo thruhikers once safely out of Massachusetts and into Vermont. Being from Massachusetts, but having left it at a young age, I'd never heard the term *Masshole* and took no offense. I imagine a few of my Taxachusetts readers will, but hey. I didn't invent either term, nor was I the person obnoxious enough to inspire some clever New Hampshireite to put two and two together and voila! An abbreviated insult!

I can see where nobo thruhikers would find Mass natives, and perhaps New Englanders as a whole, rather unfriendly and rude after the astounding and pandemic hospitality of the South. Hey, I'm from the West 25 years now, so I'm impartial. It's true, all that stuff about southern hospitality. Of course, I am white. And my hair was cut short for the trail. Anyway, moving on.

I had to go. A lot of people, guys, I was going to say, and it is mostly the guys who do this, find a snug haven like Rob's and stick there a while, rest up, veg out. I thought about it this morning, Budweiser-beaten as I was, but my mind was made up the moment someone lit a cigarette in the house and the TV clicked on and the day of testosterone loafing began. I was out the door faster than you can say "television kills and cigarette smoking sucks." Or was that the other way around? Whatever.

Once again, that's the beauty of the trek. You can always LEAVE! Just keep moving. The woods are free.

For those of you who feel trapped in shitty lives, you might ask yourselves: "What's keeping me here?" Is it a manipulative partner? Run. Is it a baby, a child? Stay. Or run from said manipulative partner and take the child with. Work out the legalities later. Is it bills? Burn 'em. Is it stuff? Burn it. Or sell it and buy a backpack. Is it depression?

Well, hopefully, at this point in my story, you know what to do with that. Walk. Walk and take your meds and don't stop until you've forgotten what you look like from lack of mirrors in the forest. Walk until you pee your pants laughing amongst your new fast-friends. For you will make friends on the AT. They'll be among the coolest, strongest ilk of friends you'll ever have.

I think this is because, on the well-trodden AT anyway, one is free to be selective. If you tire of someone on the trail, you simply pack up and walk. No one will bat an eye. So it's a weeding out process. When you run into them again days or weeks later, you'll be glad for it and so will they. It's one more example of how the Appalachian Trail is about FREEDOM in every sense of the word.

Live from *The Shining* Mountain Lodge in the eerie mists and phantom snowdrifts of a freezing August night in New England, I paint pictures for you from bed like Frida Kahlo. However, also like Frida, I mostly paint myself.

Somewhere in southern Vermont it occurs to me to ask, "Where have the fireflies gone?" Strong scent of Christmas along much of the trail yesterday, today in alpine regions, the highest of the Appalachian highs 3,000 and 4,000 feet in Massachusetts, Vermont.

Right now the smell of cool new rain-washed air and all these trees and all of this floor-level plant life just happy, exhaling oxygen in gratitude for rain, sweet rain. I'm in a position to appreciate the rain here dry beneath my sil-nylon tarp slung so low to the ground that I'm nose to tarp on my back in the dark. Almost. I have room to breathe. Distant lightning so faint, faint as the flicker of the now-distant fireflies of the South. Where have the fireflies gone? Would that I had known I'd be bidding them farewell back in...? How far back was it? Pennsylvania? Jersey? I miss them.

In New England they've been replaced by mad mushrooms red and orange and purple popping up everywhere in that graveyard dig smell of earth. To equate the lovely scent of loam with death, with all of our deaths, is this so wrong?

Speaking of death, up on Greylock gray and cold in the clouds when I walked over it anyway, young urban professionals strolled about Nature's Learning Center there in the old lodge, the yups clad in the newest and the finest REI has to offer, Golite bags for the day hikers, Patagonia jackets, and fleece by Marmot. They stroll the grounds and outside read the words of Henry David carved poorly in the wrong kind of rock such that the words are chipping away.

Thoreau. Of all the words, of all the bad-ass tough love to humanity and real love of the earth he expressed in ink and oratory, of all his tight Harvard-taught expressions of grief over the stupidity of man and the crystalline constancy of nature, clear as Walden ice, of all this, the poor yups read from the rock a bland and half-hearted ode to the view from their puny Massachusetts mountain. I'm sorry. But I think Henry David would agree. Lowell, Massachusetts, native Kerouac, too. I read it and shook my head. God help mankind if all he ever chooses to commemorate are the blandest of the bland expressions of great minds. But I digress. I'm sure many of the yups are

Ivy League graduates and thus have read all the best literature through the ages. We can hope.

Did I mention that some of my last few steps in the none-too-thrilling state forever stamped on my birth certificate were across a boring suburban town and, here comes the good part, up somebody's driveway? No kidding. The AT crosses a lot of weird turf including roads, bridges, farms, and tons of private land by way of easements, but this beat all. A thruhiker actually has to hike right up some poor Mass bastard's newly tarred driveway so close to the house you can smell what's for dinner as you pass. Then it's up through their yard, and off into the forest beyond. A short distance later, you're in Vermont. What a country!

Tonight it is the song of rocks and water wrestling in the brook below. It is the plop plap plap of raindrops dropped 20 minutes ago from sky, now reaching my tarp from high above its leafy canopy. It is the comfort of a hundred years of leafy dead matter making cushy my bed and half a dozen small trees and leafy plants here beneath my tarp and popping out all around me, like sleeping in the living room of a plant freak, and all because there are so damn many of them that I could barely find clearing enough to throw down my ground cloth poncho and make this night's home. Home away from home.

Going on five months now of life inside this tunnel of greens and gray of stone and white and shades of brown forever. Sometimes blue of sky seen through treetops but mostly not, as eyes like laser pointers scan the trail ahead for footing, obstruction, bugs, animals, mud, rock, root, you name it. Coming out the tunnel momentarily at power line easements or long gravel-surfaced roads that start and end nowhere in the wood, it's bedazzling. Coming out into these places to fluttering eyelids and retreating pupils as eyes adjust to the sudden influx of light is almost too much. But wonderful it is, too, such a flood of glorious light after so long in the dark of seeming eternal forest.

Here in Vermont a new trick: beaver-flooded sections of trail sometimes deep enough you have to wade through. Beaver dams everywhere and mud, mud, mud. Now I just want to see one of the critters in action.

So today on a dare and a bet for 10 pints of good Vermont beer, I summoned the fearless spirit of my youth, stripped down to shorts and dove into a swampy beaver pond, swam a short distance, and climbed atop a beaver mound for the amusement and photo snapping fun of fellow thruhikers Mousebait, Keytone, and White Patch. They were beside themselves with laughter and amusement, and I was happy to oblige. They didn't believe that I would actually do it. Why not? Personally, I didn't see the challenge, but I took their dare and later their beer.

Three a.m. tired, and now hunger returns as the body, awake at this unruly hour, thinks it time to eat again. Woken by the storm now passed, I thought I'd write a bit. Five months of bug bites itching, of spiders crawling, though none tonight, I'm happy to report. Five months of going days unshowered, of lousy Lipton dinners that taste queerly of Heaven after long days hiked, of blisters and split toes, sore pads of feet, tweaked knees and ankles. But then there's the more obvious bennies, the ever-growing and sculpted muscles of thighs and calves, carved from wood, carved from marble. Having never been an athlete, I find these changes in my body astounding, beautiful, sexy even.

With but 500 miles or so to go to Katahdin, I wonder: What next?

Then suddenly I stopped. Just like shutting down a jet engine with the flick of a toggle switch, I shut off weeks and weeks of mad stomping through mid-Atlantic states and came to rest, like that jet engine from the sky in *Donnie Darko*, smack dab in the Marlboro-lovin'arms of David, my New Mexico friend and brother.

Dave grew up skiing at his family's winter home at the base of Bromley Ski Mountain, what was for us AT Mile 1,650 or so, and just so happened to be out there supervising some renovations on the house when I came walking through. Did I have fun at Dave's? Does the Pope shit in the woods? Ten daze! Ten days passed like a Gaussian blur of colorful, wonderful food, a microbrew beer-smeared rainbow of steak and shrimp and chockablock omelets and burgers and salmon and fresh salads so varied in content as to be mini-jungles. And beer. Cases of carbos to restore twiggy me to some semblance of my former self, all of it top quality, all of it on Dave.

One rarely is gifted a better friend and host than my Albuquerque amigo Dave. You remember Dave? Dave who met sobo Wind Sock and in his excitement of talking trail, let fly a few mattresses down the highway? Dave from the train ride to Georgia? Dave the late arrival that day at the Albuquerque station who delivered me a six of Franziskaner Hefe-Weizen, my favorite beer in the world, but then had to detrain, who I wished would race his car ahead to Amtrak's next northern stop at Vegas, throw caution to the wind and jump aboard and ride with me across America? That Dave. My X hated Dave. I love Dave.

Dave and I pulled a handful of hikers off the trail for respite, and for those who wanted to work, there was work aplenty, and Dave paid in cash, to say nothing of the constant banquet and the plush living conditions. We were drunken fools, and we celebrated life in the manner of kings. I think Dave was sincerely proud of me for making it so far afoot, and I sucked deep of the marrow of Vermont ski chalet living that week. Not exactly what Thoreau meant by that phrase, but old Henry David would forgive me, I think.

My time at Dave's coincided with the Burning Man festival about to ignite in Nevada, and there was no question of my abandoning my plush post .4 miles from the AT to fly 4,000 miles to a dusty desert circus, the heyday of which, to this eight-time participant attendee, has passed. So I built us a man of our own. Constructed in the driveway from all manner of crap from the overflowing remodeling project dumpster, my little nine-foot-tall man looked a bit pathetic next to the real thing. Lucky for me, the real thing was far, far away. No one in attendance, not David, not Mousebait or White Patch, and not my cousin's friend or Justin himself, who had made the long drive to Manchester to deliver me my winter gear, had ever been to Burning Man.

So, after a long evening of divine cuisine and bacchanalian banter under the influence of copious amounts of various intoxicants legal and not, we assembled out front and I lit the man. The flame went out. I tried again, and again he smoldered and died. As drunk people will do, the gang drifted off into the house leaving me slightly peeved. High as I was, however, the peeve passed immediately and, like Kilgore trying to surf in Charlie's territory with sniper fire still coming from the jungle beyond, I called down the Apocalypse from above (from Dave's garage actually, and his freezer) and proceeded to slather my hesitant monument to pagan idolatry with equal parts frozen orange juice concentrate and gasoline. (Gosh, you learn the greatest stuff from movies, huh?)

I stood back this time and, standing a wooden stick match up perpendicular to the strike surface, snapped it with my forefinger. Like a tiny football kicked high and straight for a field goal, that match lit, flew, and hit my Napalm Man square on. The blast threw me back, but brought the troops scampering out of the house like fire ants to a pork rind. "I love the smell of napalm…that gasoline smell, smells like…victory," I quoted solemnly from the film while the others just stood watching, silent, reverent.

The whole time I was at Dave's, I was but a stone's throw from the trail. When I later day-hiked a portion near his house and topped the ski mountain, I could easily see Dave's house from the warming hut atop Bromley. I wonder who among our thruhiker compadres was atop the mountain that night. You couldn't have missed that blaze from 30,000 feet. Okay, I exaggerate.

I'm looking at a wallet photo, relatively old, of my nephews and me. Relatively old in the sense of their rapid growth, now four and six, perhaps half those ages in this photo. It is very dear to me, this photo. I have carried it on this entire journey, usually in the high-use zone of my map pocket, ziplock'd in against moisture with my current topo and a torn-out page from the trail data book.

In the photo, Jacob and I are wearing Hawaiian flower print shirts. Matthew's shirt is slightly stained with the dribbles of a two-year-old. Jacob, the elder, holds his brother's shirt, a kind of embrace, and I, reclining in the back, embrace them both. I have long hair that falls to my left shoulder in one big curl. With my shining forehead and goatee, I'm not real fond of my appearance that day. No matter. I don't look at the photo to look at me.

I hold Matthew's tiny hand in mine. I've come to call the photo "The Teva Ad" after some guy pointed out that we are all wearing sandals in the studio shot. I tuck the wallet print back in its AT ziplock pocket-home and proceed to try and tell the story of weeks untold. Weeks and weeks and so many small states through which I blew like an anxious wind only to stop dead in a poppy field outside a chi-chi outlet mall town in lower Vermont, the Tin Man, the Scarecrow, Dorothy, David, and me.

But the sun is setting in the west, and I grow sleepy. Just 10 miles covered today, and 12 out of the poppy field yesterday. I feel drugged, though I am not. As I said, I escaped the poppy field just yesterday.

Nearby, a hoot owl hoots. Little critters stir all about me, me back in my hammock tent again after swearing it off long ago. What is one to do? I am cowardly. So tonight the lion sleeps again like the pupa. Perhaps tomorrow I will awake with both courage and wings. I will need both to finish this thing. The days are growing shorter, and Oz, though closer than ever on the map, seems impossibly distant, impossibly irrational. Well, the daddy longlegs have mostly left, and with nights in the mid-40s, mosquitoes are almost gone as well.

Now it's Kelly and Kris again, back on the trail. They caught me up this late-August morning while sluggish-I crawled along the trail after a rough night of two-hour interval sleep sessions in my floppy squirmy hammock tent.

Kelly makes a cold tea of Tang, instant tea, lemonade mix, cinnamon, and cloves. It looks weird and lumpy but tastes great.

Mid-morning and I'm divesting here in the Minerva-Somebody Shelter of whatever foodstuffs I don't need, seeing as how I'm resupplying tomorrow in Killington; and much to my surprise, Kris and Kelly take me up on a Lipton chicken and cook it right up, a kind of second breakfast. Since Kelly boils water, I take her up on some and make up some hot chocolate and pour in a swig of Black Velvet from the plastic fifth—my second breakfast.

Sobo hiker Wood Rat drops in and my jaw drops. To call her cute is an understatement. But dammit! She's southbound! Before I can readjust my jaw, she says, "Just wanted to see the shelter," and she is gone, moving on, everything I've already seen ahead of her, my past her future. As she leaves I say aloud to Kris and Kelly, "Too bad you're sobo, love. I'd marry you right here and now."

Kris repeats a story told by Slow Poke, one of a total of two black men I have met on the trail, about when he was lost back in Georgia. Seems he'd been lost for days when he'd fallen in a creek and taken to screaming aloud as he struggled to erect his tent. Just hours before, a couple of local Georgia boys, trained trackers often hired to find lost hikers, had set out on his trail. They found him in just two hours, found him half-naked and shouting aloud, and asked him why he was shouting. "I'm shouting because I'm lost!" The two rather grizzly southerners grinned at him and replied, "You ain't lost cuz we found ya!"

It's in the way Kris tells it, his inflection, his timing, his mock accents. He told another one awhile back about a little girl and boy no more than eight years old playing husband and wife, she laying out the menu for him and he repeatedly saying something no doubt heard from an adult. She'd say, "Cereal?" and he'd answer, "All-ler-gic." So it went, Kris plugging a long list of foods into this two-word dialogue and answering himself the same to everything: "Allergic." It had me rolling. Maybe you had to be there.

The Minerva shelter is a sweet old cabin with dark oiled exterior paneling, a nice varnished wood table inside, and a ladder of chicken wire for mice to climb up the center beam of the room. I flip open the shelter register and notice where Wood Rat quickly left her mark. Beside her name, she has written her home state: California. Double dammit!

The day is sweet and warm and blue. A light breeze will cool us as we make the long climb up Killington. Jackie and Ry arrive. At last Jackie and Ry and Kris and Kelly and I are all together. It's nice, really. It's been a long time and is unique in that we all share a common start date of March 20. We've all been out here for five months. An old man going south calls us "the caboose." Vile momentum-sucking nobo basher! "Thank you very little," I sneer at him as we pass. We are indeed at the tail of the long northbound pack. But who cares! We're still going, and we ain't stopping til Katahdin's stony peak.

Now it's Clarendon Gorge and a single-lane wooden-slat Indiana Jones-like suspension bridge high over the gorge with golden waters of New England roaring through. Kris and Kelly and I arrive first. It takes only a brief glance down at the swirling deep pools and falls to stick your head under, for me to holler back, "We're going in!"

In we go! Always the first to leap fearless into any body of water especially when all hot and sweaty, it's me first, the blue blood in my prominent veins pumping double-time to the beat of trail and friends to pace. Then come Kris and Kelly. Kris and I talk of being polar bears so we could ride the marble-smooth but undeniably dangerous slide where the falls give way into the deep pools below the suspension bridge. Jackie and Ry arrive but never make it down from the bridge. I tell myself that if she were my girl, I'd get her in the water! Oh, yeah! But maybe Ry's apparent weakness in this arena comes from years of trying and failing. Maybe she's just a bore, and he's just given up.

I get some fun out of them anyway, a practical joke. The moment I see them coming and see that they see me, I duck beneath the powerful main flow of the falls and disappear into a small air pocket below. There I stay for several minutes, resurfacing only when I'm sure Jackie thinks I've drowned. I'm wicked.

Then just like that, fun time's over. Jackie and Ry cross the bridge and are gone. Tonight we summit Killington, no small feat. Scant rest for the wicked.

Wow! So many things to say, so much to write, so little time! So many great friends sending letters and e-mails and packages of support! Yet two weeks now without signal here in southern Vermont—I have been cut off from the world! Terrible timing, for in one week I'll be cut off again, for good! *Palm.net*, in what must be a violation of FCC rules, has announced they will be pulling the plug on their wireless service as of August 31!

What does this mean? It means no more dispatches from the front line of the AT Adventure! It means no more Palm magic! But we'll find a way even if I have to scrawl notes on bark and mail 'em to Justin.

Brutal climb up to Cooper Lodge on the backside of Killington Ski Mountain. I feel as though I have climbed Killington before, not on foot but by chairlift as a young boy with family skiing. Tonight it was like Kerouac's nightmare ascent of some peak in the Sierras, he inexperienced and shocked and daunted by the whole hellish jaunt. Nothing was new to me or to any of us in the crew, which I'll call The Killington Seven: Kelly, Chris, Ry, Jackie, A-Dog, T-Bot, and me, after five months and endless peaks....

Wow! I just remembered that whole bit about how after you've completed the AT, you have in essence climbed the equivalent of Mt. Everest 17 times. I thought about that a lot way back but have since forgotten it. After climbing

Killington today, the statistic returns to me in all its painful glory. I think, wow! Now with 1,680 miles down and fewer than 500 miles to go, surely I have climbed Everest, at 29,000 feet, a dozen times over!

Here atop Killington arriving in the rain, all windy and high and lonesome among the clouds, I entered the stone cabin and set about the work of tearing off wet and sweaty gear, stripping down to nothing in the near-dark of stone hut and "bathing" with my moistened washcloth. Doesn't sound like much of a comfort to you at home with showers and claw foot tubs, but it is to us. Carving off a layer of sweat is a treat not all hikers afford themselves, but I've made it a ritual.

Cold air blowing in through unpaned windows, I climbed into my warmest gear, long johns, and high-tech thermal turtleneck, wool socks dry, and Patagonia fleece sweater. Now with winter fast approaching here in weather-moody New England, I have again my North Face 700-fill down jacket, a seeming luxury item until nights like this. I throw that on and set about the work of boiling up some creek water into hot chocolate with powdered milk to make it nice and creamy and then a good slug of whiskey, Canadian, and not real hungry, thanks to having to force down gorp and Cliff bars and tuna from the packet and carob clusters, all shoved in my face on the move as I raced against time to reach this promontory before dark, shoving in the food in answer to my voracious body, shoving it in like a man shoveling coal into the furnace of an old steam train to keep it going, to make it go faster, run better, climb higher.

I arrived thus not hungry but thirsty for hot chocolate and whiskey. Now nearly two hours hence, I have completed my mission and while my compadres have tucked into bed, pots stowed and cleaned, I have had a dinner of hot chocolate only. What the hell. I skied this mountain once. Today I climbed it with claw and roughshod hobbit feet. We climbed it! What a climb it was. Both the terrain and the weather turned treacherous so quickly that it's a wonder we all made it alive. Each time the door to our stone fortress swung wide, we all breathed a sigh of relief as we got one step on human life closer to NOT having to send out a search party. Our prize is this old cabin of stone with giant wooden picnic table with so many names carved in and nine of us now shelved like warm bread out of the oven on two sets of giant bunks. Sweet.

I hear that next year they will reroute this section of trail and tear this cabin down, and for what? Shame. I often feel on this trail that I am experiencing something that will not always be, not always be free anyway. I imagine a day when the park service will find a way to charge for the whole thing, fee permits from end to end. These hundred or so free shelters I have slept in, blissful and alive and giddy with the discovery of a free America, one once dreamed of but rarely experienced in any but its more commercial aspect. I wonder if someday soon there will be fees at every shelter, as there are now at many here in Vermont and more expected in New Hampshire. Ah, screw it. The time is now. I chose well. We live and we walk and the world is but a dream far, far below this snug haven in the clouds. Thank you, world. "God be praised," I said coming in the cabin tonight. I meant it. If the climb up a root-infested, jagged, razor's edge of precipitous trail hadn't fried the nerves enough, the ensuing rain and sleet and gloomy mist of coming night sure did. One felt lucky to have arrived alive.

The next morning, we climb a short distance over the ridge to the mountaintop ski lodge that is Killington Peak. Kelly complains of tummy problems. Now, sitting here in the sun waiting for the lodge to open but digging the rest and the mesmerizing hum of the gigantor gondola landing station with all its empty gondolas whizzing by sure to soon deliver someone to open the lodge and feed us, Kelly says that what she suffers from is a difficulty comprehending another 500 miles of this. But immediately she counters this with, "What am I going to do when it's over?" "We're all going to be lost trail junkies," I say, correctly, but with no real comprehension of just how painful will be the vacuum world without these friends, this trail, these mountaintop orgasms of the senses, of the soul. "We should start a support group," Kris says. "Sufferers of Post-AT Traumatic Syndrome, or PATTS." The brightly colored airbrushed fiberglass gondolas zoom on by beneath a smashing blue sky, and it's 10 a.m. and the world below is snow white beneath a blanket of low-lying clouds. At last, employees begin spilling out of the heretofore-empty gondola cars going by, and our imaginations serve up a full olfactory sampling of the breakfast they're going to cook us, and up here it smells like Heaven. "A Heaven with bacon," Kelly adds.

Watch out when someone says, "Two can play at this game." This likely means the object of your torturous amusement has just snapped, gone completely sideways, and is about to give you a taste of whatever you've been dishing out.

This late August night, the 26th, I speak aloud to the gods. I check my watch: 2:16 a.m. I raise my titanium cook pot full of hot chocolate and Canook whiskey (in equal proportions) to the Scorpio night sky and say, in essence, "Bite me."

This is night number two bereft of sleep. Last night it was the Long Trail Lodge at the intersection of Vermont's famed "Long Trail" and the AT. When you enter Vermont from the south on the AT, you are double-timing, making miles on two famous trails at once. AT thruhikers walk about 100 miles of the Long Trail in their quest for the AT Holy Grail, then cut east and away from the remaining 160 miles of northern Vermont.

About 36 hours ago, I said goodbye to my last Long Trailers, a few lovely ladies including a lovely lass named Toco with legs that went all the way up. These three had achieved Killington Peak a day behind me, but I'd lingered and so was there for a mid-afternoon farewell. Had I a brain in my head, I would have stayed an extra day. But....

I do not. So with golden afternoon sun shining in open wood-framed windows in that mountaintop gem of river rock and mortar, and all those alpine evergreen trees in witness, I shirked a no-fault, win-win, one-night romance bird-in-hand opportunity and walked down the mountain to instead spend money on a stuffy room in a lodge by the noisy interstate.

I shared the room with long-time acquaintances Kris and Kelly and slept just three hours before being awakened by rumbling trucks on the highway. Were it not for a delightful dinner of shepherd's pie and salad and pints of beer and a shot of Tullamore Dew, all kindly provided by Still Frank in a Homer Simpson "Woo Hoo!" spirit of giving, I would have written off the Long Trail Inn as a bust. This was retired Navy commander Frank's way of celebrating "just 500 miles left!" of the trail, and I'm down with that. Bravo, Frank!

Instead, I rose from bed at 7 after five insomniac hours to a fine, full complimentary breakfast and another day back on the trail. I hit the local P.O. first, dropping a well-spent ten spot on a mail-forward that'll save my feet 10 pounds until western New Hampshire. Then I dallied at the local deli and dallied some more uptrail eating my deli lunch, and, finally, with not nearly enough time to make it to my stated destination, I launched into a 17-mile ball-buster at around two in the afternoon. Maybe if I'd been a good boy this year and not wanked too much or rode too many dirty trains through dirty tunnels or bitten the heads off too many bats, maybe I would make it by dark.

I made it. I made it with feet screaming and mind scrambled agog. I made it to a lovely lonesome large Cape Cod gray-flavored old mountaintop cabin not even listed in the guidebook but known of to those who listen and dig for special treat tips from past thruhikers or southbounders.

I made it and, boy, was I relieved. I clamored up the cabin's three-story ladder to a wide widow's walk with panoramic views of a stunning sunset moonrise green mountain Vermont world and took my ritual sponge bath there in sight of God and all Creation but hidden from the three other male thruhikers present, Impulse, Still Frank, and Paparazzi, down below. I then descended and cooked up a fancy brand-name backpacker meal given me by the Polar Bears when they went off-trail unexpectedly at the Long Trail Inn, ate it, and passed out.

Was it a day later? Two? We were just an overnight away from the next day's inevitable arrival at the New Hampshire state line when the unexpected occurred.

Correction: It was in fact the arrival of Tinker at a middle-o-nowhere road crossing in eastern Vermont that was inevitable. The element of surprise owed to my having completely forgotten triggering this event a week earlier. In a rare moment of cell service rush of e-mails atop Killington Peak some days ago, I had responded to, among many others, an e-mail from Tinker, rattling off my next week's intended itinerary so he could locate me. Off trail now for over a month, Tinker was preparing to ship off to Iraq soon and was eager to meet with trail friends one last time.

It was Friday and though Ry and Jackie and others were somewhere close by, I was hiking alone. The profile of the next few miles of trail looked like a camel with three humps or a row of cattle rumps seen through the open doors of a Bumknuckle, Vermont barn. It was hot. I consulted the map, saw a little hamlet not ON the trail but on the way, as it were. The road walk detour to the town was perfectly equidistant to the white blaze miles that would get me beyond it but with one caveat: no humps! It was a lovely walk on a flat, paved and presently empty road, and I rewarded myself for my bold foray into the town's one store of stoic locals with a pint of Ben & Jerry Cherry Garcia, my favorite of favorites.

There I am just moseying along that sunny, late summer day, tonguing my Lexan spoon for any last remnant of the now consumed frozen cow juice concoction when out of the dense forest I hear my name called out. I had just spotted the trailhead to my right, or northeast, the direction in which I was headed. To think, I almost made it into those woods unseen. But I didn't. Now two people could be scarred for life because of me. Color me unsympathetic.

"Totally spaced it," I admitted as Tinker excitedly reminded me of his plans to find me hereabouts on the trail and guided me down to his picnic blanket layout of goodies by the roadside creek where, much to my surprise, sat a dozen thruhikers, Ry and Jackie among them. Tinker the trail angel. "Well, all right!" I said, complementing him and greeting my cohorts. Among the crowd sat Dingle who apparently didn't dig my ice cream road walk story. "And just how did you get ahead of me, Jester?" he sniped. "I know I was ahead of you." As I calmly explained what had appeared to me a perfectly judicious little detour, he went all white blaze superior on me, inferring in so many words that I had cheated. Up until then a congenial enough character, he dropped a notch in my *he who is without sin throw the first stone* book. I kinda wanted to pop him one right in his self-righteous mug for trying to embarrass me in front of all the other hikers lounging creek side. But I didn't.

I let it slide. Tinker was here to see me, after all, not Dingle. Tinker, the dogged Eagle Scout and soldier-to-be had driven from road crossing to road crossing all morning shouting into the forest in search of me. I was not just a little bit flattered. The kid really looked up to me. I was honored and touched. I was also horrified by the notion that soon this strong, highly intelligent, handsome young man was about to go dodge bullets in a foreign desert for no good reason at all.

So, contrary to my strong urge to cross over into New Hampshire the next day, I suddenly found myself riding shotgun in his parent's minivan bound for a few days of R&R at the beach or wherever we wanted to go. Yes, I did say we. To my amazement, Ry and Jackie and two hikers I barely knew, Impulse and Sundown, had come along for the ride. Jackie was first to fall in. That girl just really dug hanging out with me. And what could Ry do but agree? Sundown, a pretty girl with wavy dark brown hair that coalesced into a dreadlock ponytail of sorts well down her back, had apparently hiked a lot with Ry and Jackie when I had not. Somewhat reluctant yet pliable, she fell in line with them. Impulse was the free radical in the group. Who he was and why he opted to skip school to join Pinochio and friends for a weekend of cigar smoking, billiards and morphing into jackasses, I still have no idea. I guess it was all in his name: Impulse.

In retrospect, that's pretty much what it felt like we did all weekend. We skipped trail and screwed off, and my hangover on return to the trail 48 hours later was worse than growing ten donkey tails. The consensus vote was for the beach. But it was already mid-afternoon Friday by the time the minivan got rolling, and we were on the wrong side of the state. No one else, it seemed, had any local ties, so I took it upon myself to work out lodging and fun for the night. The beach could wait until tomorrow.

So it happened that a most amazing concatenation of people and events unfolded that night at none other than my beloved aunt Mary's farm. Aunt Mary and her husband Chris welcomed five smelly thruhikers and one freshly scrubbed Tinker into their home on the spur of the moment, fed us dinner, drinks, the works. My 90-year old grandmother Bettie was also living in the house, as were my cousin Justin and his girl Jess. Everyone got along smashingly!

I suppose my use of the word concatenation here really owes to Chris. This is not a man I have ever connected with well. Some people command respect in their space, their home, by being so hospitable that you wouldn't dare disrespect them because it would be a shameful reflection on you. Ry's father and mother were just such people. My aunt Mary is such a person. Chris is not. Chris lords over his house with a frown of disapproval and a cloud of negativity. Either I'm correct in this assessment, or the man just REALLY dislikes me, and so that's all I ever see of him.

But that night, the cloud lifted. Chris shined. Or perhaps he just surrendered to the goodness of the group and let his own goodness shine through. For thruhikers generally make excellent guests. They have to. They are perpetual guests, and you don't get invited back or invited to the next place down the trail if you're an asshole. Concatenation implies an interconnection, and that night Chris interconnected with Tinker over cars and machines. He connected with Impulse over comic books, going out of his way to dig out of his vast collection and make a gift to Impulse a comic book whose hero shared the hiker's unique trail name. Chris and the girls interconnected just fine, and if my uncle had any beef with me over dropping a hiker bomb on his house, he made no indication of it. Justin, Jess, Gram, everyone had fun. The next day it was off to the beach.

As evidenced by my earlier escape to the sands of North Carolina, the call of the ocean grows strong after weeks and weeks in the woods. Going to the beach in New Hampshire, however, means going to Hampton as there isn't a whole lot more of the Granite State that touches the Atlantic. I wanted as much as anyone to feel the sand between the toes of my bare feet, maybe eat some fried clams and oysters. But Hampton on a whim with a carload of hikers presented me with a problem. Why? Because going to the beach immediately elicited the question of where we would stay the night.

Hampton is the home of my father. Rather, Hampton is, as the man himself put it, where my father lives in his wife's house. Naturally when the others found out my father lived at the beach, they thought "Great! We can camp in his yard." To Tinker, still in his teens and living at home, this was especially a no-brainer. In some alternate universe where I wasn't two decades out of the nest and hadn't burned every bridge to the nest out of fierce independence and a general long term chafing of unlike personalities, this might indeed have been a given. But it wasn't. Having to admit this to my friends and two new acquaintances in the car put me in a place of extreme discomfiture. But what really hurt was calling my father anyway just to let him know I'd be in town in hopes he could drop by the strand and see us and being told no, sorry, he didn't have time.

By now you're wondering what all this has to do with cannibalism. Well, I promise you, this latter part, this visit to the beach, has everything to do with cannibalism. It has everything to do with the laughs and the tears shared on the beach that day and with the desire, seriously, to gnaw on someone's skull like a rabid and famished savage. The grief and anger and sadness and embarrassment I suffered that day in a town I, too, had once called home, (this home of my father's wife) had everything to do with the flesh-eating that followed. For out of true sorrow comes the greatest need to laugh. And if necessity is the mother of invention, I confess that out of pure desperation I perpetrated one hell of a gag.

The gang was sprawled out in the sand across from the Playland Arcade for a good few hours that afternoon. I had forfeited much of my relaxation time by running around trying to secure us a campsite somewhere nearby. I had also spoken with my father from a payphone after having first called ahead from Mary's. It was during this latter conversation that I got word that I wouldn't be seeing him. He lived ten minutes away by car. I was crestfallen.

It was fresh from this news that I finally joined the gang on the sand. I was just in time to watch the sun sink slowly toward the arcade and finally melt away into the tar of its hot summer roof. The group was pretty subdued. Impulse was in his own world. We'd smuggled some beers down onto the beach and were playing the hide and seek game with the lifeguards. But late as it was, they were packing it up and soon gone. I remember sitting there, pounding beers clandestinely poured into some discarded Coke cup, literally a piece of Hampton Beach detritus, to drown my sorrows and watching with dull fascination and a twinge of disgust as Sundown performed a pedicure on herself there on the sand. Not only was she lancing blisters and cutting away at various layers of callus on her trail-ravaged feet, she was giving us, or herself, or whoever was listening, a play-by-play. To call it weird after 1600 miles on the trail would be wrong. That would be seeing it through you, the Reader's eyes. To us, it just was what it was. At some point she held up a nickel-sized wafer of her skin, a perfectly round specimen of callus, pleased with herself for removing it so expertly and glad to be rid of it. I think someone may have uttered a dull hoorah. Maybe the fact that all this wasn't disgusting to us contributed to what came next.

The beer was working. A hundred years of pain and rejection recently synthesized down to a spoonful of poison, drawn up into a needle and jammed into my temple upon cradling the phone after my father's goodbye: Gone. Like magic, like that orange ball of warmth and life surrendering to the arcade like a deflating basketball, the sunset and the beer made everything better. I'd grown up spending summers throwing quarters into pinball machines in that arcade, walking the boardwalk, shooting up the old west bar scene with a toy Winchester rifle that used flashes of light to make the piano player and the parrot jump to life. I'd grown up swimming all day in this surf and sitting on the beach with my sister doing just what I was doing right now: idly sifting sand through my hands.

But the more at ease the beer made me, the more honest I became in telling Tinker what he was really headed for in Iraq as opposed to all this gentle, polite policemen bullshit the military had been feeding him while concurrently teaching him to shoot weapons that would scare the crap out of you or me. He gently protested but I pressed on, seeing the confusion in his face as someone he respected told him everything he believed in was wrong. He wasn't wrong. The war was wrong. I made sure to delineate between the two. The more passionate I got about it, the harder and faster I sifted that dirty Hampton Beach sand. And that's when I found it: Sundown's callus. Somehow, in about ten minutes time, it had migrated over to me, and there it was in the palm of my hand.

By now everyone except Tinker had been into the beer or smoked a little pot. But Tinker had caught a contact high, so we were a unanimously animated group. There was a little tension over the war talk, and like it or not everyone had been at least slightly affected by the dead zone surrounding my dad and me. So, in keeping with the trip thus far, I took it upon myself to give the group something to laugh about, now and for a long time to come. The nickel of Sundown skin in my hand became the seed of a mischievous scheme, and the ringmaster corralled his audience with a booming announcement of a nare-do-well dare.

"Well, lookey what I found, kids! It's Sundown's callus. Anyone hungry?"

An embarrassed Sundown blushes while Jackie makes a puckered face and a couple of "Eeeuw!"s come from all around.

"Impulse? Feeling impulsive?" I make as though to sniff and then taste the callus, give Sundown a big grin and then turn my attention to the one I knew would do my bidding.

"Tinker! You're an eager young lad, going off to war, surely hoping to take a few good stories from the AT with ya. What's more, you're tough! You're not squeamish like the rest of this bunch." I reached into my shorts and pulled out a fiver. "I'll give you five bucks, Tinker, five dollars to be cannibal for a day and munch down this lovely little wafer of skin. Come on! How often does a man get the chance to nibble the flesh of such a fine lookin' lady as Sundown here, eh? Think what a story it'll make to tell the boys on patrol!"

By now, I'd P.T. Barnum'd up the whole affair in such a great, gravely, pirate's voice that I had everyone rolling in the sand. Sundown's red, red and redder face had earned her namesake and would have surely been the delight of every sailor for oceans around. She was mortified but had to have somehow, secretly been loving the attention as well.

Boy was Tinker an easy dare. "Five bucks?! You got a deal!" he said.

I waved the five dollar bill, he snatched the callus, popped it in his mouth and you would have thought he was in on the mischief with me from the beginning the way he chewed it for special effect before swallowing.

In the words of the little tyrant from the film *The Princess Bride*, "Inconceivable!"

The effect was fantastic, the laughter and screeches and groans uproarious. Everyone, even quiet Impulse was in tears and rolling about in a ball in the sand. I handed Tinker the five bucks and thanked him heartily through my own tears for the biggest bang-for-the-buck trade I'd ever made.

It was a little thing really, but it was just the right thing to unite an otherwise incongruous group of people, all of whom obviously needed a good belly laugh.

From there we went straight to a seafood restaurant where we met my cousin Stacey who had driven over an hour from his house in Massachusetts to come hang out with us. My father and his wife made a surprise visit after all and met the crew. When he left after not too long, my eyes went all blurry like a couple of fish tanks and I had to blow my nose about six times. We ate fried seafood like monsters, all except perhaps Sundown who was a little nauseated and in a bit of shock, I think, at having herself been eaten not an hour ago. The darkening pinks and yellows of post-sunset hung on extra long and lit up the marshes of Hampton, and I glanced at its slow farewell occasionally from our upper deck table at the restaurant. That night at the campground, everybody but Jackie, Stacey and I vanished into their quickly erected tents and weren't seen again. Stacey and I sat up all night drinking beers and catching up on lost years of each other's lives while Jackie rubbed my shoulders for hours.

The next day's hangover was ugly, and Sundown would never look at me the same again. But I didn't care about me. I was just glad to have given Tinker his wish, his weekend at the beach with Jester. He went off to war a better man for it, I think. And whether or not they care to, no one in our little group of trail runaways that weekend will ever forget sunset on the beach in New Hampshire where they witnessed Tinker eat a piece of Sundown for a fiver.

EIGHTEEN

I Live in a Bag...The Wormhole and a Wedding To Be...The 112-Pound Italian Crush...Mousilauke is Lovely and Her Name is Yazzy...Henry Miller's Fireside Chat...Meter Maid of the Forest, or How AMC Rules Could Have Cost Me My Life...They Die of Shame...Blair Witch Gummi Men...I'd Lichen You to an Asshole...Her Breath on my Face and Yazzy to the Rescue...

Jackie and I walk together. Sometimes close, sometimes not. Now and again we talk. Like a Seinfeld episode, our dialogue has no plot. It comes and goes and never really ends, just fades in and out as the distance between us fluctuates. During a long pause in the dialogue, I am deep in thought, "writing in my head" as it were and working up a theory about the nature of the backpack, when I chance to notice that Jackie, formerly a football field away, is suddenly close enough for an Eskimo kiss. If you were telepathic, this is what you might have heard me thinking:

Welcome to my home. I live in a backpack. What's a backpack, really? It is a bag, bag with shoulder straps. If you're old style, it might be a canvas bag. If you're contemporary, it's rip-stop nylon or some other high tech weave. But a bag by any other name is still a bag. Ipso facto, thus and therefore, I live, essentially, in a bag. Welcome to my bag! Come on in. Follow me now as I climb into my bag of tricks. That's it, all the way in. Come, Reader! There's room enough for two in here. This is where I live! Here's my bed over here in the corner. Okay, so it's all deflated and rolled up to the size of a loaf of bread, but it's a bed, to be sure. Note my bedding, my fluffy down feather sleeping bag. Yes, I know. It doesn't look too comfortable either, all crushed down in its compression sack to the size of a gallon coffee can. Here are my kitchen and clothes closet. My goodness, I guess everything in my bag of a home here on the trail is rather small.

But what's this? A pocket I've never been in before. Shall we peek? Why, it's a wormhole of some kind! What's that I see at the other end of that pretty spinning, swirling aurora borealis tunnel of light? Why, it's that restaurant The Mill in Damascus, Virginia! It's night, and by the look of the crowd it appears to be Trail Days. I see Ski Bum with two bottles of fine champagne and a tray of glasses. It seems there's to be a toast of some kind. The whole gang is there: Big Stick, Gordy, Munchkin, Rooster, A-Squared, Yazzy, Still Frank, Alabama, T-Bird, Maisie and, holy jeezus, there I am! My hair is long, my face filled out. This must be a wormhole through time! It appears to be Trail Days next year, and all the triumphant thruhikers are gathered in joyous reunion!

Ski Bum, looking happier than ever, has his arm around his good friend Rooster, and lovely A-Squared beside him raises her left hand and blushes, showing off her new diamond engagement ring. Ski Bum is belting out a hearty salute, and all of us are howling, glasses raised and linked in protracted toast, and a beam of unseen power shoots straight from the heart of the Universe to consummate the moment with a clenched fist of love, each of us a finger on its giant hand. Pow! Clang! Toast -made and glasses down, the band takes the lead and up we leap and down again, dancing, hoppin' like bunnies and soon the whole back deck of The Mill restaurant is a spring board, a trampoline, and even those standing still outside the tight circle of spring-loaded sprites and elves are carried aloft by the bounce. The management tries but cannot stem the tide of thruhiker triumph, the big bounce. We bounce and bounce and bounce, and I am pleased to see such unbridled joy in my face. Seeing myself there, I look happier than I've been in years.

Then Jackie appears in this kaleidoscope swirling vision, and I feel the world shift as she pulls me into the scene yet away from the pogoing crowd of friends. She is sweating, hot, her gaze intense. Suddenly, faster than my mind can follow, my friends are fading, changing, gone, each one a tree, the bouncing floor now the static earth of trail. Gone, too, is the future-me. Jackie's deep brown eyes are almost black with burning need to speak, and I notice it is day. The dazzling wormhole and the night are gone.

I am back in the present, and there is Jackie. Jackie is panting from the heat and the strain. She stands, her face just inches from mine, opens her cute little mouth and speaks. There in the woods of Vermont with Ry nowhere in sight and Hanover, New Hampshire just one good canon shot away, says, "I can't stand it any longer. I have something I must tell you."

People with near-death experiences claim time slows and sometimes stops in that near fatal second. I don't doubt this at all. Even just viewing from the engine of a train the impending, unstoppable death of suicidal woman, time slowed for me to perhaps a tenth its speed as I watched the inevitable unfold in horror.

The Universe holds far more secrets than we will ever comprehend. Time and space most certainly bend, yield, stretch, and sometimes just plain stop to accommodate the wishes, conscious or unconscious, of even one man. Where am I going with this? Down the rabbit hole, of course.

I'd been hiking on and off with Jackie and Ry forever, in trail time anyway. I admitted way back in this story to a deep attraction for this woman. From the outset, I hiked with the couple because she was beautiful, demure, flirtatious, and possessed of a quiet sexuality that drew me moth to flame. But she had Ry, and over time I came to like Ry, and only half-consciously I began to avoid them, to avoid the pain my growing love for her was causing me. Like Judas to Jesus I would thrice betray them, first as hiking partners as I ran from them in Virginia and ditched them in Pennsylvania, and finally, for the sake of love, as friends.

After months and months with only two states left and too much unrequited lust under the bridge, Jackie turned to me and said, "I've had a crush on you since I first saw you."

Crush. Now there's a word I'll care never to hear again as long as I live. It isn't love. It rings of junior high school. I should have laughed it off that moment. Alas, no. Ignoring all common sense, I took it as the answer to a long-unspoken but cogitated prayer. I wanted this woman, and now I knew she wanted me, too.

In the desert of my mind, I am on a vast dry lakebed 100 miles north of Reno, Nevada. It is the Saturday night of Labor Day weekend, and my body, despite my cerebral wanderings, is here in the southern foothills of the White Mountains, fully 1,850 miles north of Springer Mountain, Georgia. I sit in the dirt staring at the tiny flame of my luxuriously-packed-in-blue votive candle drinking a 50/50 mix of hot cocoa and Canadian Black Velvet whiskey and trying not to think about Burning Man. I'm fooling myself, pretending not to care that 3,000 miles away in a vast enchanted desert 35,000 soul mates of mine are dancing and cheering ecstatic as the Great Man of neon and fire crashes to his glorious death without me. Without me for the first time in years and years. I try not to think about it. To even talk about it would be impolite. I have guests after all. My cousin and his girl, Jess. This night of the Great Burn of 04 is the occasion of their first backpacking trip. Or maybe just first in some time. Or first together.

I intentionally skipped a rather simple 10-mile stretch of the AT just shy of Glencliff, New Hampshire, to await the weekend when Justin and Jess would be free to hike. I had chosen well. New Hampshire's White Mountains are incredibly beautiful and incredibly harsh in degree of ascent and descent, every trail a black diamond. For every 10-foot flat stretch, there is 100 feet of hard-core, just-shy-of-technical, climbing, vertical slabs and gaping synclines, the stuff of blood, sweat, and tears. The little 10-mile leader trail I reserved for J&J was just enough to give them a taste of trail life and have them begging a swift return to the land of EZ chairs, flat sidewalks, fluffy pillows, and hot showers.

A few days before, I had gained some miles on Jackie and Ry, with whom I'd been hiking steadily since Dave's house at the base of Bromley Ski Mountain in Vermont. I wasn't that far ahead of them, a couple of miles maybe, when I reached the road crossing which, upon close map inspection, turned out to be the closest the AT would come to my Aunt Mary's house in Franklin. So, even though I'd just been there a week before with the whole Tinker beach gang, I said what the hell, stuck out my thumb, and caught a ride east.

I felt mischievous, I guess. A little hide and seek with The Happy Couple was in order. Lately, I'd found myself in a constant state of attraction-repulsion with the couple. Attracted to her, repulsed by my own Christian-bred inability to seize a moment alone with her and take her, caveman-like, on a bed of moss or leaves in the magical Christmas tree-scented forest. If this sounds barbaric or rings of anything but CONSENSUAL, instinctual animal behavior, it wouldn't have been.

How do I know this? Because it had been building. Like a grain of sand in an oyster, it had been growing, layering itself from Day One. Lately the pace had quickened. A touch here, a backrub there. The holding of hands. But even without these more obvious hints, I knew. I knew the way you know the heart through the soul through the eyes. Jackie's piercing gaze spoke volumes. Then there's the language of an embrace. I've always found the embrace to be so telling, so full of unspoken language. There are the awkward hugs of homophobic men. There are the hugs of good friends. There are the hugs of lovers. Then there are the hugs of two people desperate to pull one another straight into themselves. These are often, alas, the hugs of two people who should not be hugging at all. This is how Jackie hugged me, and I her. It was the stuff of romance novels, and my heart would break a little more with every day a-hiking with The Happy Couple from North Carolina.

So I stuck out my thumb and hitched to Tilton, amazing in one hitch. I took a sunny stroll through town toward my aunt's with no luck hitching, but through the town of Tilton a nice walk nonetheless on long-familiar ground and the bonus of finding another aunt, Patty, at work at a local convenience store and a visit with her and the surprise news that my grandmother, just a week ago fine and dandy and snug in her room at Mary's, was now in the hospital.

Patty lent me her truck and I zoomed on over to Mary's and learned that Grandma, 90-something years old, had suddenly decided to go swimming and had fallen five feet off the porch surrounding the pool. She was, although doped up on morphine and probably down for the night, miraculously unbroken. That night at the VFW tavern with Aunt Patty, I shuddered to think of what would have happened had Grams actually made it IN the pool. Too weak to pull herself out of the uniformly four-foot deep water, I fear she would have drowned. In a weird way, the fall seemed a blessing.

Aunt Patty, always good for a little salty New England discourse and family-related prattle, chain-smoked and talked of the damn foolishness of men, of her lack of male companionship, and of her absolute determination to keep our family name to spite my uncle, her ex. Her cell phone rang, and as she chatted, I watched her demeanor change, her features soften. Then she hung up. She had a date, she said. Out the door we went. That was the last I saw of Aunt Patty on my Great Appalachian Adventure. Next morning it was off to the hospital with Aunt Mary. Contented by the sight of my last surviving grandparent and word of her good condition, I departed and was back on the trail in no time thanks to a ride from poor Cousin Justin who wound up late for work on my account.

From Glencliff, I roared up Mount Mousilauke to its vaulting, öber-treeline heights. In a word, Mousilauke rocked! Mousilauke cranked open the heretofore-viewless green tunnel like an electric can opener, my legs the electric power pedaling the gyro-pyro crank motor sky-opener until bamm! Blue New England sky forever above and below and me so high on adrenaline and clear sky joy that suddenly I'm sky walking, dancing on the ceiling in gravity boots past alien rock sculpture towers and to the top where whoa! Jackie! Ry! Sundown and...ooh! Who is this lovely fraulein? I spin down out of my dream-inverted world of walking in the sky, land gently on my feet, and say hello to all.

Enter: Yazzy, the azure-blue-eyed girl who would save me from myself, from my Heartbreak Fate with The Happy Couple. Sort of.

Yazzy is an athletic beauty bred for the mountains and lakes of New England. Yazzy has a cabin on a remote lake in northern New Hampshire. I didn't know all this yet...soon would. I just know I like what I see. Nice smile.

Jackie is there. I hug her hello, and as usual the hug, "hurts so good" as the song lyric says.

That night we all take up residence at a lovely shelter on the north side of Mousilauke, Jackie, Ry, Yazzy, Sundown, and me. There were others there. Kip and Ryder, and a lot of hikers out for the weekend, camping in a group behind the shelter, Ivy League college students out for one last blast before classes start.

I did what I often did whilst others spread out their gear and began cooking their dehydrated dinners of ramen and Lipton noodles. I made hot chocolate. Over thehot chocolate I inverted a liter bottle of Canadian whiskey. How long I held the bottle uncapped and inverted depended on who was watching and how much it freaked them out. The bottle has one of those governor spouts, so it's not like it comes rushing out. But it pours, fast enough. In this case, Jackie was watching. I love making that girl's big eyes grow bigger with astonishment at apparent rogue me. So I poured long.

To an innocent like Jackie, I may as well have been a Lost Boy from Never Never Land. I fascinated and horrified her all at once. I took delicious pleasure in watching her face contort in response to everything I did and said.

The shelter on Mousilauke's north flank commands a palatial view of the mountains to the north and east, as though the Dartmouth Outing Club had gone and logged a section of wood for northbound thruhikers to get a good look at their future: The Whites. The sun set behind Mousilauke thus painting all the mountains in our vista fiery orange and red. I drank my whiskey-soaked cocoa and just took it all in, refusing to stress about dinner until I'd "sat around the shanty and (got) a good buzz on," as the song lyric goes.

Perhaps the whiskey is to blame, but I don't remember a whole helluva lot about the rest of that evening. What I do recall is vivid and romantic and jolly by golly. I remember Kip pulling out a copy of Henry Miller's *Tropic of Cancer* from his pack and me just flipping out and insisting on reading a few passages aloud. I was so excited. On the trail, there are no books. No one can afford the pack weight. Besides, there is very little free time on a long-distance thruhike, despite what you might think. We hike, we eat, we sleep, we shit in the woods. With the lack of privacy in shelters and the pressure to make big miles during the day, I don't know when couples have time for lovemaking. I have yet to hear the slightest coo in the night. As for Jackie and Ry, zero public display of affection.

One couple I recall read passages from *The Lord of the Rings* to one another as they drifted off to sleep. That was Yippee and Jabberwock, and they were just adorable. Well, she was adorable, and he was handsome, and they were both intelligent and strong of character. I liked them and admired their mutual affection, but haven't seen them in forever and don't suspect I ever will again.

In any case, reading on the trail is rare. So I read some Henry Miller. I chose the raunchiest of the raunchiest of passages, the one where he talks of Tanya and "spreading the shores a little wider." Kip was rolling. I was buzzing, what did I care how many times I said "cunt?" It was Henry saying it, not me!

We had a campfire going and after most everyone had gone to sleep, I found myself still sitting watching the flames, and I was not alone. On my shoulders lay two doves nesting in my hair, the girls, Yazzy and Jackie, their heads leaning in on either side of me, their arms around my back in the near-silence of the dwindling fire. It is a sensation, a vision, a moment I will cherish forever.

One other thing I remember from that night. Falling asleep beside Yazzy, the others all around, I asked what her passion was. She said, "Being outdoors...and being happy." I liked that very much. It's so simple as to be profound.

While I expound on this story a few days later, Yazzy is out running some logging road along the Canadian border in the rain. She will punctuate this athletic act with a jump and a swim in the remote and unpeopled lake behind her cabin here in far northern New Hampshire, the air temperature outside soaring in the high 40s. A thruhiker almost by accident, Yazzy had intended to accompany her friend Anna for just a few weeks until Anna was up and running. At age 15, Yazzy had done fully half the trail with her older brother and didn't feel the need to copy her brother's thruhike.

Anna, however, quit after only a week. Yazzy figured what the hell and kept on hiking. To her credit, she made it all the way to Pennsylvania before a family outing took her offtrail a week and caused her to lose pace with all her trail friends. Back on the trail, loneliness like the Grim Reaper dropped her like a stone. Not dead, of course. Just off the trail. Until now. Sundown, one of her early-on trail friends, had made it to New Hampshire and now Yazzy was back on, if only for a few days.

Grim Reaper? Jesus. I can be so melodramatic. Ack! Who wouldn't be after walking the distance from Los Angeles to San Diego 20 times in five months?

Anyway, Yazzy's back from her swim and stoking the fire and igniting the cabin's propane wall lamps and telling Jackie, Ry, Sundown, and me a story about some guy freezing to death on a mountaintop. But before I can relate that to you, I must finish catching you up on how we got here.

Okay, so that next morning on Mousilauke I bolted ahead of the gang again, literally skipping and high-wiring it straight down the sheer rock wall trail beside beautiful falls then down out across the Lincoln access road and up the next damn mountain and over it and maybe even up another, I don't recall, and past a hut and a hundred Labor Day weekend tourists. It was a fast and furious day, and I made it to Franconia Notch in time to meet Justin and his girl, Jess. We had drinks with Still Frank in Woodstock, picked up a few sixers of Jim Beam and ginger ale, and pitched our tents in the dark in the exact spot where months earlier the same crew plus Party Girl had camped to do trail magic for thruhikers who never came.

With the exception of firefighters, I don't like men in uniform. I don't like cops or men who think they're cops just because some organization, either as ill-willed as the Nazis or as altruistic and well-intentioned as Burning Man's "Black Rock Rangers" or this new brand of pseudo-cop I've come across on the AT: the Ridge Runner. From the first Ridge Runner I encountered, back in the Smokies, I just didn't like him. If there's one thing worse than a cop, it's a cop who pretends to be your friend to get you talking, to catch you in a lie.

Meet Ratface the Ridge Runner. All I first saw of Ratface were his boots. What I heard through my half slumber that Saturday morning following my first night back in the woods with Justin and Jess was spoken in cop-tone and certainly something I never thought I'd hear whilst discreetly camping in the woods. "Would you step out of your tent please, sir."

It seems we had chosen the WRONG spot to camp. We were in a fragile eco-protection zone. Surely we'd seen the signs. It didn't matter that after 1,700 miles I had become something of a professional "camper" and knew all about the fragile zones and had done my best to hike the mandatory 1/4 mile in off the road, I was, Ratface said, off by one-tenth of a mile. Fine: $50 per person. Enter: good cop, bad cop psychology. "How many people are you?" he asked, gesturing at my cousin's tent. Three, I said. "Well, I'm gonna let you go with just one fine." Ergo: Argue with me at all on this and I'll zap you for $150.

Oh, I had reason aplenty to argue with the officious little prick. "Normally I'd let you go with just a warning, but because it's a holiday weekend I have to fine you." Great. Groovy. One-tenth of a mile! How the hell was I to know it was a holiday weekend? My kind rarely knows what day it is. I'M A

THRUHIKER! SCREW YOU, RIDGE RUNNER RATFACE, METER MAID OF THE FOREST!

Justin and his Jess and I had a nice hike despite being pulled over in our speeding tents that morning. Though I had wanted them to experience "shelter life," the shelter we arrived at that night was occupied by a handful of frat boys. We pitched our tents a little ways off. Which worms us back through Time and Space to me sitting in the dirt staring at the tiny flame of my luxuriously-packed-in-blue votive candle drinking a 50/50 mix of hot cocoa and Canadian Black Velvet whiskey and trying not to think about Burning Man.

By propane lamplight in the silence of her family cabin on this early September night, Yazzy tells us the story of a man who not so long ago bade his wife goodbye, ascended Mt. Lafayette, sat down on its west face and prepared to die. He easily succeeded in a day and a night, dying of exposure. I think of that term "paradoxical undressing" I have heard a lot recently. Apparently a result of hypothermia, a victim goes from feeling very cold to feeling too warm and thus sheds layers when they should be adding. I guess this results in many a frozen dead person being found in the nude. Paradoxical.

It seems the man was not alone in his suicidal mission. The story goes that several members of his family expired in similar fashion, the most recent, a brother or a son, walking off into the Alaskan winter never to be seen again.

Okay, but I'm getting ahead of myself. It would be a few days before I'd hear this story, When I did hear it, I didn't ask Yazzy in what season the Mt. Lafayette death took place. I should have after what I went through on Lafayette. I can tell you this much: It could easily have been last night as some night in the depths of winter. Easier in fact. In winter, the guy would have had a much harder time climbing the mountain. Snowshoes and all that. It is now early September, and trust me, last night would have done just fine for dyin'.

Or tonight.

I know this because I climbed Mt. Lafayette just hours ago. I climbed and I climbed and I damn near ran at times, pausing only to scramble up rock faces or piles of scree or stop and hold Nalgene water bottle to dripping stone for water enough to last another hour or two. I know this because for the first time in recent memory I am forced, despite pouring sweat, to don a second layer against the cold. Then a third. Soon, I am climbing in two soaked under layers, my Patagonia fleece and my North Face 700-fill goose feather jacket. I summit wearing every item of clothing I have.

Backup. Rewind.

It's a Sunday in early autumn in one of the most heavily hiked sections of the White Mountains, probably second only to Mt. Washington. I've come out of the woods with Cousin Justin and his girl, Jess, they tired and satisfied and quite DONE with hiking for a while, I'm sure. They drop me off at the trailhead near the Flume, we say our goodbyes, and I turn and face Mt. Lafayette looming above me. I saddle up with pack, cinch straps, and...and...something's missing. My Leki poles. OH SHIT, MY POLES! I turn and face the place where Justin has just driven away. Gone.

I run across Highway 93 and to the campground pay phone. A buckshot round of phone calls later, Justin is reached, via his mother on his girlfriend's cell since the battery is dead on his. Luck of lucks they stopped nearby for lunch and aren't all the way back home in Franklin. If there's one thing I'm learning about East Coasters, well, no, maybe it's just my family—they don't like driving long distances. From one end of New Hampshire to the other is like a blip on the radar screen to an L.A.-to-San Francisco 10-hour roadrunner like me or anyone from the wide-open West. Anyway, they come back. We open the trunk. No Lekis.

Immediately I see them in my mind. When we reached the car, triumphant after our bigass two-day, 10-mile dredge south from Glencliff, I planted the poles firmly in the roadside sandy dirt behind the car. And there they had stayed. I can just see us loading up the packs and me driving off. "The poles are still there," I tell Justin with all the confidence I can muster. "I just know it. We have to go back. I can't LIVE without my Lekis."

An hour later we were back at the Glencliff trailhead of the AT and, voila, there behind a whole, newly arrived lineup of day hiker SUVs, stood my $150 Leki poles. Talk about your trail magic. Justin couldn't believe his eyes. Even I, more accustomed to a trail world in which theft JUST DOESN'T HAPPEN, was pleasantly surprised.

Back to the future. I am now back at the trailhead ready to dive into the next section of the Whites. But I've lost four hours or so. I head up anyway. I bargain with the Fates of White Blazes and opt for the more direct route straight up to Lafayette. I am the ONLY hiker going uphill in a veritable human flood of day hikers huffing and puffing with dreams of Burger King sugarplums dancing in their heads and yet not so focused that they don't notice me and give me queer looks. "Where the hell is he going?" I hear one woman ask. Indeed. It is after five o'clock, and a cold fog is erasing the mountains above, and no one in their right mind would be going up...there. Lady, I'm on a mission from God.

You see, I've been secretly in love with this beautiful Italian woman since the moment I first saw her on March 20, the day she and I and her boyfriend started the journey. Or they started their journey and I alone began mine. Now I must catch her, because time is running out. That was the day the grain of sand got lodged in the oyster. Though I am pained by the knowledge that I can't win her, that I must not win her, it just isn't right, that I mustn't despite having a chance, romantic-I must see her again, must walk with her, must see her smile and feel her presence. But all this starts with a mad run up a tourist-infested mountain and a stop to pound a Foster's oil can on a rock outcropping to the further horror of the tourists, and then more running, uphill, happily rejoined with my Lekis. Poles in hand again, love in my heart, and beer in my belly, I am invincible!

I reach the hut in the cold and misty shoulder of Lafayette and out comes Doc Gnarly to greet me. He's been washing dishes for eight hours straight, he says. As trades for lodging go, this is heavy duty. But then so is Doc. Doc calls himself a humble hiker, and he probably is. But there's an alligator under that Zen walking stick of a man, one I imagine only I can see. He says maybe they'll take me on as a work-for-trade, too, what with so many tourists flooding the huts. I say thanks but no thanks. I've many miles to go before I sleep.

I'm off again. Into the mist. Into thin air. A walking human steam engine clad in naught but my shorts and a capilene long-sleeved top, my lungs bellows radiating heat. This is the mountain the guy just sat down and died on. I didn't know this at the time. Would I have been so bold had I known? Somewhere past the cairns and back into the krumholz, all light had gone out of the world, and it was just me and my headlamp.

There, somewhere on a ridgeline between Lafayette and Garfield mountains, I made my first potentially fatal error in my five months of wilderness existence.

I'd hiked too long and too far in the dark when I came upon what any sane, non-thruhiker would have called a deep, dark chasm, and I wisely went no further. It wasn't a chasm. It was just the AT, going straight down, all rocks, nice and slick, and me exhausted at this point. So I stopped. Just so. Stopped and stood there in the middle of a section of trail no wider than a skinny bear and stared at the wall of tightly packed semi-alpine trees all around me on either side. Where the hell was I going to camp? The trail here was a walled-in freeway with no breakdown lane, no exits, and not so much as a turnout to let another driver pass. The forest was more thicket than forest. I couldn't sleep in the trough of the trail. Bear, mountain lion, moose, all walked the same trails as we. Worse, so did the ridge runners. I had no choice.

So I turned to face the dense, dark clusterfuck of 10- to 12-foot tall trees and proceeded to blast straight through their barricade of branches. My mission, as clear as I could muster in my exhausted state of mind: Get out of sight of the trail, find a pocket of moss to curl up into, drop like a stone. It was that easy. Was, until I went and complicated the hell out of it.

About 20 paces into the woods, I found an adequate place to curl up fetal-cowboy-style, heaved a sigh of relief, and dropped my pack. But then my brain started going all paradoxical on me. I didn't start undressing, but it should be noted that I had shed my down jacket and my fleece an hour or so before after returning below tree line where it wasn't freezing and there was little if any wind. So I was now clad only in my usual power-hiking outfit—shorts and a short-sleeved polypro shirt.

No, the sudden odd instructions coming at me from my tired brain were more of the paranoid than the paradoxical. I blame that damn ridge runner kid and the citation system. If he hadn't put the fear in me about camping in nondesignated areas, I wouldn't have gotten it in my head that "hmm, maybe I'm not far enough back from the trail? Maybe I'll be visible at first light. Maybe THEY'LL SEE ME!" I was losin' it.

In my delirium, I hatched a plan. I would leave my pack, plant my poles in the mossy earth, walk the 20 paces back to the trail, turn, and shine my light back at my camp to see if I could see the shiny titanium of my poles. Genius, I thought. I'll win the Nobel Prize. Or maybe an Emmy. An Oscar? So back to the trail I walked. Ten paces, fifteen, twenty, boom. Back at the trail. Shine the light. No sight of my shiny poles. Good. Back into the woods. Ten paces, fifteen, twenty, twenty-five, thirty...THIRTY FIVE! Wait a minute. Holy shit! Where's my stuff?

"Oh, that's good," I thought, still capable of a little chuckle. "Good one, McKinney." So I walked back a few paces. No stuff. Then a few more. No stuff. Then a few paces to the left. A few to the right. No stuff. "Okay, now this isn't funny anymore," I said aloud to the devious trees. "Fork over my stuff!" I was just gonzo enough that had elves come to mind at that moment, I easily would have believed that this was some kind of elfish prank.

Instead, a more sober thought came to mind. Get back to the trail. "Okay, I'll just get back to the trail, figure out where exactly I went IN before by locating broken branches, and get it right this time."

Before I go any further with this story, the set designers and lighting people would like me to remind you that it was very, very dark that night. Not stormy. That's another story. But if there was a moon, it was on vacation in Pluto. Not a trickle of light from the heavens penetrated that dense forest. With my headlight off, it was cave dark. Repeat, it was very, very dark.

So I point my body back toward where my somewhat spun-out internal compass says the trail should be and begin pacing off the steps. "Five, ten, fifteen, twenty, uh, twenty-five, thirty, oh shit, thirty-five, forty. Oh shit!

Pause for a moment while every hair on my body stands straight up and that cold wave of primal fear washes down my spine.

"Where's the frikken Appalachian Trail, Jester?!!" I now ask, fully splintered from my trail name self and freaked to full awake status.

Awake, but not fully aware. I make this distinction because, for the next 20 minutes or so, I became a jabbering, bushwhacking madman. Like the college kids in *Blair Witch*, I let the "camcorder" of my internal observer jiggle, dangle, and hang by its strap as I floundered in panic. Suffice to say I don't remember what I did for those 20 minutes but jabber and walk in ever-widening circles.

Then suddenly I snapped out of it. I could hear Anthony Hopkins in that film *The Edge* saying, "You know what people lost in the wilderness die of? They die of shame." Oh, I was ashamed all right. Not only was I lost, but I'd first made a point of losing my gear so that when I, too, became lost, I would be a pig in the wilderness, naked to the elements, a dead man. Exposure. Hypothermia. Paradoxical undressing. Then I remembered something, and I froze in place and listened. I even shut out my headlamp to better concentrate and if possible attune to any unnatural sound in the forest.

Not an hour before I had noted, if only subconsciously, the sound of cars on the highway north of Franconia and the sadly departed Old Man on the Mountain. If my bearing on the trail was 12 o'clock, the sound had been coming from about 10 o'clock. I listened and I listened and I listened. I stilled my breathing, my heart rate, everything. I put my body into full stealth mode like a submarine hiding from the enemy. At last, I heard it, ever so faint. I stood up, adjusted my bearing accordingly, and walked straight to the AT, by now about 60 paces away.

The famous white blazes of the AT never looked so good! I kissed the first one I saw. Then I set about the difficult task of finding my gear. But the fear was out of it now, and I took great care to "breadcrumb" my steps back into the woods, tying toilet paper shreds to branches. When I found my pack, there was no hope of sleep. Fear does wonders for the adrenaline. I strapped in, took poles in hand, and took on that vertical chasm, that heretofore daunting dropoff, which, for its beautiful white blazes, suddenly looked like it was a bunny slope. I walked all the way to the Garfield campsites and shelter that night, quietly slipping in amidst a handful of snoring hikers at around 3 a.m., and went right into paradoxical unconsciousness, oblivious of the snores, grateful for their human sound.

The White Mountains bloom with new experiences both inspiring and, in some cases, odd. On this September 6, I am almost giddy from the previous night's brush with mortal fear. Somewhere well north of Garfield Hut, a man passes me going southbound in nothing but a blue bathrobe and carrying not a pack but a plastic grocery bag full of... something. A friend reports having seen the man hunched down hiding behind a tree. Apparently this is orientation time and colleges like Dartmouth have sent their fresh meat into the forest for a bit of bonding and, by the look of the guy in the bathrobe, mischief.

Down trail a little ways, I see something colorful dangling at eye level dead in my path. For once it is not a silkworm or a gangly nasty spider, but a Gummi Man hanging from a string. His body parts are made from various types of gummi candy. Very *Blair Witch*. Very clever. Not wanting to be selfish, I opt to bite off half of his gummi worm legs and leave him hanging there for the Dartmouth inductees.

This is a pleasant encounter and a good one to make up for what had happened a little while back. I'd been walking a particularly narrow stretch of trail when, upon seeing another hiker coming uphill toward me, I stepped off-trail to let him by. I might have known something was amiss with this dude who introduced himself as trail name Shatter. Too friendly in a Mormon-at-your-door kind of way. Shatter carried a sizable Snoopy doll on his back attached to his pack and claimed former thruhiker status, so I listened when he asked, "Can I talk to you about something?"

I said sure, not really wanting to stand there and chitchat but not wanting to be rude. "Take a look at where you're standing." What? Oh, you snake, I thought. You back-stabbing eco-Nazi hypocrite! You're going to preach to me about eco-consciousness and minimum impact hiking. I looked up from my feet and, with daggers in my eyes and a tone cold as freezer rot, said, "I stepped off the trail to make room for YOU." Sure enough, he began to preach. Okay, I'd stepped on some lichens and moss that were now horribly maimed and would go through the rest of their short lives writhing in horrible lichen pain. I'm sorry, lichens, I really am. But the nerve of that guy to lecture me after I'd hiked 1,700 miles to get to his precious White Mountains and politely stepped aside to let him pass. I would have liked to leave him writhing in horrible pain.

Instead I dismissed his gibberish with a wave of my hand, a wave that said, "Later, spook," and off I walked, straight down the center of the well-worn path. Until, of course, the next time Nature called, at which point I tromped and crashed over and through all manner of precious plant life in a perpendicular path away from the trail with all the finesse of a rutting moose. I have seen many a brand of animal scat on the trail. The bears and moose and deer all walk the well worn AT and shit on it without batting an eye. But I have also seen what I am quite sure was human shit.

Hmm? I wonder why someone would do something so uncouth as to shit right on the trail? A statement, perhaps? Something like, "Okay, you Snoopy-toting eco-Nazi, if you want my feet to stay on the trail, you got it. Enjoy my mein einigkeit mit die Natur," my 'oneness' with nature. Tricky swine, Shatter. What a most appropriate name you have. I was feeling great before you came along. And no, it wasn't me who shat mid-trail. I was having such a lovely day.

Lovely indeed. I'd awoken slow and sweet to the sound of fellow hikers chatting on the "porch" of the shelter, the mid-morning sun shining on them and me dozing late in their shadows. After last night's fright and a few more miles hiked in the dark to reach the Garfield Ridge camping area, I am just happy to be. In total, I hiked eight hard vertical miles from Franconia Notch, four of them in the dark. When I rise and rub my eyes I am greeted by friendly faces, none of them thruhikers but all intrigued by the stranger who arrived late in the night. I meet Big John from Massachusetts and his two lovely daughters and Erin the area caretaker. Before she can ask, I mention the $6 fee and ask if I should pay her now. "Later," she says smiling. "We can settle up on your way out."

The whole fee thing that began to rear its ugly head at the Massachusetts/Vermont state line is troublesome to the thruhiker after 1,500 miles of free shelters and camping all along the AT from Georgia. Some thruhikers get quite indignant about it, understandably. Alas, the victims are the poor underpaid "poo-stirrers" like Erin, the caretakers whose one big daily job is stirring the shit in the composting privies. They stir our poo by morning, and take the rap for the fee system by day.

I'm just so happy to be back among the living after feeling seriously frikken lost last night that I'm just DYING TO PAY! To myself, I'm thinking, "Ooh, ooh, let me give you six dollars for this blissful open space and sun and happy voices and...hmm, Erin, you're kind of cute." Let's just say Big John, a handsome man, had passed on his genetic good looks. His daughters were hard to, um, miss. But neither was of age, so we'll just drop that subject.

I'm in no hurry but when I finally do get my bag packed and say goodbye to the happy weekenders and accompany Erin to her big army-issue canvas tent to "transact," she won't take my money. Says she wanted to get me away from the others so as not to be unfair, but that she hates taking money from thruhikers.

Okay, then! I thank her, wish her well, and head up trail. As I go, I turn and catch her grinning gaze as she ducks into her tent and think, "Hmm, maybe she's wishing I'd follow her in there. Surely these caretakers get lonely out here?

That afternoon I meet up with Jackie and Ry again at Zealand Falls Hut. God, that woman bewitches me. I'd spent the day moving at a half-sprint listening to "Pinball Wizard" and Zeppelin's "Cashmere," racing, intent on catching my friends and sure enough found them lounging at one of the nicer huts I've seen, mostly by dint of its location smack on the edge of beautiful Zealand Falls. But did I even see the falls? No. Not really. Frank was there, and Impulse, a few others. But me, I had eyes only for Jackie.

On a trip to use the "bathrooms" at Zealand Hut, I found the usual non-flushing pit toilets prettied up to resemble a civilized bathroom, for the yups I supposed. I was astounded, however, as I went to wash my hands and discovered "motion-activated" faucets. Aha! "I see," I said to myself, "so this is what the AMC does with the $80/head lodging fee at the huts." Unbelievable. Deplorable, really. Ridiculous. Soon they'll be paving the AT for wheelchair accessibility. God help us. I surface from the shitters to Jackie and Ry. The perfect couple. The Happy Couple. I think, God help me.

They had made it all this way together and were sure to finish together. I can imagine no better segue to marriage, no better test. But as the end of the trail approached, I kept thinking less about their happiness and more about mine. I kept thinking that maybe, just maybe, there was a chance for Jackie and me. But a *crush*? Was that grounds enough to "crush" their years together? The strain of chivalry in my blood will never allow me to break and enter. She would have to jump me, and the odds of such an overt act were slim to none from this demure Italian princess. She smiled and hugged me, and my body melted into and around her tiny frame. As usual, I lifted her clear off her feet. Jackie has the bones of a bird. If you'd asked me then, I'd have said she probably even had wings.

That night at Ethan Pond Campsite, we sleep in the shelter. Jackie is right beside me, Ry beside her. It's just the way the shelters work. If enough people show up, hikers are practically sleeping atop one another. How's that song lyric go? It's a lot to take, this fortune in pain.

Earlier, a moose walked right through the camp and I missed it, off sipping spiked cocoa by the sunset-painted pond with Jackie. As I attempt sleep, I try and think of Yazzy, the sweet girl I'd met on Mousilauke. To pursue Yazzy, now that would be sane. What I'm doing to myself, to my heart and my head, right now, this is not sane. In the night, I awaken to Jackie's face one Eden's apple away from my own. I can feel her breath on my face. What can I do? Take a bite? I close my eyes and inhale. It is enough.

The next morning we head for Crawford Notch. Crawford Notch is one place along the entire AT whose name I know well. On ski trips as a boy with fellow Cub Scout and friend Gary Belcher, I learned from Gary and his brother, Craig, to call it "Nawford's Crotch," and we giggled at our dirty cleverness. On Maine's 107.5 Frank FM, it's Manfred Mann and "Blinded by the Light." As with every time I hear this song, I stop whatever I'm doing at the refrain and sing out at the top of my lungs the words, "Mama always told me not to look into the eyes of the sun, but Mama, that's where the fun is!" A glance into Jackie's eyes is definitely a glance into the eyes of the sun, a gaze, a blinding look into eyes so dark of brown they shine black. Black Hole Sun. Won't you come? Won't you come?

The weather reports call for rain, fallout from Hurricane Francis. We blaze down into the Notch wondering what we're going to do about the rain, where we might duck off the trail until the storm passes. We are far from any reasonably priced lodging and have no clue what we're going to do. We are in the trailhead parking lot no more than a minute when with that ole AT magic, who should drive up in her truck completely out of the blue, but Yazzy. Yazzy to the rescue!

NINETEEN

Escaping to Canada...Francis! Francis! Let's Just Get Naked!
Being Peter Pan is a Lonely Gig...Nawford's Crotch and the
Abduction of Yazzy...Rewriting Stevie Nicks...Holding Hands
with an Angel in a Dungeon Fit for a King...Third Generation
Coal Thrower...The Only Post Office in America Open on
Sunday...Endurance of the Monotonous...Simon Says, Cut the
Rope...

Inside you're ugly, ugly like me,
I can see thru you, see your true colors... - Staind

I am a nasty little boy. I eat pills and swill lager and kiss the girls then pull
away. I take Yaz and Jackie out on the water in the canoe and we talk of
tsunamis as the wind-whipped surface of Lake Francis slaps the hull and
tosses us hither and yon. I ask the girls what they would do if they looked
back at the dark, storm cloud-shrouded lake and saw a tsunami coming.
Practical Yazzy says she'd zip up her life jacket. Infinitely agreeable Jackie
sips her beer and smiles, says nothing. We paddle on and the early-autumn
wind sings in our ears the first few notes of summer's inevitable requiem.
After a pause, I say, "If I looked round and saw a tsunami coming, I would
passionately kiss you both, hold you tight to my heart and yell, 'Yeeee-hah!
Bring it on!'"
Back at Yazzy's cabin, Sundown and Ry sit reading in silence in the
sweltering wood furnace heat. Jackie fancies perhaps Ry has a crush on
Sundown. I wonder. An earlier observer, I'll call him Deep Throat, took one
look at Ry and said, "He's gay." Granted, I had told Mr. Throat all about
Jackie's not-so-subtle displays of affection for me and my deep affection for
her and my bewilderment at Ry's absolute lack of reaction toward all this.
"Perhaps he's bi?" Throat surmised. "That would explain why he doesn't
mind having you around, enjoys it, in fact." I don't believe it.

Out on the lake I have been lobbying the girls. Who wants to leave now? We just got here! Ry wants to leave in the morning. But today's only the ninth. Says he's antsy. Of course he's antsy. We're all antsy. We're frikken trail junkies. All we know how to do anymore is walk and walk and walk. But we left the AT and traveled fully four hours north yesterday to this blissful corner of New Hampshire woodland paradise to escape the residue of Hurricane Francis. Whoa! Francis? Ooh, that's good. Come to Lake Francis to escape Hurricane Francis! I should have been an ad man.

Now I'm sure this is EXACTLY as things were meant to be.

I unplug from my headphones a moment to throw down this comment from my bed-desk in the loft of the beautiful post-and-beam cabin: "Ry, I got antsy when we were at the beach house in North Carolina. Embrace it and relax." I don't think he's amused. But he doesn't argue the point. Either he's a colossal wimp or one of the nicest, most Zen boyfriends and human beings I've ever met.

I'd wager Sundown is the real umph behind the move to leave tomorrow.

Sundown fascinates. She never appears to see anything but what she wants to see, never focuses on anything but what is immediately at her needful attention. Her eyes do not scan a scene, a room. No, they nullify it. Ignore it completely. Or so it would seem. She speaks very little, hasn't laughed once in 24 hours, makes no eye contact, and is, I suspect, wondering why she came along. Maybe she's just avoiding MY gaze? She probably sees everything, but her downcast gaze belies nothing.

Belies nothing? Needful attention? What exactly does all this mean? I don't know. I just said it. I just say a lot of things. Use what you will and disregard the rest. It is the American way. Don't bother recycling any of my irreverently tossed-off words. They will not work to build Earthship walls nor suffice to mold into ashtrays or astronaut suites. They will not easily melt down into the raw stuff of new material goods. And they are nonrefundable. No deposit, no return. This is not Vermont, hippies! This is New Hampshire, the land of Freedom or Death, of no sales tax and cheap Canadian whiskey and no seatbelt law and no five-cent return on bottles and cans. My words then, here or on the trail in the White Mountains, are more worthless than anywhere.

Let's take the boat out, wait until darkness,
let's take the boat out, wait until darkness comes.
-Peter Gabriel

You're in a boat on a lake, its waters black as coal. You're with two women, both in their early 20s, both doe-eyed, one Italian brown like black, one blue as Walden ice. Both girls are beautiful, well-endowed, one voluptuous and earthy yet full of giggles and gin, the other lithe and tiny, soft-spoken. She'll melt your heart. They both will. Both are fertile, supple, willing, happy, and as yet unwed.

On this latter note, yes, one has a boyfriend, and after six months together in the woods, he's your friend, too. There's naught to be done about it. You're doomed. She wants you. They both do. You want them, too. Then again, you don't. An awkward first encounter with Blue Eyes has left you reticent to try again. She wanted to play but insisted on keeping her clothes on. You're too old for that shit.

Then comes Miss Italy. Too much trouble with the boyfriend thing. He will propose to her within the coming month. He has told you as much, wants to pop the question before the magic of the trail ends and Reality crashes back into their young 20-something lives. In truth, you love them both. Hell, why not love 'em all? The girls and the boyfriend. You've watched the couple succeed in their partnership and love under the harsh conditions of the trail for half a year and you know what that means: It means they should be married, immediately. They have proven in 2,000 miles that they possess what most people only dream of in a relationship. Endurance. Compatibility. Love. They belong together.

You, however, are a peregrine, a wanderer, a lost boy. You belong to no one and nothing, and unless something radical crashes into your life soon to change that, you always will be. Peregrine. (I was beginning to like this name, and in the muddle of all my trail names and nicknames, I would eventually settle on Peregrine while hiking the Continental Divide the following year.) Wanderer. Lost boy. Peter Pan, not the syndrome, the reality. Not some closet case in green tights like the guy you saw on some freak showcase TV show, but the real item. You've got a Wendy in every port, but you would trade them all for the sky, for the freedom to fly. For you OWN this freedom, as so few ever will. You know what that means: It owns you.

When you own something as magical and grand and rare as freedom, you become its caretaker and its poster child. You are duty bound to keep on flying, wandering, loving, leaving. You're in a boat on a lake, its waters black as coal. You're with two women, both in their early 20s, both doe-eyed, one Italian brown like black, one blue as Walden ice.

It is nice.

It is now. Point: There's no need to try and grab hold of it, or of them. The moment is yours now, and thus forever.

Tomorrow the residue of Hurricane Francis will pass and the exposed high rock ridges of New Hampshire's Presidential Range will be, if not sunny, at least safe to traverse again. You will be back on the trail. Blue Eyes will take to the trail at the Maine state line, well ahead of you. You and the couple will cross into Maine a few days later, together perhaps. Or perhaps not. Your heart aches for a love of your own, and being in their company pains you. Miss Italy consoles you, says to keep the faith, that maybe the girl of your dreams will finally appear in these last 300 miles to Katahdin. You doubt it, but you'll smile and say thank you, and heft your pack for the 400th time this year and walk north.

Our last sunset at Yazzy's Lake Francis cabin is like nothing I've ever seen. The earth rolls and smothers the sun to my far left, but the real action is straight across the water in front of me. It is as though the rain, in leaving, has ignited a wildfire in the hills to the north. A band of bright red and orange light rests atop the hills, undulating in flame-like waves. To complete the illusion, the burning clouds stop a few degrees above the horizon and give way to a dark, churning, smoke-gray cloud layer, which, perhaps due to it being farther off, remains outside the sun's reach.

Living in the mountains of southern California, I have seen wildfires. I have seen them close enough to fear them, helping friends frantically pack pets, precious books and photographs into escape vehicles as ash fell on us, snowflakes from the black hole sun sky. I have seen wildfires devouring forest acreage beneath towering clouds of ash, and this sunset looked every bit the part.

The sunset over Lake Francis that night hailed the end of Hurricane Francis's visit to New England with a most dramatic flair. That night for the five AT thruhikers holed up near the Canadian border, red skies at night spelled "hiker's delight." It meant we could hike again. Fair weather over Mt. Washington and his presidential buddies was almost a given.

Why then the somber mood that prevailed that night and all the next morn? Because the return to the trail meant separation. Sundown was "taking" (intentionally subjective word choice on my part) Yazzy with her to some point further north, Gorham, I think. While The Happy Couple and I, we were still back at Nawford's Crotch…er, whatever. That night while Sundown, Ry, and Jackie made a run to the store, Yazzy and I connected in a way that would, eventually, spell the end of my time with Jackie and Ry. Let's face it, the sexual tension in our little fivesome was running real high at that point. If it had been any other five people in that hot house, there would have been an orgy. With Jackie, Ry and Sundown gone, I wasted no time in breaking that tension with the Lady of the House, who now agreed that sex without clothing was much better.

The next morning we five would separate, but it wouldn't be long before my straight-outta-the-Ten-Commandments, wrong-headed desire for Jackie and my longing for companionship would combine like bleach and ammonia to create a sickening, if not deadly toxin to this writer's heart and ruin our intention to summit together, as we had by happenstance begun from Springer Mountain in Georgia together on the first day of spring, March 20, 2004.

The group dynamics of the trail have been good for heretofore depressive-submissive me. When people annoy and fluster me, more often than not (more often than I was doing before the trail) I tell them so, tell them my feelings, and speak up for myself. For example, this is me grousing down from the loft at Yazzy's cabin to those reading down below, "Can you shut off the damn blazing lantern, please?" Eloquent, eh? They do. Mind you, there were two other lanterns going, quieter lanterns and out of the direct line of sight of the loft. I would NEVER ask someone to stop reading.

"I climbed a mountain and I turned around," sang Stevie Nicks. To continue where Stevie never dreamed of taking this lyric, "I dropped to the ground and flailed around, I jerked like a hooked fish stomped by a thug, but I refused to die, oh hoh, I damn well refused to die."

Focus, McKinney. Where were we? Atop a mountain. Which mountain? Some mountain. Does it matter? Another mountain, one of several hundred mountains we've climbed since Georgia. Blow Stevie Nicks. She didn't climb a mountain, not like this one anyway, not like Lafayette. Not like Garfield or Lincoln or Washington or any o6thers in this righteous and rapacious icing on the AT Nobo Cake called The Whites. On now to the Lake of the Clouds.

Wow. What ever did I do to deserve such beauty and divine surrounds? Tonight I sit squat at the top of the New Hampshire World a pauper king, Gandhi high atop a ridge in the White Mountain range of the "Live Free or Die" state so close to Mt. Washington I feel I could touch it (just 1.7 miles in fact to the top). To my left just a few feet away tucked inside the stone foundation of perhaps the most well known of the AMC's mountaintop "huts," Lake of the Clouds, is my bed for the night. Said hut is known to thruhikers as "Lake of the Crowds," and tonight AT Mile 1,840 is no exception.

Tonight the lodge behind me is packed full of happy campers each paying $80 for the night for a bunk and two cafeteria-style meals. My fellow Dungeon mates and I, however, paid just $8. Yes, I said Dungeon. That's what they call the little emergency shelter in the basement of the Lake hut where they allow thruhikers to bunk for the night. It's the door, I think, that earned the emergency shelter its name. It's a serious, no bullshit door, more befitting a vault than a place for human habitation. Big, steel, set in the stone foundation of the hut, with a giant three-foot lever arm that comes down hard to seal the door shut against...what?

I flash for a moment on the final scenes of *The Shining,* of the brutal winds and high piling, killing snow that winter wreaks upon this place every year without fail. The door tells a story, foretells a tale of brutal winter weather not so far off on this September 11 night. Mt. Washington is home to the highest wind speed ever recorded on Earth: 231 mph. We are more than a little blessed with this window of calm weather.

The finest aspect of where I sit tonight though, is this: the sunset.

Visibility up here at the southern shoulder of Mt. Washington tonight is easily 100 miles. This means a cascading sea of blueish ribbons, mountains, hundreds of them, stretching onward to forever. Due to our present, near due east course, there's no doubt that many of those mountains have opened up their secrets to me. I have climbed them. Bagged them. Torn over and through them like some goat-footed toreador from Pamplona running with invisible bulls.

All this is mine for the viewing, for the smelling of the alpine air and the hot chocolate I brew up for warmth, for the touch of silk leggings on skin, fleece hat, and warm, warm goose down jacket, for the sounds of gaiety in the lodge behind me and the light and airy jibber-jabber of the young French-Canadian couple, Melanie and Michel, sharing the dungeon with Jackie, Ry, and me. All this is mine, is ours, for the price of one day's labor afoot, for the physical strain of eleven very steep miles up from Crawford Notch. It is mine, and my calf muscles are sore. I couldn't be happier.

I had a good cry today on a high precipice outcropping of rock beneath which dropped straight down a few thousand feet of Buddhist surreal death of air. I don't know why really. Just bawled, with Bob Dylan singing in my ear: "Mama, put my guns in the ground, I can't use them anymore, knock-knock knocking on Heaven's Door..." Could well have been a kind of purging triggered by the intense physical workout of roaring up Mt. Webster, Mt. Jackson, Mt. Franklin.

Suddenly all the pain and all the melancholic wandering of a decade or so lost and lonesome and all the loves lost, and all the death, it all welled up in me at once as I stared down at Crawford Notch, a place barely remembered from my youth but reminiscent…of something, of better times perhaps. Today is 9/11. Three years ago today the world lost its frickken mind, and me with it. Two weeks later I was in a hospital under suicide watch. A month after that, she told me I had to go. A month after that I dutifully left. Today I did again what I've been doing every day for nearly six months. Today I did a good thing, for me and, I'd like to think, for the world. I walked.

Walk with me. Want to? It's easy. And cheap! For what most city dwellers throw away in rent and utilities in ONE MONTH, one could walk the AT for six.

Climb with me. Don't believe the advertising. There is no separation between you and me, between this long walk of a daily grind and your daily 9-5. This is hard work out here. Your work is hard in different, perhaps less physical ways. The commonality, however, is this, and it is the thing that separates the men from the boys, the dreamers from the doers, both here on the trail and in the game of life. It is endurance of the monotonous.

That's the key. The Appalachian Trail, overall, is a fantastic voyage. Admittedly, it ain't six months in a cubicle, so forgive me if I err on the side of empathy. But boring it is at times. Oh, Jesus, does it get boring! There's a good reason thruhikers sarcastically refer to the AT as "The Green Tunnel." Monotony takes many forms. After 1,700 miles and more than 100 mountains, I'm so bored with climbing mountains that I generally curse the whole way up them, perhaps just to give myself something to do. Walking might be very Zen, but walking in the forest for six months, well, one can only stand so much green, so many rocks and roots, so many senseless ups and downs.

Endurance of the monotonous. Okay, don't quit your monotonous job just yet. Just climb with me. Today we will climb out of the tunnel. We will climb a tree if we have to. We will see the world from on high. Climb with me. Pretend I'm Morpheus calling you on a cell phone newly dropped in your hand. Go now. Climb out of your cubicle, straight up. If your boss sees you, tell him you heard a rat in the ventilation and are going to flush it out. (Yes, you may pack along your Swingline stapler.).) Push aside the corkboard ceiling panels. Find a pipe to shimmy up. Go for the ductwork. You see it? Find a way in.

You in? Now crawl along until you reach the vertical shaft in the ventilation. The trail here is straight up. Let's go. Find a foothold and shimmy up. Ever heard of chimneying? It's the act of using opposing force on two vertical surfaces to ascend or descend a tight spot. Think of Santa in the chimney. Now chimney the walls of that shaft. Don't lose hope if you slip and slide and damn near wet your pants when the "shaft" trail suddenly turns and drops 50 or a 100 feet straight down, slippery with moisture, the moisture of all that collective corporate breath. The Green Tunnel does this all the time, gets slippery, I mean. It's a good thing. Reduces the monotony.

Keep climbing. You're almost there now! Now shoot for the moon and blast through the roof of the forest of the high top crest of the imaginary glass ceiling of the workaday world and out into the light of endless blue, blue sky.

Welcome to the real world.

Today I added a stone to every sizable cairn I encountered, one for each and every of my precious lost. I stopped by the tall rock pile tower of a cairn of a marker of the trail here where snowdrifts obscure white blazes and the cairns are all a winter hiker has to navigate by. I stopped, chose a handsome rock from the ground, and placed it on the cairn with a prayer.

"My dearest Chris, may you be happy and comfortable in the body of your youthful, model self and living in the lap of luxury in that great Plaza Hotel in the Sky." I would place her stone somewhere high but secure. "Are you there, Chris? I think you are. Then walk with me a while, would you? Let us walk and talk as once we did." Thus would I walk a while and converse with Chris.

At the next great cairn I did it again.

"Luciano, my young brother, forgive me for not being there for you when you needed me. I just never knew. I was too wrapped up in my own black shrouds of selfish self-loathing. Now I walk as much for you as for me. May you be with Chris in Heaven. Now let us all walk together, as we did that day along the beach road in Oceanside, you and I taking turns pushing Chris in her wheelchair."

I placed a stone for Luci, and I walked on talking aloud to my spirit friends.

Tonight I am rewarded for hard miles hiked with hot noodles from my catfood can alcohol stove and hot chocolate with whiskey and golden sunset light on a warm September night. I am among friends who love me, and I know and am constantly reminded by the words of one friend whose letter I have carried with me for 1,500 miles, that I am loved by many more friends and they are out there somewhere, out beneath that green-flashing vanishing sun, out there in California, in Arizona, New Mexico. Stars descend from purplish black night, landing in my cocoa, and I know that this world will be okay again someday, if only when I pass from it and look back with a carefree grin and fading laugh.

That night in the dungeon of bunks piled three-high, Jackie deftly claims the bunk directly atop me. I imagine her weight on me, her presence, and her imagining me, just below her, close enough to touch. And touch we do. In the dark, she finds my hand and squeezes my fingers tight. When she doesn't let go, I hold on until at last sleep claims me and gravity my arm. Tonight, it is okay. Tonight, in the dreamy levity of altitude, it is more than okay.

Touching the Void of Hearts. Today, what a day, so big and airy and bright full of life and health, healthy people like ole Doctor Mike, the eye surgeon making the trek from Lake of the Clouds, the by-then short distance up to Washington. Then little Nicky from Boylston, eight years old, comes dogging it up and over all that scree, just walking along like it was a walk in the park. When I came upon Nick and his mom, Joanne, she was giving him a harsh talking-to about something. Seizing the moment, I butted in saying, "Doin' good there, Big Guy. You keep that up, maybe someday you'll be able to hike as far as I have," to which he replied, "How far?" Imagine his surprise to learn that I'd walked so very, very far. Even at eight he knew how far Georgia was and seemed to grasp the immensity of it all. I'm not sure I even do, still. With just 300 miles to go, I step toward Maine, the bright colors of autumn foliage popping out all over.

The dungeon last night, then up this a.m. early and not wanting to budge from my bunk what with all that mist outside, screw it. Wait til the fog lifts, I said. But Ry up and eager and first to go and, sure enough, that fog lifted fast as spirits on the fast track to Heaven, whoosh, and before I had my morning coffee, whammo! The peak was clear as day. To my great pleasure, Jackie lingered behind and walked with me. I filled my cook pot full of coffee from the lodge, and just to be cocky, what with all my hard-earned endurance and inborn surefootedness, I strolled past many a day hiker with both my Leki poles in one hand at the ready but not being used and the coffee a-sipping in my right, good morning, good morning, I said to all, a twinkle in Jackie's eyes as she watched me showing off.

Then suddenly, the rock pile ended, the mountain surrendered, and Jackie and I held our hands high in elated celebration. We'd done it. We'd conquered Mt. Washington, a mountain most people drive up.

The summit achieved, it was time to drop some dough on some expensive high-altitude food, two bananas, a raspberry muffin, and milk for me. Jackie made us all a gift of hot cocoa, and I, upon spying that old New England specialty, the whoopee pie, picked up three, one for each of us, and proclaimed, "Now we eat whoopee pie in the sky, woo-hoo!" All we lacked was Still Frank, the inventor of "woo-hoo" and the man who says it best.

The cog train is coming up Jacob's Ladder, awesome, scary to behold. Later from lower elevation, I will stand watching the thing climb at such a steep grade and try not to imagine the worst. But cool that train and behind me in line at the cafeteria stood Joe, the engineer, the fourth generation cog railroad man of his family. Wow. I imagine he's thrown a lotta coal at thruhikers, the tradition being that ATers "moon" the train where the trail and the train cross paths. But me, I missed that chance. Oh, I mooned it all right, but no coal forthcoming as I was far away enough that old Joe didn't figger he'd even get close.

The sun dominant over fleeting cloud cover, and, YES, it is definitely one of the best weather days of a dwindling season. Even the girls who "man" the huts said so, had hardly been a better day all summer, they said. The pure air way up here in the sky, ah! Inhale deep through the nose, "Sneahhhhhhh, haaaa!" and you'll damn near faint with fried-nostril ecstasy. Ha! I think of Bruce Willis's character in Terry Gilliam's brilliant film *Twelve Monkeys,* a lifelong prisoner of the underground now out and riding down the highway at speed, his head out the window dog-like, grinning, giddy with the freshness of the air of a world not yet made uninhabitable by the approaching deadly virus that will wipe out most of humankind. (In a nice twist, the animals survive, immune to the virus.) It's like remembering to look skyward at night to feel your problems shrink with humility as you envision inconceivable, infinite space. Nasal breathing takes practice. But what a rush. And it's free!

Eight years now since that fiction's projected date of our apocalypse, and here I stand inhaling air pure as fresh-fallen snow. There but for the grace of God go all of us. A wisp of coal smoke from the cog train is the only impurity on Mount Washington. Slightly lower down, krumholtz and spruce grow sideways obedient to hurricane force winds that bulldoze their stout branches incessant. There I will smell the scent of Christmas and chat with Ry about how fast the holiday season will come upon us this year, we the children of the forest, displaced in time, the dumb struck clock in our heads expecting to return to the world we left in late March with Easter coming up.

But now a "Boo!" it'll be. Halloween will scream on by and then turkey day; and me with that little touch of something, upset stomach, I stayed atop Washington an hour longer than Jackie and Ry and sat writing postcards to my nephews and with joyful surprise received a Kathleen postcard from Bisbee, Arizona, to the Mt. Washington, New Hampshire, post office. Wow! The only post office in America open on Sunday, the old postmaster informs me. Far out. Then roaring down the mountain, rock-hopping and dancing over scree, like Baryshnikov or a man on a wire bouncing, barely touching down and flying past all those slow day hikers, and each in turn saying, "Wow!" and "He's flying!" and me fearless and flawless and skipping like a miracle at damn near 40, one of the fastest and most agile hikers on the trail, for today anyway.

Well before reaching the hut where Jackie and Ry and I would meet and plan our next move, I heard from Mount Washington's clear radio signal Peter Gabriel's "In Your Eyes." Fast came a flood of tears as the desire to flee The Happy Couple fell strong upon me. I have sat with Jackie for perhaps an hour, she sad and struggling with what she blames on moon cycle mood swings and hating the rocks. The memory of the warmth, the strong grip of her fingers on mine last night suggest more behind the tears. Ry, as usual, has zoomed on ahead. Jackie cries softly. Her timidity is a façade, however. Psychically, I feel her bounding for me, squeezing the life out of me. I am frozen. The waters of melting ice and snow flow under us, far beneath a sea of boulders, and I feel like famed climber Joe Simpson delirious with broken leg and parched lips dragging from rock to rock, the water of true love tauntingly close, its blood of water of life cascading in my ears somewhere below, just out of reach. Screaming in my ears. DRINK ME!

But I did not drink. "Everything will be all right," I said, eyes downcast, talking to tear-blurred rocks, ill-equipped to stare this moment into the eyes of the sun. For now her eyes were on me, searching. Amazing the power of that trite little phrase, that clichéd balm. "Everything's gonna be all right," I repeat to Jackie, to me. Jackie calmed at last and was near smiling when Ry arrived, packless and backtracking at a trot, concerned lest one of us had been injured. Leaving the two alone to bond or whatever, I walked off mumbling repeatedly the cruel palliative still on my lips, "Everything will be all right."

In *A Room of One's Own*, Virginia Woolf said:

> *..the beauty of the world which is so soon to perish*
> *has two edges, one of laughter, one of anguish,*
> *cutting the heart asunder.*

I like Woolf. She believed as I do that we're all going to Heaven. She would be there now anyway, but she took the Express Train long ago. Drowned herself in a river. Less out here on the trail than in normal life, it is a daily struggle not to test those waters myself.

Fast forward again to me well up ahead, crying my eyes out to Peter Gabriel and shouting at the rocks, "Dammit! Dammit!" seeing in my mind's eye the relief on Jackie's face as I succeeded in calming her. Oh, how I had wanted to kiss those tears away, to taste their saline wine.

"Run!" said the song. "Run!" said the intoxicating ridgeline heights of the Presidentials. To complicate my overwrought emotions, the blue beauty up there on top of the New England world shot straight through me, a golden spear bound for other hearts as well.

Run far ahead of the lovers and don't look back. No matter that someone or something might still live and breathe back there. Do as Joe Simpson's hiking partner, Simon did: Cut the rope. Burn every trace of her from your heart. Make a ceremonial farewell. Do it now, or it will be YOU broken and lost in the dark, crawling with Joe over glaciers, crevasses and a boulder field the size of Texas. This love is not healthy. Run.

TWENTY

Virgin of Guadalupe Sighting on Osgood Ridge...The First Law of *Gonzo* Robotics: Walk North...Sweet Papa McKinney Hosts...Jackie of the Poppy Fields of Oz...Yellow Snow Memories...It's a Mad World...Mahousic Notch and the Importance of Secret Victories...

And I ran.

But I ran neither far nor fast enough, my desire to be in Jackie's company weighing me down, dragging me back with every forward leap.

They caught up while I sat chatting with prodigious 4K+ peak-bagger Johnny and his dog, Katahdin, a dog who had climbed them all but who would be denied the summit of his namesake. No dogs in Baxter State Park. Shame.

We spent an awkward half-hour or so at the shelter nestled between Osgood Ridge and Tuckerman's Ravine, and then set out to conquer the former. At first it went straight up. Then it went straight down, impossibly far down an impossible cascade of gigantic stones. To make matters worse, wind held court on the ridgeline, a seething rabid wind that at lesser temperatures could cut the life right out of a person, dead before they hit the ground. I have a fear of wind on high places, but this was something more. I could literally sense the presence of spirits lost here, of the people this wind-torn ridge had claimed in the past. In the late but still bright afternoon sun, I shivered as in a cave. Taking into consideration Jackie's fear of rocks, however, I steeled myself and tucked into a crevice here and there and waited for her. Ry and I, we waited for her.

I have one shining memory from that ridge, all that I will cherish of that windy descent, and that was this: Jackie, arriving at what was more or less the ridge's highest point, standing tall and brave and smiling into the wind, smiling a truly happy smile as if to say it was good to be alive and flying and smiling framed there in the late afternoon, Ry and I hunched low in the rocks just below her and looking up, amazed, at Miss Jacqueline glowing there in the low gold of the western sun. I don't know what Ry saw, but standing over me with my Arizona-California background steeped in Hispanic influence, I saw in Jackie the Virgin of Guadalupe, all fractals of windblown light and zigzag outlines of a sun grateful to find her, to embrace her and call her goddess, mother, saint.

Other than all that, Osgood Ridge sucked. It was no more to me than a broken down escalator in a mall for giants, a steep staircase to be descended with the greatest alacrity, a place of ill-written winds writing the first lines of a long list of winter death. I wanted no part of it, and I ran and skipped and hopped and danced in a manner befitting the greatest of high-wire fliers. I was a god.

That night at the base of Osgood Ridge, we camped together, Jackie, Ry, and I, our tents abutting one another atop a wooden platform. Grumpy in the morning after yet another night alone yet not alone, so close to her I could smell her in the dark, I pulled out the maps and cursed. The topo maps showed the typical pattern of AT madness I had come to expect and loathe. I had acquiesced to heading due south from Mt. Washington so as to cover the grand Presidentials. I knew that up ahead in the deep wilderness of Maine I would have to do some looping to navigate countless lakes. But today, just a hop, skip and a jump from the town of Gorham with the Maine state line close enough to spit at, the AT squirreled something wicked, south again in an ass backwards loop over the Wildcats. It was another absurd abstraction of peak bagging nutfuckers, and it had nothing to do with walking north.

Call me stupid or lazy, but I just didn't capische the abstract logic of walking south when my whole body, heart and soul, my whole *raison d'etre*, my mission and reason to be at this point and since Day One in Georgia has been to walk north. It has been my mantra, my manna, my metronome, the simple calming tick-tock rhythm to which I'd stepped and danced and run and rose daily grateful for its simplicity: walk north. It meant more to me than a thousand missed white blazes, for its singularity of purpose had kept me sane when naught else could. Walk north. It was the one law of robotics that overrode the other two and any other conflicting input: protect human life. Distilling my life down to that simple two-word command had indeed protected my life, saved it no doubt. This close to Maine, I wasn't about to change.

"No fucking way," I grumbled. "See this line straight to Gorham, and that line straight outta Gorham heading due north, that's where I am headed," I said. I wasn't kidding. The AT that I was hiking was spiritual, its white blazes mere indicators of the suggested and politically navigable way. Here at

Pinkham Notch, the white-blazed AT and I had reached an impasse. I would walk the road. I would walk as straight a line north to Maine as I could.

"Ry, take your future fiancée and follow the trail," I wanted to say. But I didn't. Wouldn't you know, Ry went for my plan. Jackie, too. So we walked to Gorham. In Gorham, we called my father. Dad, Sweet Papa McKinney, hopped in his truck and fetched us up, and took us to his lakeside cabin in Fryeburg. That night it was steak and burgers and ice cream and beers and whatever we wanted.

Dad took us roaring up a wild, winding mountain road reliving, for a moment, better days, his ski bum days at Wildcat. Then, half-deflating himself like a tired a balloon, he referred to those days as "back when I was being an idiot." Though I tried to assure him otherwise, he maintained that indeed he had once been an idiot…once, before finding God. Ironic, I thought, when 10 minutes later I referred to myself as an idiot for not being able to find or keep the right woman, and he chided me, saying something like, "Don't sell yourself your short, Son."

Thanks to Dad's hospitality, the night at his house was pleasant enough. Well, pleasant if you could call our progressive intoxication and resultant blatant amorous leanings toward one another pleasant. Jackie and I, that is. More than ever, that night, I thought, "Jesus, Ry, are you paying any attention at all?" My father was. He saw it clear as day.

The next morning as we prepared to leave, I stood looking over my father's lake and knowing that very soon it would freeze solid as granite and be run amok with snowmobiles and cars doing donuts in the snow. It was yet autumn, but just the night before, you could have rested a snowmobile, a car, a jet airplane on the tensile strength of my passion for that woman, on her *crush* on me. It felt wonderful. It felt awful.

I hadn't ever shared much more than a hug with the girl, but her body was all over me. Her sex. She was a field of poppies and I Dorothy on the road to Oz. Or was I the Scarecrow? Or the Tin Man, all brains ignoring the clunking and roaring calls of a perfectly cognizant heart? It was absurd. When the going gets weird, sometimes it's best if the weird just go.

Beside some unnamed pond just north of Gorham, New Hampshire, I awake to a sad fog over our small pond, last night's sweet sunset mirror of golden light now dull, ugly. The dew is substantial. The tent Tinker lent me is soaked inside and out. Tired and emotional last night, I had pitched it too low, and my sleeping bag is soaked from touching it. I awake fearful and very tired. The sensation is of having not slept a wink.

Jackie and Ry are ready just moments before me. I wave them off, tell them I'll catch up. They're so damn sweet. They would have waited, but....

I am grumpy and just want to plug into headphones and kill some miles. Maine's state line lies ahead 16.5 miles, a full day's hump given the difficult terrain. Instead of racing off, I get to the trailhead and contemplate going the other way. For a full hour, I stand there, frozen, pack on, equivocating, miserable.

My quandary (once again): Walk into Maine, or leave the Happy Couple and hitch ahead to meet up with Yazzy so you can have someone to take you to bed at night, so you can be loved at long last on these final 300 miles. Get away from this unhealthy attraction to Jackie, unhealthy for you for it has nowhere to go.

I flip a nickel. At two outta three it tells me to go for the "tail" on both of the first two flips. This turn of the coin is as I willed it. I want the girl. I want the escape. But I surprise myself and ignore the coin. I want to walk into Maine today, not fracture my hike into pieces I'll need to make up later. I heft my pack and walk north.

Up the next mountain, on the very top, Jackie has written me a message in broken twigs. It reads: JESTER HERE with an arrow pointing a hard left. It is written in the language of painted symbols on streets, the JESTER above the HERE like ZONE above SCHOOL as though our zillion gigabyte RAM brains can't read such messages from top to bottom but only slowly as we approach them. The twig message more likely reads, "HERE JESTER." I get it anyway and appreciate its sweetness.

I love Jackie. So sweet and soft-spoken and doe-eyed and when I lift her in a hug so light, those hollow bones like a bird. But she belongs to Ry in the way Ernie belonged to Bert, the way Mr. Rogers belonged to the neighborhood, Helen to poor doomed Troy. They are sweetness and gentility and patience and love. What the hell are they doing with me?

I meet a friendly chipmunk. He's a very busy bee. Has a mouth so full of grass it's busting out all over. Scaled up, it would be like me with a hay bail in my mouth. "You're building a nest," I say aloud. This makes me think of winter, reminds me of how close the snow is. God, I can't imagine it. Picturing this place under snow depresses me. But why?

Is it the far-distant past of my childhood winters, walking maudlin to horrid Memorial Junior High School past piles of snow dirtied to mud and car exhaust, past snow both yellow and brown. I can recall few more depressing sights from my youth of winters than dog shit-soiled snow. But deep inside I know what lies behind this angst of New England winter's approach. It is deep inside, and there it ought remain. But for the sake of my reader, I'll say this much: It was in the last brown leaves of departing autumn and first falling snows that I first learned that love does not last forever and often turns to hate. To shit. A family, once white and downy soft as winter's first hello, can turn yellow, then brown, a shit stain on a sled run. No fun.

Bye, Mr. Chipmunk. I must to get to Katahdin and then get home to Cali, where yellow snow was outlawed long ago and conscientious San Francisco yuppies follow their canines home toting turds in a bag. Ha! I'm mad. Completely cracked. Bye, Mr. Chipmunk. I have been following a bear all day. I watch as his mammoth paw-prints impress into the stiff mud of the trail before me. The bear's prints overlie the last man prints, or so it seems. I imagine the bear is just ahead of me, as though any minute the prints will give way to paws and I'll look up and..."Whoa!" there will be the bear, my first bear on the AT.

I bear down on Maine with a powerful push, a hunger to be there. Yet as I do so, I hear that down south Hurricane Ivan bears down on my beloved New Orleans with far greater power. I am concerned for my friends down there. I think of Chris and Jules and the whole Stock family. What will become of the great Miss Mae's, the landmark bar at the corner of Napoleon and Magazine? I send out a prayer for the safety, for the safe deliverance of New Orleans from the wrath of Ivan. Ivan the Terrible. Ivan the Incomprehensible to me up here in the New England woods where the winds are but gentle breezes and there are no mobile home parks to whip away, and hardly a sound at all most times when I pull off the headphones and listen. Silence.

Then just like that, with naught but a full day's intense physical labors and now pending night, I arrive and step gaily into Maine. I made it! After more than 1,800 miles afoot, I can no longer say I am going to Maine. I am here. Amazing. It feels as though I have been forever in the woods, that I've traveled halfway around the sun. I suppose in a way I have. We have. Old Man Winter approacheth. But I will beat the bastard to Katahdin. Oh, yes.

> *"All around me are familiar faces, worn out places, worn out faces. Bright and early for the daily races, going nowhere..."*

I awake the morning of September 16 like Donnie Darko, narcoleptic, knocked out of time and space, sick to my stomach. Patrick Swayze and some other guy standing over me where I lie on a golf course green, the sun behind them blinding so that I cannot see their eyes. But it's Jackie and Ry with me this morning, and it's not the sun but my own shame that's forestalling direct eye contact.

"Hide my head I wanna drown my sorrow, no tomorrow…"

As with every day for six months now, we rub the sleepies from our eyes, then we're packing, bright and early for the daily races, going…somewhere? No. Not today. Today we're going nowhere, just like the Gary Jules' song says. I can feel it in the crawling of my skin, the hollowness of my bones, the rat rattling the cage of my chest in the throes of death. "Frank, when is this gonna stop?" Donnie asks the six-foot-tall rabbit that haunts his days and nights. Today. Today I must hike on alone. I have to. I can't do this anymore.

"And I find it kinda funny, I find it kinda sad, the dreams in
which I'm dying are the best I've ever had…it's a very very
mad world, mad world."

I find it hard to tell them. I skip breakfast and pack fast. My actions are a dead giveaway that something's wrong, but it's all I can do until I find the words. I don't feel ready to speak, but they're staring at me, bewildered. Jackie walks off into the woods to pee. I seize the moment alone with Ry. "I've decided to hike on ahead," I say. "I'm going to try and catch up with Yazzy. We had a spark, she and I, and I'm starved for companionship, Ry, you know? You're lucky. You've got Jackie. I've got no one."

It's a mad world, all right.

The night before, I crossed over into Maine alone. Jackie was held back by the rocks, and Ry stuck with her. If she'd been mine, I would have stayed behind with her as well. But as the pain of her not-mine-ness grew in me, I could not but race ahead. I reached the Maine state line just before dark. Standing there at the "Welcome to Maine" sign, I fondly recalled the day Jackie and I joined hands and, upon the count of three, hopped into Virginia together with a laugh.

Now at the last state line on the northbound Appalachian Trail, I put my left arm around the sign as one would a lover, held out my right as far as I could reach, and clicked the shutter button on a disposable camera.

I had about an hour alone at the next shelter before they arrived. Jackie had a look about her that seemed to say, "Thanks for waiting for us, Jerko."

(Probably not at all her thoughts, but such a look!) They were both tapped, pouring sweat and rabid from an all-too-familiar run with the after-dark devil of determination to reach a certain point, sundown be damned.

The shelter had a recessed loft capable of sleeping six above and six below, plus a roomy front area for cooking. Unlike most shelters, there existed a front wall as well, giving the feeling more of a cabin than a lean-to. I had cooked sitting in the entryway. Finding it comfortable to sit with my feet on the ground outside, I'd cooked on a rock and watched the sunset.

Unfailingly polite and conscious of others, Jackie asked if I minded if she cooked up on the loft. I did mind. I was exhausted and ready to at least try and sleep, already cozily ensconced in my bag, head on my pillow. No, wait. Did I say cozily? Let me rephrase: I felt trapped. Trapped in my bag in the corner of the loft, and heartsick to boot. Was this some unprovoked fit of paranoia? Hardly.

You see, the moment they had arrived, well, a minute or so after her dagger-eyed stare, Jackie had complained of overwhelming hunger. I could relate, having many times pulled too-long days only to arrive so tired I didn't feel I could possibly muster the strength to cook. I, meanwhile, was three-quarters done with my two-serving dehydrated lasagna-in-a-bag dinner and adequately fed. Without hesitation, I handed Jackie the remainder and said, "Take, eat."

Here's where the story gets highly subjective. Oh, and where you might want to pause and rent the film *Donnie Darko* to follow all my references. Here's where the jet engine comes hurling through the wormhole and smashes into Donnie's bedroom and pops the question, "Did Donnie really survive just because his imaginary friend called him out of bed that night? Or is he dead? Or did just part of him die, leaving him trapped in space but dead in time?"

In all the time I'd hiked with Jackie and Ry, I recall seeing him kiss her twice. Both times the kisses were of a conciliatory nature, making up for something he'd done that pissed her off. I don't recall ever seeing her offer up a kiss. If I had witnessed regular displays of affection between the two from the get-go, would I have allowed myself to fall in love with this woman? No way. It would have been entirely different. For the sake of this story and within the limits of my memory, they NEVER openly displayed affection. Not in front of me, anyway.

Then right there in the soft light of my little rose-scented burgundy votive candle, Jackie spoon-fed her man from my dinner. She fed him and they giggled like newlyweds feeding one another from the top of a tier cake.

Cut to Donnie's bedroom: The ceiling collapses in a shower of plaster and burning steel.

Cut to me in the corner in the dark, crushed and dying. Astounding, the power of words. Twas a crush she claimed to have on me that day, the day we walked together into New Hampshire, and crush me she did.

"Children waiting for the day they feel good, happy birthday..."

I lay awake beside the pair that night feeling, in the words of Tom Waits, lonelier than a parking lot when the last car pulls away. I wanted terribly to leave that night. But I was trapped, ashamed.

"Hello, teacher...what's my lesson, look right through me..."

Outside the shelter in a locked steel "bear box" was my stuff sack full of food. Unlike the usual method of hanging food in the trees, the steel box guarantees there is no way in hell a bear is getting to your food that night. But inside the shelter, something far more vital than my food laid torn open and exposed for any creature to devour. I held my heart tight in my chest that night, felt its every liquid breath of red, red life.

In the morning I took my heart away. Saying goodbye to those two felt like administering euthanasia to your own pet, a thing I once did out of love and grief for my incurably ill Matilda, despising the thought of leaving her to die in the hands of strangers.

Despite my efforts to make it a smooth break, the vibe was clearly ugly. Ry spoke in monotone. Jackie returned my embrace with wooden arms. She was brushing her teeth when I walked away. What was that intense look in her eyes? Was it betrayal? Did she feel betrayed?

Just out of sight of the shelter but still well within earshot, I stood still and tried to speak. Were it not, I believe, for my own feelings of shame, I would have shouted these words. "I LOVE YOU, GUYS. I REALLY DO." But no words came, and I walked off alone into the woods of Maine.

"And I find it kinda funny and I find it kinda sad, the dreams in which I'm dying are the best I've ever had...it's a very very mad world, mad world..."

[Lyrics from *Mad World* by Michael Andrews and Gary Jules]

There's a reason for all the reference to the film *Donnie Darko.*

The shelter had been down a canyon of sorts, so there was no radio reception hiking out that morning. No matter. The "silence" of the forest and my own footfalls were all I could take for a while. When I later reached the next point of high elevation, I carefully searched for signal from the one last radio station I knew to be clearly audible up here in Nowhereland.

What song would you suppose came on the radio and began to play that very moment? A song not heard in the regular rotation of commercial stations, one I'd heard only once before on my hike: "Mad World" from the film *Donnie Darko.*

With the words of that haunting line, "The dreams in which I'm dying are the best I've ever had," I lost it. Right there in a narrow corridor of the Appalachian Trail, I dropped to the earth and cried as to commence the next Great Flood.

***

Mahousic Notch. The girl beside me here on Amtrak Time Warp Train #1 wants to hear the story of Mahousic Notch, the justifiably named "Meanest Mile on the AT." Suddenly I'm kind of sorry I brought it up. How many times have I told the story yet still not put it down? At my current level of success, I wouldn't profess how to be a writer, but I can tell you how to be a wanna-be writer: Tell your stories repeatedly to anyone who will listen. You'll never write a word of it.

The lovely caramel-haired, apple-cheeked girl eating cherry yogurt and sensually licking my Lexan trail spoon is Katjia. Katjia is from Slovenia, and until 10 minutes ago had never even heard of the Appalachian Trail, let alone its famed "toughest mile," the ginormous boulder-choked tight-squeeze mini-canyon that slows even the hardiest thruhiker to a crawl for upwards of two hours. Two hours to traverse one mile. That's four to six times what it would take to trek any other one-mile stretch of trail. Here north of the New Hampshire-Maine state line where most northbound hikers are pumping out two and three miles an hour, something that slows one's pace to half a mile an hour must be pretty tough. Going into it, I believed it. There's not much exaggeration among thruhikers.

I'm not exaggerating when I tell you that my Lexan spoon has never had a licking like Katjia is giving. It. Presently.

"Lexan! Nine out of ten thruhikers prefer it to those bendy *Matrix* spoons!" You know how in the first *Matrix* movie, the little bald Dalai Lama-wanna-be kid bends spoons and then says, "There is no spoon."? Well, on the AT, there is no OTHER spoon. Nor is there a fork. Or knife for most. A spoon and a cook pot, that's the lot!

"What are you mumbling about?" Katjia inquires. "Can you speak more clearly, please, Honey Butter? My English is not so good."

Sure, Katjia. How about you quit with the spoon fellatio and maybe I can concentrate!

I don't tell her this, of course, rather just smile politely as she works my spoon further into her mouth like a tongue depressor, MY SPOON that I ate with in the forest morning and night for 2,000 miles, my spoon which, as with the entire inventory of my AT trail gear, I cannot separate myself from still, now three months off the trail. Five states, four airplanes, one train and two major road trips by car, and sure as shit that backpack is still packed and ready for wilderness survival at a moment's notice. The spoon I carry in my North Face jacket pocket. The Amtrak snack bar is out of spoons. Thus the current situation.

Her yogurt gone, Katjia is now staring out at the barren west Texas landscape with tears in her eyes and gurgling "Ahhh!" to some invisible doctor as she experiments with how far she can shove the spoon down her throat. Katjia is 21 going on 12. But she listens well.

"KATJIA!" I shout, lightly thwacking her in the back of the head as I thrust my fist into her mouth and retrieve my precious trail memento. "I got the message."

A couple of the old ladies sitting nearby here in the glass-dome observation car raise a collective eyebrow at Katjia and me, but only for a second. There are other more interesting freak shows going on all around us as Train #1, currently five hours behind schedule, swaggers down the track past Marfa, Texas, like a half-full fish tank on a drunk pony. A nowhere outpost in west Texas, Marfa is surprisingly hip. It is the filming location of *Giant,* home to the mysterious Marfa Lights (watch "X-Files" much?), and a favorite getaway for Houstonian's subculture elite, my friend Stefan the most suave of the bunch.

"Zell me the story! I muss to know how you conquered da crotch!"

"Notch. Okay, okay." Concentrate, McKinney. Jeezuz. How do I transport myself to Mahousic Notch in the Maine woods while rolling through barren Texas with a burlesque Slovenian girl leaning into me with bloodshot eyes and sweet cherry yogurt breath? And that's nothing. There's this older guy twitching across the aisle and then this 20-something bohemian looking kid with an ancient, oversized cassette player behind me playing Tom Waits tunes at a volume just low enough to not get him thrown off the train but plenty loud. The older guy, this obviously suffering bastard with some kind of twitching disease, is twitching in perfect rhythm to Tom Waits. It's uncanny and appeals to my mind's obsession with all things weird. But I mention him because his outfit is all Maine: hunter's cap, thick woolen coat patterned with stag deer and pine trees and mountains and stuff.

That's my ticket out. I find my focus and target in.

Amidst all the chaos of the observation car, *I, Robot* on the video screen, Tom Waits croaking nearby, kids running up and down the aisle spreading some baloney smell, Katjia staring, and a handful of gang banger guys getting more drunk and raucous by the hour as the sun fizzles out the window to my left, I focus on twitching man's jacket. Ignoring the man and his bobbling head, I stare hard at the faux forest on his back and arms. I stare and I stare and I stare until at last I am the stag, I am the trees, I am the very fabric of nature.

There it is! "Mahousic Notch" reads the sign announcing my arrival. I'm here, deep in the woods, a good 20 miles to the nearest road in any direction. I'm ready. I've dropped down from Groton Shelter where I managed to scrawl into the shelter register the love for Jackie and Ry that I hadn't been able to express in person as I fled from them this morning in a jealous rush.

In my mind is the challenge, the impetus. On my wrist a stopwatch. At first just a little seed planted there by Ry, who said he had heard of a guy who had "done" Mahousic Notch in 38 minutes, a number that sounded like some kind of record compared to Wingfoot's and every other hiker's estimation of one to two hours.

It is now an imperative. I mean, why not? I've lost the girl I love. Okay, I conceded. Whatever. She's gone. It's just me now. Trail's almost over. I'm nearly 40 years old and in perhaps the best shape of my life. I've always had excellent balance, and even that is heightened now. I've made it into Maine. It there were ever a good time to break a leg, today would be it.

I bend and stretch a bit, rotating my ankles in preparation for turns and twists though intended to avoid the same. I lean into a tree and push at it with all my might, emphasis on the muscles in my calves. Pulling back, I stand erect and cinch every strap on my pack to glue it to my body as tightly as possible. I'm not quite sure what I'm headed into, and cannot yet see these legendary boulders from this little glade in the woods where stands the sign.

But I've heard it involves a lot of crawling, balancing, clambering, basically all things bouldering.

I have heard there are spots so tight one must remove one's pack and pass, or if alone, drag the pack through. Here I figure there must be another way: over. Where others struggle under, I will employ my billy goat balance to scramble up and over or just plain leap. I'm lucky. The ground is dry. No rain last night, so aside from some dew, the rocks should be, too.

With one foot against the sign, I hit my stopwatch and take off running like a sprinter off a starting block. In no time, I'm in the rocks and, wow, no exaggeration at all: They're huge. Imagine a flood-drainage channel through a city in which every imaginable large appliance and automobile has been driven or thrown. Hell, throw in a few shipping containers and airplane fuselages as well. I leap up onto a washing machine, prance across a prone refrigerator, scramble up a Hummer parked (as all Hummers should be) nose down into the pile, then down its other side. I slip. I slide. But nothing too serious. I leap but never land with the energy of my leg aimed anywhere but precisely perpendicular to the surface. No splits, thank you. So I go from meteor to tractor-trailer to monolith to monster truck, hop, skip, and jump.

All the while I use my Leki poles. I mean, I really USE them. I later talked to other people who explained how they were so busy using their hands they either let their poles dangle by their wrist straps or telescoped them down and packed them away altogether. My technique, never really planned, just sort of made up as I went along: Use the poles. Oh, and part two of my unplanned plan just sort of came with the motive: Keep moving.

By rarely if ever stopping, I had the benefit of the dance, the benefit of never having to dwell too long on this sketchy step or that precipice, the benefit of propulsion. The poles provided balance as well. Like extensions of my arms, they worked furiously to keep me atop the city of mammoth stones and not crawling around between and beneath them. The effect: magical! The feeling: pure fun.

Using the poles, I was able to "chimney" through wide channels in the junkyard of rocks, balance-beaming, for instance, along the razor-thin edge of a long triangular stone while using its neighbors six or seven feet away to either side as points of purchase, as the walls of my chimney, as it were.

The notch was curiously warm in parts, then a minute later in a different spot cold and damp, radical changes in temperature, part of the reason I suppose that the Wingfoot book warned of ice on the rocks at all times of the year. For water flows beneath this sea of rocks, sometimes a trickle, often a gush. Not that I ever saw it or stopped to take a sip. And man, did I want to after maybe 20 minutes of running the Mahousic Notch. It was likely the most intense workout of my life.

Work it out I did. I made it all the way, on my own. My only witnesses: a white-haired couple I encountered perhaps a third of the way through. As they were coming from the other direction, it was two-thirds of the way for them. I didn't get their names, nor they mine. They did savvy my rush, however, and deftly ducked out of the way to let me through. Not impolite, I spoke to them as I roared by, told them I was timing myself, even managing a glance at my watch to appease the woman, who had asked how much further they had to go. "I've been going 12 minutes," I told her. Gauging my speed, she quickly translated this into a half an hour or more for them.

Then I'd swear she said, "Well, now I've seen it all. Now I can go home and say I saw a crazy guy run through Mahousic Notch." The air in this section was, to my recollection, tropical. Like old Saint Nick, I let out a breathy laugh, winked, and bade them farewell as I hopped on a sleigh-shaped chunk of Maine bedrock and flew away up the Notch and into the realm of trail legends to be.

"You are like ze Spiderman!"

"Huh? Oh, yeah. Yeah, I guess I kind of am…er, was." Katjia jolted me out of my Mahousic reverie. Or maybe just saying my name had been enough. Back on the train, little had changed. The twitching guy twitched on, and the gang-banger guys got drunker. But the volume had been turned down while I'd been far away, traversing the notch like a spider.

"You are crazy man!"

"Yeah, no. Hold on, Katjia. I haven't gotten to the good part yet." I gave her back my Lexan spoon. "Stick this back in your mouth and hear me out."

I looked out the window of the train to where the last vestiges of the day's sun were pretty much gone. There remained just enough light in the sky to silhouette the rising rock formations and small mountains of far western Texas. The effect: a jumble of dark shapes. It was enough.

So I kept running. I never once took my pack off, and only once was I forced to crawl between two rocks rather than leap over them. To the purist, I may well be disqualified because of this. For you see, even in the notch where it was pretty plain that there was only one direction to go in, only one way out, the white blaze led the way. The walls of the notch were steeply pitched, impassable, thus the necessity of scrambling the stony path.

So if you say I cheated because I didn't crawl through a white-blazed crevice where an overhead path was clearly doable, well, then I guess I cheated. But hey, the way I see it, going over this mile-long rock pile was a far greater feat than going under it. So, extra credit for me. Let the crawlers crawl.

Running the Mahousic Notch made my day. It made my week. It was one of the coolest things I did on the entire breakthrough journey. There wasn't one other thruhiker anywhere present to witness my achievement. Not one. Just me.

In this unrecorded victory, I see a direct parallel to the depression that from Day One, I had been seeking to outpace. No one sees inside the mind of the depressive. The doctors who treat the mentally ill, babysitters and pill-distributors mostly, doubtful ever experience its horrors themselves. And family? Friends? Forget it. At best, you're held, as one friend put it, "at arm's length." At worst, you're not held at all. You're a pariah, a stain on the family name. Witnesses arrive too late. It's just you. Just me. At Mahousic Notch, I turned that lonesome dynamic on its head. The victory was all mine. Alone. Appropriately.

It's not something I'd recommend to anyone. Done the way I did it, it was dangerous. By the end, I was huffing and puffing like a Ford 302 with a cracked head and half a dozen blown gaskets. But, man oh man, what a thrill when the rocks ended and the path, now dirt again, hooked sharply uphill and I looked down at my watch and it read 29 minutes 34 seconds. I couldn't believe it.

When Ry had mentioned the rumored 38-minute run, I just figured that meant I could likewise do it in under an hour, 45 minutes maybe.

In a tortoise and hare sense, I hadn't beat anyone. Why? Because I had so overwrought my legs and lungs that I had to spend the next three quarters of an hour cooling off in a stream uphill. Dumping cook pot-loads of water on my body, I sent steam rising into the autumn air. I kid you not. I was hot. The Wicked Witch of the West, I had chased Miss Kansas to Oz and back and for my labors been reduced to vapors, catlike squeals, soggy shoes, and a crumpled hat.

To award me for my record Mahousic run, God and Wingfoot planted a big, fat mountain right in my path. Next order of business: Climb on. That (together with many wonderful things), is what the AT is: one long string of pain in the ass ascents and descents. What's that line from the Pink Floyd song? "Run rabbit, run, dig that hole, get things done…don't sit down, it's time to dig another one."

"That sounds terrible, Honey Butter."

"Hmm?" I looked up from the rocks of Maine, confused. The train, apparently only crawling out there in the dark night, jolted to a stop.

"Why did you do all dat if it luz so teddible?" Katjia asked, her already skewed Slovenian tongue further impeded by my spoon in her mouth.

"Because it was real, Katjia. For all the physical aches and pains, it went a long way toward healing my broken spirit. It made me feel better overall than I have felt in years, maybe ever."

"Lao, cool."

The spoon had spoken.

As my consciousness returned to the train, I became aware that the movie had ended and that the flickering light that I'd taken to be the TV was coming from somewhere outside the train. That's when I realized that the drunk gang banger guys were AWOL, no longer cruising the aisle and hooting and hollering.

I got up, crossed to the other side of the train, and cupped my hands around my face to see out past the train car's bright interior and through the tinted glass. Three cop cruisers sat fanned out facing the train. There were the three skinheads, deplaning a little earlier than planned, I imagine "Figures," I mumbled to myself. Twitching guy was also looking out the window at the live action episode of "Cops." The Tom Waits music kid had gone back to his seat or something a while back. Now the bobble of Twitching Guy's head was more of a side-to-side shake. "Yeah, I'm with you, buddy," I said.

It's easy for a sponge-like mind like mine (ooh, tongue twister) to get caught up in all the negative crap of the world around me. No doubt this is why the trail was such a boon to me. No doubt that's why my backpack, months later, remains packed. No doubt that's why I'm going back. If not that trail, then some other. I'm hooked, sister. I'm an Olympian. I ran the Mahousic Notch, the Appalachian Trail's hardest mile, in under 30 minutes. No Pantywaist here, Grandma!

"Come on, Katjia," I said, grabbing the protruding handle of the Lexan spoon and lifting her gently to her feet. "Let's go back to my sleeper and see how many ways we can prove that little bald spoon-bending kid in the *Matrix* wrong."

There is no spoon. There is no past. There is no future. There is only now: September 17, 2004, with Katahdin just three weeks away.

TWENTY ONE

Syrup Samples and a Rumored Gathering on the Outskirts of AT Land... the Dixfield Selectman/Officer Dow Slapdown... Whiteblaze.net and the Sissy "Hiker Trash" Hankshaw Tractor Trailer Triumph...Slipping it past the Geezer Freak Show...Spoils to the Victor, Toils for the Fool...Saint Yazzy and the Zip-Together Sleeping Bag Revolution...Lost Alongside Puccini in an Endless America. .the Doppler Effect on the Forest Orgasm...Squeeze this Airhorn and be President for a Night...

After pulling a 20 miler yesterday that included the dreaded Notch, I could barely walk this morning. Today then, it was ambling time, slow and painful out of my solo abode at Frye Notch Shelter, out of my cozy down bag and up and down the bumps and grinds of the remaining five miles to the B Mountain Road, all the time dreading the eight-mile stretch of road into Andover. Barren and barely surfaced, the road doesn't look good for hitching. Why didn't I notice this in the planning phase? Impossible map nuances. Too much to think about at every town stop. Postal resupply algorithms and cogitation on a strategic, militaristic scale. Not my cup of sake.

I stand my pack on the shoulder of the hard-packed dirt road (a smidgen better than a rural dirt road where there would surely be ZERO traffic), plant my poles hard in the dirt, and, with the "thruhiker by the side of the road scene" properly established, I sit down for what will likely be a long wait. I have a book with me, *Fight Club* author Chuck Paluninininichuck's (sic) latest novel, *Survivior*. It is a sick frikken book, and I like it.

I hear a car approaching before I can crack the book. Ah. Going west. Wrong direction. Before long another truck passes going the same way. Then another. I pull out the map and begin to think maybe I should hitch in that direction instead, pick up the more heavily trafficked Route 26, which makes a wide arc west then north toward Rangely, another trail town a few days ahead for one afoot, but maybe where I ought to go directly to catch Yazzy.

Map in hand, *Survivor* never gets so much as a glance when along comes a truck going toward Andover.

You see, I can't recall whether or not I sent myself a resupply package to Andover. With Andover being eight miles out of the way, I've been trying to convince myself that no, I don't have a resupply package there, and no, no one is sending care packages anymore. My Web readership went deadly silent when I proposed the "Bed and Bath" fund (a proposed cash-donation-versus-care-package scenario I slapped up on *Jigglebox.com* to help defray the higher cost of trail living through pricey, less-hospitable New England).

So there's slim likelihood that there'll be any money awaiting me there, which leaves a postcard from Kate Pearson, which I hate to miss, seeing as how she's sent me one to EVERY mail drop on the AT! But....

The "but" no longer matters as Steve Hardy and his dog, Jake, pull up and pull over, he the first to drive by heading east, and I hop in and off we go as though he were expecting me up here in his neck of the woods. Friendly as can be.

Steve's a maple syrup guy. "Been doin' it all your life?" I ask. "Nope. Had to wait until I was fo-ahh (that's Down East vernacular for "four"). I remember when I was little we had a maple out front of the house with one tap and my mother would make me wait until the jar was half full before I could take it into the house." Steve went on to tell me that he now has 2,000 taps in the forest just west of where the trail passes through these woods. Wow.

I wonder how much syrup that makes, like, how long does it take to fill, say, a gallon, with 2,000 taps, when the sap is running strong? Any educated guesses? I'm thinking sap runs pretty slow, so I guessed maybe an hour. WRONG. Steve blew my mind with this one: Try 125 gallons of sap per hour! But the sap has to be boiled down, such that 125 gallons comes down to like a gallon of actual syrup. Steve fires his boilers with wood, to boot! Wood that he cuts himself! Man, this guy is in his late sixties at least. Senior Steve Hardy is one tough mutha. I learned all of this in the short eight-mile drive down into podunk little Andover with its two general stores, one restaurant, a post office, and... and...well, not much else.

By the time we'd pulled up to the post office in town and were saying our goodbyes, I had learned a lot about how maple syrup comes to be and why it is soooo expensive. As if the gift of all that knowledge and the ride and the company of Steve and his malamute, Jake, weren't enough, out comes Steve with a fat little bottle of pack weight, uh...I mean syrup!! Pure maple! His own brew. Wow! I was beginning to think the trail magic of the South was a thing of the past. Thank you, Steve Hardy, for the syrup education, the ride, and the maple nectar, half of which I drank straight from the pint bottle, so heavenly sweet and irresistible it was.

So I'm standing in downtown Andover, AT Mile 1,917, population 8 or 12, sipping on my cherry Slush Puppie, which when I got it the old man in the store says, "Yep, 'bout time to shut that off for the season," and there's a handful of thruhikers across the street in some emptied-out old restaurant where the locals have been putting up hikers. Arms is there and Kip and Ryder and D-Bone and Munchkin, and they've all been talking up this party uptrail in Caratunk. They want to go, but now they've all smoked out and seem kind of maudlin and the trail is calling louder than the party and I'm figuring the scene like this: They're stuck, stuck on the dogma of the White Blaze, and their extreme cult- like adherence to it will not permit them to take the detour to Caratunk. (I'm wrong about this, but I don't know it yet.)

Caratunk is another trail town one sizable chunk up the trail across Maine and site of the *WhiteBlaze.com* party, on which they have consequently sold me. Some kind of intense seriousness must have been laced into that homegrown they were smoking and poof! Off they go back to the trail and leave me standing there, the lone thruhiker on the corner, Andover, Maine.

So I'm on the phone trying to make contact with someone in the outside world. Why? Perhaps just to know I exist still (in that world). I call cousins Justin and Stacey and a few friends out West, all to no avail or voice mail. I give up and stick out my thumb on Route 20 toward (no shit) Mexico.

Mexico, Maine. Check out the Maine state map sometime. Maine must have been in a real worldly state of mind when they named their towns and cities. There's a Rome, a China, a Moscow, you name it.

Now it's 3:30 pm and I've got maybe four hours of daylight to hitch a LONG way across Maine. I've got the party itch and am determined not to miss this one, having heard how much fun I missed at the post-July 4 gig in Port Clinton, Pennsylvania, called "Billville." Being in no real special hurry except for wanting like hell to catch up with Yazzy, I decide what the hell. Maybe I'll get to see my friend (and yours!), seven-time AT thruhiker Baltimore Jack.

My first ride stops almost instantly, a thin wiry guy about 45 with thick glasses strung around his head with baling wire, dried blood on his forehead and a truck bed full of odd tools and several changes of underwear. The blood, he says, came that day from all the thorny thickets surrounding his dope plants growing on some land up in the forest nearby. He's a fascinating guy with a jillion stories, and he manages to encapsulate several of them in the short 15-minute ride past Mexico and to the intersection of the next big road going my way. I thank him and he drops me on a corner in the town of Dixfield, Maine.

Now I've been rather spoiled hitchhiking-wise out here in the Appalachians. We all have. Folks living within a certain proximity of the AT just "get it" and swerve right to the curve every time without hesitation. Many rides turn out to be past thruhikers. It's great. But now here in Dixfield I'm just far enough away from the trail and close enough to the individuality-vortex of a Wal-Mart that I have a modicum of doubt. But out goes the thumb nonetheless, and with it, almost that very instant, a cop. I judiciously lower said thumb and don't raise it again until he's passed out of sight. My modicum of doubt swells to walnut size.

A few minutes go by and no one stops and I begin to remember what I must look like to the folks of this town. Grizzly, for one. I think of Joe Dirt and his succinctly written hitchhiking sign: *WON'T KILL YOU.* I surely smell, despite having caught a quick shower back at the Andover free house. (The pack holds the smell of months of sweat.) But they can't smell me from their cars? Or can they? Suddenly, there's the cop again, not approaching from the direction in which I'm looking, but just sitting there, stopped dead in the middle of the road directly across from me. Houston, we have a problem.

Officer Dow, as I soon came to know his name, in a display of astounding audacity, sits squat in the one-lane road blocking all traffic in the westbound lane of Route 2. I recall the Wal-Mart just down the road. Poor Wal-Mart shoppers.

"Whatchoo doing?" he asks.

"Uh, just trying to get up the road a bit," I lamely reply, fumbling with my dog-eared and shredded Maine state map, looking for a destination town to give him.

"Up the road, huh? Where to?" His tone is not one of concern for my well being, nor one of service. The traffic builds behind him. If he even notices, he obviously doesn't care.

Is it illegal to hitchhike in Dixfield, Maine? Who would know? Then I pull the only ace I have, the only one I've had this entire trip, though I'm not real confident that Officer Dow and I are playing with the same deck. That is to say, I don't know if he'll have any idea what I'm talking about.

"I'm just trying to get back to the Appalachian Trail, sir," I say. "I'm a long-distance hiker," and I lift my Leki trekking poles for emphasis. The traffic is piling up. Officer Dow is staring me down. No one dares beep. I finish my thought in a mumble, "...all the way from Georgia."

From the look on Officer Dow's mug, I'd say he didn't "get it." But somehow something I'd said or how I'd said it or perhaps the mystifying aspect of the high-tech-looking ski pole thingies I was carrying got through to him. Despite his "I'm a cop and I'll block traffic anytime I like, thank you" middle-of-the-road stance, he shifted his focus forward and drove off. He didn't even say goodbye! Translation: He'd probably be back.

Then Miracle #327 on this long journey began to unfold, and I watched as a big black Chevy Cheyenne pickup truck (that had been in line behind the cop) pulled a U-turn up the road and came back in my direction, pulled over and stopped. A burly Steve Donahue said, "Get in."

Just inside the truck, I had to ask. I mean, I'd seen him turn around. I knew he wasn't going my way, so...what was up? "Where you headed?" he asked, ignoring my look of confusion.

"Uh, well, Caratunk actually, but that's an awful long way, so any way along the way would be good. But hey, you're not even going my way, are you?"

Then I got the story. The truth. One of those small town truths that's stranger than fiction and the kind of grit that will always be my favorite fodder for this tap-tap-tap dance of fingers on keys I do for you, my Reader.

"I saw Joe Dow hassling you," he said, surprising me with his knowledge of the cop's name. "I'm a town selectman here in Dixfield. Where can I take you?" I'd like to think he also said something about how Dow's actions had irked him, but I wouldn't quote him on that.

Thus began one of the coolest hitches in the history of hitching, I figure. A local politician (who makes peanuts for his public service and has to work full time at the local pulp mill to make a living) drives a stinky hiker TWO HOURS out of his way (four hours round trip for him) for no good reason at all. Or to vindicate the actions of a local cop he viewed as something of a punk. Or because he was in the middle of a divorce and needed someone to talk to. Whatever. It was a pleasure. Kudos to you, Steve Donahue. If I may borrow on a line from *Fight Club,* Dixfield Selectman Steve was by far one of my most interesting single-serving friends, in the hitchhiking sense of the term.

We talked of many things, Steve and I. Good stuff about family (he'd raised a good many kids) and dreams and adventure and life and the road. Hell if I remember the details now. Because Steve was, after all, driving me to a party. And party I did for about the next 48 hours straight. Steve spoke with a kind of sadness about his soon-to-be-ex-wife. Things had gone south and stayed south for a long time. Too long. It was either leave her or go bat F-ing crazy. He was a big teddy bear of a man, a tad sad but too fulla life and (obviously) good giving nature to stay sad for long. He was working hard to start anew. I assured him that he would, that everything would be just fine. He told me all about his teenage kids with great fatherly pride, and I replied with "Right on!" and "Excellent!" and meant every word.

I wanted to buy the man dinner or a beer or something for his effort. But he wouldn't have it. It was scary when we got to Caratunk, me having never been there and suddenly realizing that I was there based on no more than a rumor heard just hours ago from very stoned friends, and Caratunk turning out to be some old historic town off the main road, empty and dead as some old museum exhibit of a town, not a soul stirring at 6 pm. I begin thinking, "Oh, shit. This is Kip's doing!" Kip with dry and sarcastic sense of humor, and none of them coming after all. "There's no party! I've been duped!"

But then I pull out the Wingnut trail guide book and reference the town and it says something about a rafting center with cabins a mile up the main road along the river and so up we go and voila! There it is! A circus tent with a bonfire and a handful of early-comers hanging around, scraggly thruhikers every one.

I'm sad that Selectman Steve didn't stop for a beer or a burger from the grill. That would have been nice. He had certainly earned it.

For the very next day, as the White Blaze party really got rolling, up drives a semi, a full-blown 18-wheeler with a load, and slows sudden to a stop there on the road between the Kennebec River and The Ferryman's Place and WOW! Out of the semi cab sprout not one, not two, but five stinky smiling hikers fresh off the trail and hitchin' and arriving in STYLE! The arrival of Big Stick and Gordy and Gaia and Sunshine and Tripod was truly a command performance that'll go down in the memories of all present as a high moment of the weekend. Better than any so-n-so celebrity rolling up to the Shrine Auditorium in LA in a limousine any day! Wow! Sunshine flagged down a semi! What do you know but truck driver Gordon parks the rig and comes down to join the party. Wow. What a day. What a weekend!

I broke down and dropped 40 bucks on one of Ferryman Steve Longley's cabins. I was eager to get out of the cold and damp Kennebec River air and into a bed and shower. I so craved a place where I could sit at a table by a little lamp and write a while about the adventures of the past weeks that, well, I just spent the dough. My idea was that I'd share it with a couple of other hikers, and so I did and maybe they'll chip in toward it and maybe they won't. I don't much care.

I can't write most times now as the temps drop below finger tolerance. So I came in here last night while a bunch of fellow thruhikers hit the bar up the street for its hot tub, Big Stick and Gordy included. I sat at the table and wrote by the light of the little lamp and drank a few Buds until Gordy and Stick returned.

Now here in Cabin Number One, Gordy holds fast in her snug bag with her teddy bear, Oliver, on the top bunk. Big Stick strums his guitar, toying with a new song he's working on. No words yet, but he's calling it "a morning song." Or I guess that's what Gordy called it. In between catnaps, Gordy speaks. "We've got only two and a half pages left in the Wingfoot book."

Evoking the seemingly far distant past with names of towns a thousand miles back, Gordy says, "That's like from Springer to Gatlinburg." I say, hoofuckingray. Someone around here is reading Kerouac's *Dharma Bums*. I'm thinking about how tired Jack was after just that two-day trip up some peak in the Sierras. Nineteen hundred miles we've come. I'm tired. Bone tired. Tired like I won't ever need to hike again for the rest of my life tired.

I shower hot and long and crawl in my bag, my goose down snuggle bag feeling better than ever with me all clean in it. Here I thought the bag itself was dirty, but it was just me every night, despite the little sponge baths I take. In that snug little cabin on the Kennebec in the good company of Stick and Gordy, I slept well last night.

I awake refreshed on the morning of September 20, the day of my six-month anniversary. Hoorah! But now it is time to motivate, time to run with the pack. Time to get out of Caratunk where we transported forth along the trail to party. Time to return to our places on the AT game board: Andover, Rangely, Stratton. I have decided to join BAMMS, the happy gang who arrived via tractor-trailer truck cab. Plan: Go back not quite so far on the trail and begin walking again in Stratton. I hear tell that Yazzy is there, so it is the best of all worlds. I'll be missing about 50 miles of trail, which I can later make up, or sooner.

Or never. Who cares? If I go all the way back, I'll end up crawling up Jackie's tail, literally. That just wouldn't be right, now would it? What with her always trailing behind Ry by a Doppler-distant orgasmic howl? You know the Doppler Effect: First you see the jet, then you hear it, that sort of thing. Of course, in the Green Tunnel, you can't see the forest for the trees. So it's a safe bet that with the devil behind the wheel, we could ride out Jackie's expressed desire to "get closer" in total auditory anonymity.

Jesus, what am I saying? "What would Jesus do?" I'll tell you what Jesus would do: He would wash the feet of that Italian goddess and suck her toes to boot. I'd be right there with the Savior, you betcha, sucking away. I'd pull a Robert Johnson for that cherry snow cone of shaved Italian Ice, sign on the dotted line at The Crossroads doorstep of The Law Firm Infernal at Louisiana, Hollywood and Vine for that fine, fine woman. But no. Relax. Finish the trail.

Jackie IS taken. That's that. End of story. To Ry the glory. Spoils to the victor. Toils for the fool. It's hitchhiking time. By the way, Happy Birthday, dearest Jackie, born September 21 in some ungodly late-model year like 1982. Eighty two, whilst a younger me got to watch his own parents beat each other black and blue. Nice to think instead of you, Jackie, in 1982, little baby innocent and new.

Some sense has returned to this mad mission of mine, this venture, this ad-venture, this tour de force of me inside nature. I have succeeded, for the moment anyway, in finding a woman to warm these ever-increasingly cold Maine nights as we close the final 187-mile gap to Katahdin.

I GIVE YOU YAZZY! Yazzy, whom I spent several days "chasing" and then finally got wise and hitchhiked forward to meet, lay with me last night snug together against the 40- degree weather, our two mummy bags of different makes and years miraculously zipping together to make one. We hiked out of Stratton, Maine, yesterday and made the whopping five-mile hike to Horns Pond Lean-to.

Caretaker Alice savvied our wish to be alone and away from the crowd at the lean-to and led us to a private little campsite all our own. Never have I seen cooler privies than the double-barrel composting setup here, proudly pointed out by Alice, the resident "poo stirrer" to use their own terminology, the caretakers of these "for pay" sites and shelters in the Northeast. A good distance from the house of poo, the site's water source looked and smelled safe enough. We drank it straight out of its mountain spring source and never got sick. I was distracted enough by Yazzy that I just plumb forgot to treat it! Then there were the Foster's oil cans, two of 'em. Foster's fat-ass cans of beer make for ideal trail "champagne," as it were. Good beer and the remains crush down light and small. Yaz and I catch a good buzz and roll joyful beneath the stars of Maine.

Next morning now and we're fine. No problems from the water.

With my usual fresh granola and hot milk breakfast I added a healthy dose of Steve Hardy's pure maple nectar. Oh, my God, is that stuff good! Sorry

Swami, but I have to disagree with you on this one. Pure maple is descended from Heaven; Aunt Jemima sucks ass. Sometimes you DO get what you pay for. Now I hear my watch alarm telling me that it's nine o'clock and time to hit the trail.

The air smells of pending winter, the sky slate gray. I cannot deny that I am entirely sick of this trail, that I wish only to finish it with all the aplomb and pride deserved of such a feat, and then make for a big double bed somewhere with down comforters and a fire in the hearth and rest, rest, rest. But onward I go. Maybe today will be better than yesterday for the presence of a lovely woman who appears to like me and who feels good to lie beside after so long alone.

First view of Katahdin! Here high atop Bigelo Peak overlooking Sugarloaf, an old fire tower at my back, we lunch on salami and sourdough bread, peanuts, and Yazzy's dinner mints. We are not alone. The aptly named Apple Cheeks (whom I just can't help but call Apple Juice!) with her red dimples, and her beau, Mighty Joy, from Oakland, California, haunt the peak with us like a couple of day hikers, out of place somehow, out of sync. I want to talk California with Mighty Joy, wanna rap homestyle with him about "Oaktown," but we may as well be standing on a Bay Area Rapid Transport platform or in an elevator for how little they warm to the Californian in me. We are a rarity out here on the AT, Californians, a fact that underscores the general inappropriateness of their aloof attitude toward me. I try to draw them out, to help them warm up to me, all to no avail.

A child's balsa wood airplane sits crashed out in the alpine scrub flora zone. Yazzy picks it up and carries it as trash, reminding me of my ex, Jill, the Deep Ecologist. Jill was great in that sense. She, too, would have picked up the plane, way out here in the wilderness. But on the streets of her native Pittsburgh or my LA, she wouldn't have batted an eye had I tossed McDonald's detritus right out the window of a moving car. Her rationale? Cities are already ruined, done for. Nature, however, is still pure. I LOVED that eco-bent philosophy, the irony of it. I loved her more than her low self-esteem would allow her to see, to comprehend.

Katahdin! To SEE him at last! Astounding! The "Grandfather" as is the native meaning of the peak's name, doesn't look so far now. It is in fact a hundred miles as the crow flies, twice that by trail. Appears but a day's journey. My perspective, however, is skewed after half a year of spectacular peak top vistas. Boo-Boo, the indefatigably quirky, and Coyote, the cartoon cute fireball, arrive as we make to go. Boo-Boo wants to Kerouac-out in the ancient tower, but finds (as literary-romantic-I did also) the nailed-up plywood battlements impregnable.

Half a mile later to the north and down now rote "stairways" of jumbled stone strewn before us, a cascade of a thousand dead washing machines, I remember that I forgot to ask Boo-Boo if he had a condom to spare. The trail in New Hampshire and Maine often greets you like a wall at your nose, straight up, or straight down. New England has yet to invent the switchback. My "man," Henry the 8th, greets condoms like a turtle greets dangers. At 37, I have yet to get clipped, to cure this inconvenience, return some of the natural ease to sex.

I slept very little last night. Reunited, Yazzy and I "slept" like two wrestling polar bears, a pair of moose in rut doing everything but. No wilderness substitute for a condom that I know of. Perhaps in direct consequence or due to some small bug in the water of last night's spring source, I felt weak at around three o'clock. Leaving the tent, I walked unsteadily, an old man, shaky on his pegs as they say. Fatigue hit me so hard I thought perhaps a flu had caught me. I sat repeatedly, once with tears welling up as I took it all in, the thousands of miles, the four billion paces, the hundred or more tent setups and breakdowns, and the fatigue-driven breakdown now upon me.

There was another factor gnawing at my gut: scowling Sundown somewhere up ahead, her face a cluster of angry muscle, angry at the world perhaps but currently said anger aimed at me for the gross sin of "stealing" her girl away. Ah, what the hell. Tom Waits, once again if you will: "Ah, there's nothing wrong with her a hundred dollars won't fix."

So we had called it a day, Yazzy and I, at just five or six miles in roughly as many hours, and dropped down a blue blaze tent site trail and set up camp and slept ALL afternoon. It was an unprecedented dreamy afternoon detour from the rigors of the trail, and I am grateful to Yazzy for going along with it. I had become so useless at this point that I literally dropped my pack on a tent platform, lay back, and blacked out. When I awoke, Yaz had the tent all ready for me. We were no sooner tucked into our joint bag than the sweet sound of rain filled the forest. (Rain is always only ever so sweet when you're tucked warm and dry inside a tent or shelter.) I closed my eyes again and slept. Bliss, you earn your kiss of a name again and again here beyond the world of men.

Now at midnight or so, I awake and write again, inspired by the strong gusts of wind roaring through the trees overhead. Wind is another element of nature with an entirely situational-relevant appeal. If you're out pushing against it under cold, gray skies, it has no appeal at all. Safe in your tent, however, it is different. It is at once exciting and scary. Blowdowns are common out here, and even a high-tech MSR Zoid tent is no protection from a falling giant. Wish us luck. Goodnight, sweet world, sweet loved ones and friends. If I die before the dawn, may my soul live on and on!

Reporting live from that part of Maine which, on a map, juts far north into Canada, an archipelago, a lake-filled land of peaks and trees and little else, of few roads and silence in quantities unimaginable by civilized man.

The Hundred-Mile Wilderness. We have achieved maximum escape velocity and are moving outward into the furthest reaches of nobo space with all the style and finesse of a tortoise two-stepping to Nirvana's "Smells Like Teen Spirit." We are limping, in essence. Limping, stumbling, bumbling, swaggering, tripping, and slipping in mud and roots and sunken puncheons over truck-sized stones and bridgeless rivers fording.

We are malnourished, under-funded, broken-hearted, bereft of body fat and fast metabolizing muscle mass. We are sick of the forest and our one ripe set of clothes, yet terrified more of what lies beyond Katahdin's close. We're in the Hundred-Mile Wilderness, the last stretch of the Appalachian Mountains, the terminus of the AT. We're ecstatic, exhausted, horrified, and pale.

The condoms slip. They are of the lubricated variety and it has been so long since I've had any consistent occasion to use condoms that I musta plum forgot that these don't work for me. Forgot that lubricated condoms don't stay on an uncircumcised "tool," can't be trusted in a pinch. It's definitely a pinch down there. The woman is young and strong. She's a helluva good hiking partner, and I'm honored she chose to join me on this final stretch, this green mile to Henry David's Kaatdn (sic). I am honored to have her with me and proud of my moment of good sense, the voice, the urge, the calling, the nickel coin-flip in my favor that led me to stick out my thumb and make the jump ahead. One small chunk of Maine, one large leap for companionship-kind. So why bring up condoms? Because, like Pop Tarts, they're hard to come by out here in the Hundred-Mile Wilderness. I bought the wrong kind and now I'm screwed. Or not screwed, as it were. You got the idea. Sex or no, I'm happy.

If it weren't for this girl, I think I might well have hopped a freight south and then west about a week ago. I am THAT DONE with this belabored journey, this "Oops! I forgot what the point was" long-ass walk halfway around the sun. I am Forrest Gump, running, running and suddenly just done. On this last day of September, I feel I have physically and emotionally reached my limit. But unlike Forrest, I have one mountain I must yet climb, and he's only 99 miles away. Seven days tops. Spiritually, I am not done. Nor topographically. So here I go. Morning campfire smoldering, coffee drunk, sun finally cracking through the wall of woods, we walk another day.

11:22 a.m. Trailside at one of a zillion ponds up here, this archipelago of water and pulp mill fodder called the Great North Woods of Maine. Three go-getters pass us, the Blues Brothers and Ranger Dan. Before them this a.m. went Swix and Squatter, checking out of Leema Brook Shelter early, tiptoeing by our tent unheard by us and thus likely privy to our morning coitus cacophony, a loon and a barn owl trapped in a double-zipped mummy bag thrashing about.

Maine Public Radio escorts me gently through today's first mile with a lullaby "lied" (German word for song) of sweet-sounding strings: cello, viola, violin. I think of Luci, of Paz and Anna. I lament that I may have offended the latter, so lovely, so volatile, so stunning and soft the day her brother died.

The forecast calls for sun and scattered clouds through Sunday. It is Thursday. The sky is blue, the sun warm, hiding from us the approaching tempest of Maine winter. I am grateful. Just one more week, God. Just give me one more week. Last night another soft bed of moss. Yellow birch, balsam, fir, the latter known by their flat leaflets, unlike pine needles that can be rolled between fingers. So says Yazzy. And ferns. Forever ferns, the rich green carpet of the forest. These are our neighbors this morning, silent and good, no fences required.

Yazzy has the legs of a horse, the strength of a Himalayan sherpa. She is a good partner, a good woman, an Alaskan dreamer, pretty blue-eyed breeder. Is she my type? I didn't think so. But, perhaps, I think again.

2:27 p.m. I sent my Piglet fleece to Tinker after giving up on ever making it into another Jester hat. I told him, if nothing else, to take a small swatch of it with him into the horrors of Iraq as a good luck charm from me, as a reminder of childlike innocence and soft cuddly things. Innocent as Piglet and Pooh.

I am disenchanted with our pace. The autumn foliage apparently so brilliant in New England, now appears dull and lackluster in the bright light of midday, and I sense it is my eyes that lack. My jaded eyes have been awash in the endless timber for six months now. I cannot see the foliage for the trees. I am bone-tired and lugging an impossible burden. Ten days of food, the signs at either end of the Hundred-Mile Wilderness recommend. I have eight. With every step, especially downhill, the added weight rattles my knees and ankles, loose bolts in creaky hinges. My days of 20-mile races are over. We'll be lucky to pull 12 miles today.

At Big Wilson Stream, the "ford" turned into a giant Plymouth Fury Wagon. Halfway across the water, she listed badly to the right like a boat punctured and sinking sideways. The "ford" was Yazzy, fording yet another bridgeless stream up here in the Maine woods where it appears they have yet to invent the bridge. They can't build walking bridges tall enough or formidable enough to withstand spring floods.

No bridge. Yazzy wanted to cry. Can't blame her. Pack half-submerged, sleeping bag and tent soaked, camera drowned. It took me a few seconds of seeming foreverness, the unbuckling of a dozen straps and unplugging of headphones from ears and disentanglement, but I finally managed to drop my pack and run to her aid, trekking poles firmly in hand and probing the rocky bottom, depth-finders and crutches-in-one navigating the fast-flowing, slick-rocked, waist-deep water. After some argument, I managed to unburden her of her pack (and pride) and get at least the former safely to the far shore. Successful in this, I went back and retrieved my own pack.

A wet and unhappy Yazzy agreed to hike on to get as close to our needed daily average. We made it 11.4 miles to Vaughn Stream and Falls where Cherokee Tears had a fire stoked and ready and welcomed us.

Awoke just now, 5:30 a.m., absolutely convinced that a downpour has begun. I leap out of our zipped-together combo mummy bag and jump outside the tent to move my pack to the cover of the rainfly. Then I remember the river roaring nearby, the waterfalls. Not a drop touches me as I stand in the dark shaking off the auditory illusion. So I pee on a tree. It is October 1, and we have just 100 miles to go. Yazzy ambles out of the tent on all fours, wobbling, a sleep-drunk bear cub rousted from hibernation. She, too, pees and we return inside, exclaiming in mumbles our surprise that the rain was not rain but river.

This is what happens to you when you sleep in a different place on a different piece of ground every night for 193 consecutive nights. You are temporally displaced. Not temporarily, temporally, as in Time with a capital "T." It would be closer to the truth to say we are permanently temporally displaced. You are a slave to every bump in the night, and like that poor bastard in TV's "Quantum Leap," you rarely know where you are, let alone who you are and how you got where you suddenly are. Yazzy, whom I've known just a few weeks now, rolls over to face me in the pale gray death light of pre-dawn and for a moment I don't recognize her, not a line, a curve, not a bone in her face.

My father worries about his memory. His father died of Alzheimer's. I am only 37, and I have perhaps the worst memory of anyone I know. Mine, however, is drug-related. I drink because I like the taste of beer and for obvious social reasons. Perhaps if I quit drinking altogether, I wouldn't need the Prozac-esque antidepressant I take, though I'm afraid it isn't that simple. Then there's the Valium to cure the anxiety caused by the anti-depressant. I knew an old lady who swallowed a dog to catch a cat to catch a spider to catch a fly....

One or all of these drugs wreaks havoc on my short-term memory. Yazzy has spoken perhaps 50 trail names in her lucid storytelling of days hiking in Georgia, The Smokies, Virginia. I recall few names and even fewer faces. Did I meet them? Probably. When this adventure is over, in all likelihood, I will read about it with wide eyes of surprise and wonder, much as you are now.

My breakfast grows cold. By the riverside, Yazzy washes her cookpan of last night's dinner, perhaps the worst burn job I've ever done on noodles. It's hard to simmer over hot coals on a campfire. The sun is up and the sky clear. I meant to listen to the presidential debates last night on Maine Public Radio, but passed out before nine. Oh, well. In the words of our Commander and Chief, Alfred E. Neumann, "What? Me worry?"

At the Long Pond Stream Shelter in Maine there is a tattered copy of *SWANK* magazine. The shelter log is full of offended hikers bitching about it. Well, why didn't they burn it? Or pack it out like trash? I recall the story of the burnt Bible from Robert Rubin's book *On the Beaten Path*. Surely if some hiker could callously roast the word of God to warm himself on a cold night, the Puritans may feel righteous in burning the *SWANK*? A wry smile crosses my face as I read a register entry by one bawdy female hiker friend who writes thanking the *SWANK* donor, saying it brought her great relief after a hard day's hike.

I make a note in my journal to buy the island in Lake Onowa, Map #3, Maine section, beneath Barren Mountain and Barren Slide. The paper companies own all of northern Maine. What do they want with an island? They don't need it. I want it. What of the train trestle at the far end of the lake? I'll take that, too.

1:10 p.m. I'm perched atop the wreckage of an old fire tower that no one in his right mind would climb (I never said I was in my right mind). Nothing left up top of the rickety steel oil-derrick-like tower but a few old wooden slats on which I now sit with 360 degrees of clear view of this awesome, man-empty Hundred-Mile Wilderness whose Cracker Jack prize at the bottom of the box is Katahdin, the great one, the grandfather. No view of Katahdin today despite crystal visibility, as another mountain hides it.

Hard hump up this bitch of a peak for "peaked-out" me. Barren Mountain. I guess. Thank God for Tool, for Maynard's impassioned wailing that never fails to reignite my tired engines. For half the damn climb it was nothing but static and my of late, ever-faithful WTOS, "The Mountain of Pure Rock!" failing me when all of a sudden on comes "Forty Six and Two" clear as a bell and whoosh! As with so many times previous on this colossal walk halfway round the sun, Tool blasts through and rockets me to the top.

9:20 p.m. Now it's talk of God, or lack thereof, and bowtie pasta with garlic freshly chopped and into the powdered alfredo sauce and carrots, too, all this by a river which tomorrow we must ford. I want to write of everything, of all the random thoughts, of the hopes and anxieties of my soon-to-come return "home," wherever that is anymore. Hotel California. Swami's Music House Studio. But I can't. Who can write that much? Try we do and hiking, too. Too much.

So I eat another of Marie Vlasic's homemade post-bummer-Burning Man '04 cookies, yum yum, and sip the last of Texas Mary's Crown Royal, a nip-bottle amount by now, intended for Katahdin, but, ahh, screw it. Cheers, Marie and Russ! Cheers, Mary! Cheers to you and to Sara and Ashley and all you've done to infuse this astronaut's mad weightless tumbling through space green and deep with love and a sense of home.

Just 84 miles to the End of the AT! Uncroixable. Now I've got young Yazzy to warm me at night and set and strike the MSR tent and talk my ear off when I'm willing with tales of everything AT, all eager and alive and excited and clueless of the Crashing Ugly Future.

My needs of companionship and sex now met, I walk the trail like a businessman awaiting his fourth commuter flight this week. I am jaded, sated and weary of the trail. At this point Katahdin is just a matter of course. I want to summit, climb down, board the flight, pop a Valium, knock back a Cape Codder (vodka/cranberry) and BE THERE. Vous êtes arrivé! No matter that THERE will soon give rise to another there, and so on, and so on. That's my crazy life.

My feet are sore, my ankles daily bruised in nasty twists that set the lion in me roaring, shaking the quaking aspens, fracturing the rocks, and rippling the well-ironed sky. When all 200 pounds of my pack and I come down on the side of a crooked foot, every gnome for half a mile around jumps out of his skin. The pain runs its course. There is no option. I get up and walk some more.

Forty degrees at dawn on the 2nd. Makes it hard to get outta bed. Winter again, or damn near. Yazzy lies beside me sipping coffee I made when I got up, rousted by Nature's call around six a.m. I can't stand to be watched while writing. Sweet Yazzy swears her eyes are closed. I can be a grumpy ass.

The sound of water on rocks was not so loud last night, but again we are creekside. Knocked down 16 miles yesterday, about 13 of them "real" AT miles and three of them magical, logical map-savvy miles, cutting down logging roads, "folding time and space," as I like to call it, achieving in a short stroke what AT engineers obviously couldn't put together for reasons of property rights, easements, whatever. Result: Shazzam! Yazzy and I hike out and reappear on the AT just shy of the next river ford and just ahead of Mighty Joy and Apple Cheeks, the young couple from Oakland, California, who had been two miles ahead of us yesterday morning. Ha. Ha. Or as the kids say, "Nanana-nanana!"

I love that shit. In my next life, I hope, well…if I don't get to be an angel with bull moose rack-sized wings who smells like cookies and attracts women in mad hordes, or an immortal eagle soaring free eternal, I hope I get to sit on some high command at FATE Central and manipulate Time and Space. The record will show that I've done a damn good job of it Down Here.

So we're on the south side of a wide river and we have to ford it because Maine hasn't invented "the bridge" yet. We both dreamt of moose walking around the tent last night, which likely means there were. Our water isn't freezing yet, so I haven't come full circle from the days of my first 100 miles, and there's a little whiskey left and Yazzy's breasts are still as warm at night as apple pies in a Mayberry kitchen window (and of equal circumference), so we may just make it to Katahdin ALIVE. Sorry, Jon Krakauer. Nothing to write about here.

Six and a half months. I'm hard pressed to remember the last time I did ANYTHING for six months straight. Jobs? Forget it. Maybe six months tops chauffeuring the dead. No, not the band but REAL LIVE DEAD people. Even school came in shorter semesters. What a freak of Life, what a monster undertaking. What joy and pain and beauty and strain. What EVER will I do next? What ever could top…this?

1:14 p.m. on Gulf Hagas Mountain, the wind is up and kicking. It spooks me. It's not a companion I want as I head into the next ascent. Five miles and three more ascents before we get to go down, making it 16 miles for the day.

Yazzy is in fine spirits now. My grim, reflective mood bothers her. She seems to have forgotten that just hours ago she was crying in her oatmeal about her dead camera battery and other camel-back-breaking-straw annoyances.

We eat our lunch of bread and salami and cheese and birdfood, and I just look at her and say, "I'm fine. I'm just done. I want this to be done. This is an endurance test at this point, that's all. Our moods rise and fall with the mountains. Be patient. Let's hike."

Now it's not feet, not like it was in Jersey with 20-mile daze. No, now it is calves burning, the back of my legs afire all the time, with every steep step, each peak ascent like a thousand deep-knee bends. Insanity. Maine, you are killing me. Metallica helps. Tool helps more.

The trail now deep in autumn leaves, obscuring roots and rocks. The future haunts me. I am neurotic without reason.

Puccini wrote, and I recently heard it played, a geographically confused opera about two lovers dying in a hot desert outside New Orleans. Today, while topping White Cap Mountain, literally the LAST peak before Katahdin, I am exalted, yet the opera rings true. I, like Puccini in Europe with his imaginary ideas about an America he has never seen, I am geographically confused. I have surmounted some 150 mountains in the East yet have no real idea where I am.

I walk a green tunnel of hastily gobbled-up government soil full of bones and blood and hunted men and haunting beauty, a far-from-virgin forest cleared and cleared and cleared again only to grow irreverent over every flickering human endeavor, a field cleared for crops a lifetime ago now supplanted by lush jungle growth; again the forest wins, and comes now FREE to ME, free and phantasmagoric, rife with dreams and inspired thoughts and all the makings of anything the mind can muster, like a Hollywood blue screen upon which anything can be made to live alongside anything else, Cajuns in the desert and bayous thorny with cactus and housecats and crows over wheat fields infinite and eternal. I walk a green tunnel.

Now with Katahdin in plain view across a valley of lakes and lowland woods, I don't know where my lovers are, in desert or swamp, and the woman

I am with takes off her underwear and hikes with a smile, ever the more aroused as the wind picks up in late afternoon and stimulates her...interest.

I am afraid of the wind, cold wind that is, cold wind atop high places. It is a recently acquired phobia, don't ask me why, how, or where from. But the joke's a good one. The joke is on me.

My young companion, unruffled by the wind and, in fact, every bit tickled by it, suddenly wants to get down and dirty right here and now on top of this mountain. Holy Jeezuz! I'm all for spontaneity and wild, animal-like sex in the woods, but this is neither the time nor the place. All I can think about is how to get down off this frikken mountain STAT, down into the safety of the trees. It is a strange juxtaposition, my fear and her arousal at, and or "of" the same thing. The wind. Wicked clit-licking wind.

Yaz mentions having been sick somewhere near Waynesboro. I think for a moment and realize that I have never, not once on this entire journey, been ill. Perhaps it's because I stayed out of the wind.

All I can tell you for sure without dragging out the topo maps and mileage reference guide (and disturb my sleeping Yazzy) is that I rest tonight at the north end of the final mountain—of hundreds crossed, crested, or circumnavigated, between me and Mount Katahdin, or Kaatdn, as Thoreau spelled it.

I rest, and yet I rarely rest well these last nights. So at two o'clock this morning, just an hour ago, I wearily rose, dressed, and stumbled out of tent ("crawled" best befits the action of entering or exiting these expedition tents), and with aid of dim headlamp made my way to the only outhouse extant for 10 miles north or south, a human-sized box on stilts. My business finished, I set out on my return trip to our tent some 50 paces away. Somewhere. Yes, somewhere in the woods not more than...well, okay, maybe it was 100 paces.

But suddenly with headlamp dim from fast-fading batteries and without my prescription glasses, I looked at the outhouse and I had a doubt. I had approached it from the rear, right? Or had it been the left? Oh, shit. Suddenly in that miscalculation alone, I had opened up about 90 degrees of dense wilderness in which to spread out my search team, me, myself, and I, and hunt down our tent. Mother of God, lost again!

Remember, forest trails are not the nicely graded walkways of parks, even BIG parks like Yosemite. The AT is itself almost completely indiscernible from the surrounding landscape, this in BROAD DAYLIGHT! Add to this the very name given this bowsprit NeverNeverland of northern Maine jutting as it does deep into Canada, "The Hundred-Mile Wilderness," and perhaps you'll get the picture.

Setting out with the privy at my back, I walked therefore a "path" that bore no resemblance to any path known to modern man. I was walking on memory, and I was thus, within a minute's time, completely lost.

How had I found the privy in the first place, you ask. Same way. Memory. I had a vague recollection of seeing the outhouse on my way into the shelter area and so knew it to be somewhere vaguely "over there."

Obviously, I found my way back eventually, or you'd be reading this in a pattern of sticks and stones laid out on some lakeshore or bald mountain top, my final words before disappearing forever into the wilds of Canada or wherever. "His final words…a story about a privy…rather banal, strange, but it's all we've got to go on. No S.O.S., just some silly thesis on comparative forest environments," or some such thing.

I'd likely be off in the trees somewhere standing nose-to-snout with the pissed-off bull moose whose moose coitus I interrupted this afternoon when the wild howling calls of bull and cow drove Yazzy and me offtrail to investigate. At any rate, I found my way back to our tent tonight by first locating a white blaze, which I followed in the wrong direction for a while, then a blue blaze, which I followed right to our tent. Go figure.

8:27 a.m. I write funny because of these fingerless gloves I'm wearing. It's the third of October and I may as well be in Alaska for what a clear post-night's rain of morning sky brings. Thirty-eight degrees. Yee-hah! It's March in Georgia all over again. But with a difference: I can see Katahdin!! I have him in my sights! I have won the hunter's lottery for the right to kill this year. Any day now, I'm going to raise my weapon, aim, and I'm going to take the giant ogre down. Mount Katahdin: DOA. Mount it on my wall.

I'm not going to do it out of mercy or some ecological "culling of the herd" or even because I'm starved and I need the meat. No, I'm going to do it for vengeance. Oh, and for the trophy to hang on my wall. I'm going to shoot the old grandfather out of pure sardonic gratitude. Thanks for the blisters!

Thanks for the shredded knee ligaments and the 147 twisted ankles! Thanks for the pain so bad in the balls of my feet that I pissed myself in Jersey. Thanks for the trip halfway 'round the sun that made me miss Burning Man, Houston's Art Car Parade, San Francisco's Art Car Fest, and my 20-year high school reunion at Torrey Pines in Del Mar, California. Thanks for the chiggers, the rattlers, the ticks, and the mice. Special thanks for denying me even ONE bear sighting in two thousand miles.

Yazzy eats her oatmeal out of the packet. Worse, she most often eats it COLD! Just add cold water, eat. Primitive hussy. I have brought warm water into her life. I am a missionary of sorts, bringing God to a half-naked jungle savage.

Today we have to ford another river. This will make three. Two thoughts: one, the logging companies that own all this land don't need the islands. Two, they should build us bridges!

10:36. The Ford was not a Ford but a Chevy. Easy. Rock hopper. Yazzy tells about a hospital visit, a severe sinus infection early in her thruhike and of her insurance company's refusal to pay for her Emergency Room visit. Cost to her: $600. Coprophagous swine!

I stop her short of more details. "Please, don't go on. That shit makes me go *Fight Club*. I just wanna go postal." I think of several good lines from Chuck's twisted book/film about wanting to burn it all down, blow it up, "...put a bullet in the head of every endangered panda that won't screw to save its species." Please, God, let socialized medicine win out over the current horrid travesty that is medical care in America. Astonish me! Make it so. Slip it past the rich scum currently running the Geezer Freak Show, I mean, The Government. Give us a miracle, water into wine, 40 days and 40 nights. All that.

It's time to walk now, another 16 today, a cakewalk into Antler's Campsite, purportedly the most beautiful site on the trail. The rain kindly did its cleansing thing last night whilst we slept. Today is all sunshine, blue sky, and the sepia-washed rainbow of summer's imminent death, which is autumn, which is right and natural, brutal, unforgiving yet natural, comprehensible unlike anything ever conceived of by Man, a thing not at all OF man.

12:40 p.m. Little Boardman Peak takes me by surprise, another goddamn hump up some useless pile of rocks. I stare up it with bared teeth, my whole lower back a tight and angry fist of sporadic breath-taking pain. An ancient back injury not felt since throwing my buddy Frank's kids into the pool a summer ago has flared up again. I curse at the mountain, small as it is, "Fuck you, peak! Fuck you! I stomp on you, fucking peak!" and so on to the not-so-distant top (only 500 feet straight up). Yazzy is, fortunately, a way back, having stopped to pee, and thus misses my tirade, a potentially frightening litany of fucks.

But I am anything but frightened. I'm envigorated, jazzed, pumped. Anger! Good clean healthy anger, victimless and so much the better for me. So much better than sadness and suicidal grief internalized, all the weight and sorrow of the world. If I seem grumpy here at trail's end, is that not righteous and good? Have I not earned the right to rage benign at irksome rocks and yet another big climb snuck up on me within kissing distance of the finish line? Every depressive should be so lucky. Every depressive should drop whatever misery they're mired in RIGHT NOW and start walking. A grump? I am a god born from the belly of a 10-year slump. Eat me, Saturn! You evil celestial prognosticator!

I think back to that day in the Doyle Hotel with Yippee and Jabberwock, Yippee fixing me with that intense stare of hers and asking (in the way one tells more than asks), "Well, are you STILL a thruhiker?" The question arose over my recent departure from the trail, my aqua blaze in which I substituted 100 miles of the AT to parallel the Shenandoah Mountains in a canoe, paddling 100 miles of the Shenandoah River. "Well, ARE YOU, JESTER? SAY IT!"

"I guess."

"No, no! No 'I guess.' Are you or aren't you still a thruhiker? Say it!" I did. Yes, I did. Yes I am. More than 2,000 miles on foot. "Yes," I said weakly at first, then stronger, catching on, "YES, I AM! I AM A THRUHIKER!"

Everything on the AT north of some geographical line I never noticed is a lean-to. In the South, they are shelters. In New England, they are lean-tos. It is 7:45 p.m. here at Cooper Brook Lean-to. Also here in the North, the privies of the South are become outhouses. Sometimes the carved and painted wooden signs bolted to trees even announce the presence of a "toilet."

Make no mistake, however, the upright, spider-infested coffin-on-stilts with a hole in it ISN'T a toilet, no matter what the $10 Home Depot butt ring and lid set might seem to imply.

Today in the mid-afternoon of my lower back spasm hobble toward Katahdin, Nature called when there was no toilet, no privy, no outhouse. I did my best to improvise and utilized, as I have learned to do, a downed tree sitting roughly toilet-height from the ground. Crude as this may sound to those of you reading from the snug comfort of your suburban "reading room," said practice is quite acceptable and about as good as it gets for the long-distance hiker adrift in a toilet-less world for six month at a stretch.

Unfortunately, due to my strained lower back, I had to concede to a slightly less-acceptable distance from the trail in answering Nature's call. In layman's terms, I had to shit just spitting distance from the wilderness sidewalk, the Great Rock and Root Highway known as the AT.

Six months ago when this journey was young, I met a man from Peabody, Massachusetts, named Rael. I didn't much care for the man at first, given what I took to be a gruff personality; but very soon I changed my mind about him, taking great pleasure in finding that my first impression had been thoroughly wrong. It got better. I soon found in the 49-year-old Rael a kindred spirit of the Monty Python kind. Rael, it turned out, had the same verbatim memory and perfectly accented recitation of line after line, sketch upon sketch of Python material, as myself. As hiking partners, we would have made a perfect match.

But it was never to be. Rael got ahead of me and I never caught up. I dreamed up and begun practicing lines of a "Holy Grail" mock sketch to perform with him at Trail Daze in Damascus, working title: "Ponty Mython and the Holy Nalgene of Appalachia." But that, too, never came to pass. That was the last I saw of Rael.

Until today.

Until smack dab in the absolutely remotest region of the AT at the least opportune time, I looked up from my too-close-to-the-trail toilet activities, and who should appear from the north (the one direction I wasn't looking, because in October the thruhike game is largely over and who the hell would be walking AWAY from Katahdin?) but Rael. Holy shit. The Pythons couldn't have written a more down-to-earth, laugh at the naked truth, "you're human and you better get used to the idea" kind of Meaning of Life reunion. Here's to you, Rael. Congratulations on your summit of Katahdin and Happy 50th Birthday, you bare-chested South Boston Napoleon with the tough facade and the Python falsetto heart. God bless you in this time of post-AT depression.

9:04 p.m. I lie atop Yazzy to quell her shivering. This is the same technique employed to raise the body temperature of a hypothermia victim, but Yazzy is hardly hypothermic. She has braved the roaring creek not two car lengths from the lean-to, and is just plain chilled. Why I use the phrase "car length" I haven't a clue. There are no cars out here. The only way in or out of here is 50 miles on foot. Exception: For the severely injured or rich, a seaplane could be summoned.

Rael spoke sorrowfully of three dead moose he'd just seen at the game warden's office outside Baxter State Park. Hunting season. The moose lottery. They'll sell you a tee-shirt, a box of chocolate moose turds, postcards of moose grazing in the golden fields, then turn tail and sell lottery tickets for the rights to kill a regal giant of the forest. Win the lottery, bag a moose.

"How hard is it to shoot a moose?" Rael asks. "They use the excuse of too many accidents with cars. Let's shoot cars instead!"

Edward Abbey would have liked that, would have been first out there with a shotgun. Then Rael. Then me, too, what the hell. We'd go about it politely, of course. Fake road blocks. Cars stopped, "Excuse me, folks, would you kindly step out of the vehicle. We're engaged in a top-secret moose protection plan here in the 100-Mile Wilderness, just need a moment to give your car the once over."

Have a heated trailer nearby. Nintendo for the kids. Coffee and donuts for the dads, maybe Oprah reruns on the TV for the wives, the volume cranked up, of course. Way loud. Loud enough to cover shotgun fire as Ed and Rael and I turn the family minivan into Swiss cheese. Have a shuttle bus ready to take the family moose-watching at the nearby favorite buck moose rutting grounds, maybe even slip in a little monster-sized moose sex ed for the kids, Nature Channel style, then back to their hotel where dad, now talked into the whole mad gonzo eco-logic of the thing, would with full empathy and confidence ring up his insurance company and explain the whole thing as a moose collision, total coverage.

When the going gets weird, the weird take to the woods. Or the beach. Failing insurrection on even the smallest moose-lottery abolishment level, there's always Mazatlan, Mexico, and Mama Margarita out there on Isla de Piedras, two home-cooked meals a day, and a palm frond hut all my own for $5/day plus another $5 or so for half a dozen liter bottles of the freshest Pacifico you can drink, right from the brewery in town. Failing that, there's the next Ice Age. I figure, either way we can't lose.

9:34 p.m. Everyone else is asleep. Spin Cycle, Impulse, Tarzan, and Yazzy. I'm the sole survivor! In the cave black darkness before me, headlamp off, one nickel-sized orange ember holds out from a campfire begun and soon neglected hours ago. I was powerless to help it. I promised Yazzy that if she cooked dinner and boiled water for my goodnight whiskey/cocoa concoction, I would lie flat out and rest my back in preparation for tomorrow's push to Antler's campsite. From there we will be just 40 miles from Baxter's front gate, then one day's walk to Kaatdn's tippy toes, sleep, rise with the sun, and summit. Finito. Fertig. Done.

I look again and the ember has gone black. Time for me to do the same.

Half a dozen stuff sacks full of food hang together on a single string. Were they the ballast of a hot air balloon hovering high above the shelter, nestled in the trees here at Mile 2,100, we could cut loose the balloon and it would surely bounce off Katahdin on its heavenly course. We are that close on this October 4.

Actually, they're a bouquet of birthday balloons for a headstand child in an upside down world. Actually, that will be enough silly metaphors out of me for now. They are an amazing sight, however, so many stuff sacks hanging together from a stick no bigger than my pen, tied to a length of parachute cord secured to a rafter overhead.

Where typically an inverted tuna can will suffice, this "mouse proof" food hanger wears a bucket for a hat, a full-blown five-gallon galvanized bucket hung like a lampshade midway down the chute cord. The food bag "balloons" twist slightly, slowly in the nonexistent breeze of peaceful dawn. All about this inadvertent piece of "thruhiker art" hang backpacks as well, also from the ceiling and likewise twisting slowly, languidly as if to say, "We are in no hurry and will hang this way forever if you wish."

Beyond the front porch-esque open front wall of this log cabin structure there is a fire pit, huge, big as a Cooper Mini, tall enough that from my vantage here on the shelter floor it half obscures the lovely stone-lined pool beyond it. Far to my right I see the white of waterfalls whose sweet auditory blanket of siren song has made for solid sleep full of few dreams and mostly just the cozy black velvet of wonderful nothingness. The pool, green from here but no doubt clear as glass up close, is fed by the falls and would make for a lovely morning dip. I make a dip of a different sort however, reaching down out of my bag with now near-frozen fingers (from writing) and read the thermometer attached to my pack. The Fahrenheit numbers are too closely bunched together on the tiny thing, but the metric message is clear: zero.

There is much about this scene I would wish to hold onto: a strong and pretty woman beside me, our bags zipped as one, she warm and supple in all the right places; beyond her, one, two, three more lumpy mummy sleeping thruhikers buried in colorful down bags against the morning frozen world; the tin roof overhead, the wood beams all around and beside and beneath me, softened, carved with decades of names, black here and there with the halo-shaped burn scars of a hundred meals cooked on alcohol stoves, the floor boards pitted and hewn with use yet glazed as well by the movements of a thousand bodies or more; and, of course, the poles, sometimes dozens of them, reminiscent of a ski lodge, all standing at attention awaiting their master's call. They, too, walk the trail, giant metal insects become organic with use: true "walking sticks."

I would freeze time and keep all this just so. But I cannot. Nature will at any moment trump me and freeze this place for real. Time to summit and go home.

Then voila! Spin Cycle, another guy I never much cared for, as he seemed stuck up, cagey, but was likely just shy and didn't talk much, well, Spin Cycle sees me fall this morning at the shelter and Yazzy gives him the lowdown on my tweaked lower back and next thing you know "crunch-crunch-crunch," the guy's a closet chiropractor! Not an hour later, I'm just whizzing up the trial, relatively pain free! I mean, it still hurts, my whole mid-section on red alert, a plate of hot coals burning, burning and sending shooting pain down my legs, but since the crunching, it's better, way better. Thank God for Spin Cycle.

I can walk again and walk I do, fully 16 miles today to the shore of some lonesome lake where an airhorn hangs from a tree and says "Squeeze me," so I do. Wow! Does that horn split the light fandango and send every late afternoon egret flying and duck squawking, and the word on the trail is that this magic horn will summon a man in a boat from far out across the lonesome lake. Fifty-four miles into the so-called Wilderness and here I am summoning a boatman who will take us to a remote hunting lodge for respite from the forest primeval, the forest of which I am so fond yet so utterly sick of, finished and DONE WITH.

Result? The boatman cometh in a flash from across the water and a dock where the usual customers are seaplanes delivering rich men with big guns and hunting permits, licenses to kill! The sun in the west setting all orange small and growing cold as the telescope of pending winter sends it further west, farther away from here. Conversely, Katahdin is so close! Magnificent it is, this grand and vaulting lone king of the land with all other mountains melted away to the south and west.

Then voila! I'm sitting in a comfy black faux leather chair beneath lamp of propane in a large cabin with many rooms to let, yet just Yaz and me here. All the boys, the men, the scant thruhiker crowd here on the island with us tonight sleep in the bunkhouse up the hill: Spin Cycle, Impulse, Two Dogs Fucking, and some guy I hadn't met before named Screamin' Steven.

Luxury! Our tab is running high here at the aptly named White House Landing, and I couldn't care less. I feel presidential! I am Teddy Roosevelt after a day of romping around Yosemite with John Muir. "Burgers, please, yes the works, and oh, put me down for one of these waffle-sized brownies, and what's that? Bud in the fridge? Two dollars-fifty a can. No problem. I'll take four. Yazzy and I walk the grounds, check out the bunkhouse and the private rooms, too, pondering the joy of sharing a bed and the displeasure of bunking with snoring men and ohh! An old four- poster bed all made up nice and knowing full well now that at close of day no new guests will arrive at this remote Alaska-esque outpost to share the house with us. So, private room it is. Private house! I mean, how could anyone else come? At dusk the ferryman closes shop and you can blow the airhorn all you want. That hardass (who barely picked us up, thanks to some previous hiker calling him a hardass) sure as shit won't answer the call.

No. This place is ours tonight. The silence is deafening, profound. I tell Yazzy how I wish we could afford to stay another night here, as checkout time is a brutally early 8 a.m. Be packed and ready to roll with your packs by the dining room door at the ring of the breakfast bell, 8 a.m. But no, we decide that to stay another night would be unnatural (and perhaps unwelcome). We are a nomadic people. This place, for all its lace and beauty, is just one more one-night stand in a string of 180 or so. Thus, no time to write. Got to shower now, then pack, then sleep, then roar across the water and back into the wilds to hike again.

I smile watching Yazzy as she sleeps sweet and warm in cotton sheets (a great luxury in trail life) on good thick mattress in old four-poster bed, and I am happy for her, feeling for a moment grand, a wealthy man. A Lord in the royal sense.

But this Lord's bowels go off like some dumb clock every night now at two in the morning it seems, causing every order, or disorder rather, of dressing in layers and locating eyeglasses and headlamp and cursing under breath as I climb from tent out over sleeping Yaz. It's 2:35 on the morning of the 5th as this time I more subtly slip from big bed but still must fully dress to make the hike to the privy high on the hill. Which gets me thinking about the bill and $60 for the two of us in private room, yet no toilet or running water or shower, all said amenities remote in outbuildings here and there throughout the property. I laugh as I think of what Timmy back home would say, a variation of it's only money. Timmy, churchmouse poor like me but rightfully proud. "Spend it!" he would say. Okay.

I just know any city folk or any ANYBODY with a real sense of the value of money not skewed and screwed like mine would find this an outrageously good deal. I fight back years of so-called poverty consciousness and choose instead to revel in this island paradise on the water's edge, on the edge of the world with 50 miles of lonesome forest all around in any direction, all this on the edge of winter, the cold wind whistling round the house tonight in the dim gray not dark of near full moon up there lending pale illumination to a low-lying blanket sky.

Wind outside, yet here in the common room of the otherwise empty guest house silence, such that one lone fly's desperate end-of-season buzz is heard loud, a death rattle really, as autumn snaps its late-start fingers, drops a tickertape parade of dazzling colors, leaves, and, in its fast retreat, glances back over birch-white shoulders and whispers, "Go! Hike now and go home, go west young man of California comforts and Pacific dreams. Go! You have done well, foot soldier. But the war ahead is not for you." Autumn old and tired turned away, and as she went dropped golden flakes of fading summer sun from Aspen fingers quaking.

In the quiet of another night on water's edge a loon cries melancholic long and lonesome as the moon and two trees rub together in the dark, one fallen against the other, a friend indeed and held up. With the help of the wind they sing a song more lonesome than the loon. My heart breaks and is daily healed here in the forest. This end comes as naturally as winter, yet I do not envy me it.

TWENTY TWO

...Hot Hiker Babes Parading Thru Baxter in the Nude...Had I Foreseen the Ugly Aftermath, Would I Have Slept? The Iconic Snapshot Reps of the AT Class of '04...Still Frank the Doo-Dah Man...the Jagged-Fanged Mechanical Vagina...Coyote Orion and Heinous Indecision...

That night, our last night on the trail before the final climb, a parade of my gonzo thruhiker peers, the group collectively calling themselves BAMMS - Gordy, Coyote, Sunshine, Munchkin, Seraphim, Big Stick, and Ski Bum among them, two-thirds of them twenty-something women and not one of them hard on the eyes, so to speak—came marching into base camp at twilight in naught but their birthday suits and packs on their backs. Hilarious. Fantastic. Ecstatic. The fireflies of the South had long disappeared, but that night the girls of The AT Class of 04 lit up the night with their "sparkler dims" as Kerouac said. A bawdy band of triumphant goddesses, they came singing through the trees for all to hear and danced into camp in NOT EVEN their underwear!

Yazzy joined them at some point after I lost consciousness. I hit the Thermarest at 6:30 p.m. and was out cold in minutes. Yazzy woke me a short time later, managed to get me to half sit up long enough to fork down some teriyaki noodles she'd kindly cooked up. Departing thruhikers from that day's summit party had given Yaz a "30-rack" of Budweiser to take and share among our gang, and next door Frank stoked up a big bonfire expecting our arrival on the scene any time. But all I could manage on that great dark yet shimmering magic song-filled night were a few sips of one 12-ounce can of beer, and down went my head again, out for the night. Yaz claims, and I vaguely recollect from the deepest of dream sleep, that she made several attempts at rousting me throughout the evening.

Was I ill? Had I drugged myself out on sedatives? Neither. I just crashed. Their final bash was my final crash. Am I sorry I missed it? A little. But not really. Not yet. I'd had the blessing of these angels' company on many, many a night and through many a hiking day and days in towns all along the way. I slept contented that night, happy for all of us, for the Dreamers-become-Doers, for us, the beaters-of-the-odds.

Had I foreseen, however, how very lonesome a victory 'twould be when all went home, myself included, and the November hours I would spend curled up in a ball against a world that couldn't or wouldn't relate, well, I might well have torn myself from sweet sleep to be among my people one more night.

6:15 a.m. Katahdin Ascent Day. The coffee is on. Last trickle of denatured alcohol ignites in cat food can stove, and I crawl back inside the double bag to give Yazzy some loving. She gets hers, but me, I'm hopeless. Still-strained back muscle bad enough that sitting up is tough, so no sex, and I'll be lucky if I can make this final ascent without crumpling a thousand feet short of the top like a termite-eaten porch. Coffee made and now already mostly cold in the short space of time spent writing these words.

"Don't you feel like it's Christmas?!" Yaz asks, her eyes buggy with excitement. I should. Today's THE DAY, after all. Frank comes by and gives the forecast. The weather, a heretofore totally ignored factor in my daily existence, essential info today. Today it is vital that the weather be good. Thankfully, it is. The forecast on the morning of October 8, 2004: mostly sunny, 71 degrees F and winds no more than 10 mph. Some two-dozen thruhikers will ascend today, a moving, rock-scrambling zoo. Time to go.

Moments later, in a fit of excitement-driven weirdness, I slip into a Jerky Boys imitation voice and shortly have Frank and Yazzy howling with laughter as the crank phone caller Sal asks to have a box welded for him to get inside to masturbate. This happens when I'm excited. All sorts of strange voices mimicked and remembered drop out of my skull and roll out of my mouth like gumballs. You never know what color you'll get. I think I am excited after all.

That's about it. We're nearly done. We have walked the Appalachian Trail. Just have to make a wish and blow out the candles now. Me, now sore of feet but feeling fine, back problems of the past few days now seemingly gone, and so up the final 5.3 miles to the summit I fly without incident and naught but one stop to rest and snack with Yaz and Frank. Closer now, very close, and it's plain to see that it's a zoo up at the top! I hear my name called out, loud and clear, as the gang already arrived cheers each new ascendants name from the summit.

Wow, what a crowd! Gordy, Ski Bum, Rooster and A-Squared, Lumber, Impulse, Cherokee Tears, Spin Cycle, Coyote, Sunshine, Big Stick, Dingle, Arms and Snax, Chef, A-Dog, Munchkin, Seraphim, Two Dogs Fucking, Yazzy, Frank, me, and on and on, or so it seems. Plenty of day hikers up here, too. With each new round of arrivals the cheers go up and resound around the rocky place and everyone is smiling and embracing and posing repeatedly with the sign, and Sunshine is the biggest showoff, shy Sunshine from my early days in Georgia. Then the group shot, "The Class of 04," and we are a motley crew and I'm glad that I am among them. I kiss the final white blaze painted, as it is, on the rock above which stands the sign, the famous sign announcing a Nobo Thruhiker's Grand Finale and take my place behind it, cigar in hand, a contented smile on my face. The champagne goes around, and I hand out a liter of whiskey packed up for the occasion. Many partake, but I'd swear Gordy killed half of it! Though hundreds have reached the summit in recent days and weeks, it's odd, but it really feels like we are IT, the iconic snapshot representation of just that shade of character that was, that IS, the AT Class of 04.

Most of the group lingers, but Yaz and I move on. I take one parting look at The Knife Edge, Katahdin's "other way down" that is every bit as treacherous as it sounds. I had wanted to do it, knew I could with my heightened agility, strength and sense of balance. But with my back out of sorts, I can only look at it and admit the impossibility of fulfilling this final desire: to walk the razor's edge. I relinquish and we retreat the way we came, walking over the same ground twice for perhaps the first time on the entire journey. Tonight we party in Millinocket, some small Maine hamlet that must veritably shake in its boots when thruhiker season peaks. God bless you, Thoreau. I tried to drink from your namesake spring but could not find the source, and your stagnant water did not look so hot.

1:53 p.m. There goes Frank: bespectacled, bald, skinny, the smile of the happiest child who ever lived, and on his birthday, no less. Frank at 52 out of the Navy, now skipping down the western slope of Katahdin, a "made man," a true blue Thruhiker with a capital T, on his way down from the summit and singing "truckin like a doo-dah man" as he goes. I don't know, but there's just something gigglicious about watching a bald ex-Navy commander in his fifties singing songs by the Grateful Dead. But that, of course, is just a reflection of my age, of my youthful naïveté, and of the fact that, pushing forty, I still think I'm twenty-something. I mean, who am I kidding? Mickey Hart has to be pushing sixty, and Jerry Garcia is a newborn Buddhist lama somewhere in Shakedown, Himalaya.

Yazzy catches up to me where I sit trailside plugged in to my headphones and writing, my chair a thickly mossed stone. I pull off the phones and, while we wait for Frank, the slowest of our ad hoc threesome, I read to her from my steno scribblings. I've been musing over Thoreau.

Early in my ascent of Kaatdn, "the grandfather," I had pictured Thoreau, his now-150-year-old tubercular dust of bones reanimated and humping it up the mount beside me. He'd have a gramophone strapped to his back, its giant cone blasting Bach, Mahler, Mozart into his head, a super-inflated, outdated, and cumbersome version of today's iPod. I would gently suggest to the poet that he might enjoy the fidelity and lightness of my "music machine." A man who cursed the "iron horse," throwing rocks at passing trains in protest of progress, Henry would not be an easy sell on the mp3 player. But eventually he would try the tiny purveyor of massive sound and he'd smile. It would be the smile of Frank when I shared a Foster's lager with him atop Killington, a smile of surprise, gratitude, and pure childlike joy.

Frank has a walking stick he calls Thumper. In Georgia, Thumper stood taller than Frank. But now, thanks to the friction of 2,200 miles, a lot of it rocky, Thumper stands roughly two feet shorter. We became a "summit team" of sorts the other day when Frank caught up with me at Abol Bridge. I'd heard, in advance of his arrival, that he was working hard to catch up so as to summit with Yaz and me. I was honored.

Frank had envisioned several ways of "Going out in style!" to finish the trail with a special flair. First, he was going to rent us a limousine out of Millinocket to pick us up at Katahdin Stream Campground and ferry us out of Baxter State Park in style. But Frank had naught but the same evil "cell phone pay phone" to work with that I, and I'm sure every thruhiker struggles with there at the Abol Bridge store. That, and not enough advance notice. He met only with voice mail and answering machines and underlings who weren't authorized to make the necessary arrangements. For a Navy commander no doubt accustomed to getting results, I thought he handled it pretty well. Rejection that is. Small town ineptitude. Communications failure.

We can visit the moon, measure the breadth of the Universe, and pro climber Rob Hall dying of hypothermia atop Everest could and did, in his final hours, dial out on his satellite phone. But could he call in a rescue helicopter? No. Helicopters don't fly that high. All he could do was reach his pregnant wife in England to say goodbye. In our little anonymous fringe world of AT Champions, a newly retired military man, a commander of six ships and six thousand men, could feed four dozen quarters into a stupid beast of a cell phone bolted to a tree in Maine's Hundred-Mile Wilderness until he was blue in the face. But could he score three Olympians a soundproof stretch limo with black leather seats and a wet bar to "roll" off the trail in a style befitting Olympians? No. Technology is the underappreciated manservant of our time. A slave on the brink of freedom, Mr. Technology labors only so far for us, then watches with wry grin as we flounder in his absence.

Technology, when tasted out here in the trees, is alkaline on the tongue. It tastes of irony and has more holes in it than Swiss cheese. Consequently, we left Abol Bridge a little less enthused, having allowed our hopes to be raised, and then dropped, one plan shot down.

Frank catches up to us and we three walk together a while. I've hiked with Frank perhaps a total of 100 miles on the whole AT, and I have never seen him fall. We all fall. Rocks and roots and that occasional temptation to look up and see the sky whilst hiking, to look left or right while under way (always a big mistake) and bam! You go down. Everyone falls. But pride dictates that it is best to fall when alone, kind of like the tree falling in the forest when no one's around. No one saw it. It didn't happen! Pride aside, falling in the company of a partner is better. There's empathy, a hand up off the ground.

So we're rambling down the trail toward the finish line, or rather, "back from the finish line" to our limo-less parking lot. It's Frank setting the pace, then Yazzy, then me in the rear. I'm rambling aloud, talking about something. A grainy rainbow of leaves falls from the trees as we walk. I reach out to catch a leaf as it falls and nearly trip in the momentary lapse of attention to the ground.

In response to something Frank has said about keeping in shape, I rattle off the one rule I remember from high school Physics 101, "A body in motion stays in motion; a body at rest stays at rest." A real no-brainer when you analyze it, but then again a salient thought in a rather brainless world. No sooner does the word "rest" fall from my lips than frumple-umpalump! Down goes Frank. Just seconds ago, a body in motion, now suddenly, as though by the voodoo of my voice, a body at rest. The timing is too bizarre, and to my horror I'm stifling a laugh. Yazzy and I help him up and, once assured he's okay, the three of us just bust out laughing. It is Frank's first fall in the company of others, and he can't help but laugh himself. We all fall.

Frank's second grandiose idea upon entering the park yesterday, the limousine now forsaken as impossible, had been to rent a cabin in Baxter State Park. Frank fancied a little extra comfort as a nice way to prepare for our final day on The Trail. When Frank offered to pay, we doubly concurred. On the AT, I learned the two operative words were Yes and Thank You. Okay, three words. Though it may indeed be better to give than to receive, there is no wisdom in the denial of kindnesses offered by big-hearted people.

Turns out the weekend of our arrival in Baxter is that park's most popular weekend of the year for tourists and day hikers. This is no without good reason. On the following Friday, the mountain would be closed for the season. For workaday people with real jobs, this was the last- chance weekend in the season to clamber up the Katahdin trail and see the foliage and breathe the alpine air of one of the few and righteously magnificent places on Earth special enough to draw Henry David Thoreau from his womb of Concord, Massachusetts, northward on a journey later told in *The Maine Woods.*

Come they did, in droves (but not so many summit climbers that our gigantic mob of finish-line-ecstatic thruhikers didn't eclipse them at the top) and had likely long ago reserved all the cabins to be had in Baxter State Park. So to The Birches we headed, the remote yet thruhiker-designated campsite, but lucked instead into a couple of lean-tos smack at the base of the five-mile trail to the top. Birches or lean-tos, either way it was $9 a head. We scored.

Still, no limo and no cabin. Two carrots dangled in the face of a comfort-hungry jackass, I'd reached out for both.

Only one who has ascended and descended half a million vertical feet in one long, physically and mentally daunting journey and lived without any creature comforts for the duration could possibly understand the drool-inspiring nature of Frank's visions of finish line comfort. If you think a limousine would be a welcome break from an office desk and an urban, traffic-choked world, imagine what it would have felt like to Frank, Yazzy, and me. To any of us who'd hiked Mt. Everest 17 times in a matter of months. Imagine.

Near the bottom of the mountain, I encounter two fortyish women hiking up. It's 3 p.m., so they can't hope to make the peak today. Or can they? When I ask how they are, one replies, "Not bad, a bit stinky, though," and pulls at her synthetic sports shirt for emphasis. "Stinky?" I ask. "Oh, you have NO idea how stinky one can get. Try six months in the same pair of shorts and shirt. You can wash them every week, and still they stink."

The shaplier of the two, with apparent hiking experience, replies with Martha Stewart conviction (oh, bad pun), "Febreze." Right. Okay, lady. "Thank you," I reply, "but after hiking 2,000 miles in them, I do believe I will be setting fire to them later this evening."

Of all the nights in the past 200 nights, this, the night of our triumph, most certainly should have been a Burger King have it your way kinda night. Alas, twas not to be. Not entirely anyway.

What did Ferris Bueller say in that restaurant scene in the movie of the same name? "You can never push things too far." Yeah, that was it. Our summit night was the night to push things as far as we wanted. I should have. I could have. I could have done anything, had anything, had any woman. I could have burned down that eerie gay quack-ass ugly box of a hotel Yazzy's mother marooned us at on the far outskirts of the town of Millinocket, Maine. Hell, jail might have been the perfect punctuation mark on my hike away from Luci's suicide and my depression and my attempted suicide, the one that brought cops to my door with guns pointed at me. Jesus! I've never done a thing in my life worth having guns and hot, nervous trigger fingers pointed at me. I should have pushed things TOO far that night. I should have insisted on staying at the little family-owned motel right beside the Blue Ox Tavern where all the hikers would gather that night.

That was my first mistake. When Yazzy's mom stopped there, I should have grabbed my shit and run. But I got back in the car, and that led straight to my second mistake. It was my first interface with civilization following a week in the Hundred-Mile Wilderness and a triumphant Katahdin summit, and it was a doozy. What, you ask, was this short-bus passenger foul-up that so deftly slammed me hard and fast back into the so-called Real World?

"Why, it was that damned visit to the ATM, Officer! That what dun it! That what made me drink that gallon of whiskey and burn all them donuts into the Wal-Mart parking lot."

Bangor Savings Bank Branch #666, Milli-knucklehead (nocket), Maine. Friday night. Frank, Yazzy, and I passengers in Yazzy's mom's car, the latter at the wheel. Now, I don't know this woman at all, but she creeps me out, by no fault of her own, I suppose. It's just that for days and days on the trail I had to hear from Yaz all about her mother's deep concern for daughter, concern about Yazzy hiking with the freak with the confessional Web site. Yazzy found it all rather humorous. I didn't.

So I'm nervous, and it's one of those ATMs you have to surrender your card to, stick it in and it EATS it for the duration of the transaction. Now, thank God my middle name is Rosenthal and I hate paying the $2 fee and therefore yank as much dough out of the machine as it'll cough up (thus reducing the percentage of "tax" on my money to minimum). Two bucks out of $20 is a lot. Two bucks out of $300? Ach, a pittance!

So I hurriedly grab my cash and receipt and jump in the compact car fulla stinky hikers and stinky gear and my girlfriend's mother, whom I'm convinced has it in for me, and away we drive. It isn't until I'm standing at the check-in counter of Millinocket's tackiest hotel (perhaps the tackiest in all of Maine) that I realize, to my horror, that I have left my ONE and ONLY debit/credit card in the jagged-fanged mechanical vagina at Branch #666, Bangor Savings, and that I will NEVER, EVER see it again.

Mind you, I mean no harm by this metaphor. I am in fact a great fan of vaginas! I just can't resist the sexual connotations rampant in everyday objects. Come to think of it, banks are rife with sexual metaphor. Remember the old-style drive-up banking with the phallic tubes that got sucked into the bank and ejaculated back out to you full of cash?! Then you've got your keys slipping into locks, and all that tension like new lovers feeling each other out mentally, and hundreds of boxes wearing chastity belts like mouths full of diamonds and gold, and vaults that safecrackers tickle open with rubber-clad fingers, and, and, and…okay. You got the point. I lost my plastic. It's a damn good thing I extracted the maximum allotted stack of twenties. And, looking on the bright side, I couldn't have lost my card at a better time on my hike. I was done. Hike over. Goin' home.

My immediate recall of that night at the Blue Ox in Millinocket (that is, directly following my two-day hangover) is both hazy and, in parts, crystal clear and diamond-dazzling delightful. Deny it though he may, the haze owes entirely to Still Frank, who bought me round after round of top-shelf whiskey to properly fete the occasion in a manner befitting his pension. I regret it not a bit and raise a bubbling glass of plop-plop fizz-fizz hangover helper in toast to you, Frank, with many thanks. However, there is no way in hell I would have gotten AS DRUNK as I did as fast as I did had I been pulling from my own stash of cash. It would have been a financial impossibility.

So what do I remember of our great summit night celebration? One, turning around every five minutes to find Frank's outstretched hand, shot of Maker's Mark or Tullamore Dew poised for a toast. Two, T-Bird and Gaia, a couple of lovely thruhikers who kindly arrived in naught but autumn leaves mysteriously plastered to their lithe and athletic bodies. Oh, yes, and watching them dance in their foliage skimpies, a wonderful sight. In particular, I recall watching Ski Bum leading T-Bird through some fancy moves, skillfully stepping to the band's jams, me mildly envious, wishing I knew how to dance and, after not too long, wishing I wasn't so damn drunk!

Maybe old Frank wasn't entirely to blame for my getting so hammered so fast on that supremely special Appalachian Trail final summit night. Maybe I snapped up those shots a little too eagerly to soothe some sadness creeping 'round inside my otherwise triumphant heart. The Fates are funny little bastards. Or bitches. I can't remember. The Muses, now they were definitely female. But the Fates? Did they even have a gender? Or did they lack reproductive organs like the Smurfs in Donnie Darko's explanation when he said, "What's the point of living if you can't have sex?" I'll bet the Fates were Smurf-like. Why else would they mess with me the way they did that night?

Why else would I have run into, of all people, Ry's dad, Terry, in our cheesy-ass hotel in Millinocket? Oh, yeah. I forgot to mention that. That, I suppose, was my third mistake of the night, although it wasn't so much a mistake as just a damn weird bit of chance. Terry and thus Ry and then Jackie, the latter two who had yet to summit but who were just hours away from their own victory the following morning.

Naturally, Terry, ever the southern gentleman, invited Yazzy, her mom, and me all out to dinner. The whole gang was there. Dad Terry and Ry and Jackie's mom and stepfather and aunt. It was then that I learned that Ry and Jackie had become engaged up on some mountain in the Saddlebacks, and what could I be but happy for them? My heart broke and my heart giggled, and I decided I just didn't give a shit, that Jackie had never been mine. No matter that I had lusted after her from Day One out of Springer. Forget about Jackie's "day late and a dollar short" Hanover, New Hampshire, slam-on-the-brakes mid-trail statement that I was not alone in my affection. Forget the sensual backrubs she'd given me on drunken nights when Ry had retired early to their tent. Forget the hugs that felt like smashing atoms together in some hidden forest particle accelerator.

Oh, and DEFINITELY forget Jackie's refusal to say goodbye later that night as they, still to hike, went early to bed, and we, "the done," went drinking. Forget that Jackie had expressed, since Hanover, her desire "to get closer" and that her refusal to let go my hand had me all but convinced that this was THE MOMENT I was supposed to sweep her away, Katahdin be damned, yank her up behind me on my trusty steed and ride off into the pulp mill-stinking Millinocket night.

The engagement news didn't hurt this knight a bit. Gollum coughs, "Bullshit!"

It's over. It's all over. Even the hundred or so miles I missed, five here, a dozen there, another 50 to chase the girl, they're done. I'll never make them up. It's not in my nature. I don't look back. Or if I do, I don't GO back. So the AT is completed, hiked, finito. Three days after our summit, for the life of me, I couldn't at this moment tell you why I did it, why I hiked through 14 states, more than 2,000 miles and half a million vertical feet. Why? Beats me. It's

Monday in America and people with purposeful lives are nose-to-it. Even though it is Columbus Day, a holiday based on a fiction, one day in a few dozen thousand days of lies, most people sit passing the hours at jobs they hate.

If I sound a bit cynical, perhaps it is the book I'm reading as I sit here fireside at Yazzy's primitive camp by a lake in New Hampshire, a stone's throw from the Canadian border. *Survivor,* the book is called. It's a sick and twisted sister-story to *Fight Club,* Chuck's opus. I read a line that makes me think of the AT, and for a moment, a flicker of the "why" crosses my mileage-stricken brain. "The whole year before baptism," he says, "every tree, every friend, every thing you saw had the halo around it of your knowing you'd never see it again." Walking the AT had this quality, afforded one a glimpse into the "halo" heavenly magic of everything, a magic we don't normally get to see. Every tree or rock or chipmunk or stream or pond or beaver lodge or human shelter I encountered, I knew I would likely never see again.

Later in the book, author Palahnuik repeats the same idea, sort-of: "Imagine you live in a house, only every day your house is in a different town." This would certainly apply to all the dozens and dozens of hostels and motels and guest bedrooms I slept in on off-trail days of rest. The trail towns, however, these I could maybe see again someday, and the hostels, especially toward the end up here in New England. Freshest in my mind, they were always a bum-rush, in and out, obscene checkout times like 8 a.m.(Heavens!!) In the eyes of this poet-athlete-drunkard, there were no halos over the heads of these innkeepers.

No, whatever auras existed owing to the absolutely transitory nature of the journey belonged to the trees, to God's four-legged creatures, to the lichen-encrusted stones, to the curve of the trail through a field, to the dance of an enchanted doe outside an ancient stone shelter in the Smokies. The halos were on the forest itself. The ability to see them was earned in the walking, just so. Walk and walk and walk in the woods until the woods become your reality, and the outside world, estranged. Mind you, however, said vision comes at a price. Here I sit on October 12 at Yazzy's Lake Francis cabin in the very northern woods of New Hampshire preparing myself, mentally, to pay that price.

Going back into The World, I'm frightened. I didn't "fit in" real well before, and I don't know how I'm going to swing it now. I've got a head full of halos! I look out and I see cobalt blue of pending winter lake of ice, its far shore a fall bouquet of multicolored haloed trees, leaves of New England autumn all aglow now as the western sun, hidden from me here in Yazzy's lakeside cabin, pours its heartfelt warmth and glory forth and at it, at the forest across the water. It is the magic hour at 6 p.m., a wood fire burning in the stove and Yaz asleep beside me here on old and tattered couch of camp house character.

There's NOTHING to do here. Nothing. That's why we came! After a man walks 2,000 miles and all the business and stresses that such entails, man needs to park his ass far away from the Things of The World and do NOTHING. Do nothing but reflect.

[As it happened, after a few months of scrambling around to find new purpose, I would in February of '05 come to the wise realization that, having lived like a bear for the better part of three seasons, I was entitled to a bear's winter rest, and thus retired into hibernation in Arizona for the winter.]

In two days, I plan to board Southwest Flight 922 out of Manchester, to bid adieu to this East Coast reality, this "place" I've been immersed in for over half a year. Yazzy, the cabins on lakes (hers, my father's), Justin, Aunt Mary, the AT, autumn color, ever-colder nights, the same one damn rock radio station I've been stuck listening to through all of Maine and the White Mountains. I'm leaving it, but I don't know what for. I have forgotten.

I get up from the couch and go outside and down to the water's edge to witness more closely the miracle of sunset. But I am quickly bored. I chide myself. How ungrateful! To think one could overdose on nature's beauty to the point of ennui.

Does the Shire still exist, Sam? Quaint and incestuous little Idyllwild nudged up in southern California's San Jacinto Mountains, my home though I have no dwelling there, per se. I have a car there. Worse. I have two cars. One functional car and one art car, a monument to my insanity, very big and very much in everyone's curious face and going nowhere for lack of a new engine. Can I go back? Is it healthy? Can one walk two thousand miles, fully FIVE MILLION paces, only to end back at a place of going nowhere? There's more, Dr. Freud.

I never met the girl of my dreams, the woman I saw in a dream hiking the Appalachian Trail, the woman who would find me. No woman, bear nor moose.

Notice how I say "no woman" and not "no women." Elly. The one I let get away. Elly came into my AT experience early, a kind of cruel joke from those manipulative swine in the Greek rendition of Heaven. They sent me a hottie with my college love Melissa Moore's lion's mane of hair on Day Two, and she went postal on me after one week. BOOM! Nutso. It took a bit to shake her (empathetic as I was to her madness but in no way capable of walking with it), but soon she was gone. Then came Pegasus, with a HUGE space in between. I had the pleasure of about 48 hours with Pegasus before my pre-arranged trail vacation to New Hampshire for the 4th of July cut that short. When months later I caught Pegasus again in Vermont, whatever we'd had in Pennsylvania seemed potentially destined to go further. In an odd sequence of events, however, she returned to the trail, whilst I, completely unplanned, wound up staying in Manchester, Vermont, for well over a week, losing Pegasus altogether.

Finally, a month before The End, I met Yazzy. There was a spark, I let her go, I chased her, we reached the summit together, and I'm with her now. But the spark is still just that: a spark. No sense at all that this is the woman I was meant to lasso across the prairie home to Hotel California with me to spend Forever with in Wherever I end up calling home. No sense that this is The One.

So I did find womEn. But, dammit, I never did see a bear in the wilds of Appalachia!! I never did see a moose in Maine!! Ah, there's nothing wrong with me a hundred dollars won't fix. Thanks again, Mr. Waits. The trail wouldn't have been the same without Tom Waits wailing and grumbling sweet gravel songs of lamentation in my ears and me wailing along with to wither the roots underfoot.

So that's how it's going to be. A little insomnia, restlessness at 4 a.m. as my flight departure approaches and those few missed AT miles plague me in the night and conflicting schools of thought, "Oh, how much easier it would be to do now with all gear at the ready and me here and in shape," and on the other side, "Hell No! It's frikken winter already, could snow any day, cold, steam of breath, ugh!" And, conflicted and needing to pee, out I go into the cold New Hampshire night of near Canada, temps in the mid-30s, and, peeing, look up at blinding clear night sky of descending Heaven and Whoa! Coyote Orion! My Patron Saint of the Road, always there for me on long night lonesome desert stretches to guide me just outside my driver's window, out and up or just above if I lean forward over steering wheel and all those silhouetted saguaro cactus flying by or nothing but sagebrush in the dead west Texas I-10 night and Pow! Coyote spirit of bold Orion brilliant and clearly outlined, defined, he guides and gives me hope, a sense that what I'm doing, where I'm roaming, is RIGHT and OKAY. Orion: my one constant in a sea of less reliable constellations.

But Orion hasn't been here this summer. Maybe it was just the dense forest canopy of most nights, shelters tucked in trees with little view of sky, but, no, it seemed Orion just wasn't around, like he knew I didn't need him to walk the well-blazed and purposeful AT. So he hid and I walked instead of driving and all was well with the world. Then Wham! Like an angel visitor my secret nocturnal Friend of the Western Road, there he is! Tilted just so as always and framed perfectly in the one open chunk of sky here in the likewise dense forest of Yazzy's Camp, far northern New Hampshire. Wow! Whoa! "What's that you say, Orion?" Go? Kerouac answers:

Go roll your bones, alone!

Close the gap in the wide toothy smile of your AT. triumph, then come home to us, to me, in the West, where we will roam again the roads of Arizona, Texas, California and New Mexico.

Yes! Together. Me and spirit brother Luci in the Beamer bolting through black night with great stereo sound and Orion overhead, we'll go to Bisbee, see Kate. New Mexico and Dave. Texas and Mary, Hunter, Stephan. Maybe even New Orleans and the Stocks, but no farther east. God bless The East and all it has given me, blessed gifts and adventure and Love, but it's time to Go Home. Or nearly so. One more week? Can I stand it? Orion says YES. Do it. Do it now. Sobo from Sugarloaf through the Saddlebacks and stroll Monday to the highway, kiss the ground and say, "Woo Hoo!" For only then will your heart be content.

I'll sleep on it. I've got another hour or two before bloodshot dawn and decision time. But I do believe the die is cast. Orion doesn't just drop by to see me every night. The message seems clear. I am clear and well rested now, enough anyway, from Katahdin and the stress of making it last week. A vision quest. Alone I'll do this one. Perhaps at last I'll see my moose, my bear.

[Postscript: Orion, Yazzy tells me, is a winter constellation, thus accounting for its summer absence. Also, Orion is for me solely a phenomenon of the hauntingly exotic open West. It was surely the stupor of 4 a.m. that made me think Orion wanted anything more than for me to come straight home, my journey at an end.]

TWENTY THREE

...Jim Beam or Heet, Boy, What'll it be? Beware the Rear View Mirror...the Prodigal Son Makes Good...the Girl Left Crying at the Airport...Looking into the Eyes of the Sun and Smiling Homeward...Wandering Vegas Airport in a Morphinated Morpheus Stupor...Rolling Out of a Depressive's Bed and Onto the Trail...Dead Men Hike No Trails.

So we pack it up and leave the quiet of the Lake Francis cabin high up in the peaked-roof attic portion of the now-vanished Old Man's house, the Granite State of New Hampshire, and head south and then east. With every mile I'm flipping out, flipping and flopping and changing my mind. Go. Don't go. There's the seat awaiting me on Southwest Flight 922 out of Manchester tomorrow, and although the ticket is open-ended, do I really want to give it up?

Cut to: complete mental meltdown in a gas station parking lot at the junction of Routes 16 and 26, the turning point where I must make my decision. I walk to the phone to change the flight and can't do it. I flip a nickel two out of three. I do it again and again and hate it, hate the outcome that tells me I must do it, but feel sure I'll never sleep again if I don't go back and finish what I started. I walk. I come to a picnic table in a small park and cry. This is madness. We have become fully lodged in the throat of the space-time continuum and we're going to choke the life out of the world if we don't do something quick.

But wait a minute! So what if all the cards are in place for an easy return to the trail? So what that Orion came out last night and said hello for the first time in months? I'm F-ing exhausted! I can't do this anymore! I'm done! I was done weeks ago. But I kept walking to make it Katahdin (not counting of course the little hitchhike pink blaze I did to make it to Yazzy so I could finish the trial...er, trail with a much-needed companion after so long alone out there). I kept walking and walking and walking until my ankles were going bad on me again and my knees were collapsing like sat-upon eggshells and my back went out...jeezus, I was a mess BUT I KEPT ON WALKING! Then I finished. Boom. Voila. Just like that it was over.

Is all this just some kind of post-traumatic AT syndrome symptom? Because if it is, man, I don't like it.

So what did I do? I walked into the gas station and ambled around. I contemplated a new round of trail rations. Unappealing junk food, all of it. Then I came to the Heet, that methyl alcohol gas line treatment shit we alcohol-stove users use on occasion when we can't find pure denatured. I stared at the bottle of Heet. It stared back. Then my focus shifted. Behind the Heet were glowing cases where cold beverages sat awaiting my attention. I gave the Heet a miss and grabbed a sixer of Jim Beam and ginger ales in the can. I calmly walked to the counter. I paid. I walked out to the truck and cracked one open. I took a swig and I knew. I knew the truth.

There is no truth. There is only choice. The truth is bullshit, the truth in the exact-mileage, bean-counter sense of the AT and what it means. "Endurance is more important than truth," Bukowski said. Had I not endured enough? Two hundred and twenty-two daze on the trail in the woods with no outdoor plumbing and stinking socks and going to bed at night sweaty all over despite the outside temperature, sweaty from 10 hours of hard physical work. I had endured plenty.

I looked up at the center rearview mirror and remembered a line from an old road-race movie from the sixties, when a racecar driver tore the mirror off the windshield and tossed it out the window saying, "What is behind me is not important!" Yazzy returned from the pay phone and chuckled as she saw the sixer of booze. I chuckled back. "Drive, woman!" I said. "Drive SOUTH! Away from Maine. I'm done. I'm done, Yaz. I just want to go home."

New England shimmering now in golden light of sun, the sun a bobbing apple in the barrel of mountains, hills running the New Hampshire/Maine line and all the leaves in the full burst of autumn color, the crescendo! The colors, they are clearer now in my joyful eyes of decision made. Going home. Home to the idea of home. Zeppelin and Moby and Petty and the Beasties mix it up on Yazzy's stereo truck rolling past bright white homes and jeans hanging on the line to dry, North Fryeburg enroute to Daddy-o's for a final visit. Let's see if he can embrace the occasion a little better than has been done thus far. Out now. Over and out. Too much beauty passing our October window to be looking down to write.

October 14. Bach's Cello Suite #1 in G major lifts me high in jet-ascending rush of strange New England farewell. Up then we rise over densely populated Manchester, the suburbs beautiful "Today Only!" by dint and loving brush of autumn leafy color, the colors of God, the colors of pending winter death and sleep and change. A thief in broad daylight I bid you adieu, New England, and steal away (just in the nick of time) to golden shores of western dreams, to California, straight back to my private suite in that Forever Hotel where checkout time is flexible, but leaving for good? Impossible. Southwest Flight #922 has lifted me already, in the short space of this page, high aloft past showers just beginning straight up and into blue blue skies where all the world below is white and soft and forgiving as deep, deep sleep.

Where now is my Appalachian Trail? Where now is my daily friend and spirit guide over mountain after mountain, mile after mile? I look down now at the biggest white blaze I have ever seen. Sting sings in my ear 'bout how he's sending out an S.O.S. Good thing. We're going to need some guidance, some counsel, to deal with a blaze the size of all the world below this plane.

Yazzy's gone, tears in her blue eyes and running down soft cheeks as I heft my pack for the last time in New Hampshire, in New England, on the whole East Coast for anywhere a continent away from the AT World. Good-bye, sweet Yazzy, hiking partner and lover sweet there at long journey's brief Maine end. You leave me curbside and drive your burnt orange pickup away as bade by cops and security lights and all the rushing madness that is airports and fear combined.

I go inside and run the gauntlet, anxious a bit as I'm set aside for secondary invasion of personal privacy and wanded down and removed of shoes and hat and zippers, et al. Anxious only should they produce my little pill stash and start asking questions. Pain killers, antidepressants, more pain killers of a more prescription-level nature, as many colors in that little jar as all the autumn leaves now falling dead in suburban yards below.

My fears were for naught. Free to go. Free. That's the key word in all of this, folks, in every paragraph of every page of prose and poetic rambling and just straight reportage, the sum total of which is fast approaching 200,000 words from six months on the Appalachian Trail. Free. Freedom. Live free or die. I picture the Old Man on the Mountain, roll a quarter between my fingers, see his face restored. He is gone now, New Hampshire, but I see him as Ben Obi-Wan Kenobi, vanishing by Vadar's saber but not before reminding the evil one, "You can't win, Darth. If you strike me down, I shall become more powerful than you can possibly imagine." New Hampshire, you are stronger now than ever, and the Old Man lives on in your collective, freedom-pumping heart.

I leave you, New Hampshire, but I take with me your spirit, your license plate slogan, words to live by. Freedom IS NOT "just some people talking" so stated in the lyrics of Desperado. In the case of the AT, it's just some people walking. A lot of people. We walked and conquered. We walked ourselves ragged and at end our conquests are all internal. It is quiet here at the end. Hardly a woo or a hoo.

Heading straight into the western running sun, chasing him as it were. We will not beat him to Cali, nor even to my layover destination of Vegas. But it will be fun to be on-course with him for a change, after all these months of late afternoon shine and warmth like a kiss on my left cheek, always on the left or the back of my neck as I balance-beamed over bog bridges following bear tracks in the Maine mud or Spiderman-walked up steep sloping bald tops above tree-line or alongside minimal alpine growth or even in dense forest, letting only a flickering strobe of healing western sun reach me in the darkening woods of moss and lichens and roots savage and unruly, stones drunk on snakebite and rolling about thus to trip me up after some hoary saber-toothed rattler dropped by to sharpen his teeth on them.

I've said it before and I'll say it again, how can a poet fly and not be dazzled beyond all cure? One thousand seven hundred fifty miles from Vegas, says the pilot, just 20 miles out of Baltimore. How can the mind fathom such a distance until the feet themselves have walked every mile?

Don't feel bad if you can't. I just DID walk all that way and more, and I cannot comprehend it. I am humbled by this Earth, humbled by God's big key lime pie planet over which I now soar in whipped cream splendor agog at the rolling hills and mountains of water-retaining air. This is the pilot's world, where he lives every day. How could not the pilot become poet?

Same way I suppose that I could walk the East Coast Earth from near end to end and sometimes have nothing at all to say, just complaints about sore feet, and see the AT as nothing more than an oblique "green tunnel" as it is often called. You get sick of anything after too much of it. I could not, after summiting Katahdin, stand the thought of saddling up another day, of stomping up the Saddlebacks, the mountains I missed in my Sissy Hankshaw, thumb-wagging pink blaze for companionship.

Now I've left a girl crying at the airport with no hope or promise of anything more than what we had on the trail, a trail romance short-lived but pleasant. I hope she'll be okay. I'm eating airline peanuts at 450 miles per hour. How I got here, I moved virtual money from my virtual online account to someone else's, to the guy selling his Rapid Rewards flight voucher on eBay, and he made a virtual "gift" of his tickets to me and an hour later Southwest Air sent me an electronic mail message saying the tickets were mine now and "here are some code numbers to make all this virtual shit seem more real." Something like that.

I told my dad this last night at the bar at the Black Horse Tavern near his place in Maine. Dad took Yaz and me to his favorite tavern for a celebratory dinner and drinks. I don't recall the last time I've seen him so proud of his prodigal son. It was as though I were just that: the wayward son returned to Grace. Six months later I would be lost again, his pride befuddled. But who cares? Last night we had it all: he, his champion son; me, a father's beaming pride. I said, "Isn't that amazing? I never met the seller, never handed anyone any cash, never even saw the money myself. A friend electronically deposited money for me into my account a week ago and I bought me an e-ticket to ride." Then voila! I'm on a plane shredding the white blaze sky at damn near the speed of sound.

To celebrate my departure, to make this weird transition from Yazzy and AT and Dad and Aunt Mary and Justin and New England, from all of this to the Big Unknown awaiting me in California, I pulled a Matrix and ate not the red pill, not the blue, but the purple one. For 222 days on the trail, I carried one 30-milligram fentanyl capsule duct-taped to the back of amigo Mike's inspiring send-off card. It was along for the ride for one reason: the guy who fell while rock climbing, wedged his arm in a crevice, and, after hanging there a few days, hacked off his own limb with a Swiss Army knife.

Now I figured, if this happened to me, or if I fell and broke a leg or a buncha ribs and was far offtrail, or ontrail but in what we call "a bubble," an area of trail empty of thruhikers for a day or so in either direction, well, I'd need the purple. Turned out I never did. Made it through with flying colors.

So, nothing left to do now but EAT the EVIDENCE! Gobble it down before some Patriot Act-jacked airport security stooge DEA wannabe gets his rectal probing rubber-clad fingers on it screaming, "Traitor! Terror-monger! Drug fiend!" bringing the Culture of Fear crashing down on my Bambi-hugging six-month pseudo-reality with brute and ugly force.

Result: We're high now.

Oh, yes. Thirty thousand feet and cruising. Back pain from pulled muscle of high-strung, taught sinew body of athlete, Olympiad, alas unaccustomed to the hip-swivel movements of *coitus alpinium*. Translation: Hike, hike, wee! Hike, hike, whippee! Hike, make love, get up, bend over a stream and.. OUCH! *Hikerus Interruptus.* Pulled the muscle in the Hundred-Mile Wilderness and voila! Along comes Spin Cycle to the rescue, a bear-sized man whose too-quiet demeanor and penetrating, seemingly patronizing looks had me avoiding the guy at all costs. Irony of ironies, it turns out the former TV ad man is not only a teddy bear sweet guy but an angel chiropractor to boot! Okay, a novice, but it doesn't take a pro (just a bear) to lift a six-foot twig like me off my feet, my arms folded across my chest, and basically "bounce" me off his chest for the desired effect. CRUNCH! Trailside spinal alignment. Amazing. Sure there was still pain, daily. But without hero Spin Cycle, it's possible I might not have walked out of the wilderness of my own volition.

Where was I? Oh, yes. Back pain of past two weeks: gone.

Aches in knees brutalized by endless steep descents in Vermont's Greens, New Hampshire's Whites, and Maine's...blacks and blues: gone. Hangover from last night's Jim Beam and ginger ale celebration with Dad and Yazzy at the Black Horse Tavern? Gone. Sore feet? Gone. Sore airplane-seat ass? Gone. Shouting noise of drunk, Vegas-bound seatmates: diminished.

Sustained on air by pills.

All the morphine doesn't seem to have addressed is the congestion in my influenza-addled head and throat sore. Or maybe it did for a while but has by now worn off. Hell if I'll reveal my source, but let's just say the pills are old, and I split the 30-milligram pill in half figuring I'd save half for the second five-hour chunk of this rather long flying day. Out of Fryeburg at 11 a.m., airborne at 3, down in Baltimore at 4:20, airborne again at 5 with a five-hour run to Vegas, two hours on the ground in that psycho-deliriunk airport, then off again for a one-hour run to Ontario, California. Oh, yeah. Then the two-hour drive to Idyllwild. Home at Swami's by midnight, or 3 a.m. by my East Coast clock. Long day.

Flying over the Continental Divide now, the Rockies already snow-covered to a certain elevation. I think of Flyin' Brian Robinson, Triple Crown Champ, running over all those razor ridges lit with the pink alpine glow of reflected sun on their western faces. I peer down upon that white jungle of massive jags and think: No F-ing WAY.

I'm done. I've done my Great Hike. I don't need to hike the Continental Divide or the Pacific Crest. Homey don't need no Triple Crown to make him The Man! I just need rest. Jeezus, I want to sleep for a week. Maybe I'll throw down, spend the cash on one of those motels that rent by the week, just check in, hang the DO NOT DISTURB sign on the knob, and lay there until I get bedsores. I am that tired. Please, God, let there be some peace at Swami's and some nook for me to crawl inside and hide a while. I told Yazzy today on our approach to MHT that if the plane started going down, I would just cackle and hoot. "Yee-haw! Bring on the Big Sleep, Baby. I HAVE lived 'a good life, enough to base a movie on,' as Jim Morrison said. I'm done."

But far from going down in flames, this plane and everyone on it gets higher by the minute as Vegas-jazzed passengers liquor up for a night of celluloid fun. It's some guy's fortieth birthday, so suddenly the whole crew is prancing down the aisle with a toilet paper roll bedecked in plastic Southwest captain's wings and a small can of juice on top: the effect is more mock-wedding cake than birthday cake, but what the hell. We all sing the song as the last of the bright pink and orange light of Thursday, October 14, makes the engine and wing out my window look like a Mary Kay car, and far below the Colorado River winds and wiggles its way toward California.

To get the gamblers in the mood, the crewmembers have us all write our seat number on a dollar bill and toss it in a hat. Little boy Nathan is chosen to do the honors and pulls out Seat 3-A, the Asian woman directly behind me who has been kicking my seat for hours wins the pot. I'm too tired and stoned and tired and exhausted and stoned and wore out and bone dry dead on my 2,000-mile-ragged feet and bony, hiked-off ass to even flinch, either earlier at her kicking or now at my not winning. Congratulations, Asian kick box lady from Baltimore. Live long and prosper on your $102 booty.

Did I mention I'm tired?

Did I mention my last-surviving grandmother's parting words to me the other day were, "Have a nice life." Did I mention that Baltimore Jack locked me in the porta-potty at the Caratunk party and then proceeded to run at it like an offensive lineman? Did I mention that I let all my fellow Katahdin summiters sign my back in the Blue Ox Tavern in Millinocket on the night of our festive farewell? Yah, that's how that night of top-shelf whiskey wound out. For lack of an art car or a canvas, I yanked off my shirt and made myself the canvas. You should have seen the sheets on my hotel bed the next morning.

The lights of Vegas have grown bright below. Brighter. Now darkness below and that sense that the ground is very close. The screech of tires, the roar of thrusters in reverse. Vegas. Time to find a bar and await my final flight.

Eight p.m., Pacific Standard Time. I amble into the only bar in this "wing" of the massive Vegas airport. Already spent my obligatory dollar on 25-cent poker, betting 50 cents a hand, my Vegas excitement prolonged only momentarily by one jacks-or-better "winning hand." Some win.

Made my way over to another machine and in my morphinated Morpheus stupor took a good minute to realize the slot machine-looking R2D2 thingy with a video screen monitor featuring dancing Vegas showgirls was in fact an ATM machine. This elicited a smile. The irony never ceases.

All I can say is thank Colonel Sanders or Lord God the Big CPU in the sky or Skynet or whoever is running this virtual reality for allowing me to pop out of the woods and, sans the PayPal credit card, go online and use pass codes and keystrokes and other imaginary matrix magic to buy my little blonde inner Charlie Bucket a Golden Ticket on Wonka Airlines and get the "F" out of Foliage Land and back to the Land of the Warm and the Weird.

I'm sure most of you have noted this point, but for those who haven't, take if from a now and again closet cynic: Civilization is a bad case of hemorrhoids for those without a whole lotta luck, a faerie godmother, or a briefcase load of pixie dust. It helps to have your own private Tinkerbell to sprinkle it on. I fortunately do have luck in abundance and a Tinkerbell so hot and deft with the dust she makes Julia Roberts look a homely fool. Thus has civilization, in the form of a federal endowment for the certifiably creative, has likewise been kind to me.

I much enjoyed the lonesome call of the loons on New England ponds on quiet nights. I felt a kinship with the loon. I felt a measure of gratitude for the bird. Were I not myself a court-certified loon, this entire AT trip would have been a lot more difficult but not impossible. Remember the story of the young homeless guy picked up by a sheriff somewhere north of Atlanta. The sheriff was driving the young man to the county line as is so often their practice, when he took an interest in the guy and asked him what he wanted out of life, what he liked to do. The man replied that he just liked to walk, that he walked all the time, everywhere. So the sheriff did the man a favor. He dropped him at the southern terminus of the AT, pointed to a white blaze and told him to follow the blazes north and just keep walking. The man had nothing but the clothes on his back and a bucket with a few personal effects and food. As the story goes, he made it a long, long way, if not the whole way. There's something so indescribably peaceful about waking up every morning with but one task for the day, one responsibility on your mind. Walk north. Walk north.

Do I feel patriotic in these politically nauseating and twisted times? Yes I do. Not because of my NEA grant. Not because I have any love-loss for the foul degenerates holding my government hostage at the moment.

It's the people. It is the people of this nation, and this grand and magical 2,000-mile path of freedom that have transformed this closet ex-patriot into a man in love with his homeland again. It is the trail angels and the thruhikers and the hostel-keepers and the past thruhikers and the section hikers and even those loony southbounders! It is that there exists this AMAZING path of freedom and kindness and beauty and hope and dreams straight through the heart of the whole East Coast Appalachian corridor and that YOU, anybody, can drop what you're doing TODAY if you so choose, abandon the cubicle, and set out on this path and walk and experience a degree of freedom you may never have imagined possible. Best of all, you can walk these 2,000 miles for FREE. The total cost of all permits on the AT (if you stealth the Whites and Baxter): $0.00.

"How can I just abandon my job, my credit card debt, my mortgage? How can I abandon my family?" Well, this last one is a toughie. But I'm not talking to the "kinda just bummed out" people. I'm talking to the people so depressed that they daily have to fight the urge to drive off a bridge on their way home from work. I'm talking to you with *The Bell Jar* under your pillow, you stockpiling painkillers or Xanax or Valium. I'm talking to you who know where your buddy hides his gun, to you making the plan to end all plans. What matters your debt, your employment record, your car loan, what matters any of these things if you're DEAD? I'm sorry if that sounds harsh, but I've been there. I don't, however, have children. But even to you who have a family dependent on you, what good are you to them laid out on a stainless steel table at the morgue?

There is another way. I used to argue with a friend who would ask, "Why can't you just change your life, go to a different country, become a different person rather than taking your life?" I would explain to him that a severely depressed person can barely crawl out of bed or tie their shoes let alone plot out a whole new identity, a new life, travel expenses, all that. But I do believe that on the Appalachian Trail I have found an exception to my answer and a possible positive answer to my friend's question. Professional outdoorsmen and gear suppliers and hikers who planned for months for the AT and probably most everyone I hiked with will disagree with me on this point, but I'm the suicidal depressive guy who thruhiked the trail and they're not, so here goes.

I believe a severe depressive could literally roll out of bed and onto the trail, even without their shoes tied. I believe that the camaraderie and the trail angels and the preponderance of like-minded seekers and the shelters and the excess of gear and food that fills hostel "hiker boxes" and the forest itself, the stunning change of environment, would help provide for and pick up that person and propel them along until the day (and it wouldn't be long, I bet) they'd find the energy to tie their shoes and the enthusiasm to walk in them.

My friend's other question was this: "If you were alone, marooned on a desert island, would you kill yourself if you didn't take your medicine?" In a nutshell, is my depression truly the result of a chemical imbalance in my brain, and would I die without seratonin reuptake inhibitors? Maybe. I don't know. I tried, unsuccessfully, to go without my meds on the trail. But I'm no model patient. At every trail town I drank, knowing full well that alcohol, even if it was just a couple of beers, is a depressant. After about a thousand miles, I could drink myself unconscious on beer and get up the next day and hike off both the physical and psychological hangover in a matter of hours. I had altered my body chemistry. For the better. For the waaaaay better. I was a machine. Besides, I needed the carbohydrates provided by the beer. But, as the man on TV says, "What you are about to see is very dangerous. These men are trained professionals. Don't try this at home."

If you've managed to read this whole book, then you're not as close to the brink as you may think. But just in case, as you crawl out of bed into untied shoes, grab a month's worth of your SRIs or your MOAs or whatever it is you take to maintain some semblance of sanity in this world and carry them with you. Take them as prescribed. Nature if you'll pardon a few California-isms, is blue-sky bitchen. It's rhododendron tunnel tubular. It's rock-stomping radical. It did it for me, and I bet it can do it for a whole lot of other people who have lost their way and can think of no other option than death.

I may be wrong. But one thing I'm sure of: You can't walk, you can't avail yourself of this corridor of beauty and freedom if you pull that trigger or chug down that bottle of pills.

Dead, so far as we know, is dead. And dead men hike no trails.

***

As it happened, I would see Jackie and Ry again several months later at the Trail Days celebration the following May. Communication would be sparse between us during the intervening winter. I would write to her the way I always write, expressing my honest emotions, my struggles with my feelings for her, with my return to the "real" world. Her letters were quite different, not unfriendly but curt and impersonal as though addressing a group of distant relatives, updating them on her life newsletter-style. I hadn't been communicating with Ry at all, embarrassed as I was at my own honesty in relating "our story" to my Web audience. So, with the story told in all its gory romance novel detail, I more or less tried to put the two of them out of my mind.

When I saw Ry at Trail Days, I waited for him to hit me. I wanted him to hit me, in a primitive man-protects-his-woman kind of way. Instead he was nice to me, too nice. They were both too nice. Great, I thought. I picked the two nicest people on the planet to fall into a lover's triangle with. I felt shamed. I felt sorry for them and hoped that someday when a less noble man came to steal his woman away from him, Ry wouldn't be so nice. Now I just love them both.

Upon my return to California right after the trail, I visited with family and spent a few weeks trying unsuccessfully to adjust to my "home" town of Idyllwild. I took off to Houston on a whim in November and spent a whole month leading up to and including Christmas in Texas where, using my newfound thruhiker superpowers, I made it snow on Christmas Day for my friend Mary's young daughters Sara and Ashley. It was apparently the first such snow in nearly a century, and it made both the girls and their mother quite happy.

But in so doing, I missed spending Christmas with my nephews in San Diego, a terrible sin that left me sad. We drove to New Orleans to join my friends Jules and Chris, sons of the celebrated beat poet Robert Stock, in ushering in what no one knew would be a most devastating New Year for that city and nearly the entire Gulf Coast. There, for my sins, I was jumped and punched in the face by a threesome of wildly dressed and quite drunk French Quarter girls when I tried to take their picture on New Year's Eve in New Orleans, apparently also a sin.

After a bit of aimless roaming around the southwest on Amtrak early this year, I landed at Bisbee Kate's Straw Bale House halfway between the old mining towns of Tombstone and Bisbee, Arizona just a rifle shot from the

Mexican border. There I stayed for three glorious months, writing and editing and sleeping in a high loft in an octagonal house of straw that I came to refer to as Sanctuary, a nod to the 1970s film *Logan's Run*. With no electricity or running water, I made do with rainwater collection, candles and oil lamplight, my propane-fueled camp stove. I charged my iBook laptop and mp3 player off my car battery every night, and every morning I got a good workout pushing my car up to bump-start speed on a nearly flat dirt desert road. This was my vacation, my hibernation. The night Hunter Thompson shot himself, I filled the desert night with banshee cries and big explosions, drunk with grief and dancing around a giant bonfire like a spirit-possessed tribal witchdoctor and occasionally hurling the eight-ounce camp stove propane canisters into the fire and diving for cover.

With Hunter now gone and my true trail love emotionally unplugged from me (and soon to be married), I took up with a stripper named Bettie and lost myself in her 24/7 sensuality, her mango-ripe body of pure sexual power and movement. We lasted a month. Perhaps in much the same way all that hiking had altered my body chemistry, a month of sex and my mentor's death altered it again, this time not for the better. It seemed like it happened overnight that suddenly I couldn't drink one beer without succumbing to dangerous levels of fear and self-loathing, namely in the presence of other people, even close friends. So I stayed isolated in the desert as much as possible, drank only water and tea for a month and worked at editing this book. As plans came together for the journey east to Trail Days and points beyond, I began to feel better. Hibernation had apparently ended. The nomad, the peregrine in me called.

The day I left Arizona, I first crossed the border into Mexico and had my twice-abscessed molar pulled, the one that haunted me on the trail at Pearisburg yet afforded me oodles of good drugs, pain killers later employed to keep walking on mangled ankles. The dentist's office is so close to the border in Naco, Mexico that on the walk back I greeted the female U.S. Border Patrol agent on duty with a Cheshire Cat grin full of blood as I hissed out, "A-vare-a-schken" to her citizenship query. As I drove away and out across the vast sea of sagebrush and cacti that is the southern Arizona desert, blood poured from the as yet unclotted hole in my mouth. For reasons I can't explain, yet feeling very Tyler Durden, I adjusted my rearview mirror and used my forefinger to paint my face with my blood. Soon I was an Indian, a warrior, a native on the hunt. I liked the way it looked.

On the AT, if I hadn't beaten depression for good, I had at least learned HOW to beat it for a while, maybe forever with proper discipline. Perhaps now it was time take it one step further, from walker to warrior. Flying down the border highway at 80 mph in my dead friend's sports car, my long dirty-blond hair whirled and crackled electric in the bright sunlight of the open sunroof. I downshifted, whipped the wheel hard to the right and onto a dirt road shortcut into New Mexico. The savage, red-streaked face in the mirror smiled a knowing smile, knowing that everything would be different now. From here on out, everything would be better.

-The Beginning-

EPILOGUE: OR WHERE ARE THEY NOW?

The following is hardly a comprehensive list of all the hikers mentioned in this book. To read more about these hikers and many others, visit WhiteBlaze.com, or the more comprehensive TrailJournals.com, where you will find the personal accounts of endless hikers written in their own words, thus opening up a virtually endless read on the lives of thruhikers worldwide.

Elly returned to her commune in Virginia after the trail. She says she worked through a lot on the trail. Last I saw of her was an e-mailed photograph of her bald as Sinead O'Connor which threw the Jody Foster likeness out the window. Personally, I loved her long and dready mane.

Maine Sail and Christa made it through their summer apart, he on the AT, her in Africa. The two live in Missoula now where Maine Sail is finishing his degree, and a July wedding is planned! Maine Sail says he got himself a dog to accompany him on his "gonzo hikes of the future." I'm thinking if I had me a Christa, I wouldn't be taking no dog hiking!

Mouse Bait and **White Patch** seemed an unlikely pair when they met on the trail yet made it to the end together. Last I heard, Bait, a native Mainer, was headed south to set up house keeping in Florida with Patch. Go, Mouse Patch!

Franko & Bennie, traumatized by the Dismal Falls incident, shaved their heads bald and joined a cult that live in trees and avoid flowing water at all costs. Honestly, I don't know what Bennie's up to, but Franko was indeed bald and happy to see me at Trail Days '05. He works a corporate job he hates but is saving up and intent on a PCT thruhike in '06.

Party Girl now lives in Bullmoose, Wyoming where she works at the local outdoor outfitter and has fallen very much in love with a Zamboni operator & fly fisherman with a young son. I don't know if there is a Bullmoose, WY. I just made that up in case Her Gorgeousness, one of the hottest women on the AT in '04, has any stalkers. Love ya, PG.

Still Frank is still cool as a moose. Retired from the Navy in his early fifties, he says everyday feels like Saturday. After the AT, Frank left Ohio and bought a house in Illinois to be closer to his mother. He spent last summer trimming out the new house and volunteering all over the place to keep his naval commander brain from flipping out. Frank intends to be the first person to successfully thruhike all eight of America's National Scenic Trails. Meanwhile, he works in nature photography and plans on canoeing the entire Mississippi in '06 and has invited me to copilot. I just may do it!

Tinker was shipped off to Iraq short of completing the trail, was overseas at *war* during the editing of this book (during which time I tensely awaited bad news). He returned home & safe in time for Christmas, 2006. God Bless him.

Coyote, clever as her namesake, had already lined up her next adventure while on the AT in '04 and was off to Jima, Ecuador as a Peace Corps volunteer a few months after completing her thruhike. If anyone can set the world on fire with love & energy, Coyote can.

Dingle took a job in the AMC hut system in the White Mountains of New Hampshire shortly after the trail. Though he lost his Skirt, I can't imagine that working with all those fit young granola girls in the secluded huts of the Whites left him pining for long.

Scholar went off-trail after three months on the AT in '04 but returned this year, started from the beginning and reached Katahdin's summit on 10/6/05. Now a bona fide trail junkie, she has the PCT is in her sights for the near future.

Sunshine, like Scholar has become an AT junkie. She thruhiked it again this year and is probably out there still hiking in the snow with some cute young boy Sherpa at her side. Of all the people I met on the trail, Sunshine seems to have blossomed most of all in the AT school of society-weary and half-crazed peak-bagging fishies. Swim on Sunshine, you crazy diamond.

Gordy, Cyberdine and **Ski Bum** all live and work together now in Colorado. Based out of Leadville, America's highest city at 10,200 feet elevation, they all work as wilderness therapy instructors for Trailhead Wilderness School, improving the lives of at-risk youth through immersion in nature. I had a lot of fun with the Leadville gang this past summer!

Big Stick was being rowed away in a ranger's canoe on a lake in Yellowstone National Park when last I saw him. After just 20 miles of a planned 500-mile trek together, a heel spur had apparently done him in. I truly hope he's well although he hasn't spoken to me since. He Wu Wei'd a good deal of high-dollar sponsored gear out of my 2005 CDT "Suicide Awareness Hot Hike" including a flight to Yellowstone, then walked without a word to me since. I guess there's not a lot of etiquette required of practitioners of conscious inaction.

Baltimore Jack lives in a mock cabin in the forest in Hanover, New Hampshire. I say "mock" because behind the cabin façade is a Spaceship Enterprise-like command center from which Jack, ATCIA Chief of Protocol, keeps a close eye on all AT-related affairs.

The Garland 5, the hiking family I called the von Trapps, reached Katahdin's summit on October 3, 2005, completing an epic two-year thruhike! Left homeless and jobless in late '03, the amazing Garlands somehow managed to hike half the trail by late '04, then four months later summon the enthusiasm to pick up where they'd left off and hike another season! Wolfsong, Starfire and Alden, 14, 12 & 10 when they began, all had a birthday on the trail. At last report, Mama "Clothesline" Garland's home-schooled children, so much the wiser from their journey, were all tested and admitted into Mensa, and Papa Fotoman was getting lots of work in computer consulting. The Garland 5 truly are a credit to the AT.

Yazzy wiped away her airport tears and got right to work finding a job in late '04. She's now in her second season working at a ski resort in Vermont, has a new boyfriend and sounds very happy. Her real trail name is way cooler than Yazzy but, feeling the need to protect her identity, I gave her a choice, and she concurred with Yazzy.

Jackie and **Ry** married June 18, 2005. They are now living in Asheville, North Carolina where she enjoys working with at-risk youth in an outdoors setting similar to the Leadville, CO crew. Ry is a teacher and (God help him) aspires to be a writer. As a side note, on the day of their betrothal, I got obscenely drunk, beat myself to a pulp with a 4-foot piece of rebar, snorted enough powdered dilaudid to kill a horse, jumped off a cliff into the Atlantic, drowned and was met by my late-uncle David, himself lost to the sea off the Maine coast at Acadia decades ago, who sat me down in Heaven, put his arm around me and kindly said, "She's not the one, Peregrine. Peace, little brother. You did right. The one, the last woman you'll ever love, she's coming. Besides, you've felt true a couple of times in this life. I died too young, never had true love." With that I felt shame, and there's nothing like shame to get you booted out of Heaven and back to this world lickety-split.

His Madnesty Lord Duke Jester Gadget Malcovich Peregrine Jack (a.k.a. Rick McKinney), now divides his time between writing and editing; filling his web site *Jigglebox.com* with alternately incendiary, inspirational, and heart-breaking gibberish; and, in Don Quixote fashion, bush-whacking the scrub deserts of the Arizona-Mexico border region with an American flag cape and a machete in search of terrorists posing as cacti. Nightly, he watches the breath-taking Arizona sunsets with his angel companion Luciano, the two of them lying on their backs on the roof of Luci's old smoke black BMW 535i, heads thrown back, the blue concave sky inverted in their minds, turned convex. Positioned thus, Luci & Rick become astronauts floating high above the Blue Planet, bedazzled by space and irreverent of the petty affairs of men.

ACKNOWLEDGEMENTS

I have so many friends to be thankful for, so many people who have in one way or another contributed to the realization of this book since I first set fingers to keyboard in February, 2004. My highest gratitude goes to my cousin Justin Alessandro, without whose countless hours of work this material would never have made it up on Jigglebox.com where it gained incredible momentum, peaking at over 1000 readers a day, apparently inspiring many, not the least of which me, to continue. Heartfelt thanks to:

My young nephews Jacob and Matthew for just being alive and growing, riding shotgun in my front map pocket, now a wrinkled photo but one I gazed at every day with love & well-wishings; Mom, Dad & Sis for their love; Timmy and Bruce for your unflagging ground support from Base Camp Idyllwild; Mary Forbes for your love and support across the board; Kate Pearson & Gregg Snyder for the divine gift of "Sanctuary," a top secret desert hideaway wherein I was able to collect the scrambled fragments of my mind into this cohesive whole; Harrod Blank for being the greatest single human concentration of powerful, positive and motivational energy on the planet, and every other members of my huge Art Car Family who, collectively, have given me reason to live through one, long unpublished decade; Hunter Mann for your genius rambling phone messages always so full of praise; Michael Strickland for returning to me with such beautiful words; Scott Beale of Laughing Squid for floating the Jigglebox for years; Dave Cuneo for true friendship; Nayber for da shoes; Mama & Papa O for unparalleled southern hospitality; all the Trail Angels & hosts who make the AT pure magic; seven-time-thruhiker Baltimore Jack for embodying, like a drunken boxer, the intoxicating spirit of the AT parallel world; Shawnee for the great cover design; Scott Roberts for insight; Pam Johnson for the superior editing you accomplished whilst I was off running around the mountains of Colorado; Nick, Gordy & Hobo, Ski Bum, Deia, Taylor Bones, and Leslie and Kathy & Chris of Proving Grounds, and everyone else in Leadville for the open-armed hospitality that made me want to stay there forever and may soon call me back. Thank you to the few women who brightened a handful of my many, many otherwise lonesome nights on the AT with your tender companionship.

My deepest empathy and love to Sara Grant, Judy Haas, Brian of the Cirques, Steamboat Matt and all suicide survivors who met my mission with open hearts.

Special thanks to Blister Sister, Tilly, Cynthia, Marie Vlasic, Rebecca Lowe, and many more who kept me in goodies, praise and love on both trails. To Naomi Havlen, Autumn Phillips, Dan Bennett, Kit O'Carra, Todd Johnson, and everyone else who went to bat for me in the bat-infested jungle that is suicide, the well-buried epidemic. To Rich Rudow of Trimble Outdoors, Kris Wagner of Backpacker Magazine, Carol Blayden of MSR, Dwight at JetBoil, to Merrell, Leki, SteriPen and Mont-Bell of Japan, a major "Domo arigato!" to you all.

Thank you to everyone on the trail who inspired me to write, even and especially those of you who (God forbid) find your likeness not to your liking. As said in the opening Disclaimer, this is not reality. This is my distorted recording of what I saw, through my borderline personality dis-ordered, God-boggled eyes. There's no such thing as non-fiction, and objectivity is a myth created by the tight-assed, now-elderly scions of old school journalism.

Forgive me if you are not in here. You are not forgotten, merely misplaced in my scattered brain. If I don't hand in this book soon, I shall surely go mad or self-immolate like a Buddhist monk aflame in protest of this mad, mad world.

FINAL WORD

Free speech is like driving in America.
It's not a right; it's a privilege.
If that sounds wrong to you,
suit up and prepare to fight.
Fight to set it right.

The author wishes to thank God, Tinkerbell, Zeus,
Buddha, Allah, Morpheus, the late Hunter Thompson
or whoever is out there keeping the light on for us,
keeping the Internet free for wise-ass Thomas Jeffersons
writing amok anything they please in the name of freedom,
knowing full well that freedom has never been free.

To everyone who has ever been harassed, beaten,
pepper sprayed, threatened, jailed, or at worst
eliminated for want of freedom, my sincere apologies for
what must seem a most self-centered life of morbid obsession.
Suicide, however, is rarely undertaken by the rational mind.
If the suicidally depressed were rational & organized,
I for one would proffer my life in your stead,
giving of it thus, rather than taking it,
rather than wasting it entirely on a
lost battle with bad brain chemistry.

Dead Men Hike No Trails is the direct creative result of
freedoms afforded to and exercised by:
jigglebox .com

Printed in the United States
54312LVS00003B/44